STUDIES IN THE ENGLISH RENAISSANCE

John T. Shawcross, General Editor

SALVE DEVS
REX IVDÆORVM.

Containing,

1 The Passion of Christ.

2 Eues Apologie in defence of Women.

3 The Teares of the Daughters of Ierusalem.

4 The Salutation and Sorrow of the Virgine
Marie.

With diuers other things not vnfit to be read.

Written by Mistris *Æmilia Lanyer*, Wife to Captaine
Alfonso Lanyer Seruant to the
Kings Maiestie.

AT LONDON
Printed by *Valentine Simmes* for *Richard Bonian*, and are
to be sold at his Shop in Paules Churchyard, at the
Signe of the Floure de Luce and
Crowne. 1611.

Aemilia Lanyer
Gender, Genre, and the Canon

MARSHALL GROSSMAN
EDITOR

THE UNIVERSITY PRESS OF KENTUCKY

For Jacob

Publication of this volume was made possible in part by a grant
from the National Endowment for the Humanities.

Copyright © 1998 by The University Press of Kentucky
Scholarly publisher for the Commonwealth,
serving Bellarmine College, Berea College, Centre
College of Kentucky, Eastern Kentucky University,
The Filson Club Historical Society, Georgetown College,
Kentucky Historical Society, Kentucky State University,
Morehead State University, Murray State University,
Northern Kentucky University, Transylvania University,
University of Kentucky, University of Louisville,
and Western Kentucky University.

Editorial and Sales Offices: The University Press of Kentucky
663 South Limestone Street, Lexington, Kentucky 40508-4008

98 99 00 01 02   5 4 3 2 1

Frontispiece: Title page of *Salve Deus Rex Judaeorum* (1611), courtesy of the
Folger Shakespeare Library

Library of Congress Cataloging-in-Publication Data
Aemilia Lanyer : gender, genre, and the canon / Marshall Grossman.
    p.   cm.
    Includes bibliographical references (p.   ) and index.
    ISBN 0–8131–2049–7 (cloth : alk. paper)
    1. Lanyer, Aemilia—Criticism and interpretation.   2. Christian
poetry, English—History and criticism.   3. Women and Literature—
England—History—17th century.   4. Lanyer, Aemilia. Salve Deus
Rex Judaeorum.   5. Canon (Literature)   6. Literary form.
I. Grossman, Marshall.
PR2296.L27Z56   1998
821′.3—dc21   97–39283

Manufactured in the United States of America

Contents

Preface

In 1989, having been scheduled to teach the then required undergraduate survey course in Renaissance and Baroque Literature at the University of Maryland, I found in my mailbox a large packet from my colleague Jane Donawerth. The invaluable contents of this packet, which had been assembled by a college committee on women in the curriculum, were a reminder of my obligation to include works by women in my syllabus, and a carefully culled collection of readings, draft course materials, and suggested approaches. Not the least of these collegial gifts was a country-house poem, "The Description of Cookeham," by Aemilia Lanyer. Intrigued by this poem and the ways in which it would affect my teaching of other poems in its genre, and fortunate in my proximity to the Folger Shakespeare Library, I read through one of the two copies of the *Salve Deus Rex Judaeorum* (1611) held there. Thus began my engagement with the poetry of Aemilia Lanyer and what it could teach me about the dialectical interrelations of gender, genre, and canonicity. Selections from Lanyer became a staple in my courses, and, when Susanne Woods's edition of the poems came out in 1993, the volume in its entirety became a required text.

Having become evangelical about Lanyer's merits, I soon connected with a network of aficionados with whom I organized a session on her work for the 1992 MLA meeting in Toronto. The earliest versions of the essays by Lewalski, Berry, Woods, and myself included in this volume were presented at that meeting. Plans for a collection of essays began thereafter.

As with most matters in scholarship, the path from idea to book was lengthened by detours and along the way required the solace of many helpers. Most notably Jane Donawerth, having introduced me to the poet and the field, not only by handing me Lanyer's poem, but also by initiating me into a network of collaborative scholarship, remains a prime resource. David K. Miller gave me the opportunity to discuss Lanyer at the Strode Center for Renaissance Studies at the University of Alabama, listened to my ideas through a summer of lunches in the Folger garden, and put me in touch with the University Press of Kentucky when it was time to seek a publisher. Susanne Woods, Ann Baynes Coiro, Barbara Lewalski, Boyd Berry, Kari McBride, Achsah Guibbory, Janel Mueller, Karen Nelson, and Leeds Barroll shared their works and sources with me, as well as their advice. Special thanks go to Amy Stackhouse for her keen editorial eye and her invaluable and generous help with numerous scholarly chores. John Shawcross made brilliant suggestions about possible contributors, offering encouragement and a careful reading of the manuscript. I am also indebted to the comments and suggestions of an anonymous reader for the University Press of Kentucky. As always, the staff of the Folger Shakespeare Library provided attentive service, a quiet, collegial environment, with free coffee all day, cookies every afternoon, and, not incidentally, all the books I asked for. I cannot imagine a greater privilege for a scholar than the one conferred by my Folger reader's card.

The title page of the 1611 *Salve Deus Rex Judaeorum,* reproduced as frontispiece, is courtesy of the Folger Shakespeare Library. Versions of two of the essays included here have appeared previously: Achsah Guibbory, "The Gospel According to Aemilia: Women and the Sacred in Aemilia Lanyer's *Salve Deus Rex Judaeorum,*" in *Sacred and Profane: The Interplay of Secular and Devotional Literature, 1500-1700,* ed. Helen Wilcox, Richard Todd, Alasdair MacDonald (Amsterdam: VU University Press, 1996); and Janel Mueller, "The Feminist Poetics of Aemilia Lanyer's "Salve Deus Rex Judaeorum," in *Feminist Measures: Soundings in Poetry and Theory,* ed. Lynn Keller and Cristianne Miller (Ann Arbor: University of Michigan Press, 1994). I thank VU Press and the University of Michigan Press for permission to reprint these essays, both of which have been revised for this volume. Unless otherwise noted, all citations to Lanyer refer to Susanne Woods, ed., *The Poems of Aemilia Lanyer: Salve Deus Rex Judaeorum* (Oxford: Oxford University Press, 1993).

Introduction

I will begin with some meager and probably by now familiar facts. Aemilia Lanyer was the daughter of Baptist Bassano, a Christianized Venetian Jew, who was a member of the queen's music, and Margaret Johnson, his common-law wife. In 1592, at the age of twenty-three, she was married to Alfonso Lanyer, also a musician and a participant in a number of military expeditions. By her own report, she spent some time in her youth in the household of Susan Bertie, Countess of Kent.

She comes to our attention because in 1611 she did something extraordinary for a middle-class woman of the early seventeenth century: she published a small volume of religious, epideictic verse, the *Salve Deus Rex Judaeorum*. This book was printed by Valentine Simmes for Richard Bonian.[1] There seem to have been two impressions in 1611; only nine copies are known to survive, six of these are of the second impression. Two presentation copies—one for Prince Henry, the other for Thomas Jones, Archbishop of Dublin—make strategic omissions among the dedicatory poems, reflecting the likely responses of the intended recipients.[2]

In 1978, A.L. Rowse, in the service of his own tendentious identification of Lanyer as the "dark lady" of Shakespeare's sonnets, brought out a modern edition of the *Salve* under the problematic title, *The Poems of Shakespeare's Dark Lady*. Happily, Oxford University Press has since brought out an edition edited by Susanne Woods of the Brown University Women Writers Project. Unlike Rowse's edition, the Oxford edition has Aemilia Lanyer's name on the title page, includes reliable biographical and textual introductions, and is suitable for classroom use.

The emergence of Lanyer from dependency on a presumed connection to Shakespeare into, so to speak, her own write, is, of course, part of a broad and significant movement toward recovering women's voices long hidden behind the disadvantages of gender that hampered them in their own time and a patriarchal canon that continued to cultivate deaf ears into ours. The publication in accessible form of lost or little known writings is a necessary step. Having become available to readers only recently, much writing by early modern women still needs to be assessed and understood in its own terms. This next step is complicated by the fact that the protocols with which we read the principal genres of early modern literature turn out—now that we consider the fact—to be gendered. Thus, serious attention to the writings of early modern women is rewarded with access to what amounts to parallel, yet distinct and frequently contentious, constitutions of familiar genres, the pleasures of a new and valuable text, and an opportunity to rethink the canonical poetry of their male contemporaries. Paying serious attention to Aemilia Lanyer's poems in praise of noble women and of sacred devotion, for example, a reader learns to recognize the masculine assumptions underlying established genres and comes to understand how and why Lanyer's project necessarily rejects ideological assumptions that seemed previously to define certain kinds of writing. Such a reader learns to hear the merits of a poet who speaks a language in some ways structurally opposed to the hegemonic voices represented by, say, Ben Jonson and John Donne. Reading her well is important both for Lanyer's work and the work of her male contemporaries, because each significantly affects the way we read the other. The essays collected in this volume engage the task of reading Lanyer well, not in terms of any possible biographical interest in Shakespeare but in terms of her intrinsic merit and in terms of her complex poetic contemporaneity with male poets—John Donne, Giles Fletcher, Ben Jonson and Andrew Marvell—as well as with antecedent and contemporary women writers—Christine de Pizan, Mary Sidney, Rachel Speght. Thus we aim to move slowly toward an early modern literary history reshaped by an appreciation of the ongoing conversations among works in a gender integrated canon.

The "Salve Deus Rex Judaeorum" is a religious poem, presented in a volume apparently designed to solicit patronage; the long title poem, in ottava rima, deals primarily with the Passion, but the title page lists four parts as though they were separate poems, which they are not: 1. The Passion of Christ; 2. Eves Apologie in defence of Women; 3. The Teares of the Daughters of Jerusalem; and 4. The Salutation and Sorrow of the Virgine Marie.[3] As these titles suggest, the poem everywhere and continually projects a female subject for a female reader, even, and complexly, in the section on the Passion, which presents the Crucifixion as a crime perpetrated exclusively by men. This central poem is prefaced by ten dedicatory verses, all addressed to women: Queen Anne, Princess Elizabeth, "all vertuous Ladies in generall," Arabella Stuart, and the Countesses of Kent, Pembroke, Bedford, Cumberland, Suffolke, and Dorset. Some of the dedicatory poems are purely formal, others seem to presume some acquaintance, even intimacy, with the noblewomen to whom they are addressed. In the dedicatory poem addressed to her, in a strikingly intimate digression in the body of the title poem on the Passion, and again in an appended country-house poem, "The Description of Cooke-ham," Margaret Clifford, Dowager Countess of Cumberland, is identified as the principal patron of Lanyer's poetry and of her religious conversion.

The dedicatory poems are followed by a prose address "To the Vertuous Reader" in which Lanyer says that she has written "this small volume, or little booke, for the generall use of all virtuous Ladies and Gentlewomen of this kingdome," and in which she takes occasion particularly to chastise "some [who] forgetting they are women themselves, and in danger to be condemned by the words of their owne mouthes, fall into so great an errour, as to speak unadvisedly against the rest of their sexe" (p. 48). Such turncoat women ought, "for their owne ease, modesties, and credit," "referre such points of folly, to be practised by evill disposed men, who forgetting they were borne of women, nourished of women, and that if it were not by the means of women, they would be quite extinguished out of the world, and a finall ende of them all, doe like Vipers deface the wombes wherein they were bred, onely to give way and utterance to their want of discretion and goodnesse" (p. 48). Previewing her reading of the Passion in terms of gender conflict, Lanyer goes on to remark that "such as these [i.e., the aforementioned womb-defacing Vipers], were they that dishonoured Christ and his Apostles and Prophets, putting them to shamefull deaths" (p. 48-49).

In the body of the "Salve Deus" Lanyer reiterates this analogy between the dishonorers of women and the crucifiers of Christ in her description of Gethsemane as:

> That blessed Garden, which did now embrace
> His holy corps, yet could make no defence
> Against those Vipers, objects of disgrace,
> Which sought that pure eternall Love to quench. [ll. 363-66]

She thus sets up an inverse or negative typology between Eve and the exclusively male perpetrators of the Crucifixion. As Christ's sacrifice makes good Adam's sin, the sin of Christ's male crucifiers makes good Eve's fall: by it men forfeit dominion over women:

> Then let us have our Libertie againe,
> And challendge to your selves no Sov'raigntie;
> You came not in the world without our paine,
> Make that a barre against your crueltie;
> Your fault beeing greater, why should you disdaine
> Our beeing your equals, free from tyranny?
>   If one weake woman simply did offend,
>   This sinne of yours, hath no excuse, nor end. [ll. 825-32]

Lanyer also calls on Pilate's wife—who, she says, spoke for all women, when she "a message sent, / That thou should'st have nothing to doe at all / With that just man" (ll. 835-37)—to witness that women never consented to this singularly decisive crime.[4] Thus, although she works in the established genres of the poetry of praise, Lanyer's aggressive position on the *querelle des femmes* is anything but occasional or contingent. Rather, it forms a unifying structure that integrates the various parts of her book. Whereas normatively the poetry of praise evokes the singular superiority of its patrons, Lanyer's good women exemplify and exculpate woman in general.

How might we further contextualize this skillful and intellectually strong innovation? The first two essays in this volume—by David Bevington and Leeds Barroll respectively—explore Lanyer's life and the social contexts in which she wrote. Until the publication of Susanne Woods' edition in 1993, most of what we thought we knew about Aemilia Lanyer, apart from what can be learned from the *Salve* itself, came from two dubious sources: Simon Forman, the astrologer, who, if his case-records are to be believed, seems to have acted as something of a resident psychotherapist to the courtly set in Jacobean London, and A.L. Rowse, whose information derives in roughly equal proportions from Forman's diaries and from an unusually vivid imagination of the day-to-day life of Shakespeare and his presumed associates. Rowse's assertion that Lanyer is the "dark lady" of Shakespeare's sonnets has been useful in drawing attention to the *Salve* and his edition made available an authentically rare text. Were Lanyer, in fact, the "dark lady" of the sonnets the association would provide a fascinating occasion to reflect on Shakespeare's work as well as hers and it would considerably broaden our view of the literary middle class in early modern London. The identification, however, is founded on evidence that can be fairly summarized as follows: Shakespeare and Lanyer were both alive in London at the same time. They were both—in drastically different ways—associated with the Lord Chamberlain, Henry Cary. Being of Italian descent, Lanyer may well have been dark, and her poems suggest—to Rowse—that she may have been just the sort of woman who, Rowse imagines, would get under Shakespeare's skin. In the present volume, Bevington reviews the available facts about Lanyer's life and evaluates Rowse's argument in detail to conclude that the case is not only, as Barbara Lewalski has remarked with characteristic restraint, "not proved," but wholly improbable.[5] Along the way to this conclusion, Bevington reviews the extent of our knowledge of the circumstances in which Shakespeare's sonnets were produced and offers a thoughtful consideration of the relations between art and biography.

If not Shakespeare's "dark lady," who, then, was Aemilia Lanyer? According to Forman and Rowse, Lanyer, in her youth, was the mistress of Henry Carey, Lord Hunsdon, who kept her in some style (at least) until she became pregnant and then arranged for her to be married "for color" to Captain Alfonso Lanyer. The liaison with the Lord Chamberlain may explain how Lanyer came to presume to some degree of personal relationship with the extraordinary group of noblewomen to whom the *Salve* makes its address, but her residence in

Susan Bertie's household, which, if it actually occurred, would presumably have preceded her relation to Cary, suggests that her parents were able to give her a relatively genteel upbringing. Leeds Barroll examines Lanyer's bid for patronage and her claims—implicit and explicit in the *Salve*—to be acquainted with the aristocratic women addressed in the volume. Looking deeply and carefully into the opportunities Lanyer would have had to become acquainted with the noblewomen she addresses, Barroll challenges us to consider the difficulty of reconciling what we know of the social world of early seventeenth-century England with Lanyer's self-representation and what has become the received account of her life. In so doing, he provides an unusually detailed picture of aristocratic life in early seventeenth-century England and of the limited opportunities open to a middle-class woman of literary talent.

There are a few other facts about Lanyer's biography that I think worth mentioning at the outset. Forman reports that Aemilia believed that Captain Lanyer had some hope of a knighthood as a reward for his military service. He never was knighted, but he was granted a patent "for weighing hay and straw coming to the city of London, and to take for his service therein 6d. for every load of hay and 3d for straw."[6] When Alfonso Lanyer died he left this lucrative grant to Aemilia who subsequently entered into an agreement with Alfonso's improbably named brothers, Innocent and Clement, to surrender the patent in lieu of an annual grant of half the profits. Apparently her husband's brothers did not pay her according to the agreement and she sued, winning a partial settlement in February of 1634. In this her experience was to mirror on a smaller scale that of Margaret and Anne Clifford, who, after the earl's death, entered into nearly endless litigation against George Clifford's brother and nephew, attempting to establish Anne's claim to her father's northern estates. The obstacles presented by the rule of (male) primogeniture to patrimonial inheritance by widows and daughters is reflected in the dubious addition "dowager" to the title of widowed noblewomen—like Margaret, Countess Dowager of Cumberland—living on wealth reserved to them by prearrangement after their husband's titles and estates have passed to male heirs. Lanyer makes wry reference to this patrilineal arrangement in the *Salve,* when she names Christ as "the Husband of [Margaret's] Soule" who by "dying made her Dowager of all" (ll. 253-57). Her suit against her late husband's heirs represents her participation in an important rite of passage for women standing in the line of heritable property in this markedly and engrossingly litigious period of English history.

"The Description of Cooke-ham," taking for its occasion not the dwelling of the Clifford women on the estate (as, for example, Jonson's celebration of Penshurst as an estate on which the "lord dwells") but their leave-taking, provides another and more extended dramatic reference to the peculiar legal institutions of patrilinear inheritance as they affected the lives of real women.

Although Lanyer's problems with her late husband's male heirs postdate the *Salve Deus Rex Judaeorum,* they are of interest because they suggest how common such litigation was and because they fulfill, in a sense, the poems' attempt to establish a community of female interest across class lines of which Lanyer was painfully aware. Issues of class and the complex interactions of class and gender are thus, appropriately, a persistent theme in the essays here presented.

Beyond and beside the opportunities her work affords for a better understanding of gender and class identities in early modern society and of the dynamics of canonization and literary reception, Lanyer claims our attention on her own poetic merits. Her poetry is varied, subtle, witty, and provocative, and excepting the biographical essays by Bevington and Barroll that open the volume, each of the essays presented here represents, first and foremost, an attempt to read Lanyer as a poet whose work is capable of sustaining the sort of open-minded close attention to language, rhetoric, and thought with which we are accustomed to approach the works of, say, Donne or Jonson.

Barbara Lewalski explores Lanyer's subtle manipulation of established genres—the Book of Good Women, the country house poem, a variety of dedicatory poems—to create a work unified by its imagination of a distinct female community and its displacement of the "hierarchical authority of fathers and husbands." Lanyer challenges the patriarchal hierarchy of the seventeenth century through her skillful and, in Lewalski's view, intentional manipulation of genre and the commonplaces of biblical exegesis; by so doing, she also challenges some of the new historical orthodoxies of our time, by seizing a feminine agency from within the very discourse of patriarchy.

Kari Boyd McBride engages another leitmotif of contemporary scholarship—patronage—using a discussion of Lanyer's patronage-seeking poetry and its modern reception as primary documents from which to consider "the gendered nature of much theorizing about patronage and about women poets, as well." After reviewing the brief history of Lanyer criticism, McBride recenters the discussion on the way in which Lanyer's peculiar melding of the poetry of praise directed toward patrons and Christian devotional epideictic "fundamentally altered the context in which patron-client relationships were supposed to have functioned."

Patronage conventions and religious topoi are further examined in Susanne Woods's inquiry into "Vocation and Authority in Aemilia Lanyer." Noting Lanyer's "unapologetic assertion of poetic vocation" in the *Salve Deus Rex Judaeorum,* Woods studies the "intricate complex of patronage conventions . . . and self-assertion" through which Lanyer derives the authority of a public voice. Woods shows how, by placing the traditional (male) authority of patronage and Petrarchan inspiration in the service of a divine subject, Lanyer supports "a vision of nature and art which seems particularly to invite the agency of the Godly woman poet."

Taking an avowedly "historicist approach," Janel Mueller concedes Lanyer's implication in a number of "essentialist" assumptions about the innate features of men and women and universalist assumptions about the divine motives of sexual difference. But because, like Lewalski, Mueller perceives, in Lanyer's poetry, the appropriation of a specifically feminist poetic authority from within the constraints of her historical context, she sees also an opportunity to address a more generally urgent scholarly need: to develop "an eventual set of useful generalizations about the conditions that empowered female authorship in preindustrial and pre-Enlightenment Europe." Mueller turns for context to the works of Christine de Pizan and Giles Fletcher in order to situate the *Salve Deus Rex Judaeorum* as exemplary of feminine authority, and she explores how Lanyer establishes a powerful feminine perspective by melding the genres of verse panegyric addressed to patrons and devotional meditation on biblical subjects.

My own contribution, "Aemilia Lanyer and the Gendering of Genre," continues the emphasis on genre, focussing on Lanyer's country house poem, "The Description of Cooke-ham." In an effort to explore the expression of historical and gender relations in the processes of canonization and the conventions of reading, I consider the obscure fate of Lanyer's poem in relation to the originary status ascribed to Jonson's "To Penshurst." To demonstrate the gendering of the country house poems, I examine the implication of the rhetorical figures and strategies of Jonson's poem in the legal institutions of patriarchy, most notably patrilinearity and virilocality—the assumption that after marriage the bride will reside in her husband's house—and the resistance offered those same institutions by Lanyer's figures of matrilineal genealogy and maternal immediacy.

Continuing the exploration of maternal resistance Naomi J. Miller focusses on Lanyer's "representations of women as at once mothers and others" to examine "the relationship between maternity and subjectivity in early modern England," a relation bearing not only on "those women who claimed the actual title of mother, but also upon all the other women who found their speaking positions (pre)determined by masculine judgments of their (pro)creative capabilities." Miller shows how Lanyer's verse engages a language that "reconfigures the mirroring potential of verse" to construct "femininity in female-authored terms."

Building on the work of Keith Wrightson and Alan Sinfield, Michael Morgan Holmes articulates a more rigorous notion of the substance and processes of the feminine community invoked by other contributors. Contextualizing the *Salve* with Donne's "Sapho to Philaenis" and Marvell's "Nymph complaining for the death of her Faun" and "Upon Appleton House," Holmes argues that Lanyer's poems "forthrightly draw eroticism and religion together in such a way as to emphasize the homoeroticism involved in women's love of

Christ." Thus in Holmes's reading the figures of maternal and sisterly affection give way to an erotics of feminine desire and the engagement between a feminized Christ and "her" female lovers.

Achsah Guibbory returns us from body to spirit by taking Lanyer's feminist theology seriously. Guibbory is specifically interested in Lanyer's reading of Christ's message regarding the place of women in Christian devotion with respect to the contradictory construals of women's connection with God in the Protestant culture of early modern England. Returning to questions of poetic authority, she argues that Lanyer presents her poem "as a true Gospel, inspired and authorized by God." As such the *Salve* represents Christ's Passion as "a message for social as well as spiritual change, . . . founded on a critical and independent reading of the Scriptures which recognizes the New Testament as not simply the Word of God but a series of texts, written by men, in which all parts are not equally authoritative." Guibbory finds that Lanyer uses the gospel form to subvert worldly authority by asserting a "fundamental discontinuity" between Christ's teaching and that of his disciples on issues of sexual equality and the subjection of women.

In the volume's concluding essay, Boyd Berry's tightly focussed reading of Lanyer's use of digression as a rhetorical device serves to show how her language "enacts an interrogation of gendered issues of power and control." In Berry's reading, Lanyer's digressions provoke "discrepant readings in a multiply digressive moment as a way of marking both female powerlessness (consoled by religious sentiment) and an almost scornful sense of unrepentant, female power."

Is Aemilia Lanyer a canonical poet? The essays presented here work together to explore the ways in which Lanyer enters the canon by disrupting it. By developing a contrary voice out of the literary historical materials of scriptural tradition, established (male-dominated) genres, the patronage system, and the everyday social actualities of the patriarchal legal institutions which governed the descent and management of property—both material and symbolic— in early modern England, Lanyer also genders as male a canonical voice that had passed itself off as neutral; *her* difference undermines the claim to disinterested indifference implicit in *his* voice when it speaks for a gender-neutral and undifferentiated *man*kind.

Presumably Aemilia Lanyer wrote more than the slim volume now extant, and it is doubtful that we have now enough of her poetry to sustain the kind of perpetual inquiry that creates and maintains canonicity. I would argue, however, that we cannot teach early modern literature without her. By gendering its voices, Lanyer contributes crucially to the necessary re-formation of the canon, not as a positive and ultimately oppressive body of positively asserted works, but as a dynamic site of dialectical struggle out of which social agency forms, reforms, and adapts in response to the material conditions of its various lives. In the jargon of dialectic, her voice is the negation of the negation of gender in seventeenth-century literary history; it allows us to hear the complicities and contradictions of genre and canonization.

In the *Areopagitica,* Milton spoke famously of books "as lively, and as vigorously productive, as those fabulous Dragons teeth; [that] being sown up and down, may chance to spring up armed men"[7]—perhaps a masculine and military metaphor for the present context, but an apt one. One measure of canonical agency is the books a book instigates. In this respect the *Salve Deus Rex Judaeorum* has been, in recent years, "vigorously productive." For the benefit of readers interested in following this production, Karen Nelson offers an annotated bibliography of works by, collecting, or about Aemilia Lanyer.

NOTES

1. The *Salve Deus Rex Judaeorum* was entered in the Stationer's Register 2 October 1610 and published late in that year but is dated 1611 on the title page (see Woods, "Textual Introduction," p. xlvii). When referring to the publication date, we have used the title page date of 1611 throughout the present volume.

2. See *The Poems of Aemilia Lanyer: Salve Deus Rex Judaeorum,* ed. Susanne Woods (New York: Oxford University Press, 1993), "Textual Introduction," pp. xlvii-li. The copy prepared for presentation to Prince Henry is discussed by Leeds Barroll in chapter 2.

3. The structural significance of the divisions given on the title page is discussed by Janel Mueller in chapter 6.

4. For this episode see Matt. 27.19.

5. "Rewriting Patriarchy and Patronage: Margaret Clifford, Anne Clifford, and Aemilia Lanyer," *The Yearbook of English Studies* 21 (1991): 87-106.

6. "The humble petition of Emilia Lanyer . . ." 1634/35, PRO/SP 16/57.

7. John Milton, *Complete Prose Works,* ed. Don. M. Wolfe, et. al. (New Haven and London: Yale University Press, 1953-80), 2, 492.

1

A.L. Rowse's Dark Lady

David Bevington

The wrong road always leads somewhere.
—G.B. Shaw, "Preface to The Dark Lady of the Sonnets," 1910

In what may be his most notorious claim to have solved a literary riddle through historical "method," A.L. Rowse announced to the waiting world in 1964 and then in 1973 that he was hot on the trail of the identity of the "dark lady" in Shakespeare's sonnets. Despairing at first of a solution, he then triumphantly proclaimed "The Problem Solved" in his 1973 edition of those poems. His candidate: Aemilia Lanyer, the daughter of a court musician who became the mistress of Lord Hunsdon and the mother of an illegitimate child (Henry) by him, at which point she was conveniently married off to another musician named Alfonso Lanyer. Rowse persuaded himself that she was also Shakespeare's mistress and the subject of that poet's bitter reflections on female infidelity. But history can sometimes surprise us all. The woman whom Rowse thus brought to scholarly notice as a woman of easy virtue has satisfied almost no one as a potential candidate for the "dark lady." Aemilia Lanyer has, however, turned out to be a woman of considerable substance in her own right as author. Simply by discovering her, Rowse has done much more for her reputation than he could have imagined possible.

 In order to understand the significance of A.L. Rowse's search to find out "who Shakespeare's mistress was," something needs to be said here about Rowse's method of analysis. He writes, with captivating grace, and draws upon an extensive knowledge of English social life and aristocratic family history. All this makes for a beguilingly persuasive reading of the Shakespeare sonnets as autobiographical. The Earl of Southampton stands before us as a convincing original of the young lord to whom the sonnets might have been addressed. Southampton's reluctance to marry Burghley's granddaughter and Oxford's daughter, Lady Elizabeth Vere, in 1590 and in the years immediately following; his ambivalent physical beauty corresponding to that of "the master-mistress of my passion" (Sonnet 20); the nearness in theme of the sonnets urging that the young lord marry and beget children to parts of *Venus and Adonis* (published 1593), in which Venus pleads with Adonis to "Make use of time" and to obey "the law of nature" insisting that he is "bound to breed" (ll. 129, 171); the plausible resemblance of Southampton to Adonis, as well as to the young lord of the sonnets; Southampton's role as patron for Shakespeare's two published poems in 1593; the Countess of Southampton's protective interest in her son's marrying—these are circumstances that Rowse properly calls to our attention. When the sonnets refer flatteringly to the beauty of the lord's mother (2.9-10) and allude to the lord's father as no longer living (13.13-14), the family constellation seems recognizable. The Second Earl of Southampton had died in 1581, leaving young Henry Wriothesley to inherit the title at the age of eight.[1]

Similarly, Rowse aptly depicts for us a Shakespeare to whom Southampton was a godsend and hence a likely subject of adoring portraiture in the sonnets. Shakespeare was no longer young in 1592 and thereabouts. He lacked the advantages of university training and networking that started Lyly, Marlowe, and Kyd toward rapid success in their careers. Shakespeare was burdened by the early 1590s with a wife in Stratford eight years his senior and three children. Difficult plague years in 1592 and 1593 threatened his career in the theater just when it was beginning to gather momentum. As a player without university credentials he was bound to be in a subservient social position with respect to Southampton, dependent on him, no doubt genuinely grateful, and quite possibly struck by the young man's gentility and social sophistication.[2]

If we could stop there and read the sonnets in those terms, few critical problems would arise—other than a lack of originality in any such claim dating back to Edmund Malone. Rowse's method carries him a good deal further, and is based on a number of problematic assumptions. First, for Rowse the sonnets "were autobiography before they became literature." They "were written straightforwardly, directly, by one person for another, with an immediate and sincere impulse." These and other statements assume a one-to-one correspondence between autobiographical event and the writing of a sonnet sequence. It follows that the analyst's chief task is to discover enough about "the historical circumstance in which they were written" to allow a "flood of light" to pour in upon the text. The second assumption, then, is that historical research, rigorously pursued, will uncover information enabling the analyst to make the one-to-one correspondences. The researcher will find the original lying behind the literary portrait since, as is axiomatically stated, that literary portrait is bound to have a living original.[3]

"Here is where the historian comes in." That is in effect the third postulate of the method. Historians and literary critics are collaboratively in need of each other, possessing as they do the separate strengths and training of their respective disciplines. No one could quarrel with this formulation. On the other hand, its ramifications here are troubling. Historians do things that literary scholars are not trained to do, and presumably vice versa, though Rowse's apparent generosity to the other side ("I cannot express how much I owe to the work of the literary scholars who have done so much to illuminate Shakespeare's work for us") is almost at once qualified by hostile references to "the blunt perceptions of a New Critic," and the like. It turns out that one needs "greater sensibility, a subtler perceptiveness—as well as an intimate knowledge of the manners of the age—just how things were between men of such differing positions and status [as Shakespeare and Southampton], to be able to interpret the Sonnets." The historian doing the work must also possess "an equal feeling for literature." One would be well advised to call on the resources of a social historian on such an occasion, one deeply versed in Renaissance aristocratic codes and wise enough in the way of men of this world to see what is going on.[4] In other words—and here, I think, is the fourth postulate of the investigative method—one needs A.L. Rowse.

This barely unstated assumption that only a historian like Rowse himself can be trusted to unlock the historical meaning of the sonnets leads him into pursuit of further one-to-one correspondences that cause increasing unease. If (so the method goes) the sonnets are autobiographical about Southampton and Shakespeare, then the trained historian can also find straightforward equations for other figures, arriving "through the accumulation of attested evidence" at "certainty." No mystery need surround the identity of "Mr. W. H.," to whom the publisher, Thomas Thorpe, dedicates his first edition of the sonnets in 1609: Mr. (i.e., "Master") W. H. "is" the Countess of Southampton's third husband, Sir William Harvey. Thorpe wishes Harvey "all happiness and that eternity promised by our living poet" because Harvey had remarried in 1608 after the death of the countess in 1607 and was about to start a family, thereby embracing the sort of eternity—perpetuation of self through the procreation of children—that the sonnets celebrate. Harvey is "the only begetter of these ensuing Sonnets" in that he got them for Thorpe, presumably from the countess's papers, still in their proper order. Thorpe's greeting from "the well-wishing adventurer in setting forth" echoes current excitement about the Virginia Company and its plantation in the New World, in which adventure Southampton was interested.[5]

This is a plausible reading of a much-disputed passage, but its certitude and its dismissive attitude toward "innumerable people" who have been led "astray" by other options is neither endearing nor persuasive. For one thing, Thorpe is talking about himself as "the well-wishing adventurer" who is "setting forth" in publishing the sonnets. The metaphoric appeal is to overseas adventure, surely, but any Londoner could respond to that stirring proposition, and might think of England's nautical daring generally without specific reference to Virginia, let alone to Southampton. Because the sonnets had evidently been in private circulation in manuscript for some time prior to 1609, we can have no assurance that the collection Thorpe obtained came from the countess's private copy, if she had one. The ordering of the sonnets in Thorpe's edition increasingly makes sense to readers today, but Rowse's suppositious account of their provenance from 1590 or so until 1609 (a long while) offers no evidence supporting the present order. "Begetter," according to the *OED*, can mean "one who begets; a procreator," or, figuratively, "the agent that originates, produces, or occasions." Thorpe's context, with its wordplay on the idea of the begetting of children and of setting forth on an adventure, supports the literal and figurative meanings for which *OED* gives contemporary examples; the dictionary quotes Thorpe as fitting into the figurative meaning. The other Renaissance illustrations speak of God as the begetter. Rowse's reading of "obtainer" is possible, especially since "beget" can mean "to get, acquire," but "obtainer" remains a historically undocumented definition of the word "begetter," and in any case is not the only meaning. For that reason other critics have justly searched for someone who might assume the role of the inspirer of the sonnets. Harvey was never on good terms with his stepson Southampton, and it was to Southampton that Shakespeare was presumably connected. I will not rehearse the other possible candidates for "Mr. W. H.," other than to say that disagreements are numerous and that the lack of consensus is not likely to be owing to the circumstance that Rowse is right because he is a historian while the others are simply wrong. Rowse's case for Harvey is flawed by the very thing he likes best about it: its simplicity based on personal judgment and training, and its unwillingness to deal with complex and multiple meanings of words.[6]

Even in the matter of identifying Southampton and Shakespeare as the main figures of the sonnets (along with the "rival poet" and the "dark lady"), Rowse's interpretation moves swiftly from plausible biographical links to his perceptions of the emotional states of the protagonists. True enough, Shakespeare reveals in his dedication to *The Rape of Lucrece* in 1594 a warmth, gratitude, and personal closeness not as fully expressed in the dedication to *Venus and Adonis* in 1593, but this is easily accounted for by Southampton's continued support and by Shakespeare's growing success under that protective arm. It does not follow that Shakespeare "fell for the young lord to whom he owed all this."[7] In the sonnets, to be sure, the poet is enamored of the young man; he is at various times elated, tortured by his own failings, thankful for friendship, tortured by physical absence, jealous, reproachful, fatalistic, bitter, serene. Yet much or all of this could be a heightened imaginative dramatization, extrapolated from a real but more mundane relationship that Shakespeare as actor and budding playwright enjoyed with a young aristocrat.

Even if he took as his narrative "source" such a dependent relationship, Shakespeare was fully capable of bringing to that situation the intense poetic creativity that he brought to other depictions of jealousy and affection in his plays and poems. One can even imagine that Shakespeare found Southampton a bit insufferable and precious (as we tend to do), and that he maintained a decorous silence in the sonnets about his personal reservations lest he alienate the young man and his family. About such a speculation we cannot possibly know the truth, but it is as plausible as Rowse's scenario, which suffers from the serious weakness of positing that art models itself directly on living circumstance. This is the same naive assumption about creativity that has led a number of Oxfordians to argue that Polonius, for example, is a roman à clef likeness of Burghley, and that only an influential courtier would have known enough about Burghley's mannerisms and methods of dealing to have executed the portrait.[8]

No less simplistic is Rowse's conclusion that the difference between Shakespeare's first supposedly "artificial" plays, *The Comedy of Errors* and *The Two Gentlemen of Verona*, and the vital "new dimensions" of *A Midsummer Night's Dream*, *Love's Labor's Lost*, and *Romeo and Juliet* is to be accounted for by "the inspiration of love" that came to Shakespeare from his relationship with Southampton, as well as from private sponsorship of production. "We now know," insists Rowse, that *Love's Labor's Lost* was written "as a private skit on and for the Southampton circle" in 1593, and that *A Midsummer Night's Dream* was adapted for the private nuptials of the Countess of Southampton to Sir Thomas Heneage in 1594, while *Romeo and Juliet* reflects the feud between Henry Long and Southampton's dear friends Henry and Charles Danvers that led to Long's death in 1594.[9] These judgments are reductive, first, in their dismissive view of Shakespeare's first two plays (if they are indeed the first and in this order; Rowse likes certitude about dating); second, in their supposition that Southampton's friendship was Shakespeare's main source of emotional support, as though he had nowhere else to turn; third, in their insistence on private productions of plays written for the popular stage that provide nothing more than circumstantial evidence of any courtly occasion and that could in any event be linked to other courtly festivities or marriages; and fourth, in their suggestion that an artist like Shakespeare writes beautifully when he is in love and less so when he is merely carrying out apprenticeship exercises. Romantic biographies like Sullivan's about Beethoven used to pursue similar sorts of antitheses: happiness produces the symphonies in a warm key, especially 2, 4, 6, and 8, while suffering produces the Eroica, 5, 7, and 9.

It follows from all that has been said that the dating of the sonnets can be firmly ascertained with reference to the biographical circumstances of Shakespeare's relationship with Southampton. Shakespeare's sonneteering for

Southampton "comes to an end when he achieves financial security and independence with his purchase of a share in the Lord Chamberlain's company," the money having been provided, according to an early tradition,[10] by Southampton himself, "generous as ever." The "dark lady" sonnets, 126 to 154, are not later in time; rather, they overlap, spelling out the unstated reasons for the poet's difficulties with the young lord as expressed in Sonnets 33-42, for example. (In fact, since those sonnets say nothing about a female or a rival, this reading of them is pure speculation.) Topical references all fall for Rowse into the early 1590s, with a terminal date in the spring of 1595. The "painful warrior famousèd for fight" in Sonnet 25 who is "from the book of honor razèd quite" is Ralegh, who fell from favor in 1592; this is made "certain" for us, despite the plethora of others who fell at other times, like Essex in 1601. So too with the line in the same sonnet announcing that "The mortal moon hath her eclipse endured." To Rowse, intent on the early 1590s, this can only mean the threat to Queen Elizabeth's life in the Lopez conspiracy of 1594, but then the queen also survived a time of crisis when Essex rebelled against her. The topical hints in Sonnet 124 about "thrallèd discontent" and "policy, that heretic" are indeed, as "anyone can see," politico-religious, but to say that is not to limit fears of Catholic meddling in English affairs to 1594-95 as Rowse would do. In sum, the insistence that Sonnet 104's reference to "three winters cold" is a chronicle of the years 1591-92, 1592-93, and 1593-94 imposes the kind of tidy neatness on dating that Rowse brings also to matters of verbal interpretation, speculation about emotional states of mind, and views on the relationship between art and biography.[11] Rowse's distaste for "non-historians" who range "blithely" over a number of years is part of his inability to see the limits of his own argument.

Rowse arrives "with certainty" at the identity of the "rival poet" as well. Marlowe best fits Rowse's search for a poet whom Shakespeare might have called "a better spirit" (Sonnet 80) and who, with "the proud full sail of his great verse" (Sonnet 86), competed so effectively for the young lord's approval. Rowse emphasizes that this description of Sonnet 86 is in the past tense, as appropriate to one who died, as Marlowe did, in May of 1593. Though we have no evidence of connection between Southampton and Marlowe, Rowse is sure that he sees the narcissistic young lord figured in Leander, with his dangling tresses and white skin. Rowse finds significance in a similarity of theme between *Hero and Leander* and *Venus and Adonis,* especially in the sexual ambivalence and in the urging of the beautiful young man to reciprocate the amorous love that is offered him—for which a literary analysis might well suggest a generic connection and literary models out of Ovid. Rowse has no doubt that the two poems were written in a direct competition for Southampton's favor.[12] Other major poets of the era, like Chapman, are not in the running in

Rowse's project of identification of the "rival poet," mainly perhaps because the chronology of their work is less favorable to them.

The grand prize of identification is of course the "dark lady," the prize being all the more inestimable because of the difficulty of the assignment. All of Rowse's method points to this Garden of the Hesperides. We see him arising out of his long-held conviction that "we are never likely to know who Shakespeare's mistress was"[13] in 1964 and earlier, to the triumphant discovery in 1973 that his doubt on the subject was simply, in the last analysis, a sign that even he had not pursued the correct method of research with sufficient rigor. "The Problems Solved," announces the title page of Rowse's 1973 edition of the sonnets. The historian's method is "triumphantly vindicated."[14]

The successful conclusion toward which he has been reaching prior to 1973 is not simply to identify the "dark lady" of the sonnets but to know, biographically, "who Shakespeare's mistress was." He expects to find a lady who is "no better than she should be"—much along the lines also of Elizabeth Vernon, who in 1598 could boast of having "caught" the eligible Southampton in marriage "in the usual way," that is, by getting pregnant, or Elizabeth Throckmorton, by whom Sir Walter Ralegh was caught also "in the usual way" in 1592, or Anne Hathaway, by whom, and by his own "sportive" nature, Shakespeare had been "trapped" at the age of eighteen. The "dark lady" was even more sinister than these, for she disrupted the significant friendship that Shakespeare had formed with Southampton. She must have been, in Rowse's view, something of a challenge to Shakespeare, tyrannical and promiscuous but also bright and personally aroused to anger by him, perhaps even something of a poet in her own right, capable of revenge in her writings.[15]

"Defrauded by his sex" and thereby given no option of a physical relationship with Southampton, even if Southampton's own inclinations may well have been closer to Marlowe's (who was undoubtedly homosexual, in Rowse's view), the "highly sexed and heterosexual" Shakespeare loved the young lord with the self-denigrating and idealized passion we see in the earlier sonnets. When, however, Shakespeare became "infatuated" with the "dark lady" toward the end of 1592, "the snake had already entered Paradise, and destroyed its pristine innocence, with a woman." She did not keep the poet waiting long in his craving for fornication (Sonnet 129). Shakespeare made the mistake, as chronicled in the sonnets, of introducing Southampton to his own mistress, thus apparently initiating the young peer into heterosexual experience but at the cost of a painful rivalry made all the more distressful by Southampton's own emotional disengagement from the affair and by the woman's cynical alacrity in taking up with a wealthy and unattached young aristocrat. Shakespeare himself may have taken away from the affair as his grim prize a sexually transmitted disease. The woman was, in short, "a bad lot." The Lady Rosaline in *Love's Labor's Lost*, with her dark complexion and coquettish way of torturing Berowne, is another wry tribute to Shakespeare's obsession with the "dark lady"; *The Rape of Lucrece,* 1594, expresses Shakespeare's contrite revulsion after the fact at his own carnality in the affair.[16] What reader of *The National Inquirer* or the London tabloids would not wish to know the identification of this notorious woman?

Clues line the path of the researcher well before the discovery. The lady in question must, from the evidence of the sonnets, be a gentlewoman but also a "lady of pleasure" who has had other lovers before. Probably she has been married; certainly she has broken her "bed-vow" (Sonnet 152). She and the poet have broken off and then renewed an unsatisfactory relationship, in which her power over him is physical only. Others hold her in low esteem and cannot see what attracts the poet to her, especially since she is unfashionably dark of complexion. She is given to scorning him in the presence of others. "No doubt she was socially superior to him." Perhaps Shakespeare's candor "helped to get the young man out of her clutches." Evidence for the biographical veracity of the whole account lies in its vivid "realism" and "power of the portrait," so unlike anything found in other Elizabethan sonnet sequences.[17] (This generalization forgets Sidney and Spenser, and assumes that the vividness of Shakespeare's sonnets can arise essentially from actual experience rather than from the extrapolations of an extraordinary poetic imagination.)

In Sonnet 128, Rowse argues, Shakespeare "tells us" that the "dark lady" "is musical." The sonnet describes how the lady often plays what appears to be a spinet or virginal or harpsichord, the "jacks" of which "kiss the tender inward" of the player's hand. The term "jacks" is oddly used; technically it means the upright pieces of wood fitted to the back of the key-levers and provided with quills to pluck the strings as the keys are pressed down by the performer. The *OED* suggests that the use here in Shakespeare and by some later writers is erroneous, since the description in the sonnet applies better to the key itself rather than to the jack. If Rowse knows all this he declines to say so, for he glosses "jacks" simply as "keys," and also does not acknowledge a pun on the idea of "common fellows," as in line 13: "Since saucy jacks so happy are in this." I would interpret Shakespeare's use as poetic license for the sake of a conceit, not error, but I am less inclined to be charitable toward the editor in this case, whose liking for straightforward, commonsense interpretation misses several significant nuances and puts in question the editor's musical expertise.[18]

More importantly, can we take this one indication of musical rendition as evidence that the "dark lady" must be "musical"? Ladies at court and in good families were expected to play of an evening, in the Renaissance as in later eras. There is no hint of professional performance; quite the reverse. The lady plays "oft," and the poet-listener says nothing of her training or skill; the sonnet seems to invoke the kind of occasional, amateur playing suitable for a lady of breeding. Indeed, Rowse envisages, in the supposed romance of Shakespeare and the "dark lady," various "pleasant intervals" when the lady "played the virginals to him," taking pity on the man she enjoys torturing.[19]

The person whom Rowse proposes as the living model for the "dark lady," or rather states flatly that she "was" the "dark lady," is Emilia Lanier or Aemilia Lanyer—Rowse prefers the first spelling, though he uses both. From Simon Forman's Diary (a chief source for Rowse) and from parish records and other documents it appears that Aemilia was baptized on January 27, 1569, in the parish church of St. Botolph, Bishopsgate, outside the City walls to the northeast.[20] Her father, aged twenty-seven at the time of her birth, was Baptist Bassano, a native of Venice (Bassano is in the state of Venice) and "one of the musicians of our sovereign lady the Queen's Majesty."[21] The Bassanos had come into England in Henry VIII's reign, and continued on as royal musicians until the time of the Civil War. Like many or most such musicians imported from Italy and the Spanish peninsula to satisfy Henry's passion for music, the Bassanos appear to have been Jewish, closely associated with Anthonius Moyses, Anthony Symonds or Simon, Anthony Cossin (i.e., Gershon), and others, some Ashkenazim (especially the wind players) and some Sephardim (the string players). Bassano was a common name among the Jews of Northern Italy, though borne by some Christians as well. The Bassano coat of arms, displaying silkworm moths and a tree (presumably mulberry), is aptly suited, since Jews had introduced silk-farming into Italy.[22]

Aemilia's mother was Margaret Johnson, a name suggesting that Aemilia was half Jewish-Italian and half-English. The husband's will refers to Margaret as "Margarett Bassany also Margarett Johnson my reputed wieff"; whether this description implies a common-law relationship is not clear.[23] The parents died and were buried in St. Botolph's, Bishopsgate, Baptist on April 11, 1576 (Rowse says May 11) and Margaret Bassano (as she is recorded in the parish register) on July 7, 1587.[24] Baptist left in his will (dated January 3, 1576) a bequest of £100 for his soon-to-be-seven-year-old daughter to be paid on her twenty-first birthday or upon her marrying, together with the rents of three houses or tenements to be shared with Aemilia's older sister Angela after the death of their mother. Baptist's fortunes, according to Forman (whom Aemilia consulted as an astrologer in 1597), had declined before he died, to the point that he was beginning to be "miserable in his estate," but he evidently was not destitute. Margaret was appointed executrix.[25] When she died in 1587, Aemilia was eighteen.

Forman reports that Aemilia was brought up in Kent—a circumstance that is later confirmed by her dedication of a poem to "the Lady Susan, Countess Dowager of Kent," warmly thanking that noble person as "the mistress of my youth, / The noble guide of my ungoverned days."[26] Aemilia was married on October 18, 1592, at St. Botolph's, Aldgate, when she was twenty-three, to

Alfonso Lanyer, three years her junior.[27] As a resident of Longditch, Westminster, near the bridge leading to Canon Row, Lanyer and his wife enjoyed a proximity to Whitehall and an influential courtly set. His family were, like the Bassanos, professional musicians, having come from the vicinity of Rouen in the 1560s; they were to stay on at court in their musical function into the Restoration period. Alfonso Lanyer lived until 1613, having proved to be a difficult husband.[28] Meantime, Aemilia's sister Angela had married a gentleman named Joseph Holland some time prior to 1576; she is described as married in Baptist Bassano's will of that year.[29]

An astrological figure that Forman cast for Aemilia on May 17, 1597, provides the notation that "she was paramour to my old Lord Hunsdon that was Lord Chamberlain and was maintained in great pride; and it seems that, being with child, she was for colour married to a minstrel."[30] Henry Carey, first Lord Hunsdon (1524?-1596) maintained a relationship with her for some time: "The old Lord Chamberlain kept her long," says Forman. Hunsdon was about forty-five years her senior. The affair might have started when she was about nineteen. The device of marrying her to a "minstrel," that is, to Alfonso Lanyer, was a common way of providing a cover of respectability and some financial support for the pregnant mistresses of great men.

Her son, Henry, presumably named for Lord Hunsdon, was born in early 1593, only a few months after her marriage in October of the previous year. Aemilia later was suffering difficulties of pregnancy when she visited Forman on June 3, 1597. She seems to have been prone to miscarriages, though she did give birth to a daughter, Odillya, in December of 1598. This child died in September of the next year and was buried at St. Botolph's, Bishopsgate—the parish of her own family, not that where she was married. Her son Henry became a flautist at court, married in 1623, had two known children, and died in 1633.[31]

Although Aemilia gained some favor and attention at court, she seems to have had a bad marriage with Alfonso Lanyer—not surprisingly, perhaps, given the motives that might have prompted a young musician to provide a facade of respectability for Lord Hunsdon's affair with her in return for a suitable financial settlement and other assurances of continued support. Aemilia was "maintained in great pomp," says Forman still in 1597, with "£40 a year" given her by Hunsdon presumably at the time of her marriage in 1593, enough so that she was "wealthy to him that married her, in money and jewels." Again, "She hath been favoured much of her Majesty and of many noblemen, and hath had great gifts and been made much of—a nobleman that is dead [i.e., Hunsdon] hath loved her well and kept her and did maintain her long." Soon, however, according to Forman, she was plagued with difficulties at home. "Her husband hath dealt hardly with her, and spent and consumed her goods. She is now [in

1597] very needy, in debt and it seems for Lucrese [i.e., lucre's?] sake will be a good fellow, for necessity doth compel."[32]

Forman's own low opinion of Aemilia Lanyer as available for money may well be the result of his attraction to her and his ultimate frustration with their relationship. Here was a classy young woman coming to him for astrological consultation, telling him of her affair with Hunsdon, her marital troubles, her difficult pregnancies, and the like, and anxiously seeking his advice as an astrologer about her and her husband's prospects. Would Alfonso prosper in his venture at sea with the Earl of Essex, out of which the young adventurer hoped to be knighted? About herself, Aemilia longed to know "whether she shall be a lady, and how she shall speed."[33] The situation was fraught with erotic potential, and Forman, something of a lady's man by his own account, took up the gambit he thought he saw.

His reply to Aemilia's queries—inaccurate enough as matters turned out, like most such fortune-telling—was that "She shall be a lady or attain to some further dignity," while her husband "shall speed well and be knighted hardly," that is, with difficulty, only to die within two years of his coming home. Encouraging her thus, Forman went on to see what there was for him in all this. Having been told by his astrological figures that Aemilia had the mind of one who "seems she is or will be a harlot" and who also "useth sodomy," Forman proceeded to wonder if the lady might not receive him sexually. Entries in his Diary for September 11 and 20 at least imply that matters proceeded to rather intense foreplay but not to sexual intercourse (or "halek," in Forman's demure euphemism). Forman tortures himself with the questions, "Best to do a thing or no?" "whether it were best to send to her to know how she did, and thereby to try whether she would bid the messenger bid his mistress round to him or no? Thinking thereby what he might goodly bolden thereby to see her." Whether Forman obtained more complete success ultimately is debatable and unimportant. Plainly he was intrigued, baffled, titillated. Other entries in his Diary attest to an interest in exploiting women sexually, and reveal what we would call a distinctly misogynistic turn of mind.[34]

Forman complains in the upshot of this series of encounters that Aemilia Lanyer "was a whore, and dealt evil with him after." He suggests that the Lanyer household might have been used by others in search of sexual adventure. He has a low opinion of her husband as well. Whether the accusations have any real basis or are the product of his own disappointment with Aemilia, and his knowledge that she had been Hunsdon's mistress, is a question we must ask. As late as January 7, 1600, we see Forman casting his own horoscope to know "why Mrs Lanyer sent for me and quid a sequitur whether she intends any more villainy or no."[35] Such at any rate is the man from whom most of our information about Aemilia's personal life proceeds.

Rowse's candidate for the "dark lady" rests on dubious qualifications. First of all, says Rowse, she was "no better than she should be." Taking Simon Forman at his word, Rowse envisages a woman who was dissipated enough to provoke all the manifestations of self-disgust we hear from the poet-author of the sonnets. Is there any evidence, however, outside of the account of a misogynistic astrologer who may well have been piqued by his own lack of success with her, that Aemilia was in fact profligate? She evidently was Lord Hunsdon's mistress and bore him a child, but to draw further inferences of wantonness from this circumstance is very hazardous.[36] Aemilia Lanyer does seem to have had some acquaintance at court. Was she, as Rowse first insisted, "very brown in youth"?[37] Rowse found this detail, implicit no doubt also in her Italian heritage, to be highly significant, though he then dropped the dubious item after the first excitement of discovery when, under Stanley Wells's more careful examination of Foreman's case-book, the key word turns out to be "brave" rather than "brown."[38]

Rowse gets other crucial details wrong. Aemilia did come from a musical family, to be sure. She had a close relationship with Lord Hunsdon, the patron of Shakespeare's company, the Lord Chamberlain's men. She consulted Simon Forman as an astrologer, who often went to see Shakespeare's plays. Shakespeare's landlady, Mrs. Mountjoy, also visited Forman. So did Shakespeare's fellow actor Augustine Phillips.[39] But Rowse was incorrect to suppose that her husband's name was William or Will, and that the bitter sexual punning on that word in the sonnets thus offers biographical particularity.

How well does this candidacy serve? One might wonder if Southampton and Shakespeare would have quarreled over such a lady, but the evidence is plain that Lord Hunsdon found her worth keeping and that Simon Forman could not stay away, for all his need to despise her and perhaps himself. Still, would Shakespeare and then Southampton have thought it prudent to pursue a lady who, in 1592-94 (Rowse's years for the sonnet narrative), was for most if not all of this period the mistress of the Lord Chamberlain? Hunsdon became Shakespeare's patron in 1594 when Shakespeare joined the Lord Chamberlain's players. Hunsdon may have kept Aemilia as his mistress after her marriage to Lanyer in 1593; such an arrangement was not uncommon, and Forman's phrase, "The old Lord Chamberlain kept her longer," might seem to lend support to such an interpretation. In any case Aemilia had been Hunsdon's mistress in 1592-93 and perhaps well before. If the sonnets were autobiographical in these terms, would a smart poet have missed the opportunity to exploit a dramatic conflict like that? Or would a person with any grasp on sanity not have stayed away from such obvious trouble?[40]

Even if one were to believe Forman that Aemilia Lanyer was a kept woman and still worse, the circumstance would not render her unique. Nor would her being dark of complexion—if we can trust Forman about this detail, and if we take seriously the idea that Shakespeare as imaginative poet had to stick to the facts. The musicianship, mentioned in passing in the sonnets, is the accomplishment of many a young lady whom Hunsdon might have kept, and in no way points to a family background in professional musicianship. The name "Will" is one of the most common of English first names, even if Shakespeare needed a real circumstance to devise wordplay on his own name, and even if Rowse were correct in supposing that Aemilia's husband's name was Will in the first place. The wry joking about "Whoever hath her wish, thou hast thy Will, / And Will to boot, and Will to overplus" (Sonnet 135) might seem to have more caustic point if Will were the name of the young aristocratic friend who is two-timing the poet, not the lady's spendthrift husband.[41] If the husband were to be brought into a roman à clef narrative, why doesn't Shakespeare hint at a husband who abuses his wife and spends all the money she brings in from the aging great lord who keeps her, as evidently was the case with Lanyer and his wife?

All that can be brought to Aemilia Lanyer's candidacy is an argument about probabilities: that the alleged whorish reputation, the courtly favor of the queen, the purportedly dark complexion, and the musicianship are unlikely to be found together in any one woman present on the scene in 1592-94 unless that woman is the "dark lady." Yet even these few characteristics, each of them common enough at the time, are problematic or uncertain. The focus on these characteristics ignores other seemingly relevant and piquant circumstances, such as Hunsdon's protective interest in Aemilia Lanyer and Alfonso Lanyer's role as the jealous, irresponsible husband.

Rowse's account is also unbalanced in that it ignores the woman who lived long after Forman had seemingly passed out of her life. Recent studies, and this present volume, focus instead on the married gentlewoman who became "the first Englishwoman to publish a substantial volume of original poems, and to make an overt bid for patronage as a male poet of the era might, though in distinctively female terms."[42] Sometime in the early 1600s she enjoyed the hospitality of Margaret and Anne Clifford at Cookham, where, by her own account, she experienced a religious conversion and dedicated herself to the vocation of writing poetry. Her poems, published in 1611, were to include a tribute to that royal manor in her "The Description of Cooke-ham." Her bid for patronage seems not to have been rewarded with any permanent bestowal of favor at the Jacobean court, and insecurities of income seem to have plagued her; although her husband was awarded a patent in 1604 to collect revenues from the weighing of hay and grain in London, by all accounts he was a spendthrift. After becoming a widow in 1613, Aemilia claimed her share of these revenues in many petitions and lawsuits against the members of Lanyer's family.

When she set up a school "for the education of noblemen and gentlemen's children of great worth" in the well-to-do district of St. Giles in the Fields in 1617, she found herself imbroiled legally with her landlord. She claimed, in her chancery case against him, to have been left "in very poor estate" by the death of her husband. The school venture lasted two years, after which little is known of her other than that she evidently lived near her son Henry and his family in St. James, Clerkenwell. On her burial record for August 3, 1645, she is listed as a "pensioner," suggesting that she enjoyed at least some small income.[43]

The picture overall is of a determined, independent woman who made a significant contribution to the Renaissance poetic corpus, and whose largely unsuccessful quest for patronage is eloquent testimonial of what it must have been like for a woman of her social status—partly Italian and Jewish, it would seem, and in any case from a family of court musicians with uncertain claims to gentry—to survive at the Jacobean court. Rowse's defamatory portrait, derived largely in fact and in spirit from Simon Forman, would hardly prepare one for the woman that Aemilia Lanyer turns out to be.

Rowse's recurring Victorian phrase, that Aemilia Lanyer "was no better than she should be," is, interestingly enough, a variation on what George Bernard Shaw says about Mary Fitton as his whimsical choice for the "dark lady" of the sonnets—"no better than she ought to have been."[44] Blithely disclaiming all semblance of historical accuracy, Shaw writes his play on the "dark lady" of the sonnets as a "brief trifle . . . full of manifest impossibilities," taking as its point of departure the theory of Thomas Tyler, Frank Harris, and others that the sonnets were written in the late 1590s to the young Lord Herbert, soon to be the Earl of Pembroke, who had gotten with child a young lady whom Rowse calls "another of those frail ladies, the maids-of-honour," Mary Fitton.[45] Herbert was a great patron of the theater, and later of the Shakespeare First Folio. Mary's blonde complexion has ruled against her candidacy of late, but at the end of the nineteenth century she was very much in evidence, along with Maria Thompkins and Mrs. Davenant, the mother of the poet and keeper of a tavern in Oxford, to name but two. These ladies have all disappeared, but Shaw's perfectly fantastic "dark lady" lives on as a kind of comic rebuttal of Rowse's utterly serious crusade on behalf of, or against, Aemilia Lanyer.

One wonders if Rowse knew Shaw's jeu d'esprit. Shaw's "dark lady" is, to my mind, closer to what we know of Aemilia Lanyer than is Rowse's "dark lady." She is intelligent enough to know that she has to put up with a poet-wooer whose nature it is to laugh at his own infatuation and to dress her down as a woman whose "breasts are dun" and whose breath "reeks" (Sonnet 130). She must have been, says Shaw, a person of real substance to have kept Shakespeare on his toes as a sonneteer. Shaw presupposes the same sort of correspondence between the sonnets and Shakespeare's own personal life as does

Rowse, but at least Shaw comes away with a lively respect for whatever lady it might have been.

Rowse's case for Aemilia Lanyer as the "dark lady" is not a strong one, and indeed would hardly be worth discussing if it were not for the ironical circumstance that he discovered for his own purposes a woman who has now assumed a significance her discoverer did not begin to grasp. We need to consider who Aemilia Lanyer was in the full dimensions of her life, and especially who she became after Simon Forman's brief acquaintance with her in 1597 and even to some extent before that: the woman who was acquainted, albeit marginally and in a dependent relationship, with Lord Hunsdon, the Countess of Kent, the Countess Dowager of Cumberland, the countesses of Bedford, Suffolk, and Dorset, Princess Elizabeth, Lady Arabella Stuart, and Queen Anne, and who published *Salve Deus Rex Judaeorum* (S.R., October 2, 1610). We certainly need to wonder whether Forman's disapproval of her, and then Rowse's no less denunciatory view, may stem from a not untypical male response to a "whore" (Forman's term) or a "cocotte" (Rowse's)[46] who is "no better than she should be," with a resulting dislocation of judgment and a skewed evaluation of Aemilia Lanyer's accomplishment as a human being.

NOTES

1. Rowse, Introduction, *Shakespeare's Sonnets,* ed. with an Introduction and Notes by A.L. Rowse (London: Macmillan, 1964), pp. xi-xii, xxx. Hereafter referred to as "First Ed."
2. Ibid., pp. xiii, xvii-xx.
3. Ibid., p. vii; *Shakespeare's Sonnets: The Problems Solved. A Modern Edition, with Prose Versions, Introduction, and Notes,* 2d ed. (London: Macmillan, 1973), p. ix, hereafter referred to as "Second Ed."; and A.L. Rowse, *Shakespeare the Man* (New York: Harper & Row, 1973). Rowse extensively repeats himself, using verbatim the phrases and sentences of his earlier work, not only in his second edition of the sonnets, where the practice is understandable, but also in what purport to be separate scholarly publications, such as *Shakespeare the Man* and *William Shakespeare: A Biography* (New York and Evanston: Harper & Row, 1963).
4. First Ed., pp. vii, xvii; Second Ed., p. x, where Rowse specifically attacks Hyder Rollins's *New Variorum Shakespeare* edition of the sonnets for its "total pessimism" and "the assumption that all these questions are unanswerable."
5. First Ed., pp. vii, xi-xii; *William Shakespeare,* p. 200.
6. In *William Shakespeare,* p. 200, Rowse supposes that the sonnets were "folded and put away," not privately circulated. He argues that Shakespeare uses "begetter" in the sense of "to get or acquire," though his one example, from Hamlet's address to the players, "you must acquire and beget a temperance that may give it smoothness" (*Hamlet,* 3.2.7-8), does not certainly use the words "acquire and beget" in apposition as meaning the same thing; the passage can well mean "you must acquire and produce or call into being a temperance. . . ." Compare *Love's Labor's Lost,* 2.1.9, cited by the *OED* sv. "beget" v. 4: "His eye begets occasion for his wit." In fact, even the word "acquire" in the Hamlet passage need not mean

"come into possession of from someone else," as Rowse proceeds to apply it to "Mr. W. H." and Harvey; the first meaning of "acquire" in the *OED* is "to gain, obtain, or get as one's own, to gain the ownership of by one's own exertions or qualities." Textual references in this essay are to *The Complete Works of William Shakespeare,* ed. David Bevington, 4th ed., updated (New York: Longman, 1997).

7. First Ed., p. xix.

8. See, for example, Richard F. Whalen, *Shakespeare: Who Was He? The Oxford Challenge to the Bard of Avon* (Westport, Conn., and London: Praeger, 1994), pp. 71-72 and 76-77; Charlton Ogburn, *The Mysterious William Shakespeare: The Myth and the Reality* (New York: Dodd, Mead, 1984); and Dorothy Ogburn and Charlton Ogburn, Sr., *This Star of England: William Shake-speare, Man of the Renaissance* (Westport, Conn.: Greenwood Press, 1972). More orthodox Shakespeare scholarship too has long taken the view, going back to Edmund Malone, that Lord Burghley stood for the portrait of Polonius.

9. First Ed., p. xix; Second Ed., p. xv; *William Shakespeare,* pp. 203-22.

10. E.K. Chambers, *William Shakespeare: A Study of Facts and Figures,* 2 vols. (Oxford: Clarendon, 1930), 2, pp. 276-77. See First Ed., p. xxx.

11. First Ed., pp. xx-xxiii; *Shakespeare the Man,* pp. 87-90; *William Shakespeare,* pp. 165-66, 181-83.

12. First Ed., pp. xxiv-xxvii; Second Ed., pp. xix-xxi and xliii; *Christopher Marlowe: A Biography* (London: Macmillan, 1964), pp. 165 ff.; *William Shakespeare,* pp. 175-77.

13. First Ed., pp. xxx, and *William Shakespeare,* p. 197.

14. Second Ed., p. x. The announcement was first made in "Revealed at Last, Shakespeare's Dark Lady," *London Times,* January 29, 1973, p. 12.

15. This point is developed, after Rowse had learned that Lanyer was a poet, in his edition of *The Poems of Shakespeare's Dark Lady: Salve Deus, Rex Judeorum by Emilia Lanyer* (London: Jonathan Cape, 1976), p. 20 and passim. For an interesting discussion, see Lorna Hutson, "Why the Lady's Eyes Are Nothing Like the Sun," in *New Feminist Discourses: Critical Essays on Theories and Texts,* ed. Isobel Armstrong (London: Routledge, 1992), pp. 154-75.

16. First Ed., pp. xvi-xxi; Second Ed., pp. xix, xxxiii; A.L. Rowse, *Ralegh and the Throckmortons* (London: Macmillan, 1962); *Shakespeare the Man,* pp. 87, 91-92, 100-5.

17. First Ed., pp. xxxi-xxxiii.

18. Second Ed., p. xxviii; *Shakespeare the Man,* p. 91.

19. Second Ed., p. xxx.

20. Parish Register of St. Botolph's Bishopsgate, Guildhall Library 4515/1, naming the child "Emillia Baptyst." The date fits with what we know elsewhere of Aemilia's age, and the parish is that of her parents' residence. Cited in Woods, *Poems,* Introduction. Rowse implies a birthdate after May of 1570 when he says that Aemilia was "a girl of only six" when her father was buried on "11 May 1576"—actually April 3. Rowse, Second Ed., p. xxxviii.

21. Rowse, Second Ed., p. xxxix, cites Prerog. Court Cant., Prob/11/58, f. 21.

22. Roger Prior, "The Bassanos of Tudor England," *Jewish Chronicle Literary Supplement* (June 1979); Prior, "Jewish Musicians at the Tudor Court," *Musical Quarterly* 69 (1983): 253-65; Prior, "More (Moor? Moro?) Light on the Dark Lady," *Financial Times* (October 10, 1987): London Section, Other Page, p. 17; and H.C. De Lafontaine, ed., *The King's Musick: A Transcript of Records Relating to Music and Musicians (1460-1700)* (London: Novello, 1909). I agree with Barbara Lewalski, "Imagining Female Community: Aemilia

Lanyer's Poems," in *Writing Women in Jacobean England* (Cambridge, Mass.: Harvard University Press, 1993), pp. 213-41, esp. p. 395, n. 5, that Prior's evidence about the Bassano family crest adds to the likelihood of their having been Jewish, but does nothing to strengthen Rowse's contention that Aemilia Lanyer is the "dark lady." The case rests chiefly on puns like "moor" and "moro" (Italian for "mulberry tree"), Bassanio and Bassano, Launcelet and Lanier, etc., and on presumed analogies between the Moor's illegitimate child in *Titus Andronicus* and Aemilia's child Henry (who was not illegitimate, in fact, though probably conceived out of wedlock), and still more. Rowse was unaware of the likelihood of Aemilia's Jewish ancestry when he made his discovery of her.

23. Prorog. Court Cant., Probate 11/58, f. 153, quoted in Lewalski, "Imagining Female Community," p. 395, n. 6. S. Schoenbaum, *Shakespeare's Lives,* new ed. (Oxford: Clarendon, 1991), p. 558, assumes that Baptist and Margaret, "although unmarried, lived together as man and wife."

24. J. Pulver, *A Bibliographical Dictionary of English Music,* pp. 41 ff., cited in Rowse, Second Ed., p. xxxviii, and the Parish Register of St. Botolph's, Bishopsgate, Guildhall Library 4515/1, cited in Woods, *Poems,* Introduction. Biography is briefly discussed in Elaine Beilin, "The Feminization of Praise: Aemilia Lanyer," in *Redeeming Eve: Women Writers of the English Renaissance* (Princeton: Princeton University Press, 1987), pp. 177-207, esp. pp. 181-82, and Maureen Bell, George Parfitt, and Simon Shepherd, *A Biographical Dictionary of English Women Writers, 1580-1720* (Boston: Hall, 1990), p. 123. See also Leeds Barroll's essay in this volume, chapter 2.

25. Prerog. Court Cant., Probate 11/58, f. 154, and Forman's account in Bodleian ms. Ashmole 226, fol. 95v, cited in Rowse, Second Ed., p. xxxiv, and Woods, *Poems,* Introduction.

26. Simon Forman's account in Bodleian ms. Ashmole 226, fol. 110v; and "To the Ladie Susan," ll. 1-2, in Woods, ed., *Poems.*

27. Register General of St. Botolph's, Aldgate, 1571-1593, Guildhall Library 9221, cited in Woods, ed., *Poems.* Rowse first identified the husband as William Lanier; Second Ed., p. xl. As Woods explains, Rowse evidently misread Forman's entry of May 13, 1597, regarding "Millia Lanier" as about "William Lanier," and then realized his mistake the next year, in 1974, since in *Simon Forman: Sex and Society in Shakespeare's Age* (London, 1974), pp. 96-117, he renews his argument for the identification of the "dark lady" but without claiming that she was married to a man named William. The difference is significant, since Aemilia's supposed marriage to "another Will" (Second Ed., p. xl) tempts Rowse into autobiographical speculation about the wordplay on "Will" in several of the sonnets. See *Shakespeare the Man,* pp. 93-94.

28. Pulver, *Bibliographical Dictionary,* p. 282, cited in Rowse, Second Ed., p. xli; *Shakespeare the Man,* p. 105; Woods, *Poems,* Introduction.

29. The will refers to "Angela Hollande nowe wieff of Joseph Holland gentleman." Prerog. Court Cant., Probate 11/58, f. 153, quoted in Lewalski, "Imagining Female Community," p. 395, n. 6.

30. Bodleian ms. Ashmole 226, f. 95v, cited in Woods, *Poems,* Introduction, and in Rowse, Second Ed., p. xxxiv, and *Shakespeare the Man,* p. 106, but see note 23.

31. *The Parish Register, 1539-1660, of St. Margaret's, Westminster,* ed. A.M. Burke (London: Eyre & Spottiswoode, 1914), p. 62, records the baptism of "Odillia," daughter of Alphonso Laniere, on December 2, 1958. *The Registers of St. Botolph, Bishopsgate,* trans. A.W.C. Hallam, 2 vols. (London, 1889), 1, p. 324, record the burial of "Odillya Lanyer" on

September 6, 1599; see Guildhall, microfilm 4545/1, cited by Lewalski, "Imagining Female Community," p. 395, n. 12. Odillya was thus baptized at St. Margaret's, Westminster—the parish church one would expect, as Woods, *Poems*, Introduction (p. xxiv), points out, for residents of Westminster, whereas she was buried at St. Botolph's, Bishopsgate, where Aemilia herself had been baptized and where her parents had been buried, in a parish to which her husband had no connection.

32. Bodleian ms. Ashmole 226 fols. 95v, 110v, and 201, and ms. 54, cited in Woods, ed., *Poems*, and earlier by Rowse, Second Ed., pp. xxxiv-xxxv; *Shakespeare the Man*, p. 107-8, but with several misquotations.

33. Bodleian ms. Ashmole 226, fol. 122v and 201, and ms. Ashmole 354 ("Geomantica"), fol. 296 (situated before fol. 252), for the dates June 16 to September 2, 1597, cited and discussed in Woods, *Poems*, Introduction.

34. Bodleian ms. Ashmole 354, fol. 250 and 296, cited in Woods, ed., *Poems*. See Rowse, Second Ed., pp. xxxiv-xxxvi.

35. Bodleian ms. Ashmole 236, fol. 250, cited in Woods, ed., *Poems*.

36. Schoenbaum, *Shakespeare's Lives*, pp. 558-59, briefly quotes Forman's comment about Aemilia's willingness "for lucre's sake" to "be a good fellow," and concludes, affirmatively, "So she was promiscuous."

37. Bodleian ms. Ashmole 225, fols. 95v, 110v, 201, June 2 1597 entry.

38. Schoenbaum, *Shakespeare's Lives*, p. 559, relates Stanley Wells's discovery of "braue" for "browne" (in a Radio 4 broadcast on April 22 and then in a letter to *TLS*, May 11, 1973, confirmed by John Carey in *The Listener*, May 3), The *Times* beating a quick retreat from its premature announcement that "A.L. Rowse discovers Shakespeare's Dark Lady," and Rowse's subsequent retelling of the story in *Simon Forman: Sex and Society in Shakespeare's Age*, still clinging to his identification of Aemilia as the "dark lady" but saying nothing about "brown" or a husband named "Will." "Nowhere," observes Schoenbaum, "does Rowse allude to past errors." See also Susan Snyder's review of *Shakespeare's Sonnets: The Problems Solved*, in *Shakespeare Quarterly* 25 (1974): 131-33. For a review of the often *ad hominem* controversy in *The Spectator, The Observer*, and elsewhere occasioned by Rowse's edition in 1973, see Louis Marder, "The 'Dark Lady': Demise of a Theory," *Shakespeare Newsletter* 23.3, #125 (May 1973), p. 24; Marder, "The Dark Lady, Rowse, and His Critics," *Shakespeare Newsletter* 23.4, #126 (September 1973), p. 35; and Paul Ramsay, *The Fickle Glass: A Study of Shakespeare's Sonnets* (New York: AMS Press, 1979), pp. 20 and 169, n. 5.

Prior, "More (More? Moro?) Light on the Dark Lady," argues that the presumed white mulberry tree in the Bassano coat of arms, and thus presumably in her own, signifies the paradoxical "dark lady" who is "black" but also "fair" and "bright." The argument relies too extensively on purported analogies between the plays and Shakespeare's imagined relationship to Aemilia Lanyer. See note 22 above.

39. Lewalski, "Imagining Female Community," p. 394, n. 3.

40. Rowse, *Shakespeare the Man*, p. 113, finds it "a piquant thought" to imagine Shakespeare's being presented to the patron of his newly formed acting company in 1594, having "succeeded him for a time with his mistress, in the seat of her favours."

41. *Shakespeare the Man*, pp. 93-94, assumes without arguing the case that "Will" in Sonnet 135 is the woman's husband. The idea that "Will" might be the young aristocratic friend is unthinkable in Rowse's terms since that aristocrat "is" Southampton. Yet the sonnet plainly addresses the "thou" of the sonnet sequence, and clearly here "thou hast thy

Will" laments the aristocrat's success with the woman. The husband's presumed right to possess her sexually has never been presented as a problem to the poet.

42. Lewalski, "Imagining Female Community," p. 213.

43. The known facts about Aemilia Lanyer's career after 1597 are aptly presented by Woods, *Poems,* Introduction, and by Lewalski, "Imagining Female Community," pp. 216-18. For further discussion of Lanyer's finances, see Leeds Barroll, chapter 2, in this volume

44. Shaw, Preface to *The Dark Lady of the Sonnets,* 1910, *Misalliance; The Dark Lady of the Sonnets, and Fanny's First Play: With a Treatise on Parents and Children* (New York: Brentano's, 1914), p. 109.

45. Rowse, *William Shakespeare,* p. 298.

46. Second Ed., p. xxxvi. Rowse repeats his presumably witty distinction in *Shakespeare the Man,* p. 108. "Cocotte" is not in *OED. Webster's New Collegiate Dictionary,* 2d ed., glosses "cocotte" as "a young woman of loose morals; a strumpet."

2
Looking for Patrons

~

LEEDS BARROLL

In recent years, the emerging body of scholarship on Aemilia Lanyer and her work, suitably represented by the present volume, attests to a new critical awareness of the importance of women writers to early modern cultural history. My own recent work in another area of that history—the court of Queen Anne, consort of King James—has been tangentially but not directly related to this burgeoning research, so perhaps it is not surprising that a period spent considering the phenomenon of Lanyer's life and work produced for me more questions than answers. Thus this essay must be more interrogative than assertive, querying two aspects of the poet's early modern life and subsequently offering some suggestions about a later problematical phase of it.

My questions have to do first with Lanyer's relationship to the Countess of Kent, the subject of eight dedicatory stanzas at the beginning of the *Salve Deus Rex Judaeorum,* and then, in quite a separate vein, with the status and activities of Lanyer's husband, Alfonso. Finally, I shall consider some points to be made about Aemilia Lanyer's bid for patronage with her 1611 volume of poems, suggesting several nonliterary reasons (aside from Lanyer's gender) for the probable failure of this bid. Thus the general focus of this essay is Lanyer's social milieu, her own relationship to it, and some of the problems it raised for her.

The proposition posed by Aemilia Lanyer's publication effort displays the heart, I think, of the early modern social situation as defined, if not by race, then certainly by gender and (this often not adequately stressed) by class. That is, Lanyer was obviously no male—no Samuel Daniel or Ben Jonson: she enjoyed neither the gendered privilege of wandering London alone without thereby being called "whore," nor the social background of associations at public school or university that might be parlayed into access to male or female nobles who sponsored learning. Rather, from what seems to be known about her, Lanyer was, in 1610, a female Londoner, probably a Jew, married to a gentile instrumentalist associated with the production of royal music.[1] That is, she was a Londoner living perhaps in the middle of the income scale of those citizens who owned houses. She was nowhere near as rich as Joan Alleyn, whose father (the entrepreneur Philip Henslowe) and husband (Edward Alleyn) shared the same entertainer-servant class as Aemilia's father and husband; nor did she approach the gentility of another actor's country wife, Anne Hathaway, with her Arden connections. Rather, in the years before her volume of poems was published, Aemilia seems identifiable solely as the wife of the Christian Alfonso Lanyer of London of St. Botolph's parish in Bishopsgate, with no discernible special wealth. She thus seems, significantly, as far from the nobility of the persons invoked in her volume as from the moon.[2]

Nevertheless Lanyer's book was evidently designed to do the traditional job of inventing her as a poet writing within the pale of aristocratic sanction. For very few early modern English writers who were not penning modestly-paying plays or broadside ballads attempted to present themselves as did the remarkably successful John Taylor the Water Poet, that is, *sui generis,* removed from the Virgilian and Horatian traditions of magnificent patronage. Shakespeare, the player, sought a Southampton for his early poems, and Samuel Daniel, although a university man, required the Countess of Bedford, the Countess of Cumberland, and several other nobles. In such a socio-literary context Lanyer's volume obviously required equivalent patronage to be competitive. Her bid, further, warrants close scrutiny since Lanyer's dedications have led us not only to infer biographical facts about her, but have also, perhaps, had the effect of softening our sense of the real rigors of Lanyer's life by seeming to impute to her something of an aristocratic background.

In this regard, the first three dedications of her volume—to the queen, Princess Elizabeth, and Lady Arabella Stuart—seem overly optimistic and un-realistic gestures (more on this subject later). That is why Lanyer's fourth dedi-cation, to "the Ladie *Susan,* Countesse Dowager of Kent and Daughter to the Duchesse of Suffolke," is biographically intriguing because it goes beyond mere hope to claim a prior association. For in the first lines of this dedication Lanyer writes of Kent as "you that were the Mistris of my youth, / The noble guide of my ungovern'd dayes." The second stanza adds:

> And as your rare Perfections shew'd the Glasse
> Wherein I saw each wrinckle of a fault;
> You the Sunnes virtue, I that faire greene grasse,
> That flourisht fresh by your cleere virtues taught:
>   For you possest those gifts that grace the mind,
>   Restraining youth whom Errour oft doth blind.
>   ["To the Lady *Susan,*" ll. 7-12]

These, the only lines (with one exception, to be noted below) connecting Lanyer's young girlhood to an atmosphere of patronage, suggest a supervisory status on the part of the Countess of Kent or at least a powerful exemplary status. Kent was the "glasse" or ideal against which Lanyer could compare her own shortcomings, and, in a second image, the "sunne" of virtue generating Lanyer's efflorescence and keeping her from "Errour."

Such description, of course, has prompted critical interpretations of Lanyer's early years that suggest a relationship to a nurturing aristocracy, despite the nonaristocratic—and even nongentry—circumstances of her parents. Lanyer's father, Baptist Bassano, one of "the musicians of our sovereign lady the Queen's Majesty" and described in his will as a "native of Venice," was living, we know, with Margaret Johnson, his common-law wife, and was probably a lutenist, as were others in his first family.[3] Thus Bassano must have received, like the playing members of the families of Lupo and Lanière (Lanier) who had filled many of the musician posts at the English Court, an annual salary ranging from £20-£40 a year.[4] But although financially comfortable enough to provide a portion for Aemilia's older sister, Angela, to marry a self-styled "gentleman," Joseph Holland,[5] Bassano's support of his family would have ceased at his death in 1576, when Aemilia was seven. Four uncles on her father's side had all died by the time Aemilia was nine (see n. 32 below). In more straitened circumstances she then presumably lived alone with her mother, her sister having married in that same year. Thus by 7 July 1587, when her mother was dead, Lanyer was a single young woman of eighteen, possessed of all her mother's "leases, goods, and chattells."[6] It was in such circumstances that Lanyer was forced to wait for three years, until she turned twenty-one in 1590, before she could inherit the £100 her father had left her, presumably for a marriage-portion. Within such chronological (and social) parameters, Aemilia Lanyer's early access to aristocratic patronage is, in the end, imagined only with difficulty since the interest Aemilia might have inspired in titled women of learning could not, at this stage, plausibly have derived from any writing she had yet done. These facts seem especially relevant to the case of the Countess of Kent.

The countess was daughter of the Duchess of Suffolk, Catherine Willoughby, who in 1534 had married Charles Brandon, First Duke of Suffolk.[7] Brandon died in 1545. The widowed Catherine saw the dukedom go briefly to Henry Brandon, her husband's eleven-year-old son from a previous marriage, who himself died at sixteen, half an hour before a second son, Charles Brandon, also died from the same disease. In 1551, then, with Charles Brandon's immediate male line exhausted, this dukedom became extinct. Thus by 1553 (the year Mary Tudor came to the English throne), the thirty-three-year-old Catherine Willoughby had been eight years removed from the dukedom of Suffolk when, as dowager duchess, she married Richard Bertie. By this second husband Catherine had two children, a daughter, Susan, born in 1554, and a son, Peregrine, born in 1555. Susan was the noblewoman memorialized by Lanyer at the beginning of the *Salve* as the "daughter of the Duchess of Suffolk."

The dowager duchess and her second husband went into exile on the Continent with Susan and her brother for the remainder of Queen Mary's reign, only returning in 1559 to the countess's elaborate manor house of Grimsthorpe in Lincolnshire after the accession of Queen Elizabeth, Susan being five years of age. In 1570, at the age of sixteen, Susan married Reynold Grey of Wrest, and, of course, left Grimsthorpe. Known at time of his marriage as "Master Grey," Susan's husband was restored as Earl of Kent by 28 March 1572, and Susan became Countess of Kent.[8] A year later, on 15 March 1573, the earl died, his death-record at St. Giles without Cripplegate attesting to his London residence in that ward and thus to the Countess of Kent's hypothetical availability to the Londoner Aemilia Bassano, who was living on the other side of town in St. Botolph's without Cripplegate.[9]

Because the Earl and Countess of Kent had been childless, however, the heir to the earldom was the earl's thirty-three-year-old younger brother, styled until then Henry Lord Grey of Ruthin. Susan Bertie Grey, now nineteen and Dowager Countess of Kent, and presumably unable to continue living in the new Earl of Kent's inherited residence, may at this time have been invited to live at Court.[10] If so, the invitation was presumably issued at the behest of Queen Elizabeth, who often kept a benevolent watch over younger ladies of the peerage in Susan's situation—certainly the queen would take an angry interest in Susan's remarriage in 1581.

In this context, we might recall Simon Forman's note that in 1597 Aemilia told him that she "was brought up with the Countess of Kent." But if, as Lanyer herself writes in her poem, Kent was "the mistress of my youth," this situation is unlikely to have obtained between 1570 (when Susan married and left Lincolnshire for London) and March 1573 (when the Earl of Kent was buried). For Aemilia (christened January 1569) cannot have been older than four when the Earl of Kent died.[11] Thus, if the succeeding Earl of Kent, together with the countess his wife, took possession of the house and lands even as soon as forty days after his brother's death, the former earl's nineteen-year-old widow would presumably have gone to Court or returned to her original home soon afterwards, and thus have stopped residing in the city a number of months before Aemilia turned five.[12]

Further, even if one grants the possibility that the countess might have demonstrated sustained intellectual interest in such a small girl during this four-year period of her London residence, Aemilia Bassano's actual presence in the Kent household is nevertheless not easy to envisage. It is hard (albeit not impossible) to suggest a set of circumstances in which the very small daughter of a Court lutenist might obtain to a mentoring relationship with a countess.

Who would have introduced the child, and why? Her mother, it is true, might for some reason have worked in the countess's household occasionally, bringing her baby daughter with her—Lanyer later noted to Simon Forman that she "was brought up on the bankes of Kent," but there were servants aplenty in Elizabethan London and the "Kent" reference is misleading.[13]

Nor is it any easier to imagine a relationship between Lanyer and the Dowager Countess of Kent in the latter part of the poet's childhood, after the death of her father and the remarriage of her (much older) sister in April 1576, when she was seven. During this period, except for the possible company and help of her uncles' widows—whoever they were—Lanyer and her mother were alone together.[14] They would presumably have occupied their original dwelling, Lanyer's mother having the rents and use of three houses in Bishopsgate left to her by her husband, and so it is not likely that they lived in want.[15] But in these even more difficult circumstances, how could Aemilia have established a relationship with the Dowager Countess of Kent, especially if the countess were now at Court, as is commonly assumed?[16]

Having left the houses of the Kent earldom in Cripplegate when Lanyer was four, the dowager countess remained a widow until 1581. Shortly before her marriage, on 19 September 1580, Kent's mother, the Dowager Duchess of Suffolk, died, and by 28 December 1580 Susan was back at Grimsthorpe with her father Richard Bertie.[17] Nine months later, on 30 September 1581, she was at Stenigot in Lincolnshire where she remarried outside of the peerage. Susan's new husband, Sir John Wingfield, nephew of the Dowager Countess of Shrewsbury, lived in Withcoll,[18] and although Susan's English place of residence at this time is not certainly known, presumably she lived in Lincolnshire where her new husband was located.[19] But by 31 October 1587 (shortly after the eighteen-year-old Aemilia Bassano's mother died),[20] Susan was with her husband on the Continent at Bergen-op-Zoom in the Low Countries, where Wingfield had a military role under the command of Susan's brother, Lord Willoughby. Indeed, this situation led, in early 1589, to the couple becoming prisoners in Breda.[21]

Susan was soon released and by 20 May 1589 was back in London, but apparently in some financial hardship because seven years later, in September 1596, after her husband had died at Cadiz, she wrote Robert Cecil that she had been living on credit for seven years, and that her husband "lost all his worldly substance in her Majesty's service . . . by which losses he hath left me and his poor child in most miserable estate." Indeed, the countess "had not one penny in my house . . . to buy meat either for myself or child, till her Majesty most like a gracious princess, hearing of my misery, sent me forty pound." Further, she had "sold and mortgaged all, so I have neither plate nor jewels left, but only three score and ten pound a year."[22]

Thus, any relationship that might have developed between Aemilia Bassano and the young Dowager Countess of Kent after 1581 (when the countess married in Lincolnshire) could only have begun in 1589, after the countess's return from the Low Countries. At this time Aemilia perhaps still qualified as "youthful" (her description of herself in association with the Countess of Kent), she being twenty and the Countess of Kent thirty-three. But the effort to put Aemilia Bassano together with the Countess of Kent from, say, 1589 until Aemilia's own marriage in 1592 when her "youth" might be said to have ended, is as problematic as the earlier scenarios.

Again, how would Lanyer as a young woman and the countess have met? With respect to the countess, there is some indication that she had no fixed abode in London when she returned in 1589. Her husband's estate was presumably in Lincolnshire, and when she was in London, her letters place her variously. In November 1595 she was writing "from my house in Barbican St." which actually belonged to her brother Peregrine Bertie who referred to his "great mansion house called Willoughby House or Barbican" on the west side of Red Cross St. in Cripplegate.[23] In September 1596 she wrote of her husband's death from Sion House which was on the north bank of the Thames in Isleworth and far enough from the center of the city then to be considered as a place for the Court of the Exchequer to meet during plague in 1560.[24] During June and July of 1597 she wrote several times from Greenwich.[25] Whether this was at Court or in a residence it is not certain, but she seems to have remained there at her "lodging" at least until the end of July, when she attained for herself and her son the £100 annuity that she had asked the Crown for in June.[26]

The point is that Aemilia Bassano and the Countess of Kent, waiving their social differences, seem to have moved along divergent paths. In 1589 Aemilia, probably living at her property in Bishopsgate, was a single woman, age twenty, with a married and much older sister and no living parents, waiting for the £100 that would come to her when she was twenty-one. In the same year, the Dowager Countess of Kent was living in London, in various locations, in straitened circumstances (at least in an aristocratic context) and with a child, the son to whom she referred in her letter to Cecil (see above).[27] So at this point Lanyer's claims to aristocratic propinquity (at least through the Countess of Kent) are puzzling.

On the other hand, it was presumably some time prior to her own marriage in 1592 that Aemilia Bassano had reportedly become the mistress of the first Lord Hunsdon, Lord Chamberlain. How this relationship came about is also not easy to determine. The contributing circumstances seem obvious only if we situate Aemilia at one or the other of the queen's palaces—a fact by no means established. For clearly it was no simple matter for someone in Aemilia Bassano's position simply to walk in off the London streets and to encounter the Lord Chamberlain of England "at Court." And even if Aemilia in her early womanhood had become acquainted with the Dowager Countess of Kent, Susan herself was not only suffering financially but presumably was still in disfavor with Queen Elizabeth for having married without permission. The queen's one-time gift to Susan of £40 in 1596, when Elizabeth was informed of the death of Susan's husband, hardly constituted a full pardon.[28]

In the foregoing discussion of the circumstances mitigating against a relationship between Aemelia Lanyer and the Dowager Countess of Kent, I do not mean to argue that the two never met, nor indeed that the relationship implied in Lanyer's complimentary verses could not have existed. After all, one might counterargue, was it any easier for Lanyer to become the mistress of Hunsdon than the protegé of the Countess of Kent? Yet most scholars writing about Lanyer assume that Aemilia's report to Simon Forman about her association with Hunsdon is borne out by other circumstances in her life, so that she must have found a mode of access to the Lord Chamberlain. Moreover, the last lines of Lanyer's dedication to Kent seem frankly to demonstrate a loyalty to and knowledge about Susan that in themselves strongly suggest a personal connection of some sort, even if not as exalted a one as Lanyer would have us believe.

> And since no former gaine hath made me write,
> Nor my desertlesse service could have wonne,
> Onely your noble Virtues do incite
> My Pen, they are the ground I write upon;
>> Nor any future profit is expected,
>> Now how can these poor lines go unrespected? [ll. 43-48]

Given the dowager countess's known financial circumstances, Lanyer's lines insist on her own sincerity because her gesture cannot possibly be motivated by the anticipation of monetary gain. She is not disingenuous. She is factual. And since a notice of the countess's funeral in 1617—which, incidentally, does *not* include Aemilia among the mourners—establishes that the countess was very much alive prior to the publication of Lanyer's book in 1610, there is still a fifteen-year period not examined in the foregoing analysis during which a friendship may indeed have been established (although this period would not, of course, have coincided with Lanyer's "youth").[29]

My concern, then, is not whether this friendship existed, but the means by which we decide that it did. There is a danger in taking Aemilia Lanyer at her word without corroborating evidence, and without due consideration of other factors—such as her need to insert herself into an aristocratic context—that might have prompted her (along with many other aspiring poets of the period) to use dedicatory verses for self-aggrandizing purposes. I would propose that we examine what seem to be even *probable* assumptions more closely than heretofore so as to contextualize Lanyer's career as fully as possible.

If Aemilia's relationship to the countess of Kent has been exaggerated in some accounts of Lanyer's life, her relationship with her husband has been frequently undervalued. That Alfonso Lanyer participated in the effort to promote the *Salve* is evidenced by one copy whose title page bears an inscription in a contemporary hand, "guift of Mr. Alfonso Lanyer," signed by Thomas Jones, Archbishop of Dublin (Woods, p. xlix).[30] But Alfonso's connections extended elsewhere. Indeed, what is remarkable about him is that despite his modest social status as a court musician, his entrepreneurial initiatives succeeded in connecting him, at least indirectly, with several powerful figures at Court. Thus, somewhat ironically, it may have been Aemilia's own husband who was best positioned to promote her bid for patronage.

Aemilia's marriage to Alfonso on 18 October 1592, approximately two years after she gained the £100 annuity left her by her father, was logical, for she was a member of one family of musicians marrying into another such family, many of whom interacted.[31] Both families, too, were extensively employed at Court.[32] Alfonso's father was Nicholas Lanier (1), not to be confused with the famous composer Nicholas Lanier (2). Lanier (1) owned considerable property in Greenwich and served the Crown as a musician from 1561 until his death in Greenwich between 28 January and 1 July 1612. Alfonso also had five brothers and four sisters, the brothers being employed musicians. One of them, John Lanier, was the father of Nicholas Lanier (2) who was thus Aemilia's nephew, at least by marriage—a fact implied by Susanne Woods in 1994.[33] Alfonso, about five months after his marriage, was earning more than £30 a year with a yearly livery allowance £16/2/6, William Daman's particular status as court musician having reverted to Alfonso after Daman's death.[34] Despite a variety of ventures, Alfonso maintained his profession, for at Queen Elizabeth's death in 1603 he was listed as a recorder-player to the queen and given an allowance for mourning livery for her funeral, and he was a royal musician under James up to his death in 1613.[35] As his wife, Aemilia must have lived surrounded by musicians, and, indeed, there is no reason why she might not herself have been one, even though she would not have been employable as such.

But aside from his music, Aemilia's husband was engaged, like other court musicians, in various entrepreneurial activities presumably derived from contacts with the Court bureaucracy.[36] Apparently somewhat more ambitious than his fellows, Alfonso was after preferment, for by 16 June 1597 he had joined Essex's expedition which had been readying for sea since at least May, the ships actually leaving on the expedition (usually known as the Islands Voyage) on 10 July.[37] (Aemilia began visiting Simon Forman on 13 May 1597.) Although Essex commanded both sea and land forces, the fleet was under the general orders of Lord Thomas Howard (future Earl of Suffolk and future Lord Chamberlain under James I) and Sir Walter Raleigh, and aimed at destroying the Spanish war fleet in the harbor of Ferrol or to capture Spanish merchant ships and invest the Azores.[38] "The presse of gentlemen" (ambitious, like Lucio and his friends in *Measure for Measure,* for knighthoods through military service) was to be very great, according to John Chamberlain who in June alluded to this expedition. But in the end the venture was unsuccessful and the fleet sailed back to Plymouth in order to be demobilized in October. But as soon as the force was in harbor, on 28 October 1597, it was sent out again immediately to intercept the new Spanish Armada then discovered to be at sea. When the enemy force was dispersed by storms (by 5 November) the fleet and force seem finally to have been demobilized and Alfonso presumably returned home.[39]

Alfonso continued to pursue his extramusical ambitions, and to follow Essex. For although it has not been noticed, a letter written in 1602 to support a suit by Alfonso, mentioned his Irish service (see below). Essex arrived in Ireland April 1599, the expedition staying there, with Essex and then with Mountjoy, until 2 January 1602. Since he somehow came to know the Archbishop of Dublin and also the Earl of Southampton (with Essex in Ireland)— see below—Alfonso must have used his time there well. Later, in 1602, Alfonso also knew Sir Robert Wroth (not yet married to Mary Sidney) since the two men were involved in a lease.[40] Finally, and most interestingly, Alfonso seems to have been (personally?) acquainted with John Bancroft, the future Archbishop of Canterbury! For when Bishop of London in 1604, James now being on the throne, Bancroft wrote a letter for Alfonso supporting his effort to attain the patent for hay and grain referred to by Woods (p. xxv) that he finally received in the same year.[41] In his letter to Cecil supporting the suit, Bancroft praised Alfonso's service in Ireland (although the bishop himself was not there) and referred to Alfonso as "mine old fellow and loving friend." According to the bishop he and "Captaine Alphonso Lanier" both served the Lord Chancellor (Sir John Fortescue). Further, Bancroft indicates that Alfonso had been "put in good hope of" Cecil's favoring of the suit "by the Earl of Southampton."[42]

The association with Bancroft is provocative but difficult to interpret. Bancroft was in charge of the pikemen who at Ludgate resisted Essex's insurrection in 1601 and he was at Royston with a retinue to greet James in his 1603 progress south from Scotland to ascend the English throne. Whatever the case, and perhaps because Southampton was being publicly supported by King James in the first years of his reign, Alfonso attained his suit in 1604. Thus, in the case of Aemilia's husband, there is some indication that if any one in the Lanier family had useful Court contacts, it seems, unexpectedly, to have been Alfonso, a man able to secure the support of the Earl of Southampton and of the future Archbishop of Canterbury in a suit, and acquainted with Wroth. The implications of this situation for our understanding of Aemilia Lanyer's biography are, however, unclear and my own analysis can deal with only one aspect of this important issue.

This consideration has to do with what Bancroft's letter suggests about Aemilia's activities between 1597 and 1605. In the summer of 1597, the same summer as that in which the Countess of Kent was in Greenwich seeking her annuity, Aemilia Lanyer seems to have been resourceless enough, from the viewpoint of any "advancement" she may have sought through Court contacts, to discuss her prospects with Simon Forman. She had consulted him from 13 May to 29 September 1597 when she asked, among other things, "whether she shall be a Ladie or noe" (Woods, p. xxii). Presumably she was thinking of Alfonso's possible knighthood—a hoped-for reward resulting from the Islands expedition. Sometime after her 1597 visits to Forman, Alfonso must have returned home from the Islands Expedition and the Spanish Armada activity, by early 1598 since Aemilia's short-lived daughter Odillya was baptized in December 1598. But assuming that Alfonso then left to rejoin Essex, he would have gone before spring 1599 because the earl was in Ireland by 15 April. Although Essex's premature return from that country would bring him to England that summer, there is no way of telling when the gentlemen and soldiers of the expeditionary force would themselves have been allowed back, the English army remaining largely intact in Ireland. Indeed, it was not until sometime between 21 October 1601 and 2 January 1602 (Mountjoy's defeat of the Spanish and Irish at Kinsale on the former date and the surrender of the Spanish garrison in January 1602) that the army was likely to have begun returning to England. In the interim, of course, from the summer of 1600 until his execution in February 1601, the noble whom Alfonso preferred to follow, Essex, was in serious trouble. Southampton, whose support Alfonso had for his 1604 suit, was still in Ireland as of 28 May 1600 (Chamberlain 1:95), although he soon left. Alfonso himself was surely back in London by 1602 when he and Sir Robert Wroth were involved in their lease (see n. 40).

The bearing of this minutely focussed narration on Aemilia's probable activities is that Alfonso's wanderings would have freed her—as his earlier expedition did when she went to see Forman—from attendance on her husband.[43] Further, by 1600, Aemilia's son Henry would have been seven and it was at this point that he might have begun his musical apprenticeship, passing from her maternal supervision to that of his paternal (Lanier) uncles or of his paternal grandfather to be trained in the profession. For trained he was, since ultimately, in 1629, when he was twenty-one, he was appointed flute player in the royal music at Court.[44] So in 1600, without direct responsibilities to a resident husband or to any child (Odyllya having died), an independent Aemilia alone would have been in a very plausible position for that association with Anne Clifford and her mother, the Dowager Countess of Cumberland, which scholars have identified as crucial to her career and which assumes Lanyer's sojourn at Cookham.[45]

Having posed two general questions concerning Aemilia Lanyer's relationship to the Countess of Kent and to Alfonso, her husband, I shall conclude this essay by suggesting some unconventional activity in Lanyer's preparation of her 1611 volume, activity that might have deeply compromised her bid for patronage—if patronage is what she sought. I refer especially to her rhetorical way with one noble, the Dowager Countess of Cumberland. Lanyer not only gave the dowager countess her primary dedication, but she went further to tie Cumberland, rhetorically, so closely to the poem that her prominence is almost a monopoly. The volume begins with the thirty-nine-line prose dedication to the countess, continues with dedicatory verses to other nobility, and then introduces the "Salve Deus" proper with a 256-line preamble directed yet again to Cumberland, after which the same countess is invoked three more times in italicized marginal glosses which mention her name.[46] And, of course, there is the last, retrospective, poem, on Cookham, in which the countess and her daughter, Anne Clifford, later Countess of Dorset, are the implicit topic throughout (just as Robert Sidney is the implicit topic of Jonson's "Ode to Penshurst"). Obviously, the problem with such an emphasis, from the viewpoint of the poet seeking patronage of multiple dedicatees (as Lanyer seems to have been), is that it wagers all on one throw. For by stitching the countess into the fabric of the poem, Lanyer was, perhaps inadvertently, hierarchizing the other nobles whom she also solicited in this work, and in an unconventional, if not inexpert manner.

The subsequent dedications in Lanyer's volume reinforce this mistake in judgment. Again, a comparison here with Samuel Daniel's and Ben Jonson's (and Lady Mary Wroth's) modes of cultivating court patronage is instructive. Certainly, contemporary attitudes about gender may have defined the successes of these men to a large degree, but even had Aemilia Lanyer been male, the pattern of dedications in her volume would have been ill-advised because it did not sufficiently weigh in with the influential circle of Anne of Denmark which operated as the cultural center at Court.[47] Daniel, in contrast, took care to focus most of his dedications consistently on the so-called Essex circle that surrounded the queen, and that included, first, the countess of Bedford, the queen's only English Lady of the Bed Chamber (who aided him materially), as well as such nobles as the Earl of Devonshire, the Earl and Countess of Hertford, and the Earl of Pembroke. When Daniel did offer dedications to such politically inactive nobles as the Countess of Cumberland and her daughter, he was careful not to imply that their status rivalled that of more powerful members of the peerage.

Lanyer, in contrast, was much less adept in prioritizing her dedicatees. The complete list of nobles in Lanyer's dedications comprises, in this order: Queen Anne; Princess Elizabeth; "vertuous Ladies in generall"; Lady Arabella Stuart; Susan, Dowager Countess of Kent; the Dowager Countess of Pembroke; Lucy, Countess of Bedford; Margaret, Dowager Countess of Cumberland; Katherine, Countess of Suffolk; and Ann [Clifford], Countess of Dorset. But in William Harrison's *Description of England* the degrees of these last six ladies "according to the anciency of their creation" would have ranked them as follows: Kent, Bedford, Pembroke, Cumberland, Suffolk, Dorset.[48] Lanyer's major mistake (as regards any hope of penetrating the queen's circle) might have been the placing of the extremely influential Countess of Bedford *after* the Dowager Countess of Pembroke, a strategic error that could only have been compounded by the multiple ways in which Lanyer foregrounded the countesses of Cumberland and Dorset throughout the volume.[49]

Lanyer's choices of dedicatees for her volume proved unfortunate in other ways as well. One of them, a very intellectually gifted woman, Lady Arabella Stuart, King James's first cousin, sequestered at Court since his accession, began a fall from grace in late 1609 as a result of her secret efforts to marry a potential claimant to the throne, William Seymour, grandson of the Earl of Hertford. The unauthorized marriage took place on 21 June 1610, but by the time Lanyer's volume came out several months later, Arabella was already under confinement in the Tower. Although she tried to escape from England the following June, she was captured and returned to prison, where she eventually died, under severe psychological stress, in 1615.[50]

Aside from such an unpreventable misfortune, the unconventionality of Lanyer's bid for patronage is especially emphasized in the presentation copy of her edition that she (or her husband?) prepared for Prince Henry, with the prince's coat of arms on the cover. Its dedications attest to the complexity of the Court patronage game that this particular volume seems to be playing in that the number of dedications has been reduced from that in the other issues of the edition. The revisings are interesting and illustrative of the difficulties such a volume faced.[51] Because she (or Alfonso?) could hardly change the body of her poem, the dedication to Cumberland clearly had to stay, whatever its political valences. Nor could Cumberland's daughter be omitted, although retaining Anne Clifford would also have been of little use in gaining access to the members of the royal family.[52] But beyond these retentions, the only other dedications in this Prince Henry copy comprised several members of the royal family itself—Queen Anne and Princess Elizabeth—along with the countess of Bedford, the Queen's only Lady of the Bed Chamber. Strangely, there was none to Prince Henry himself.[53]

Because this presentation copy has, as Woods noted, the name "Cumberland" written in ink at the center top edge of the first (blank) leaf preceding the title page, it has been suggested that the dowager countess was meant as the conduit for the volume to the prince.[54] But arguing against this and other scenarios for the transmission of the gift is the actual failure of Lanyer's bid, arising not only from the unlikelihood that Cumberland would have had direct access to Prince Henry, but also from the unlucky circumstance that Henry's newly-attained status complicated *any* access to him. Noted in the Stationers' Register in October 1610, Lanyer's volume was seeing the light four months after Henry, as Duke of Cornwall, had been invested as Prince of Wales. At this investiture he assumed control, as was customary, of his own palace, complete with court, courtiers, and artists. Reportedly, Henry, a popular, strong-willed person of definite tastes, administered this court in a firm, even autonomous manner (*SPV*, 11:516).

It has been suggested that because Henry was a lover of music, and Aemilia Lanyer was the wife of a musician, her volume might have come to the attention of the prince via the well-known Nicholas Lanier (2), traditionally regarded as Prince Henry's master of music. But this hypothesis immediately raises questions of class. Lanier was only a musical servant whose access to the prince would have required intermediaries (first gentlemen, and then nobles), an improbable scenario, especially since there is no record of Henry ever having met with those artisans whose work he provably contemplated at the court of King James—the plays of William Shakespeare, for instance.[55] More fundamentally, the traditional claim that Nicholas Lanier (2), the singer, composer, and painter, whose music was used in some of Ben Jonson's later masques, was indeed the Music *Master* at the court of Prince Henry seems to have been rejected both by musicologists and historians of the Court. Prince Henry was quite interested in music, but it was the famous Alfonso Ferrabosco who had instructed him in that art and dedicated *Ayres* to him in 1609. Nicholas Lanier (2) was certainly one of the musicians at the prince's court, but other artists, such as Walter Quinn, John Bull, and the Italian Angelo Notari were also in attendance.[56] Thus there is as yet no reason to assume that Nicholas Lanier enjoyed a special status at this new court.

In any event, gaining access to Prince Henry at his court would have been a matter of connecting with those aristocratic channels that were defined as such in *Henry's* terms. These would of course include Queen Anne, his mother and political ally, and the Countess of Bedford, the queen's favorite lady. As the aunt of Bedford's husband, and as a patron, like Bedford, of Samuel Daniel, Cumberland theoretically could have made an overture to the countess on Lanyer's behalf. But unlike the situation in Anne's court, such an overture in Henry's court would probably have required yet another step. For the most influential person in the prince's newly-constituted circle, especially in matters pertaining to the arts, was John Harington, brother of Lucy Bedford, and best friend for the previous seven years of the sixteen-year-old Henry.[57] Thus although in the end the Countess of Cumberland might well have indirectly initiated high-level interventions on behalf of Aemilia Lanyer, we cannot be certain how amenable Lucy Bedford would have been to sponsoring Lanyer's volume, especially considering the Pembroke/Bedford *faux pas* of Aemilia's original hierarchy of dedicatees, nor do we know what John Harington's influential opinion of the matter would have been.

Whatever the case, as regards both royal offspring that she tried to connect to her volume, Lanyer was overtaken by circumstances. Henry died in November 1612, a little more than two years after her volume appeared in the Stationers' Register (2 October 1610) and his court was dissolved before the end of that year (Chamberlain, 1:399). Nor was Lanyer any more fortunate with Princess Elizabeth, access to whom would, incidentally, also have been dominated by the Countess of Bedford since Elizabeth was brought up from seven years of age in the country great house of Lord and Lady Harington, Bedford's parents.[58] Princess Elizabeth's marriage to the Count Palatine in 1613, several months after Prince Henry's death, and her subsequent removal from England, signalled the end of any hope that Lanyer may have harbored for the princess's patronage.

The nub of the foregoing series of speculations is that the vexed question of Aemilia Lanyer's bid for aristocratic patronage—its motives, its modes, its practical prospects for success, and even its relationship to her marriage—needs, I suggest, further examination. But in emphasizing the disparities between Aemilia Lanyer's background and her ambitions, the activities of her husband, and also what appears to be her lack of sophistication or her unconventionality regarding the politics of patronage, I do not mean to insist that she did not gain access to the Court—and through her own efforts—or that the biographical allusions in her work were constructed as fictions. Yet in vying for Court patronage, she was competing in a very tough arena, against accomplished male poets (already privileged because of their gender) with considerable political awareness and very powerful sponsors. What I am suggesting is that we attempt, with great and respectful care, to situate Lanyer's admirably bold bid for patronage within the hard exigencies of her social milieu, attempting neither to idealize nor to diminish her status and accomplishments. As a female poet with a nonaristocratic social and educational background, Aemelia Lanyer was seriously handicapped as a player in the Court game, yet one could argue that these are the very factors that make her Court failures understandable, and her presumed relationships with Kent, Cumberland, Hunsdon, and perhaps other nobles, so remarkable.

NOTES

1. That Aemilia's father was one of a family of Ashkenazi Jews who were wind-players from Venice, see Roger Prior, "Jewish Musicians at the Tudor Court," *Musical Quarterly* 69 (1983): 253-65, esp. p. 257. For other studies of the Bassano family, see Prior, "A Second Jewish Community in Tudor London," *Jewish Historical Studies* 31 (1988-90), 137-52, esp. p. 150 n.4, and, most lately, David Lasocki with Roger Prior, *The Bassanos: Venetian Musicians and Instrument Makers in England, 1531-1665* (Aldershot: Scolar Press, 1995), ch. 6: "The Bassanos' Jewish Identity."

2. To this effect, too, see Lisa Schnell's very suggestive article on Lanyer's ambiguous rhetorical relationship to the Countess of Cumberland and to the problem of "degree" in "'So Great a Difference is there in Degree': Aemilia Lanyer and the Aims of Feminist Criticism," *Modern Language Quarterly* 57 (1996): 23-35.

3. See Susanne Woods's documented account, pp. xv-xvii in *The Poems of Aemilia Lanyer.* Margaret Johnson, not coincidentally perhaps, had a name associated with musicians too. Woods notes this connection in "Aemilia Lanyer and Ben Jonson: Patronage, Authority, and Gender," *Ben Jonson Journal* 1 (1994): 15-30 (hereafter cited as Woods, *Jonson*), alluding to John Johnson of the "Queen's Musicians" who died in 1594, leaving a widow Alice 25 January 1595 (*Calendar of State Papers Domestic Series,* ed. Robert Lemon and M.A.E. Green (London: HMC, 1856-72), 4:4—hereafter cited as *SPD*). To Woods's suggestive discussion here one might add Francis Meres (whose list of Shakespearean plays is one of our earliest sources for his activities in the 1590s), who names Edward Johnson as one of England's "excellent musicians"—see Diana Poulton, *The Life of John Dowland* (Berkeley: University of California Press, 1982), p. 51, and Robert Johnson's selection over Dowland as the composer of the music for Chapman's *Masque of the Middle Temple* (Poulton, p. 82).

4. See Poulton, *The Life of John Dowland,* p. 74.

5. For Holland, see Woods, p. xvii n.8.

6. She must frequently have been in touch with her sister since her sister's husband, Joseph Holland, is named several times in the will of Aemilia's mother, a will the existence of which at the Guildhall I was apprised by Susanne Woods who, with her usual generosity, has furnished me her transcription.

7. See *Complete Peerage,* ed. H.A. Doubleday, et al. (London: St. Catherine's Press, 1910-59), 12.1:460-462. Hereafter cited as *Peerage.*

8. All dates in this essay are English New Style (the new year beginning in January but the calendar still ten days behind the Continent's).

9. Grey appears to have lived in the parish of St. Giles without Cripplegate. For these matters, see *Peerage,* 7:170-171. John Stow, *A Survey of London,* ed. Charles L. Kingsford (Oxford: The Clarendon Press, 1971 [1908]), 2 vols, 1:300, notes the survival of the memorial inscription to "Sir Henry Grey, Knight, son and heir to George Grey Earl of Kent 1562" and "Reginald [Reynold?] Grey of Kent."

10. Henry, Sixth Earl of Kent, married Mary Cotton whose former husband, the Third Earl of Derby, had died 24 October 1572 (*Peerage* 7:172). After this latter marriage Mary would have been a possible "Countess of Kent" in documents about a living person until 16 November 1580 when she died.

11. Susanne Woods has kindly indicated to me that further examination by her, Katherine Duncan Jones, and the Bodleian paleographer fails to return any determination

as to whether the Forman manuscript reads "bankes of Kent" or "contes of Kent," the first letter of "contes" being still obscure. Woods agrees with their suggestion that "w the contes of Kent" is the more probable meaning. For Aemilia Lanyer's baptismal-date, see Barbara K. Lewalski, "Imagining Female Community: Aemilia Lanyer's *Poems*," in *Writing Women in Jacobean England* (Cambridge: Harvard University Press, 1993), p. 214 n. 7; and for Forman's remarks, see Lewalski, p. 215. Lanyer's Christian baptism is part of the vexed context of Jewish assimilation in Tudor England, a context that includes her father's appointment of Stephen Vaughan and John Austen, gentiles, as executors of his will. For the two names, see Prior, "A Second Jewish Community," p. 148 and n.

12. One reason for assuming this interim, as most critics have, as a time of Susan's residence at Court, rather than at Grimsthorpe with her parents, is the fact that over a year and a half after Susan's remarriage (6 February 1583) the Countess of Shrewsbury was still trying to allay Queen Elizabeth's displeasure over the fact. Nevertheless, it is important to remember that there is no documentary evidence for Susan residing at Court at this time. The queen's desire for control over the remarriage of a widowed dowager countess whose brother and mother were Willoughbys d'Eresby did not require a Court acquaintance with Susan.

13. "Kent" has, in this context, been vaguely associated with the countess ("of Kent"?) but if the reference is to the "bankes of Kent," this may more plausibly be taken as a reference to the royal court, which was often at Greenwich, or to some residence there—but see n. 11 above. The dowager countess signed letters from Greenwich in the 1590s: see n. 22 below. But, as we shall see, Nicholas Lanier, Aemilia's father-in-law, also had property in Greenwich.

14. It is of course possible that the dowager countess did not go to Court nor to her parents' home after the death of her husband, but moved to a new residence in London. Nonetheless, even if this rather unlikely scenario proved true, the basic problem remains: how did Aemilia, as a child, gain access to the countess's sphere of influence?

15. See Woods, *Poems,* p. xvi n.3.

16. Mother and daughter, presumably, would be together for eleven more years, Lanyer's mother dying in 1587.

17. See *MSS of the Earl of Ancaster* (Dublin: HMC, 1907), p. 6—hereafter cited as *Ancaster.*

18. For Wingfield as Shrewsbury's nephew, see *Calendar of the MSS of the Marquess of Salisbury Preserved at Hatfield House,* 23 vols., ed. M.S. Giuseppi (London: HMC, 1883-1976), 5:30 (hereafter cited as *Hatfield*), and for Wingfield see *Peerage,* 7:171-72. Both the Earl and Countess of Shrewsbury wrote Walsingham in an effort to enlist him in appeasing the queen about the marriage (*SPD,* 2:95).

19. Stenigot and Withcoll were respectively 6 and 3.5 miles southwest of Louth in Lincolnshire: see W. White, *History . . . of Lincolnshire* (Sheffield, 1842), pp. 352; 448.

20. For her death, see Lewalski, n. 19, and Woods, *Poems,* p. xviii n. 11.

21. See *Ancaster,* pp. 273-77.

22. See *Hatfield,* 6:365-66. The countess may either have been in Greenwich or in her house in the Barbican where she was living in 1595, for writing to Robert Cecil then, she alludes to both places: see the entry for 23 November 1595 (*Hatfield,* 5:465). The countess was in Essex in 1602 before December 8—*MSS of J. Eliot Hodgkin* (London: HMC, 1897), p. 274—probably en route to or from her deceased second husband's holdings in Lincolnshire.

23. See Stow, 1:302.

24. See Daniel Lysons, *The Environs of London* (London, 1792-96), 4 vols. 2.2:448-449. Sir Francis Knolleys had been appointed its keeper by Queen Elizabeth in 1560 but by 1 November 1596 Sion House seems to belong to the Earl of Northumberland, who writes Cecil from there (*Hatfield*, 6:466), about two months after Kent wrote from there. Thus he may have extended her his hospitality, perhaps because of some association with her brother who had assumed command of the Northern Marches.

25. 18 June 1597, 24 June 1597, 5 July 1597: see *Hatfield*, 7:258, 268, 289.

26. See *Hatfield*, 14:16 and *SPD*, 4:454 (9 July 1597).

27. See above, n. 22. Even this narrative is not *completely* probable because the dowager countess's holdings through her husband would presumably be in Lincolnshire. She could have been living there (see n. 22) and coming up to London only to pursue her requests to Robert Cecil, staying then at the various locations from which she dates her letters. Robert, Lord Rich, for example, wrote the Earl of Sussex 26 September 1601 to inquire whether the Barbican was for rent (*Ancaster*, 351), probably because Lord Willoughby had died 25 July 1601 (*DNB*). But the Barbican in effect belonged to the Countess of Kent for her brother (Lord Willoughby) left his son "all his lands and tenements in Barbican and Golden Lane" only "after the decease of Susan Countess of Kent" (*SPD*, 6:64-65). Sidney Lee notes that Willoughby had spent much time in military commands on the Continent, returning in 1596, only to leave in 1598 for the north where he had been appointed governor of Berwick-upon-Tweed in February 1598 (*DNB*). Thus the Barbican must often have been available to his sister.

28. Interestingly, before the Countess of Kent obtained her £100, Aemilia was actually receiving an annuity almost comparable to Kent's. For Simon Forman observed that Lanyer in 1597 "hath £40 a year" (Woods, p. xviii) and "was wealthy to him who married her [1592] in money and jewels," presumably because she had her £100 from her father and half the rents from the three houses (Woods, *Poems*, p. xvi n. 3)—while Kent, as she herself observed in 1596, had "sold and mortgaged all, so I have neither plate nor jewels left" (*Hatfield*, 6:366).

29. Although the *Peerage* article on the Kent earldom traces the countess only to 1602, there is an account of her funeral available (see *SPD*, 9:510). That the Dowager Countess of Kent was the woman under discussion is clear from the fact that Mary Cotton Grey who became Countess of Kent after the death of Susan's husband herself died in 1580. Her husband did not remarry and he himself did not die until 1623. Thus, between 1580 and her own death in 1617, Susan, albeit dowager, was the only extant "Countess of Kent." That Susan probably lived in the city is suggested by a document describing her brother's funeral with the Countess of Kent's departure from his Lincolnshire residence. See Margaret Whitworth, "Original Document," *The Lincolnshire Historian* 2.3 (1955-56): 23-26.

30. This copy, Woods remarks, retains dedications to the queen, Princess Elizabeth, the Countess of Cumberland, and the Countess of Dorset (p. xlviii).

31. For example, in 1634, Aemilia's relative, Henry Bassano, a musician, would be acting as the deputy of her brother-in-law, Clement Lanier, a musician, in a law proceeding involving rights that Aemilia had given over to Clement regarding a grant that she had inherited from her husband. See *Records of English Court Music*, ed. Andrew Ashbee, 8 vols. (Aldershot: Scolar Press, 1986-), 8:117 (hereafter cited as *RECM*) and Lasocki with Prior, ch. 7, n. 42.

32. On 16 August 1585 Mark Antony Bassano (one of Aemilia's first cousins) is referred to as "one of her Majesty's musicians"; on 23 February 1584 Arthur Bassano (another first cousin) was described identically (and as living in Aldgate—*SPD*, 2:202, 204, 260) as was Jeronimo Bassano (also a first cousin) on 4 September 1598 (*SPD*, 5:90). On 25 November 1611 there was another reference to Andrew (Andrea) Bassano (still another first cousin) who was tuning virginals for the Court. (Presumably Arthur, Andrew, and Jeronimo are the Bassanos referred to in 1594—*Hatfield*, 13:519). A Thomas Bassano replaced John Phelps in the office of court musician on 29 July 1615 (*SPD*, 9:299). Further, a list of court musicians appearing before 18 March 1606 shows twenty-three musicians of whom four are Aemilia's first cousins on her father's side, one is her husband, and another—Jerome Lanier—is her brother-in-law (see *Hatfield*, 24:65). Wendy Thompson described the Bassano family (presumably at the time when Aemilia was born) as a group of five brothers; see *The New Oxford Companion to Music*, ed. Denis Arnold (Oxford: Oxford University Press, 1983), 1:182. Lasocki and Prior describe these siblings as "the second generation" of immigrating Bassanos. See ch. 3 along with the very useful family-tree table of Bassanos (pp. xxiii-xxx).

33. See Susanne Woods, "Aemilia Lanyer and Ben Jonson: Patronage, Authority, and Gender," *Ben Jonson Journal* 1 (1994): 15-30

34. Alfonso was already a court musician at this time, but now he succeeded to Daman's *place*, presumably to the 20d. per day in addition to the £.16.2.6 per annumm wage. William Daman (Damon, Damano) was a Walloon composer and flautist brought to England in 1561 (?) by Lord Buckkhurst (better known as Thomas Sackville Earl of Dorset, author of the "Introduction" to the *Mirror for Magistrates*). Daman is best known for his harmonization of the tunes from the Sternhold and Hopkins metrical psalter published posthumously in 1591. For these matters, see *RECM*, 8:28, 30, 45; *Grove's Dictionary of Music and Musicians* (London: Macmillan, 1954), 2:585-86, which should be consulted in conjunction with *The New Grove Dictionary of Music and Musicians* (London: Macmillan, 1980), 5:169.

35. Alfonso, Jerome Lanier, and William Ballard shared a grant in 1601 (*RECM*, 8:52). For Alfonso's mourning livery in 1603, see *The King's Musick*, ed. Henry Cart De LaFontaine (London, 1909), p. 45. John Hussey on 22 November 1613 was granted the "office of musician" in place of "Alfonso Lanier deceased." See *SPD*, 9:210. Lasocki with Prior, despite their assumption that the Countess of Kent was "Aemilia's guardian" (p. 102), offer a useful account of Alfonso and Aemilia with hitherto uncollected details of Alfonso's financial and social circumstances.

36. Jeronimo Bassano was awarded the privilege of calfskins in 1598 (*SPD*, 5:90); John Lanier (Alfonso's brother) received a grant in 1598 and a re-grant in 1599 (*SPD*, 5:94); and on 14 October 1619 the court musicians Alphonso Ferabosco, Innocent Lanier, and Hugh Lydiard were awarded the authority to dredge the river Thames of "flats and shelves" and to sell the detritus (*SPD*, 10:85).

37. Alfonso's thinking here is suggested by Forman's comment (see Woods, p. xx) that Aemilia's "husband was gone to sea with therle [the earl] of Essex in hope to be knighted."

38. See John Chamberlain, *Letters*, 2 vols., ed. N.E. McClure (Philadelphia: The American Philosophical Society, 1939), 1:30 and Wallace MacCaffrey, *Elizabeth I: War and Politics* (London: Edward Arnold, 1993), pp. 279-80.

39. See J.R. Dasent, ed., *Acts of the Privy Council of England* (1542-1604), 35 vols. (London, 1890-1907), 28:62-63, 99-100; *Hatfield*, 7:492.

40. See *Hatfield,* 12:278; 16:274.

41. See Woods, p. xxv and *RECM,* 8:55. The twenty-year grant was made to Alfonso to have by himself and his deputies the weighing of hay and straw to be brought to London and Westminster or their suburbs or within three miles, and that Lanyer might get both from buyer and seller recompense for this effort, recompense not exceeding 6d. per load.

42. See *Hatfield,* 16: 274, which calendars the notice which is to be found in the Cecil Papers with the names of the attendees: see vol. 106, fol. 130. See Lasocki with Prior for a different discussion of this matter.

43. This line of thought, of course, is speculative, delineating one way in which some-one in Lanyer's position might behave with regard to both her child and her household.

44. For these matters see the much-neglected *Supplementary Volume* to the fifth edi-tion of *Grove's Dictionary of Music and Musicians,* ed. Eric Blom and Denis Stevens (Lon-don: MacMillan & Co., 1961), pp. 254-58.

45. See Barbara K. Lewalski, "The Lady of the Country-House Poem," in *The Fash-ioning and Functioning of the British Country House,* ed. Gervase Jackson-Stops et al. (Wash-ington, D.C.: The National Gallery of Art, 1989), p. 265 n. 29.

46. See Woods, pp. 51, 57, 62, 101, 108, 122.

47. See Barroll, "The Court of the First Stuart Queen," in *The Mental World of the Jacobean Court,* ed. Linda Levy Peck (Cambridge: Cambridge University Press, 1991), pp. 191-208.

48. See William Harrison, *Description of England,* ed. Georges Edelen (Washington, D.C.: The Folger Shakespeare Library, 1994), p. 122. Suffolk and Dorset do not appear in Harrison's list because, although their titles were ancient, they had been newly recreated: Suffolk in 1603, Dorset in 1605.

49. It is hard to overestimate the value assigned to precedence at Court. The experi-ence of Penelope Rich, totally implicated in her brother Essex's 1601 rebellion, is a case in point. In order for her to recapture her (pre-rebellion) position at Court, it was necessary to promulgate an act restoring her precedence at Court over all daughters of earls except the daughters of the Earl of Oxford (first in precedence) and Arabella Stuart, the king's cousin (*SPD,* 8:32). Cf. the Venetian ambassador's long discussion of precedence in 1610 (*SPV,* 11:508-9).

50. For Arabella's activities in early 1610 see Chamberlain, 1:292-94. For the 1610 secret marriage and attendant events see *The Court and Times of James I,* ed. Thomas Birch (London, 1849), 2 vols., 1:124; *Calendar of State Papers . . . of Venice,* 35 vols., ed. R. Brown et al. (London: HMC, 1864-), 12:19, and G.P.V. Akrigg, *Jacobean Pageant* (Cambridge, Mass.: Harvard University Press, 1962), pp. 113-24. For Arabella's marriage, see P.M. Handover, *Arabella Stuart* (London: Eyre and Spottiswoode, 1957), p. 263.

51. The Victoria and Albert copy is one of the eight copies surviving from the second issue, defined by a five-line printer's imprint (as opposed to the four-line imprint of the first issue), both issues bearing the dates "1610." See Woods, pp. xlvii-li.

52. It is true that Anne Clifford had danced in two masques given by the queen in the two years prior to the publication of the *Salve—The Masque of Beauty* of January 1608 and *The Masque of Queens* of February 1609—yet she participated in these masques not because she was close to the queen but because she was an unmarried young woman of high nobility who was also a first cousin of the Countess of Bedford's husband. Clifford was not married to Dorset until 25 February 1609. Thus in 1610, even though, previous to the end-of-year

publication of Lanyer's poems, Clifford as Countess of Dorset also danced in Queen Anne's *Tethys' Festival* during the June installation of Henry as Prince of Wales, her country residence does not seem to have put her in a position to offer Lanyer special access to the nobles who dominated the circles around the two monarchs.

53. When Ben Jonson had configured a presentation-copy of *Cynthia's Revels* to the Countess of Bedford with the Bedford crest stamped on the sides of the vellum wrapper, he wrote ten lines of dedicatory verse printed on a special leaf. See W.W. Greg, *A Bibliography of English Printed Drama to the Restoration* (Oxford: The Bibliographical Society, 1939), 1:290.

54. See Woods, *Poems*, p. xlviii.

55. See *Malone Society Collections*, 15 vols. (Oxford: Malone Society, 1907-1993), 6:48-50.

56. See Roy Strong, *Henry Prince of Wales and England's Lost Renaissance* (London: Thames and Hudson, 1986), p. 173 and nn. 80-85 (note 82 is misprinted as note 80). Nicholas Lanier (2) was obviously employed at Henry's court for he wrote Dudley Carleton on February 1613, three months after Henry's death and two months after his court was dissolved, that the world was so altered since the death of his master that he knew not which is "the more dangerous attempt, to turn courtier or clown" (*SPD*, 9:174).

57. Another appointee to the household of Prince Henry with a possible connection to Lanyer was Peregrine Bertie, the second son of the deceased Lord Willoughby, the Countess of Kent's brother, Peregrine thus being her nephew. But Susan Countess of Kent, one of Lanyer's dedicatees, was, we recall, absent from the pages of this special dedicatory copy to Prince Henry. Bertie was one of the group of young men created Knights of the Bath for Henry's investment six or seven months prior to Lanyer's publication. Correr, the Venetian ambassador, had remarked that the prince, "who wishes this solemnity to prove as magnificent and pompous as possible," paid special attention to the list of these knights, crossing out the names of those who were not to his liking. See *SPV*, 11:503-4; John Stow and Edmund Howes, *Annals* (London, 1615), sig. 4G-4G4.

58. Furthermore, great affection seems to have characterized the association because when Elizabeth married in 1613, she continued to correspond with Lady Harington, who eventually went to the Continent to visit her former charge, as did Lord Harington, who died during this trip. See *Peerage*, 6:321-26.

3
Seizing Discourses and Reinventing Genres

Barbara K. Lewalski

Aemilia Lanyer—gentlewoman-in-decline, daughter and wife of court musicians, cast-off mistress of Queen Elizabeth's Lord Chamberlain, Henry Hunsdon (to whom she bore an illegitimate child)—is the first Englishwoman to publish a substantial volume of original poems, *Salve Deus Rex Judaeorum* (1611). These poems are now beginning to accumulate the kind of scholarship and criticism that will enable us to assess and properly value their cultural significance and their often considerable aesthetic merit.[1] My interest here is in Lanyer's appropriation and rewriting, in strikingly oppositional terms, of some dominant cultural discourses and a considerable part of the available generic repertoire, as she introduces a forceful female authorial voice into the Jacobean cultural scene.

Lanyer's volume challenges patriarchal ideology and the discourses supporting it, opposing the construct of women as chaste, silent, obedient, and subordinate, and displacing the hierarchical authority of fathers and husbands. Her book as a whole is conceived as a Book of Good Women, imagining a female community sharply distinguished from male society and its evils, that reaches from Eve to contemporary Jacobean patronesses. The volume incorporates a wide variety of genres—dedicatory poems of several kinds, a prose polemic in defense of women, a meditative poem on Christ's Passion which contains an apologia, laments, and several encomia (the "Salve Deus"), and a country-house poem ("A Description of Cooke-ham"). Her dedicatory poems emphasize the legacy of virtue from mothers to daughters—Queen Anne and Princess Elizabeth, Margaret and Anne Clifford, Catherine and Susan Bertie, Katherine Howard and her daughters—a legacy that redounds upon their female poet-client and celebrant, Lanyer. The qualities Lanyer associates with her gallery of good women—heroic virtue, extraordinary learning, devotion to the Muses, and high poetic achievement—implicitly challenge patriarchal constructs of women and help to justify her own poetic undertaking. The challenge to patriarchy is quite explicit in the dedication "To the Ladie Anne [Clifford], Countesse of Dorcet,"[2] as Lanyer protests in strikingly egalitarian terms the class distinctions and privileges produced by male structures of inheritance:

> All sprang but from one woman and one man,
> Then how doth Gentry come to rise and fall?
> Or who is he that very rightly can
> Distinguish of his birth, or tell at all,
> > In what meane state his Ancestors have bin,
> > Before some one of worth did honour win? [ll. 35-40]

The title poem, "Salve Deus Rex Judaeorum," disrupts our generic expectations for a meditation on, or a narrative of, Christ's Passion, by its sharp focus on the contrast between the good women associated with that event—Pilate's Wife, Mary, Mary Magdalene, the women of Jerusalem, even Eve—and the evil men: the cowardly apostles, the traitor Judas, the wicked Hebrew and Roman judges, the tormenting soldiers, the jeering crowds. The country-house poem, "Cooke-ham," celebrates an estate without a lord—or indeed any male inhabitants—but with a virtuous mother and daughter as its defining and ordering principle.

Lanyer's multiple dedications to Queen Anne and nine noblewomen rewrite cultural and literary discourses pertaining to courtiership and patronage. They make an overt bid for patronage much as a male poet-client might: Spenser, for example, dedicated *The Faerie Queene* principally to Queen Elizabeth but secondarily, in seventeen appended sonnets, to powerful (chiefly male) courtiers and patrons. By contrast, Lanyer reaches out only to women, showcasing as principal dedicatee, not Queen Anne but Margaret Clifford, Countess of Cumberland, whom she credits with nurturing her talent and commissioning her country-house poem. This is apparently the first English instance of female patron and female literary client.[3] Unlike Spenser also, Lanyer both honors her dedicatees as individuals and displays her own poetic talent by devising dedications in different genres: odes in a variety of stanzaic forms for the queen, the Countess of Kent, and the Countess of Suffolk; sonnet-like poems for Princess Elizabeth and Arabella Stuart; a long dream-vision narrative of 224 lines for Mary Sidney (Herbert), Countess of Pembroke; a prose epistle for Margaret Clifford; a verse epistle for Anne Clifford in which Lanyer calls upon the conventions of that genre to sanction her presumption in offering to teach Anne proper moral attitudes and conduct. These dedications construct a female community of patrons to support a female poet who celebrates them and all womankind.

The concluding prose epistle, "To the Vertuous Reader," reaches beyond the named dedicatees to a general female audience (and to well-disposed male readers as well). This is a polemic, a brief but hard-hitting contribution to the

querelle des femmes, that centuries-old controversy over women's inherent wor-
thiness or faultiness, chiefly managed by men as a witty game.[4] Lanyer's bibli-
cal examples were conventional, cited in numerous defenses of women to ar-
gue women's natural abilities, their moral goodness (equal or superior to men),
and the honors accorded them by God and Christ. Lanyer supplies to the
genre heightened passion and rhetorical power:

> It pleased our Lord and Saviour Jesus Christ, without the assistance of man, . . .
> to be begotten of a woman, borne of a woman, nourished of a woman, obedient
> to a woman; and that he healed women, pardoned women, comforted women:
> yea, even when he was in his greatest agonie and bloodie sweat, going to be
> crucified, and also in the last houre of his death, tooke care to dispose of a woman:
> after his resurrection, appeared first to a woman, sent a woman to declare his
> most glorious Resurrection to the rest of his Disciples. [pp. 49-50]

Most notably, she argued the God-given call of many "wise and virtuous women"
(not merely queens) to exercise military and political power "to bring downe
their [men's] pride and arrogancie." Her examples are Deborah, Jael, Judith,
and Hester "with infinite others, which for brevitie sake I will omit" (p. 49).
The discourse she here seizes upon, biblical exegesis, is employed even more
boldly in her Passion poem.

    The title of Lanyer's volume refers only to that Passion poem, and the title
page promises, somewhat misleadingly, a collection of religious poetry: *Salve
Deus Rex Judaeorum. Containing, 1. The Passion of Christ. 2. Eves Apologie in
defence of Women. 3. The Teares of the Daughters of Jerusalem. 4. The Salutation
and Sorrow of the Virgine Marie. With divers other things not unfit to be read.* In
fact the title poem is a long meditation on the Passion and death of Christ
(1,840 lines) in which the other items listed (and more) are incorporated as
embedded kinds. The genres of religious and devotional literature were long
identified as safe and perhaps even laudable for women writers, but Lanyer
reconceived her Passion poem in decidedly unsafe terms that challenge funda-
mental assumptions of patriarchy. Identifying women with the suffering Christ,
she argues their moral and spiritual superiority to men by contrasting the many
kinds of female goodness displayed by the women in the Passion narrative with
the multiple forms of masculine evil. More daring still, she presents Christ and
Christ's passion as subject to female gaze and interpretation—by herself as
woman poet, and by the Countess of Cumberland, her patron. The countess is
eulogized in framing passages of 776 lines (more than a third of the whole) as
chief meditator upon, as well as exemplary image and imitator of, her suffering
Savior.

    This poem incorporates several kinds. One is the religious lament or com-
plaint—the tears of the Magdalen, of Christ himself, of penitent sinners—
usually focussed on Christ's Passion. This was usually, though not exclusively, a

Counter-Reformation genre: the best-known English example was probably Robert Southwell's *St. Peters Complaynt,* in which Peter laments Christ's Passion and his own cowardly denial of Christ.[5] Lanyer's stanzas on the tears of the daughters of Jerusalem and on the grief of the Virgin are complaints—but voiced by Lanyer as she apostrophizes those personages rather than by the characters themselves. The segment called "Eves Apologie" is a rhetorical *apologia* or defense. It may even be a direct response to the frequent outbursts of misogyny in Southwell's poem, as when Peter berates the woman who questions him, laying his and all men's sins, at woman's door:

> O Women, woe to men: traps for their falls,
> Still actors in all tragicall mischances:
> Earths Necessarie evils, captivating thralls,
> Now murdring with your toungs, now with your glances.[6]

Another important constituent genre is the Passion meditation, often featuring, as in Lanyer's poem, erotic elements from the Song of Songs. This was also a popular Counter-Reformation kind, but the third part of Giles Fletcher's baroque *Christs Victorie and Triumph* (1610)[7] provides a suggestive Protestant analogue. Also, Lanyer's very long framing passages eulogizing Margaret Clifford find suggestive analogues in the frames of several meditative poems addressed by poet-clients to Mary Sidney, Countess of Pembroke, associating her with Christ and his Passion: for example, Nicholas Breton's *The Countesse of Pembrookes Love,* and Abraham Fraunce's *The Countesse of Pembrokes Emanuell.*[8]

Lanyer adopts a variety of stances toward her material: sometimes narrating and elaborating upon events, sometimes interpreting them as a biblical exegete, sometimes meditating upon images or scenes, often apostrophizing participants as if she herself were present with them at these events. She also calls upon a variety of stylistic devices. Stanzas 10-18 comprise an embedded psalmic passage, a melange of psalm texts—chiefly from Psalms 18, 84, 89, 97, and 104—that praise God as the strong support of the just and the mighty destroyer of all their enemies.[9]

> With Majestie and Honour is He clad,
> And deck'd with light, as with a garment faire;
> . . . .
> He rides upon the wings of all the windes,
> And spreads the heav'ns with his all powrefull hand;
> Oh! who can loose when the Almightie bindes?
> Or in his angry presence dares to stand?
> . . . .
> He of the watry Cloudes his Chariot frames,
> And makes his blessed Angels powrefull Spirits. [ll. 73-90]

This has application to the much-wronged Countess of Cumberland and may be a gesture of discipleship to the Countess of Pembroke and her psalms.[10] Lanyer uses rhetorical schemes—especially figures of sound, parallelism, and repetition—with considerable skill; her apostrophes often convey strong feeling; she describes and sometimes dramatizes scenes effectively; and the inset rhetorical speeches such as "Eves Apologie" are conducted with force and flair. Also, her baroque descriptions yield nothing to Giles Fletcher:

> His joynts dis-joynted, and his legges hang downe,
> His alablaster breast, his bloody side,
> His members torne, and on his head a Crowne
> Of sharpest Thorns, to satisfie for pride:
> Anguish and Paine doe all his Sences drowne,
> While they his holy garments do divide:
>   His bowells drie, his heart full fraught with griefe,
>   Crying to him that yeelds him no reliefe. [ll. 1161-68]

Lanyer manages her surprising fusion of religious meditation and feminism by appropriating the dominant discourse of the age, biblical exegesis. She thereby claims for women the common Protestant privilege of individual interpretation of Scripture, and lays some groundwork for the female preachers and prophets of the Civil War period. Her most daring exegetical move is to rewrite the Adam and Eve story within a narrative of Pilate's wife appealing to her husband for Christ's release. The *apologia* for Eve pronounces her virtually guiltless by comparison with Adam and Pilate, ascribes to Eve only loving intentions in offering the apple to Adam, and identifies woman as, through that gift, the source of men's knowledge:

> Our Mother *Eve*, who tasted of the Tree,
> Giving to *Adam* what shee held most deare,
> Was simply good, and had no powre to see,
> The after-comming harme did not appeare:
>   The subtile Serpent that our Sex betraide,
>   Before our fall so sure a plot had laide.
> . . . .
> If *Eve* did erre, it was for knowledge sake,
> The fruit being faire perswaded him [Adam] to fall:
>   No subtill Serpents falshood did betray him,
>   If he would eate it, who had powre to stay him?
>
> Not *Eve*, whose fault was onely too much love,
> Which made her give this present to her Deare,
> That what shee tasted, he likewise might prove,
> Whereby his knowledge might become more cleare;
> He never sought her weakenesse to reprove,

> With those sharpe words, which he of God did heare:
>> Yet Men will boast of Knowledge, which he tooke
>> From *Eve's* faire hand, as from a learned Booke.
>
> If any Evill did in her remaine,
> Beeing made of him [Adam], he was the ground of all;
> . . . .
>> Her weakenesse did the Serpents words obay;
>> But you [Pilate] in malice Gods deare Sonne betray.
>
> Whom, if unjustly you condemne to die,
> Her sinne was small, to what you doe commit. [ll. 763-818]

This exegesis underscores the susceptibility of biblical texts to interpretations driven by various interests: the Genesis text had long been pressed to patriarchal interests, so by a neat reversal Lanyer makes it serve feminist ones. Taking Eve and Pilate's wife as representatives of womankind, while Adam and Pilate represent men—who are far more guilty than Eve because responsible for Christ's death—Lanyer concludes with a forthright demand for gender equality:

> Then let us have our Libertie againe,
> And challendge to your selves no Sov'raigntie;
> You came not in the world without our paine,
> Make that a barre against your crueltie;
> Your fault beeing greater, why should you disdaine
> Our beeing your equals, free from tyranny?
>> If one weake woman simply did offend,
>> This sinne of yours, hath no excuse, nor end. [ll. 825-32]

"The Description of Cooke-ham" (210 lines of pentameter couplets) may have been written and was certainly published before Ben Jonson's "To Penshurst."[11] We cannot be sure just when or how long Lanyer was at Cookham with Margaret and Anne Clifford, or just what kind of patronage stands behind her claim that this sojourn led to her religious conversion and confirmed her in her poetic vocation:[12]

> Farewell (sweet *Cooke-ham*) where I first obtain'd
> Grace from that Grace where perfit Grace remain'd;
> And where the Muses gave their full consent,
> I should have powre the virtuous to content:
> Where princely Palace will'd me to indite,
> The sacred Storie of the Soules delight. [ll. 1-6]

At the least she seems to have received some encouragement in learning, piety, and poetry in the bookish and cultivated household of the Countess of Cumberland.

Whichever came first, "Penshurst" and "Cooke-ham" draw upon some of the same generic resources and offer, as it were, a male and a female conception of an idealized social order epitomized in the life of a specific country house. Jonson's poem, an ode, established the genre of the English country-house poem as a celebration of patriarchy: it praises the Sidney estate as a quasi-Edenic place whose beauty and harmony are centered in and preserved by its lord, who "dwells" permanently within it. However false to social reality, the poem constructs a social ideal: a benevolent and virtuous patriarchal governor; a house characterized by simplicity and usefulness; a large extended family with lord, lady, children, servants, and retainers all fulfilling their specific, useful functions; the harmony of man and nature; a working agricultural community of interdependent classes linked together in generosity and love; ready hospitality to guests of all stations, from poets to kings; a fruitful and chaste wife and mother embodying and transmitting the estate's ideal fusion of nature and culture; and stability ensured by the religion and virtue passed on from the lord and lady to their progeny.[13] Penshurst is imagined as a *locus amoenus* harmonizing pastoral and providential abundance with georgic cultivation.

Lanyer's country-house poem conceives the genre in very different terms, displacing patriarchy. It is not celebratory but elegiac, a valediction lamenting the loss of an Edenic pastoral place inhabited solely by women: Margaret Clifford, who was the center and sustainer of its beauties and delights, her young unmarried daughter Anne, and Aemilia Lanyer. Lanyer's poem, like Jonson's, draws upon the "*beatus ille*" tradition originating in Horace and Martial, praising a happy rural retirement from city business or courtly corruption, but Lanyer replaces the male speaker and the virtuous happy man with women. Another strand is classical and Renaissance pastoral and golden-age poetry. Yet Lanyer owes most to poems like Virgil's First Eclogue, based on the classical topos, the valediction to a place. Rewriting that model, Lanyer makes the pastoral departure a matter not of state but of domestic politics—the patriarchal arrangements pertaining to Margaret's widowhood and Anne's subsequent marriage.[14]

The generic topics that became conventional after Jonson's "Penshurst" are managed very differently by Lanyer. The house itself (which belonged to the Crown, not the countess)[15] is barely mentioned. The estate is, as we expect, a *locus amoenus,* but the pastoral pathetic fallacy is exaggerated as all its elements respond to Margaret Clifford's presence and departure as to the seasonal round of summer and winter. The creatures welcome her presence with an obsequiousness like that of the Penshurst fish and game offering themselves to capture, but Lanyer does not, like Jonson, invite us to smile at the exaggeration:

The swelling Bankes deliver'd all their pride,
When such a *Phoenix* once they had espide.

> Each Arbor, Banke, each Seate, each stately Tree,
> Thought themselves honor'd in supporting thee.
> The pretty Birds would oft come to attend thee,
> Yet flie away for feare they should offend thee:
> The little creatures in the Burrough by
> Would come abroad to sport them in your eye. [ll. 43-50]

There is no larger society: no extended family, no servants, no villagers, no visitors, no men at all. The only male presences are from nature or the Bible: an oak tree serves the countess as a kind of ideal lover, sheltering her against the too fierce onslaughts of the (also male) sun, and receiving her farewell kiss before she departs. She also enjoys in meditation the spiritual companionship of the psalmist and the apostles. Female aspects of nature, Philomela and Echo, serve as emblems: at first their voices bring praise and delight, but at the ladies' departure they sound their familiar tones of grief and woe, associating their sad stories with this new example of women's wrongs and sorrows. The final passage effectively heightens the pathos of the ladies' departure as all the elements of the *locus amoenus* transform themselves from summer's beauty to wintry desolation:

> Those pretty Birds that wonted were to sing,
> Now neither sing, nor chirp, nor use their wing;
> But with their tender feet on some bare spray,
> Warble forth sorrow, and their owne dismay.
> Faire *Philomela* leaves her mournefull Ditty,
> Drownd in dead sleepe, yet can procure no pittie:
> Each arbour, banke, each seate, each stately tree,
> Lookes bare and desolate now for want of thee;
> Turning greene tresses into frostie gray,
> While in cold griefe they wither all away.
> The Sunne grew weake, his beames no comfort gave,
> While all greene things did make the earth their grave:
> Each brier, each bramble, when you went away,
> Caught fast your clothes, thinking to make you stay:
> Delightfull Eccho wonted to reply
> To our last words, did now for sorrow die:
> The house cast off each garment that might grace it,
> Putting on Dust and Cobwebs to deface it. [ll. 185-202]

By writing and publishing her poems under her own name, Lanyer also intervened in the era's developing discourse about authorship, claiming authority for herself as a woman writer. At times she invokes the humilitas topos to excuse the "defects" of her sex, but she also boldly claims the poet's eternizing power, promising Margaret Clifford that her poems will endure "many yeares longer than your Honour, or my selfe can live" (p. 35). She authorizes her poetry on several grounds: For one, the excellence of her subject—Christ's Passion, and all the worthy women she celebrates. For another, Nature: though Lanyer's poems display considerable knowledge of classical rhetoric, the Bible, and poetic traditions, she assigns learned poetry to men, and to women a (perhaps superior) poetry based on experience and on "Mother" Nature, source of all the arts:

> Not that I Learning to my selfe assume,
> Or that I would compare with any man:
> > But as they are Scholers, and by Art do write,
> > So Nature yeelds my Soule a sad delight.
>
> And since all Arts at first from Nature came,
> That goodly Creature, Mother of Perfection,
> Whom *Joves* almighty hand at first did frame,
> Taking both her and hers in his protection:
> > Why should not She now grace my barren Muse,
> > And in a Woman all defects excuse. ["To the Queenes most Excellent
> > Majestie," ll. 147-56]

She also claims divine authorization for her poetry: a postscript recounts that the title of the volume was "delivered unto me in sleepe many yeares before I had any intent to write in this maner;" significantly, she concludes, "that I was appointed to perform this Worke" (p. 139). She finds further sanction by assuming a place in a female poetic line: in her dream-vision poem to the Countess of Pembroke, she invites the countess to accept her as her own poetic heir.

Lanyer's case would seem to indicate that dominant literary and cultural discourses do not define women's place and women's speech with the rigorous determinism seen by some theorists—at least they do not when women take up the pen and write themselves into those discourses. Lanyer's oppositional writing was, it seems, deliberate: the evidence of genre transformation and subversion of dominant discourses argues for considerable authorial intentionality. Lanyer seems to have regarded the several literary genres she uses, as well as biblical exegesis and the discourses relating to patronage and authorship, not as exclusively male preserves but as common human property, now ready to be reclaimed for women. Her little volume delivered a formidable challenge to Jacobean patriarchal ideology as it appropriated and rewrote these genres and discourses, placing women at the center of the fundamental Christian myths—Eden, the Passion, the Community of Saints. Like other early modern women writers, she could do little to change the repressive conditions of her world. But she was able—no small feat—to imagine and represent a better one.

Notes

1. Some important recent studies include: Elaine Beilin, "The Feminization of Praise: Aemilia Lanyer," in *Redeeming Eve: Women Writers of the English Renaissance* (Princeton: Princeton University Press, 1987); Lynette McGrath, "'Let Us Have Our Libertie Againe': Aemilia Lanyer's Seventeenth-Century Feminist Voice," *Women's Studies* 20 (1992): 331-48; Janel Mueller, "The Feminist Poetics of Aemilia Lanyer's 'Salve Deus Rex Judaeorum,'" in *Feminist Measures: Soundings in Poetry and Theory,* ed. Lynn Keller and Cristianne Miller (Ann Arbor: University of Michigan Press, 1993): 331-48 (reprinted in revised form in this volume as chapter 6); Wendy Wall, "Our Bodies/Our Texts?: Renaissance Women and the Trials of Authorship," in *Anxious Power: Reading, Writing, and Ambivalence in Narrative by Women,* ed. Carol J. Singley and Susan E. Sweeney (Albany: State University of New York Press, 1993), 51-71. See also Lewalski, "Imagining Female Community: Aemilia Lanyer's Poems," in *Writing Women in Jacobean England* (Cambridge: Harvard University Press, 1993).

2. Anne Clifford was the only surviving child of the dashing adventurer and privateer George Clifford, Third Earl of Cumberland, and Margaret (Russell) Clifford. In 1609 she married Richard Sackville, Earl of Dorset, and in 1630 Philip Herbert, Earl of Pembroke and Montgomery. She is remarkable for the sustained lawsuits she carried out with her mother, to claim property denied her by her father's will. That struggle and much else about her domestic life, Court associations, and family are recorded in several autobiographical and biographical works, the most remarkable of which is a *Diary* of the years 1603, and 1616-19, published in *The Diaries of Lady Anne Clifford,* ed. D.J.H. Clifford (Wolfeboro Falls, N.H.: Alan Sutton, 1993). See Lewalski, *Writing Women,* chapter 5.

3. Margaret Clifford's literary and clergy clients include Robert Greene, Thomas Lodge, Samuel Daniel, Henry Lok, Edmund Spenser, Samuel Hieron, Henry Peacham, William Perkins, Richard Greenham, and Peter Muffett, among others. See Lewalski, *Writing Women,* chapter 5.

4. For discussion of the English controversy and its gamesmanship, see Linda Woodbridge, *Women and the English Renaissance: Literature and the Nature of Womankind, 1540-1640* (Chicago: University of Chicago Press, 1984).

5.[Robert Southwell], *Saint Peters Complaynt* (London, 1595); rpt. with other Southwell poems in 1595, 1597, 1599, 1602, 1607.

6. *Ibid.* (1607), p. 14.

7. "*Christs Triumph over Death*" is Part III of Fletcher's *Christs victorie and triumph in heaven and earth, over and after death* (Cambridge, 1610).

8. Nicholas Breton, *The Pilgrimage to Paradise, Joyned with the Countesse of Pembrookes Love* (Oxford, 1592); also, *A Divine Poem, divided into two Partes: The Ravisht Soule, and the Blessed Weeper* (London, 1601). Abraham Fraunce, *The Countesse of Pembrokes Emanuell* (London, 1591).

9. See especially Psalm 104:

> 2. Who coverest thy self with light as with a garment: who stretchest out the heavens like a curtain. 3. Who layeth the beams of his chambers in the waters: who maketh the clouds his charriot: who walketh upon the wings of the wind. 4. Who maketh his angells spirits; his ministers a flaming fire. . . . 32. He looketh on the earth, and it trembleth: he toucheth the hills, and they smoke.

10. First published in 1823, the psalm versions of Sir Philip Sidney (Psalms 1-43) and the Countess of Pembroke (Psalms 44-150) were widely circulated in manuscript; they were especially noteworthy for stanzaic and metrical variety. Margaret Clifford had for some years been estranged from and virtually rejected by her husband, a notorious womanizer.

11. From internal evidence it is clear that "Penshurst" was written sometime before the death of Prince Henry in November, 1612, as a reference to him (l. 77) indicates, but the poem was first published in Jonson's *Works* (1616). Lanyer's poem was written sometime after Anne Clifford's marriage to Richard Sackville on February 25, 1609, since she is referred to as Dorset, the title her husband inherited two days after the marriage, and before the volume was registered with the Stationers on October 2, 1610. If Jonson's poem was written first, Lanyer might have seen a manuscript copy.

12. None of the extant records or letters identify Lanyer as a client or a member of Margaret Clifford's household, but there are few such records. During the period September-November 1604, Margaret Clifford dated five letters from "Cookham in Berkshire" (Longleat, Portland Papers, vol. 23, ff. 24-28), and this may be the period of residence. Anne Clifford's *Diary* (p. 15) records one visit to Cookham in 1603, but has nothing before 1603 and then skips to 1616, so has no occasion to mention Lanyer.

13. For an extended comparison, see Lewalski, "The Lady of the Country-House Poem," in *The Fashioning and Functioning of the British Country House,* ed. Gervase Jackson-Stops, et al., (Hanover and London: National Gallery of Art, 1989), 261-75. See also Grossman's essay in the present volume (chapter 7).

14. The valedictory mode of this poem suggests a permanent rather than a seasonal departure, probably related to the countess's permanent departure to her dower residences in Westmoreland after she was widowed in 1605. Anne would have departed with her; she was married to Dorset in 1609.

15. Cookham belonged to the Crown from before the Conquest until 1818; it was annexed to Windsor Castle in 1540. The manor was evidently granted or leased to Margaret's family (the Russells) and occupied by the Countess of Cumberland at some periods during her estrangement from her husband in the years before his death in 1605, and perhaps just after.

4
Sacred Celebration: The Patronage Poems

KARI BOYD MCBRIDE

The forms and dynamics of patronage and patronage poetry constitute a significant field of early modern scholarship, as the continuing production of articles, monographs, and collections attest. Yet the difficulty and even embarrassment some readers of Aemilia Lanyer have evinced when confronted by her patronage poems speak to the gendered nature of much theorizing about patronage and about women poets, as well. As Lorna Hutson has noted, early critical response "display[ed] a tendency to account for [Lanyer's poems'] embarrassing length, inappropriateness and apparent sycophancy by referring to the lady's notorious past."[1] Poets such as Edmund Spenser and Ben Jonson are understood to be writing in—and modifying and challenging—the epideictic tradition, but discussion of Lanyer's patronage poems initially devolved into a skeptical critique of her presumption upon tenuous or nonexistent aristocratic connections balanced by a kind of grudging Johnsonian compliment, "it's not that Lanyer wrote well, but that she wrote at all." Only the sustained work of second-generation Lanyer scholars has begun to bring her patronage poetry into critical focus.

This study is part of the ongoing project to read Lanyer's poems against the larger literary and social culture of patronage. Building on the work of Hutson, Ann Baynes Coiro, Mary Ellen Lamb, Barbara Keifer Lewalski, and others, I wish to suggest here that the patronage poem functioned to construct a transgressive female authority for Lanyer only because she fundamentally altered the context in which patron-client relationships were supposed to have functioned, substituting a religious sphere for the courtly one. That change in political and social context revalues everything in the patronage exchange—Lanyer's relative position vis-à-vis her patrons, her function as author, the significance of her book, and the meaning produced by her rhetoric. Rather than figuring herself and her book as humble supplicants for aristocratic favor, Lanyer's poetic assumes preemptively a divine favor that is most audacious in her repeated claims to offer her readers Christ, the Word that her poetry paradoxically makes flesh. And if Lanyer's poetry incarnates Christ to become a means of salvation for her readers (as she repeatedly suggests), then the banquet scene that adumbrates the hospitality topos of patronage poetry becomes a eucharistic meal with Lanyer its priestly celebrant. She, rather than a titled patron, is host—both provider of the feast and, in her identification with Christ, consecrated body. It is on these transgressive terms, I suggest, that Lanyer constructs the patronage relationship, combining traditional social and generic forms with a radical theology to claim authority and poetic identity.

Interest in the poems that preface Lanyer's *Salve Deus Rex Judaeorum* has constituted a significant subspecies of Lanyer criticism since her (re)discovery by scholars early in this century. Charlotte Kohler saw them as part of a project of "art for lucre's sake," and A.L. Rowse called them "sycophantic," chastising Lanyer for advocating a meritocracy based on virtue while writing dedications to "grandees."[2] Later readers, while commenting on the poems' "obsequiousness" and "hyperbole,"[3] have seen them as integral, not secondary, to Lanyer's poetic. Elaine V. Beilin, acknowledging that the dedications "may seem at first to be the most dubious part of Lanyer's work," links them to "the poem's central purpose." She argues that, "In the dedications, Lanyer concentrates on the spiritual gifts of women, expressing her intention most clearly in the image of the wise virgins prepared for the bridegroom."[4] Barbara Kiefer Lewalski has further argued that "these dedications as a group portray a contemporary community of learned and virtuous women with the poet Aemilia their associate and celebrant." She suggests that the dedications "rewrite the institution of patronage in female terms, transforming the relationships assumed in the male patronage system into an ideal community." Lanyer, says Lewalski, "comprehends all the dedications within the thematic unity of her volume, addressing these ladies as a contemporary community of good women who are spiritual heirs to the biblical and historical good women her title poem celebrates."[5]

Recent critics have complicated the assessment of Lanyer's patronage poems, providing alternatives to both poles of analysis: to the chastisement of Lanyer's effusiveness and to the alternative postulation of a sisterhood of women. Ann Baynes Coiro notes that "studies devoted to early modern women writers have emphasized an idealized sisterhood among them, even though these studies discuss highly varied configurations of women across several generations and even across continents." She argues, on the contrary, that, particularly in their use of epideictic forms, "Lanyer and Jonson have more in common with each other than does Lanyer with other important women writers of her generation."[6]

Mary Ellen Lamb points out that "the language of Lanyer's dedications to women was not unusually celebratory by early modern conventions." Further, she suggests that "[t]he dedications do not create a stable vision of a community or family of women patrons; even textually, membership in such a group fluctuated among copies according to marketplace considerations as dedications were added or dropped."[7] Rather, Lamb sees the patronage poems and the patronage system behind them as forming the agon in which Lanyer wrestled with gender and class issues. Hutson has argued that the entire *Salve* is an attempt to produce "a poem which celebrates woman as an effective reader and agent" and that the female patrons, foremost among whom is Margaret, Countess of Cumberland, model, along with biblical women, this power to discern virtue: "For it is not that [Lanyer] wrote a narrative of Christ and absentmindedly kept apostrophizing the Countess of Cumberland because she could not keep her mind off the richest woman in England. Her subject . . . is reflexive; it is the reading subject, the encounter of the patron's mind with the text, which is celebrated as a textual resource."[8] Likewise, Coiro argues that the prefatory poems combine "criticism of the aristocratic ladies studded with inestimable wealth, promotion of a leveling Christian radicalism, and, at the same time, a wonderful degree of self-promotion."[9] I wish to articulate here an understanding of Lanyer's patronage poems that draws on these insights, assuming that the poems are central to Lanyer's poetic and suggesting that they contribute to our definitions and understanding of epideictic rhetoric by their redefinition of the genre. That is, Lanyer's self-authorizing is dependent on her transformation of the patronage poem in the service of a literary identity that such forms had not hitherto invoked: the female, middle-class poet. The poems thus serve to authorize Lanyer in the poetic tradition apart from any lack of support (financial or otherwise) she might have hoped to receive from the powerful women whose names she invokes.

The patronage poem is, of course, a genre designed to construct and empower the poet by tapping the potential of the more powerful patron. Part of a larger culture of patronage that defined seventeenth-century social and political relationships—a culture that was being challenged and altered by, among many other things, the continuing rise of the middle class and the proliferation of printed works—the patronage poem was in many ways backward-looking without being outmoded. Middle-class poets like Aemilia Lanyer and Ben Jonson, who distinguished themselves from the aristocratic circle of poets by publishing their works in print rather than (seemingly reluctantly) allowing them to circulate in manuscript, embody the emerging challenges to the system of patronage and to the primacy of the aristocracy.[10] So their poems, while they could not help but hold out hope for the kind of jackpot reward—long odds on an income for life—that is the promise of literary patronage, used the generic form as a context for constructing literary authority in the meantime. As Robert C. Evans has argued, the system of patronage allowed for a "complex and dialectical" relationship between client and patron and offered "opportunities for irony, ambiguity, paradox, and equivocation" to the artist who could exploit its possibilities.[11]

Like Ben Jonson, Aemilia Lanyer exploited the genre's rich complexity to construct and promote herself as author. But Lanyer was restricted because of her gender in the means available for self-representation, in the kinds of roles she could play as supplicant. She did not have the public and professional persona Jonson had developed as dramatist and poet—nor could she, as a woman writer. Likewise, she did not have the aristocratic family ties of Mary Sidney with the added advantage of a protective, genius, poet brother. Further limiting Lanyer was the fact that, for a variety of reasons central to her polemical project, Lanyer made her suit exclusively to female patrons. And while there existed an acceptable form of address for the female patron, that discourse was inappropriate to Lanyer in a number of ways. Traditionally, the male author employed the language of love as the framework for defining the client-patron relationship when addressing patronage poems to women. As Maureen Quilligan points out, "Petrarchism had . . . become an overtly political language, developing into a substitute political discourse, especially during the reign of Elizabeth."[12] Even into the reign of James I, that amorous discourse continued to provide a pretext for articulating a social dynamic that would otherwise invert the realities of gender hierarchy too radically, particularly after the death of Elizabeth I had made "women on top" cease to define courtier relationships in general.[13] But such conventions left Lanyer without a rhetoric of patronage, for she could no more speak to her female patrons in Petrarchan similes[14] than she could place herself at the table of a patron in the manner of Ben Jonson at Penshurst. After all, even Barbara Gamage Sidney is neither seen nor heard in "To Penshurst"; her ladies-in-waiting have no place at the table. Quilligan argues that Mary Wroth solved the problem of rhetorical positioning by redefining the female in the Petrarchan economy vis-à-vis the male; Lanyer, I would argue, deleted the male from the exchange, remade the banquet scene that figured noble hospitality, and introduced alternative rhetorical forms that allowed her to position herself authoritatively in relationship to her patrons.

These features are merely part of a larger generic revision whereby Lanyer appropriated the conventions of patronage poetry to her service by redefining the context in which such poems are presumed to circulate. In Lanyer's *Salve,* the mise-en-scène of courtier politics that define such poems has a parallel in the spiritual setting defined by the presence of Christ. In Coiro's words, "the prefatory company of women shift in and out of the two spheres."[15] But since the religious context in some sense justifies the existence of aristocratic privilege

and certainly takes precedence over the courtly world in a Christianized soci-
ety, I would suggest that the secular sphere is not merely paralleled but is super-
seded in Lanyer's poems by the religious order. In that sphere, her station is
equal—or perhaps even superior—to that of the patrons she celebrates. So, for
example, the titled women addressed in Lanyer's poems are positioned in this
religious hierarchy beneath the biblical heroines Lanyer's text praises, and in
place of the social structure predicated on a divine-right monarchy, Lanyer
substitutes a society of grace and virtue predicated on the person of the deified
Christ whose humiliated and demeaned body is displayed at the center of her
poem. That founding paradox of Christian dogma—of power disguised as
humbleness—allows Lanyer to appropriate the topos of humility that defines
the poet's relationship to powerful patrons, turning it into a claim of divine-
right authority. Thus Lanyer's rhetoric of patronage subverts the traditional
motifs of epideictic, effacing rather than delineating the class distinctions that
separate her from her patrons. The praise apparently directed to the noble-
women repeatedly devolves to biblical heroines, to untitled virtuous women,
and to Lanyer, first among equals in her repeated identification with Virtue
and with the humbled Christ.

Nonetheless, the trope of hospitality that is so important to the definition
of client-patron relationship remains central to Lanyer's self-fashioning. In-
deed, those poems function more as invitations to a banquet than as dedica-
tions in the traditional sense.[16] But Lanyer evokes the theme of hospitality that
had traditionally defined class relationships only to subvert the hierarchy it
implied. As Michael C. Schoenfeldt has noted, practicing hospitality "announces
prestige in the political arena, for the ability to feed others is an index of social
status." When Lanyer invites a handful of noblewomen and "all vertuous ladies
in generall" to a feast, she is taking a position of authority, for "the giving of a
feast is a sign of power . . . [and] the acceptance of another's fare is a mark of
submission." By her actions she co-opts "a mode of behavior through which
the aristocracy parades its power over others."[17] In other words, she has used
the very social means by which the noblewomen to whom she addresses her
poem might express their power over her and turned that social form into a
poetic trope that articulates her own authority—and all in a manner that seems
to offer service rather than challenge.[18]

Lanyer's banquet draws on a number of biblical models, most notably, as
Beilin notes, the Matthean parables that figure Christ as bridegroom and be-
lievers as wise virgins ready to be called to the wedding banquet. The allusion
to that spiritualized marriage calls to mind other biblical passages involving
marriage, including Luke's images of feasting in the presence of the bridegroom
and the imagery of the Song of Songs that, in the Christian "spiritual" reading,
figured the relationship between the individual Christian and Christ as that of
bride and bridegroom. Perhaps most important to Lanyer's conception of fe-

male community is the imagery of the eschatological vision of a renewed Jerusalem from the Book of Revelation (itself a re-visioning of the deutero-Isaiah messianic prophecies) that figures the end times as a wedding supper for the Lamb and his 144,000 elect. Lanyer merges these images into a prophetic vision of her own, one that displaces men (who had traditionally modeled the community of saints, even when figured as brides) and places women at the center. Instead of a male-defined church, Lanyer figures "virtuous women" and herself as priests who have the power to consecrate and incarnate language.

It is to this multiply sanctified banquet, disruptive of client-patron relationships, that Lanyer invites nine titled women and "all vertuous Ladies in generall." Queen Anne, wife of James I, is the "welcom'st guest" at the feast for which the poet has "prepar'd my Paschal Lambe" (ll. 84, 85). Next in honor to the queen is the Lady Elizabeth, her daughter, whom Lanyer "invite[s] unto this wholesome feast" (l. 9). "All vertuous Ladies in generall" are invited to "Come wait on" (l. 3) the queen, and are counseled to "Put on your wedding garments every one" (l. 8) and to "fill your Lamps with oyle of burning zeale" (ll. 13) for "The Bridegroome stayes to entertain you all" (l. 9). Her book offers them access to heaven where they will experience "a second berth" (66). "The Ladie *Arabella*" is invited to "Come like the morning Sunne new out of bed" that her "beauteous Soule" might be embraced by "this humbled King" (ll. 12-14). The poem addressed to "the Ladie *Susan*" repeats three times the invitation to attend Lanyer's feast:

> Come you that were the Mistris of my youth,
> . . . .
> Come you that have delighted in Gods truth,
> . . . .
> Come you that ever since hath followed her
> In these sweet paths of faire Humilitie. [ll. 1, 3, 31-32]

She is invited both to "grace this holy feast" (l. 6) and to "[t]ake this faire Bridegroome in your soules pure bed" (l. 42). In the poem to Mary Sidney, Countess of Pembroke, Lanyer "invite[s] her Honour to my feast" (l. 206). Lucy, Countess of Bedford, is asked to "Vouchsafe to entertaine this dying lover," and counseled to let her thoughts "Give true attendance on this lovely guest" (ll. 16, 22-23). Katherine, Countess of Suffolk, is asked to allow her "noble daughters" to feed "On heavenly food" and to know in Christ "a Lover much more true / Than ever was since first the world began" (ll. 51-53). The dedicatory poem to Anne Clifford recalls the parable of the bridegroom again: "One sparke of grace sufficient is to fill / Our Lampes with oyle, ready when he doth call / To enter with the Bridegroome to the feast" (ll. 13-16).[19] So rather than invoking the patron-client relationship in the manner of Jonson by figuring herself as a guest at an aristocratic banquet, Lanyer figures herself as hosting her "patrons" at a feast that is the image of eucharistic and eschatological banquets. Lanyer is thus a sacerdotal and sanctified "host" who "patronizes" her noble guests.

Lanyer's authority as priest and host is underscored by her merging of the heavenly marriage banquet with her book, as she does particularly in the poem "To the Lady *Elizabeths* Grace":

> Even you faire Princesse next our famous Queene,
> I doe invite unto this wholesome feast,
> Whose goodly wisedome, though your yeares be greene,
> By such good workes may daily be increast,
> Though your faire eyes farre better Bookes have seene. [ll. 8-12]

Here a kind of rhetorical slippage makes the "wholesome feast" into a "Booke" that increases "good works." That notion is underscored by Lanyer's claim in the poem to Queen Anne to have "prepar'd my Paschal Lambe" (l. 85), the "figure of that living Sacrifice" (l. 86) and the means of salvation. Her invitation to Anne—"this pretious Passeover feed upon" (l. 89)—figures the queen as a laywoman while Lanyer assumes a sacerdotal function that recalls Abraham's sacrifice of Isaac, Moses's and Aaron's roles at the first Passover, and the contemporary image of a priest celebrating Eucharist. Again, Lanyer and her book function as the "host"—she *to* her noble patron and the book *as* consecrated bread.[20]

Once they are figuratively seated at Lanyer's holy banquet, her noble patrons are displaced and disempowered by the presence of biblical heroines who outrank the titled guests. In contrast to the biblical men of the "Salve Deus," whose virtue and spiritual fitness are called into question, the biblical women whom Lanyer names are both models of empowerment and of womanhood: they have traditionally feminine characteristics such as beauty and chastity, but they play nontraditional roles in the biblical narratives. The much-anthologized poem "To the Vertuous Reader" and an extended section of the "Salve Deus" (ll. 1465-1616) present six women of the Hebrew Bible as models of female virtue and power: Deborah and Jael of the book of Judges, the Queen of Sheba of the first book of Kings, Esther and Judith of the books bearing their names, and Susanna, whose story formed one of the additions to the book of Daniel in the Vulgate and stood as a separate book in the Apocrypha of the Elizabethan Bibles.[21] Though some of these biblical figures are "titled"—the Queen of Sheba, Esther, and Judith, for instance—they are linked by divine favor in Lanyer's analysis to the untitled virtuous women for whom she is spokeswoman; they, thus, displace the noblewomen of the poems. Lanyer's choice of female figures here is telling. She could have chosen women who modeled obedience or patience, typical female virtues, for the Bible offers many examples of such women. Instead, Lanyer has chosen women whose lives signify independence. Susanna is the most "traditional" female character, one willing to defend her chastity to the death; the Queen of Sheba is unique to the biblical narrative as a woman equal in status to that greatest of kings, Solomon; the other women play central roles in the military and strategic defense of Israel.

Further, these women, though occupying varying periods and purposes in the biblical narrative, share one negative quality: their purpose is unconnected to generation and lineage. As "breeding" is a duty that defines noblewomen's lives more significantly than middle-class women's, Lanyer's selection of these women distances them from her patrons. Lanyer has chosen five women who are not valued for their procreative ability, as are other strong biblical women such as Tamar, Hannah, and Ruth. Instead, Lanyer's biblical heroines are narratively independent of the genealogical concerns of much of the Bible. When the biblical narratives introduce Deborah, Jael, and Susanna, they are linked to their husbands—Deborah is the wife of Lappidoth, Jael is the wife of Heber the Kenite, and Susanna is the wife of Joachim—but the men then disappear from the text, never to be named again, and we never hear whether the women have children or not. The Queen of Sheba is utterly independent of men and children and is the equal of Solomon; she enters and exits the narrative attended only by her great retinue. Raised by her uncle, Esther is an orphan who is groomed as a concubine and becomes a queen; children are never mentioned. Judith's widowhood is important to the narrative, as is Susanna's chastity, but their childlessness is not. The presence of these childless women in a narrative mildly obsessed with the theme of the barren woman (and God's merciful ending of her affliction) is remarkable, and Lanyer's singling out of these women cannot be accidental.

Rather than being defined by their subservient relationship to men or the patriarchal concerns of the Bible, these women are defined by their superiority to or even violent dispatching of men. In a twist on the biblical pattern of introducing women by reference to their fathers or husbands or children, Lanyer instead introduces some of the biblical heroines by the names of the men they destroyed, linking the women to the exercise of the will of God "who gave power to wise and virtuous women, to bring downe [men's] pride and arrogancie" ("Vertuous Reader" ll. 31-33). Likewise, in the "Salve Deus," Lanyer introduces her heroines as "Those famous women elder times have knowne, / Whose glorious actions did appeare so bright, / That powrefull men by them were overthrowne" (ll. 1465-67). However, while the women co-opt many of the strong characteristics of men, they do not seem either "male" or androgynous, for many of the women Lanyer has chosen as models are noted for their beauty. While the Queen of Sheba and Deborah are powerful national leaders, their appearance is not mentioned by the biblical text. But the beauty of Judith,

Esther, and Susanna is integral to the narrative. Judith and Esther use make-up and heighten their beauty to serve God's purpose by seducing men in order to overthrow them. Susanna, on the other hand, is persecuted *because of* her beauty. In none of the narratives are women condemned for being attractive, an omission that is, in itself, an anomaly in the religious text.[22]

Given the characteristics that Lanyer delineates in her pantheon of biblical heroines, it is surprising that, in the poem to Queen Anne, the queen's authority seems to depend on her ability to bear children. She is initially invoked in the first dedication as "Renowned Empresse" and "great Britaines Queene," titles more appropriate to, because reminiscent of, the deified Elizabeth—an initial displacement that deflects the praise seemingly directed toward Anne.[23] This questionable empowering of Queen Anne is immediately displaced again, as the third title bestowed on her by Lanyer is "Mother of succeeding Kings." The ironic nature of this compliment is underscored by Lanyer's poem to Princess Elizabeth. She is overtly compared to the dead and semi-divine queen— indeed, one stanza of the two-stanza poem is about Elizabeth I—and is characterized ambiguously as "next our famous Queene" ("To the Ladie *Elizabeths* Grace," l. 8). The apostrophe, "Even you faire Princesse next our famous Queene, / I doe invite unto this wholesome feast," says that only Anne precedes Elizabeth on Lanyer's guest list, but it also is a sore reminder that Elizabeth will not be the "next" queen, as neither she nor her mother can be queens in their own right. Thus their actual or potential mothering of kings subsumes any independently-wielded authority. Such praise of women for their childbearing abilities is particularly suspect, given Lanyer's choice of non-mothering women as biblical heroines (and the way in which she excludes from the country-house poem the genre's obsession with female fertility). This doubtful praise shows Lanyer to be a consummate *bricoleuse*, for she has made use here even of women's powerlessness: women's inability (in all but the most unusual cases) to inherit titles and property in a patrilineal system becomes a tool for Lanyer's building of her own authority relative to titled women.

Also important here and later is the fact that Queen Anne is asked to "view" and "reade"—asked to practice an act of virtue and authority normally reserved for men. Hutson, for instance, argues that a woman's (specifically Margaret, Countess of Cumberland's) ability to read virtuously is central to Lanyer's poem and to her self-fashioning as author, and, indeed, Lanyer's presumptuous claim for women's virtuous power lies behind this passage.[24] But, as Coiro has pointed out in her discussion of Lanyer's address to Queen Anne, "the queen is being subjected throughout the poem to a sustained critique for failing to provide . . . patronage to Lanyer" as did Elizabeth I.[25] And while Lanyer's invitation to Anne seems to defer to her, she is, in fact, repeatedly asked to confirm Lanyer's authority: "Vouchsafe to view that which is seldom seene, / A Womans writing of divinest things" (ll. 3-4). While Lanyer is empowered to write "of divinest things," the queen is merely the observer—and potential patron—of Lanyer's actions. Lanyer later asks the queen to "behold . . . faire *Eves* Apologie" and "To judge if it agree not with the Text" (ll. 73, 76). Here, as Hutson has suggested, a woman is given the virtuous power to read rightly, but, at the same time, the queen's authority is checked, as she is being asked merely to confirm Lanyer's right reading of the Bible. Succeeding stanzas delineating the queen's virtues remain under the shadow of the initial displacements and Lanyer's undermining of all royal authority. For instance, the third stanza, which seems to credit Queen Anne with goddess-like virtues, ends abruptly with a cryptic couplet that, again, questions her standing: "How much are we to honor those that springs / From such rare beauty, in the blood of Kings?" (ll. 17-18). It isn't clear here whether the couplet is a rhetorical question or dead serious: should we, in fact, honor "blood" at all? Parallel tirades against class hierarchy (in, for instance, the dedication to Anne Clifford) suggest that Lanyer is here questioning the validity of the entire social order rather than praising the female representative of its highest level.

This patronizing rhetorical gesture of displacement and subversion is subsequently repeated when Queen Anne is likened to "faire Phoebe," an ambiguous glory that pales when "*Apollo's* beames" appear that

> doe comfort every creature,
> And shines upon the meanest things that be;
> Since in Estate and Virtue none is greater,
> I humbly wish that yours may light on me:
> That so these rude unpollisht lines of mine,
> Graced by you, may seeme the more divine. [ll. 31-36]

Anne seems again to be praised, by being likened to the moon and its mythic parallels, only to have that compliment deferred to Queen Elizabeth and then to be dimmed by a greater light. Even this praise is devalued when "Apollo's beames" shine on Lanyer, for she then becomes equal to the moon, by implication the equal of Elizabeth I and perhaps superior to Anne.[26] Further, it is not clear who possesses "Virtue and Estate"—Phoebe? Apollo? the queen? Lanyer? All possibilities seem implied in the vertiginous rhetorical construction, resulting in a confusion of meaning that leaves Lanyer, the maker of the verse, at the center. Moreover, while on the surface that stanza asks for the queen's gaze again—the result of the queen's "shining" on Lanyer's work is that "graced by you, [it] may seem the more divine"—the encoded message empowers Lanyer rather than the queen. The construction seems to invoke the queen's power to make things divine, but the sentence implies that Lanyer's work is already divine; the queen's gaze can only make it "seem the more" so.

Twice in the poem to Queen Anne, Lanyer links her virtuous poetic authority to poetry's mimetic potential, repeatedly comparing her book to a mirror. Here again a religious context displaces or augments the merely poetic argument. Queen Anne initially is told to "Looke in this Mirrour of a worthy Mind, / Where some of your faire Virtues will appeare." (ll. 37-38). But syntax subverts this seeming deference to the queen's virtue, for it is unclear whether the "worthy Mind" is Lanyer's, the maker of the poem/mirror, or the queen's, of which the poem is a mirror. Lanyer's apology that her mirror cannot reflect the whole of Anne's virtues, being "dym steele" rather than "chrystall," is hedged by the claim that the poem/mirror is, nonetheless "full of spotlesse truth" (ll. 40-41). While Lanyer's poem seems unable to reflect Queen Anne, it can contain all of a truth that the term "spotlesse" associates with both the sinless Christ and the immaculate Virgin Mary. The poet able to mirror the central figures of the Christian narrative whose poem at the same time cannot express all of Queen Anne either communicates a disinclination to mirror her or implies that "all" of Anne contains "some" that is not Christ- or Mary-like.[27]

Further, as John C. Ulreich has suggested, "When Queen Anne looks in the glass [of Lanyer's poem], she sees . . . not herself, but the image of her Lord. Since she cannot be the source of that reflection, it must derive from the power of the maker of that mirror."[28] In other words, the *subject* of Queen Anne's gaze—"He that all Nations of the world controld" (l. 45)—subverts the authority with which Lanyer seems to credit the queen. For Christ is "Crowne and Crowner of all Kings" (l. 49), the king of kings who is both the justification for and the challenge to all monarchy. So, while the religious order is the source of the divine right of kings and the machinery of privilege ("No bishop, no king," said James I, astutely), here, rather than supporting the earthly sovereign in her rank, the presence of Christ the King supersedes the queen's claim to authority. Though this (and the previous stanza) seem to speak of the power of rule, Anne is displaced by a higher authority, and all hierarchy is called into question by this subversive king who "tooke our flesh in base and meanest berth" and who is "[t]he hopefull haven of the meaner sort" (ll. 46, 50). When Lanyer says that "my wealth within [Christ's] Region stands, . . . [and] in his kingdome onely rests my lands" (ll. 55, 57), she has divested herself of all allegiance and submission to Queen Anne or any other human authority.

Lanyer's seemingly humble offer of her book to the queen must be placed in the context of this subversive portrait. Comparing her state on earth to what she expects in heaven, Lanyer says,

Though I on earth doe live unfortunate,
    Yet there I may attaine a better state.

In the meane time, accept most gratious Queene
This holy work, Virtue presents to you,

In poore apparrell, shaming to be seene,
Or once t'appeare in your judiciall view:
    But that faire Virtue, though in meane attire,
    All Princes of the world doe most desire. [ll. 59-66]

Lanyer's presentation to the queen happens "In the meane time," this brief moment before eternity while Lanyer is temporarily the queen's inferior. Further, the one presenting the "holy work" is, once again, Virtue itself. Lanyer/ Virtue/Christ "in the meane time" appear "in poor apparrell," but even in this "meane time," they are what "all Princes of the world doe most desire." While "all royall virtues" (l. 67) may reside in the queen, Lanyer is one with virtue itself. Further, her seemingly deferential offer—"I hope . . . / You will accept even the meanest line / Faire Virtue yeelds"—inscribes instead the queen's subjection to Lanyer. For both Lanyer and Virtue construct the poetic portrait of Queen Anne: it is "by [Virtue's] rare gifts you are / So highly grac'd, t'exceed the fairest faire" (ll. 70-72). Thus Lanyer claims already to possess that which Queen Anne might merely discover in Lanyer's work. Again, while seeming to defer to the queen, Lanyer has, in fact, subverted the realities of social position and power to construct her own authority in the source of earthly titles, Christ.

Lanyer's self-fashioning in the dedication "To the Ladie *Anne,* Countesse of Dorcet," relies on similar rhetorical techniques, wherein praise of Anne is repeatedly deflected in such a way as substantially to negate that praise. This technique, in the context of an extended rant against the class system in which Lanyer distinguishes between true nobility and inherited title, produces a poem that serves to bury rather than praise Anne Clifford. Lanyer's authority here derives again from a displacement of secular patronage relationships by a religious sphere. Indeed, the poem to Clifford illustrates, perhaps more clearly than any other, how Lanyer's evocation of the religious order subverts the privilege of title. "God makes both even, the Cottage with the Throne," she claims; "All worldly honours there [in heaven] are counted base" (19-20). In the higher "reality," Lanyer's status exceeds Clifford's, for in Lanyer's work, Christ is always identified as enfleshed in an unhonored body. Like Lanyer and her book, Christ is only seemingly poor and without title; in the more "real," religious world, however, they are a means to salvation, the image of ultimate authority. Lanyer's "praise" of Clifford thus becomes a lecture on the vanity—the nothingness—of earthly honors. Lanyer and her poetry are the ones truly deserving of honor, for they exist in the world of true reward in which Christ is not crucified, but enthroned.

The initial stanza of the poem, which contains the actual dedication, seems to praise Clifford:

To you I dedicate this worke of Grace,
This frame of Glory which I have erected,

For your faire mind I hold the fittest place,
Where virtue should be setled & protected. [ll. 1-4]

However, while Lanyer has "erected" an undoubted "worke of Grace" and "frame of Glory," Clifford's mind is merely the place where virtue "should" reside, not necessarily where it, in fact, does reside. The stanzas that follow reiterate the disjunction between what should be in Clifford's "faire mind" and what is actually there, as Lanyer repeatedly distinguishes between inherited honor and "real" (that is, heavenly) honor, tacitly allying herself with the dispossessed and truly honorable Christ, and implying Clifford's lack of virtue *because* of her title:

Titles of honour which the world bestowes,
To none but to the virtuous doth belong;
. . . .
But when they are bestow'd upon her foes,
Poore virtues friends indure the greatest wrong:
    For they must suffer all indignity,
    Untill in heav'n they better graced be. [ll. 25-26, 29-32]

In a passage that seems to echo the Lukan "sermon on the plain" ("Woe be to you that are rich: for ye haue receiued your consolation"), Lanyer implies that she, Virtue's friend, will gain her reward in heaven while Clifford has the "title of honour" perhaps unconnected to true virtue, to be enjoyed only in this life.

The distinction between earthly and heavenly virtue is part of a larger attack on privilege that recalls the time "When Adam delved and Eve span":

What difference was there when the world began,
Was it not Virtue that distinguisht all?
All sprang but from one woman and one man,
Then how doth Gentry come to rise and fall? [ll. 33-36][29]

Further, Lanyer argues, even if one's ancestor, the original recipient of the title, deserved it, who is to say his offspring, "although they beare his name," are equally virtuous? They may not "spring out of the same / True stocke of honour" (ll. 41, 43-44). The significance of the suggestion that successors do not always inherit their ancestor's virtue becomes apparent in the following stanzas when Anne Clifford is markedly distinguished from her mother, Margaret, Countess of Cumberland. While Cumberland is figured as truly virtuous, her daughter is repeatedly admonished to imitate her mother, implying that Clifford does not yet possess virtue, and suggesting the possibility that she may never be like her mother in that respect.[30] Clifford is merely one "In whom the seeds of virtue have bin sowne, / By your most worthy mother, in whose right, / All her

faire parts you challenge as your owne" (ll. 58-60). It is only by the "right" of
her "most worthy mother" that Clifford might have "faire parts," but not in
her own "right." A later stanza repeats this distinction: Clifford is pictured as
"Heire apparant" of a "Crowne / Of goodnesse, bountie, grace, love, pietie" (ll.
65-66). It is hers "By birth" (l. 67), says Lanyer, but "The right your Mother
hath to it, is knowne / Best unto you" (ll. 69-70). It is only by imitating the
Messiah (as figured in Isaiah) that Clifford can possess virtue unto herself:

> And as your Ancestors at first possest
> Their honours, for their honourable deeds,
> Let their faire virtues never be transgrest,
> Bind up the broken, stop the wounds that bleeds,
> Succour the poore, comfort the comfortlesse,
> Cherish faire plants, suppresse unwholsom weeds. [ll. 73-78][31]

The catch here is that Clifford can see any virtues she might posses (only?) in
Lanyer's verse: "In this Mirrour let your faire eyes looke, / To view your virtues
in this blessed Booke" (ll. 7-8). Lanyer's book is additionally figured as a Dia-
dem, merged with the "Crowne / Of goodness" (ll. 65-66) to which Anne is
heir, and, by association, with the crown of Jesus—both the crown of thorns of
the false dishonor of this world, and the crown of glory that is appropriately
his. It is only by wearing this multivalent crown—that is, by reading Lanyer's
verse—that Clifford can become like her mother:

> If you, sweet Lady, will appeare as bright
> As ever creature did that time hath knowne,
>> Then weare this Diadem I present to thee,
>> Which I have fram'd for [your mother's] Eternitie. [ll. 61-64]

Clifford's support of Lanyer's poetry is linked to Clifford's attainment of the
virtue she lacks. For the sign of her virtue is the support of Lanyer's book; to be
like the Messiah is to be Lanyer's patron. If Clifford engages in messianic acts
of mercy, she will show her true lineage (be truly descended from her mother). A
slippery parallel construction links the resulting (true) fame to Lanyer's success:

> So shal you shew from whence you are descended,
> And leave to all posterities your fame,
> So will your virtues alwaies be commended,
> And every one will reverence your name;
> So this poore worke of mine shalbe defended
> From any scandall that the world can frame:
>> And you a glorious Actor will appeare
>> Lovely to all, but unto God most dear. [ll. 81-88]

A final admonition suggests that Clifford's gratefulness to Christ for her redemption can be expressed by reading Lanyer's book: "Therefore in recompence of all his paine, / Bestowe your paines to reade . . . " (ll. 139-40). Meditating on Christ's Passion thus should engender in Clifford a compunction productive of patronage.

The poems "To the Ladie *Arabella*," "To the Ladie *Susan*," and "To the Ladie *Lucie*" repeat these techniques of subversive celebration, but with less venom than the address to Clifford. Lanyer pictures Arabella Stuart arising like the sun accompanied by Athena and the Muses, only to beg her to "spare one looke / Upon this humbled King, who all forsooke" (ll. 11-12), implying again the superiority of Lanyer's host/book to Stuart's mythologized power. Susan Bertie, Countess of Kent, is addressed as "[t]he noble guide of my ungovern'd dayes," implying a more egalitarian mentoring relationship than the servant-master one that certainly existed. In those days, says Lanyer, "your rare Perfections shew'd the Glasse / Wherein I saw each wrinckle of a fault" (ll. 7-8). The image of the older Bertie's wrinkled face overwhelms the sense of the passage and is underscored by the following line that figures the younger Lanyer as the "faire greene grasse, / That flourisht fresh by your cleere virtues taught" (ll. 9-10). And Bertie's face seems here to display faults that served as cautionary injunctions to Lanyer rather than being a reflection of Lanyer's own faults. Bertie is also effaced by reference to her "most famous Mother" (l. 23) and is pictured as one "that . . . hath followed her, / In these sweet paths of faire Humilitie" (ll. 31-32). Again, as in the poem to Anne Clifford, the mother's virtue is primary. The poem "To the Ladie *Katherine* Countesse of Suffolke" again substitutes a religious for the secular context and makes the claim of Lanyer's postscript "To the doubtfull Reader" that the poem was divinely commissioned "by celestiall powres" (l. 8). That claim authorizes Lanyer, "a stranger," to speak to a "great Lady," and even to pair herself with Suffolk: the divine commissioning is something to which "wee [both Lanyer and Suffolk] must needs give place." Lanyer's summary preview in that poem of the "Salve Deus" ends by comparing once again the possession of "wealth, . . . honour, fame, or Kingdoms store" with the virtues embodied in the divinity of Christ (ll. 89-96), implying again Lanyer's real authority compared to Suffolk's.

Lanyer's address "to the Ladie *Marie*, Countesse Dowager of *Pembrooke*" evokes the religious context in place of the courtly one by its setting in a heavenly pastoral landscape.[32] The poem is cast as a *visio* and Lanyer initially pictures Mary Sidney surrounded by a host of goddesses (Minerva, Bellona, Dictina, Flora).[33] But that classical context is displaced by the invocation of "great *Messias*, Lord of unitie" (l. 120) and the divine subject of Mary Sidney's psalm translations. Sidney, whom Lanyer repeatedly praises for her poems, is, ironically, trapped in the celestial landscape by virtue of her poetic fame; while she seems to have been set apart as the most famous—she is the one whom "*Minerva chose,* / To live with her in height of all respect"—she is "Fast ti'd" to the Graces "in a golden Chaine" (ll. 3-4, 7). It is an odd scene that at once praises Sidney "to the heights" and enchains her in the heavenly realm. Later in the scene, in spite of Minerva's seemingly preemptive praise for Sidney, the goddesses hold a singing contest which, nonetheless, Sidney wins before the battle has begun. Again, the praise serves to fix Sidney forever in the heavenly landscape, for the goddesses agree to sing her psalms "continually, / Writing her praises in th'eternall booke / Of endlesse honour, true fames memorie" (ll. 126-28). A favorable comparison of Mary Sidney's poetic abilities with her brother Philip's has the effect of making her seem to share prematurely in his death as well. Her "beauteous soule hath gain'd a double life, / Both here on earth, and in the heav'ns above" (ll. 153-54). Her "pure soule" is sealed "unto the Deitie" so that "both in Heav'n and Earth it may remaine" (ll. 164, 165). The poem ends with a reaffirmation of Sidney's placement in a heavenly context—"my cleare reason sees her by that streame, / Where her rare virtues daily are increast" (207-8)—and with Lanyer presenting the *Salve* to Sidney. Again Sidney's poetry is praised above Lanyer's: Sidney's "faire mind on worthier workes is plac'd, / On workes that are more deepe, and more profound" (ll. 215-16). But the subject of Lanyer's poem subverts that praise:

> Yet is it no disparagement to you,
> To see your Saviour in a Shepheards weed,
> Unworthily presented in your viewe,
> Whose worthinesse will grace each line you reade. [ll. 217-20]

Lanyer excuses her "unworthy hand," but immediately follows that humble statement with a mention of Christ's "faire humility" (ll. 221-22), allying herself with his paradoxically humble and glorified state. So Lanyer's poem to Sidney, while seeming to construct a hierarchy of poets in which Lanyer is far beneath Sidney, ironically places Sidney so high as to remove her from the worldly context of patronage relationships. Sidney is displaced by the greatness of her fame and by Lanyer's greater affinity to the subject of her poem, the abased and exalted Christ. The religious context both imprisons Sidney and authorizes Lanyer.

A contrast to these subversive patronage poems is the praise addressed "To all vertuous Ladies in generall"—by implication, all those who hold title to virtue rather than earthly honors. These women, with Lanyer at their head, are figured as priests, positioned both in a clerical hierarchy parallel to the secular, aristocratic one and, at the same time, tied closely to an otherworldly—and superior—order. The first couplet that addresses these women removes them from the world of the Petrarchan economy that objectifies women through the praise of their beauty. The poem is addressed to "Each blessed Lady that in Virtue spends / Your pretious time to beautifie your soules" (ll. 1-2). These women are figured instead as the brides of Christ, wearing the colors that Petrarchism had borrowed from the Song of Songs, but here transplanted to another realm by their apocalyptic association with Christ:

> Let all your roabes be purple scarlet white,
> Those perfit colours purest Virtue wore,
> Come deckt with Lillies that did so delight
> To be preferr'd in Beauty, farre before
> Wise *Salomon* in all his glory dight. [ll. 15-19]

They are told to imitate a host of classical goddesses and the Muses, but more significant here is Lanyer's admonition to "Annoynt your haire with *Aarons* pretious oyle" (l. 36) and to present Christ with "Sweet odours, mirrhe, gum, aloes, frankincense" (l. 41), for these actions co-opt the biblical power of the Aaronic priesthood and of the Magi of Matthew's gospel, those who recognized the divinity of the humble child in the manger. This empowerment of women by co-option of male religious roles reaches its apogee when Lanyer calls on these virtuous women "To be transfigur'd with [not *by*] our loving Lord" (l. 51), imagining them as participants with—or even equals to—Jesus at his transfiguration.[34]

None of the noblewomen Lanyer addresses receives such exalted praise, a fact that is underscored by the final stanza of the poem, in which Lanyer seems to apologize for not naming these women individually as she did the noblewomen:

> Yet some of you me thinkes I heare to call
> Me by my name, and bid me better looke,
> Lest unawares I in an error fall:
>   In generall tearmes, to place you with the rest,
>   Whom Fame commends to be the very best. [ll. 73-77]

Yet Lanyer's rhetoric allows here for the possibility that she dishonors virtuous commoners by placing them in the same category that Fame calls "best." And even this seeming confession of an error must be placed against the undermining of earthly fame in deference to the true honor of heaven in Lanyer's other patronage poems. Such a distinction is made in this poem as well, where the women are advised that they should "Of heav'nly riches make your greatest hoord," for "In Christ all honour, wealth, and beautie's wonne" (ll. 53-54). Even Lanyer's promise that she will "bid some of those, / That in true Honors seate have long bin placed" (ll. 85-86) is, typically, subverted by the statement that their presence is to insure that "my Muse may be the better graced" (l. 88).

The subversive self-fashioning Lanyer achieves through this rhetoric is repeated in the prose address "To the Vertuous Reader" which precedes the title poem. This much-quoted passage begins, "Often have I heard, that it is the property of some women, not only to emulate the virtues and perfections of the rest, but also by all their powers of ill speaking, to ecclipse the brightnes of their deserved fame: now contrary to this custome, which men I hope unjustly lay to their charge, I have written this small volume, or little booke, for the generall use of all virtuous Ladies and Gentlewomen of this kingdome . . ." (pp. 48, ll. 1-7) Lanyer seems initially to set up a parallel construction in which the actions of "some women" will be balanced against Lanyer's actions "contrary to this custome." But instead of the expected disclaimer—"contrary to this custom I will not eclipse the brightness of their fame"—Lanyer defers meaning through a generalization that does not follow in either sense or syntax from the first clause: "contrary to this custom, I have written a book for all virtuous women." The phrase that follows continues to defer meaning and begins to distinguish between the powerful patrons and the less powerful category that Lanyer inhabits: "I have written this small volume, or little booke, for the generall use of all virtuous Ladies and Gentlewomen of this kingdome; and in commendation of some particular persons of our owne sexe, such as for the most part, are so well knowne to my selfe, and others, that I dare undertake Fame dares not to call any better" (p. 48, ll. 5-10). These "particular persons of our owne sexe" are less important than "all virtuous Ladies and Gentlewomen of this kingdome," the (unnamed) famous subsumed under the general category "our owne sexe" while Lanyer's peers are styled doubly and are, paradoxically, linked to royalty ("kingdome"). Further, Lanyer in this construction becomes the one who controls and constructs the status of these women: it is Lanyer's (and others') knowledge of these women that prompts Fame to call them "famous."

The next sentence seems to provide the missing conclusion that promises meaning. Some may attempt to eclipse the fame of those they emulate, but Lanyer has written her book: "to make knowne to the world, that all women deserve not to be blamed though some forgetting they are women themselves, and in danger to be condemned by the words of their owne mouthes, fall into so great an errour, as to speake unadvisedly against the rest of their sexe" (p. 48, ll. 11-15). Here again the famous have been replaced by "all women," and it becomes clear that the purpose of the patronage poems that precede this address is not to increase the fame of the eponymous women of those poems, but to redeem the category woman and to advance Lanyer's authority. For here again it is Lanyer who functions as Fame, "mak[ing] knowne to the world" the goodness of women.

Like Lanyer's address to "virtuous ladies," the poem "To the Ladie *Lucie,* Countesse of Bedford," and the prose address "To the Ladie *Margaret* Countesse

Dowager of Cumberland," while not engaging in the subversive rhetoric that displaces the titled women of the other patronage poems, serve to coalesce Lanyer's position of primacy among the truly noble virtuous women and to underscore her role as poet-priest whose celebration has consecrated her book as host. The poem to Bedford is a little gem, perhaps the most polished and accomplished single piece of Lanyer's work, that figures Lanyer/Virtue unlocking the "closet" of Bedford's breast, the site of her true "selfe" that becomes an "arke" and a "bowre" where she entertains "the true-love of [her] soule, [her] hearts delight." At the same time, Bedford is invited into the openings in Christ's body made by his "most pretious wounds [where] your soule may reade / Salvation, while he (dying Lord) doth bleed" (ll. 13-14).[35] So, here again, Lanyer's book is the host (for) Christ, the "lovely guest" (l. 23), and a means of salvation.

Likewise, the prose dedication to Cumberland offers her "rich treasures, Arramaticall Gums, incense, and sweet odours" which are named only to be eclipsed by Lanyer's ability to "present unto you even our Lord Jesus himselfe" (p. 34, ll. 4-5, 7). Lanyer here claims equality with—or perhaps superiority to—the Ur-pope, Peter. "[A]s Saint *Peter* gave health to the body, so I deliver you the health of the soule" (p. 34, ll. 9-10)—that is, her incarnational book. Implied in that promise is her ability to deliver "The sweet incense, balsums, odours, and gummes that flowes from that beautifull tree of Life" (p. 34, ll. 14-15), the rood as well as the tree in Eden that Adam and Eve never touched even in their sin, but that Lanyer seems to be able to harvest with impunity.[36] On the contrary, in opposition to the Genesis tradition, Lanyer claims that the fruit of this tree "giveth grace to the meanest & most unworthy hand that will undertake to write thereof" (p. 35, ll. 16-18). However "unworthy" her own "hand writing," the presence of this Tree of Life in her work will assure its perfection: "[It] will with the Sunne retaine his owne brightnesse and most glorious lustre, though never so many blind eyes looke upon him" (p. 35, ll. 25-27). Thus Lanyer cajoles and flatters her patron into seeing the divinity within her work: "Therefore good Madame, to the most perfect eyes of your understanding, I deliver the inestimable treasure of all elected soules" (p. 35, ll. 27-29). Eyes of perfect understanding will see the true worth of Lanyer's work; only flawed vision will detect flaws, just as the truly virtuous who hold title in the heavenly realm can see divinity in the humbled Jesus. And Lanyer's repeated merging of herself with Virtue and priesthood and of her book with Christ and the eucharistic meal makes Lanyer the one who possesses all virtues and dispenses all honors, controlling here even the ultimate sacrifice of the Christian narrative.

Lanyer's patronage poems, then, use traditional forms but in innovative and subversive ways that allow a middle-class woman to speak authoritatively to royal and noble women. By placing her relationship with her potential patrons in a hierarchy defined by religious rather than courtly values, Lanyer has altered the terms of the patron-client relationship. As both Lanyer and her book are allied to the humbled Christ, her authority eclipses that of any potential patron, garnering for her perhaps the only reward that she could hope to receive for her book. Lanyer is also empowered to speak authoritatively about the central mysteries of Christianity for which she serves as priest-poet whose words "celebrate" not titled women but a kind of eucharistic banquet. Lanyer, her book, and Christ all are figured as "hosts" to her patrons, and the "Salve Deus" becomes not merely a meditation on the Passion, but somehow the "real presence" of Christ, a gift superseding anything her patrons might offer her. Lanyer's use of epideictic does not reinscribe class distinctions, as the invocation of a religious order well might, offering a heavenly reward in recompense for patient acceptance of earthly submission and suffering. Rather, Lanyer's repeated reference to the values of another world resembles a kind of liberation theology: the use of biblical prophecy to fire and fuel revolutionary political doctrine demanding the end of social and economic inequalities. Hers is a realized eschatology, a vision of the kingdom of heaven here and now, that calls for earthly hierarchies to be transformed by the values of the New Jerusalem. Her patronage poems, thus, not only stand in relationship to early modern epideictic, but also serve to place Lanyer in the lineage of religious visionaries such as John Bunyan, Margaret Fell, Anne Hutchinson, and John Milton.

Notes

This study has benefited from the thoughtful comments of Meg Lota Brown, Marshall Grossman, and John C. Ulreich.

1. Lorna Hutson, "Why the Lady's Eyes Are Nothing Like the Sun," in *Women, Texts and Histories, 1575-1760,* ed. Clare Brant and Diane Purkiss (London: Routledge, 1992), p. 16.

2. Kohler quoted in Betty Travitsky, *The Paradise of Women: Writings by Englishwomen of the Renaissance* (Westport, Conn.: Greenwood Press, 1981), p. 29. A.L. Rowse, *The Poems of Shakespeare's Dark Lady: Salve Deus Rex Judaeorum by Emilia Lanier* (New York: Clarkson N. Potter, 1978), pp. 20-24.

3. Travitsky, *The Paradise of Women,* p. 92. Barbara Kiefer Lewalski, "Of God and Good Women: The Poems of Aemilia Lanyer," in *Silent But for the Word,* ed. Margaret Patterson Hannay (Kent, Oh.: Kent State Univ. Press, 1985), p. 206.

4. Elaine V. Beilin, *Redeeming Eve: Women Writers of the English Renaissance* (Princeton, N.J.: Princeton Univ. Press, 1987), p. 183.

5. Lewalski, "Of God and Good Women," p. 212; *Writing Women in Jacobean England* (Cambridge, Mass.: Harvard Univ. Press, 1993), pp. 221, 220. Ideal community is also the theme of Lewalski's earlier article, "Re-writing Patriarchy and Patronage: Margaret Clifford, Anne Clifford, and Aemilia Lanyer," *Yearbook of English Studies* 21 (1991): 87-106, a theme reiterated in her contribution to this volume (see chapter 3).

6. Ann Baynes Coiro, "Writing in Service: Sexual Politics and Class Position in the Poetry of Aemilia Lanyer," *Criticism* 25 (1993): 358, 359.

7. Mary Ellen Lamb, "Patronage and Class in Aemilia Lanyer's *Salve Deus Rex Judaeorum*," in *Women, Writing, and the Reproduction of Culture in Tudor and Stuart Britain,* ed. Mary Burke, Jane Donaworth, Linda Dove, and Karen Nelson (Syracuse: Syracuse Univ. Press, 1998).

8. Hutson, "Why the Lady's Eyes Are Nothing Like the Sun," p. 21.

9. Coiro, "Writing in Service," 368.

10. For a discussion of the gendered politics of print versus manuscript, see Coiro, "Writing in Service," esp. pp. 358-60. Coiro argues that Mary Wroth's publication of her prose constituted "a breach of social and sexual decorum" (p. 360). On print culture, see Martin Butler, "Jonson's Folio and the Politics of Patronage," *Criticism* 25 (1993): 377-80, esp. p. 378, and Arthur F. Marotti, "Patronage, Poetry, and Print," in *Patronage, Politics, and Literary Traditions in England, 1558-1658,* ed. Cedric C. Brown (Detroit: Wayne State Univ. Press, 1991), pp. 21-46.

11. Robert C. Evans, *Ben Jonson and the Poetics of Patronage* (Lewisburg, N.J.: Bucknell Univ. Press; London and Toronto: Associated Univ. Press, 1988), p. 24.

12. Maureen Quilligan, "The Constant Subject: Instability and Female Authority in Wroth's *Urania* Poems," in *Soliciting Interpretation: Literary Theory and Seventeenth-Century English Poetry,* ed. Elizabeth D. Harvey and Katharine Eisaman Maus (Chicago: Univ. of Chicago Press, 1990), p. 325.

13. See, for example, Arthur F. Marotti's discussion of John Donne's use of Petrarchan conventions in his verse and prose correspondence with the countess of Bedford. "John Donne and the Rewards of Patronage," in *Patronage in the Renaissance,* ed. Guy Fitch Lytle and Stephen Orgel (Princeton: Princeton Univ. Press, 1981), pp. 207-34.

14. Indeed, Lanyer overtly rejects that form of address in her poem "To all Vertuous Ladies in generall," as will be discussed below.

15. Coiro, "Writing in Service," p. 368.

16. In fact, it is only the poem "To the Ladie *Anne,* Countesse of Dorcet," that dedicates the book to its addressee: Lanyer begins that poem, "To you I dedicate this worke of Grace" (l. 1).

17. Michael Schoenfeldt, "'The Mysteries of Manners, Armes, and Arts': 'Inviting a Friend to Supper' and 'To Penshurst,'" in *"The Muses Common-Weale": Poetry and Politics in the Seventeenth Century,* ed. Claude J. Summers and Ted-Larry Pebworth (Columbia: Univ. of Missouri Press, 1988), pp. 63, 64.

18. Similarly, in his discussion of Ben Jonson's "Inviting a Friend to Supper," Schoenfeldt argues that "[b]y entreating the guest to compensate for the host's lack of prestige, Jonson emphasizes the political component of the occasion even as he attempts to palliate it" (65). So Lanyer repeatedly asks Queen Anne to compensate for the deficiencies of her feast/book: "Reade it faire Queene, though it defective be, / Your Excellence can grace both It and Mee" (ll. 5-6).

19. The central purpose of the two prose pieces that precede the *Salve*—addressed to Margaret, Countess of Cumberland, and "To the Vertuous Reader"—is not so clearly to invite them to Lanyer's feast, as is the case with the poems. However, Margaret of Cumberland, while not overtly invited, is addressed in a compliment that invokes the wedding feast of the New Jerusalem by placing Christ in a begemmed, paradisal landscape: "I present unto you even our Lord Jesus himselfe. . . . I deliver you the health of the soule; which is this most

pretious pearle of all perfection, this rich diamond of devotion, this perfect gold growing in the veines of that excellent earth of the most blessed Paradice, wherein our second *Adam* had his restlesse habitation" (ll. 6-7, 9-14).

20. The merging of host/guest, eater/eaten calls to mind George Herbert's similarly ambiguous "Love (III)," which is not to suggest that he had read Lanyer's poem, but simply that the idea is embodied in the paradoxes of incarnation, crucifixion and resurrection, and Eucharist.

21. Jael, a character in the Song of Deborah, appears only in the dedication, while the Queen of Sheba appears only in the "Salve Deus," but there twice. The other four women are mentioned in both places.

22. By highlighting these stories, Lanyer presents a complex commentary on women's desirability. Being desired by men can bring women power over men, but can also result in abuse by men. But, either way, it is the men, not the women, who are condemned both by the biblical texts and by Lanyer's allusion to this group of texts. As in "Eves Apologie," where Adam is condemned for being seduced to sin by Eve's beauty, it is men who are wrong if they objectify and abuse women for their beauty. That beauty is, in itself, good, and can be an instrument of God's will, though it doesn't ultimately define a woman's virtue.

23. Also dismissive of the queen is Lanyer's implication in the "Salve Deus" itself that "Sith *Cynthia* is ascended to that rest / Of endlesse joy and true Eternitie" (ll. 1-2), her place can be filled only by Margaret, Countess of Cumberland (rather than, as is more logical, Queen Anne).

24. In "Why the Lady's Eyes Are Nothing Like the Sun," Hutson compares Lanyer's self-authorizing project to humanist assumptions about reading embodied in Shakespeare's Sonnets 82 and 20: "The relation between masculine author and masculine patron/reader emerges as inherently 'virtuous' (in the Renaissance sense of conducive to good action, rather than to theoretical speculation on the nature of good)" (p. 18).

25. Coiro, "Writing in Service," p. 367.

26. A similar contest for "Apollos beames" occurs in the poem to Mary Sidney. See note 34 below.

27. Lanyer later confesses that Christ's "worth is more than can be shew'd by Art," but in another slippery construction that merges her book with Christ ("To the Ladie *Anne*," l. 144).

28. John Ulreich, personal communication.

29. Many readers have pointed out the similarity between Lanyer's lines and the popular rhyme.

30. The stanzas that follow—lines 57-144 of this poem—are absent in the version of Lanyer's book (STC 15227) that omits three other poems as well. The second version (STC 15227.5) also resets a portion of the *Salve* that contained an error of indentation (on D4 verso) in the original version. The two versions of the *Salve* show many differences in orthography, but the introductory poems are constant in this respect, implying that they were not actually reset, but simply expanded.

31. The passage is from Isaiah 61.1: "The Spirit of the Lord God is upon me, therefore hathe the Lord anointed me: he hathe sent me to preache good tidings unto the poore, to binde up the broken hearted, to preache libertie to the captives, and to them that are bounde, the opening of the prison." The admonishment to "Cherish faire plants" while "supress[ing] unwholsome weeds" recalls the scene of judgment in Matthew 13 where the wheat is distinguished from the tares—also an action of the (Christian) Messiah. All quotations are from the Geneva Bible (which Lanyer often follows with literal accuracy).

32. I have argued at length elsewhere that Lanyer uses conventions of the initiatory pastoral poem to claim poetic vocation (and displace mentor poets, among whom she figures Mary Sidney) in "The Authors Dreame to the Ladie *Marie,* the Countesse Dowager of *Pembrooke*" (as well as in "The Description of Cooke-ham"). See my "Remembering Orpheus in the Poems of Aemilia Lanyer," *Studies in English Literature, 1500-1900* 38 (1998).

33. This poem may, again, disparage Queen Anne. Two of the goddesses in the scene, Aurora and Phoebe, who may represent Queen Anne and Elizabeth I, are engaged in a struggle for primacy. Aurora triumphs when she persuades the sun—James I?—to shine too brightly on Phoebe, "That his bright beames may all her Beauty marre, / Gracing us with the luster of his eie" (ll. 67-68). "Thus did *Aurora* dimme fair [*Phoebe's*] light, / And was receiv'd in bright *Cynthiaes* place" (ll. 73-74). (The text says *Phoebus,* but that cannot be correct.) The association of Elizabeth with the moon in all its mythical guises makes Queen Anne the only logical candidate as a rival here. If so, her fame seems to arise from questionable motives and a questionable (male) source.

34. The account of the transfiguration appears in Matthew 17, Mark 9, and Luke 9.

35. Christ is actually modeled here on St. Sebastian ("all stucke with pale deaths arrows"), that most homoerotic of saints, a figuring that dovetails with the feminized Christ of the "Salve Deus."

36. It was for fear that man would "put forthe his hand, and take also of the tre of life and eat and liue for euer" that Adam and Eve were banished from the garden (Gen. 3.22).

5

Vocation and Authority:
Born to Write

SUSANNE WOODS

And knowe, when first into this world I came,
This charge was giv'n me by th'Eternall powres,
Th'everlasting Trophie of thy fame,
To build and decke it with the sweetest flowres
That virtue yeelds.
    —Aemilia Lanyer, "Salve Deus" (ll. 1457-61)

Aemilia Lanyer's unapologetic assertion of poetic vocation in *Salve Deus Rex Judaeorum* is one of its many remarkable qualities. The voice of the public writer infuses and connects the dedicatory poems, the "Salve Deus" narrative, and "The Description of Cooke-ham."[1] Although either Lanyer or her publisher uses the book's title page to derive authority from husband and king, the work gains its magisterial tone through an intricate complex of patronage conventions—all addressed to women—and self-assertion.[2] In this essay I want to examine her use of some of those conventions, in particular as they allow her to affirm her own agency within the interconnected traditions of humility and grace, in order to illustrate how she contextualizes and embeds her more direct and radical claims of authority. In the process I hope also to account for some of the assurance she brings to her authoritative voice.

The multiple meanings of "author" in the early seventeenth century emphasized free agency, with the primary citation in the *OED* underscoring the confusion between the words "author" and "actor" in the early modern period (a result of their common derivation from the Latin "auctor," or "agent").[3] Renaissance theories of the female role followed Aristotle and others in assuming a natural feminine passivity, which restricted if it did not altogether deny female agency. As Thomas Elyot summarized in 1531, "the good nature of a woman is to be milde / timerouse / tractable / benigne / of sure remembrance / and shamfast."[4] More familiarly, Ben Jonson in his praise of the patron and writer Lucy, Countess of Bedford, made a particular point of her ability to act freely, associating it with an unusual, "manly" character:

> Onely a learned, and a manly soule
>   I purpos'd her; that should, with even powers,
> The rock, the spindle, and the sheeres controule
>   Of destinie, and spin her owne free houres.[5]

While women of the earlier seventeenth century were expected to defer authority (in both word and action) to men, many of them nonetheless struggled to act in the world through the authority of print even though, as Wendy Wall puts it, "female authorship was a tricky business."[6] Women's early claims to authority included authority derived from obedience (Saint Teresa obeying her confessor or a Protestant woman her conscience, as in Elizabeth Melville's *Godlie Dreame*); from a male-authored "original," which allowed women to act as translators (Anne Lok's translation of Calvin or the Countess of Pembroke's of Garnier's *Antonie*); or from Godly material (the countess's psalms or Lanyer's poem on Christ's Passion).

Lanyer insists repeatedly on the last of these, the authority she receives from her divine subject matter, which she combines with the traditional male authorial validations of patronage and Petrarchan inspiration. A key word throughout the book is *grace,* which she uses more than ninety times.[7] The reciprocity of grace was a familiar idea to Renaissance readers in all three contexts: religion, where the humble prayer of the creature invites the vivifying love of the Creator; society, where the lowborn writer's eternizing power is elevated by the grace of the highborn patron; and Petrarchan devotion, where the lady graces the personal service of the lover by an empowering attention. As she addresses her female patrons and claims her right to speak to them and for them, Lanyer uses these three traditions to support a vision of nature and art which seems particularly to invite the agency of the godly woman poet. Lanyer's handling of these familiar materials provides her with a strategy that overrides, with only limited direct argument, traditional views of female reticence and inactivity.[8]

The ease and assurance with which she handles that strategy may well derive from Lanyer's early relationship to the Elizabethan Court. As daughter and wife of Court musicians and mistress to the Lord Chamberlain, Aemilia Bassano grew up in and around Elizabeth's Court. She told Simon Forman that during her youth "She hath been favored moch of her mati [majestie] and of mani noblemen & hath had gret giftes & bin moch made of."[9] In the first dedicatory poem of the *Salve,* addressed to Queene Anne, Lanyer claims that "great *Elizaes* favour blest my youth" (l. 110). The poem that follows, to Anne's daughter, the Princess Elizabeth, devotes the first of its two stanzas to rhapsodizing on the queen whose name the princess bears, "the *Phoenix* of her age," "deare Mother of our Common-weale" (ll. 4, 7). Elizabeth is mentioned in the first line of the "Salve Deus" poem in her poeticized persona, "Cynthia," with the implication that Lanyer had addressed poems to her during her lifetime and now turns to the Countess of Cumberland in her stead:

> Sith *Cynthia* is ascended to that rest
> Of endlesse joy and true Eternitie,
>
> . . . .
>
> To thee great Countesse now I will applie
> My Pen, to write thy never dying fame. [ll. 1-2, 9-10]

Lanyer 's familiarity with female power comes from direct contact with it, with consequences for how she deals with traditional notions of weakness and humility.

In addition to her direct invocation of powerful women patrons, Lanyer uses the *humilitas* topos, one of the foundations of patronage poetry, to create a vision of exemplary female authority in a specifically Christian context.[10] The Pauline notion that human weakness enables and makes visible God's strength finds its corollary in patronage poetry where the poet's humility allows the greatness of the patron to inspire and make possible a worthy tribute by the poet. Both of these ideas often came clothed in the language of courtly love, which conventionally assumed that the beauty and virtue of the lady could empower the lowly and unworthy lover.

A striking confluence of all three of these conventions of humble access occurred in the poetry addressed to Queen Elizabeth I, God's agent on earth, the ultimate patron, and the mythic Virgin Queen, whose existence as both woman and queen complicates the picture considerably. Elizabeth encouraged poetry which served both to join and sometimes to muddy the various kinds of grace a poet might seek from a queen: God's grace, the enabling grace of an earthly patron, and the energizing grace of the lady's favor. In the courtly love tradition the lady is addressed as if she were the feudal lord to whom the petitioning vassal pledges fealty. Courtly love poetry addressed to the queen made those conventions literal. While poetry in the courtly love tradition idealized and objectified the lady in order to provide an occasion for male speech and to encode a fiction of female power, poetry addressed to the queen had to deal with the reality of God's regent.

Consider, for example, the difference between Samuel Daniel's cheerful acknowledgment of the useful but anonymous "cruel fair" and Sir Walter Ralegh's more complex and tortured address to his displeased lady, who is also his monarch. Daniel endures his suffering in the sure knowledge that the inspiration of the lady, even or especially through her cruelty, authorizes the poet: "O had she not beene faire, and thus unkinde, / My Muse had slept, and none had knowne my minde." Ralegh, on the other hand, uses the standard convention of female cruelty (his lady's beauties "be the Tirants that in fetters tye / Their wounded vassalls") for very different purposes. Explicitly, he seeks to come to terms with the paradox of a power which both vivifies and mortifies. Implicitly, he appeals to the lady's pity in hopes of activating the queen's grace. His suffering is more clearly linked to the real-world experience of a vassal in his prince's displeasure. The queen's tyrannical beauties

> nor kill nor cure,
> But glory in their lastinge missery
> That as her bewties would our woes should dure
> Thes be th'effects of pourfull emperye.[11]

Ralegh very probably wrote these lines in the tower, where he had been placed at the queen's displeasure over his marriage to Elizabeth Throckmorton. This incarceration—an unmistakable symbol of Elizabeth's complex interweaving of political and Petrarchan power—occurred in June, 1592, while Aemilia Bassano was presumably still at Court under the protection of Elizabeth's Lord Chamberlain, Henry Carey (she was married to Alfonso Lanyer in October, 1592).

Of course poetry in general played a notable role in the game of power in Elizabeth's Court, as professional poets vied for favors from the queen and other patrons, some of whom were prominent women.[12] Daniel's first principal patron, for example, was the Countess of Pembroke, followed by the Countess of Cumberland and Queen Anne. The "prince of poets," Edmund Spenser, sought and received Queen Elizabeth's patronage with Ralegh's help. While Spenser and other poets who lacked regular personal access to the queen do not approach Elizabeth intimately as lover to lady, they do make much of her personal beauty as well as her regal power. Most importantly, Spenser and other poets proffer their stance of humility in response to the queen as lady, as prince, and as divinity. Aemilia Bassano Lanyer grew up among these gestures, at Court herself from about 1588 until 1592 and a reader of Daniel and other contemporary poets.[13]

When Lanyer approaches her patrons she therefore speaks from within a well-established and familiar tradition of poetic humility graced by ladies, patrons, and queens. That she is herself a woman is, on the one hand, an additional reason for humility beyond her lower social standing, and so one more reason for the power of grace to reveal itself. On the other hand, as a woman she participates in the tradition of grace that she invokes.

The poem to Queen Anne illustrates the complexity of the author's stance. Lanyer's book may be "defective" (l. 5), but her "rude unpollisht lines / . . . Graced by [the queen] may seeme the more divine" (ll. 35-36). "More" is the important word here; Lanyer assumes that her divine subject matter is itself the first authority. The poet holds up a "Mirrour of a worthy minde" (l. 37), presumably the mind of the queen, who reads and sees her virtues reflected in the poem, but also and inevitably the mind of she who makes the mirror, "Which is dym steele, yet full of spotlesse truth" (l. 41). The poet is the giver of the gift. Similarly, while Lanyer acknowledges her low social status, she also suggests that her lowliness empowers her authority: "faire Virtue, though in meane attire, / All Princes of the world doe most desire" (ll. 65-66).

Identification between woman patron and woman poet, between she who graces and she who is graced and who together are graced by divine grace, is most pronounced when Lanyer describes the volume's main poem, "Salve Deus Rex Judaeorum," which she commends to the queen. "I have writ in honour of your sexe," she tells Anne about the daring "Eves Apology" section (l. 74), but of course it is also in honor of the author's sex as well. The figure of Eve, the author tells her queen, is designed to be a gracious hostess, to "entertaine you to the Feast" (l. 83) where the poet has, like a good cook, "prepar'd my Paschal Lambe" (l. 85): "This pretious Passeover feed upon, O Queene, / Let your faire Virtues in my Glasse be seene" (ll. 89-90)

In sum, there is an ongoing and subtle tension throughout the poem between the petition and the gift, between the poet distinct and humble and the poet identified with her lofty dedicatee. To some extent this is a feature of all patronage poetry. The proems to the several books of Spenser's *Faerie Queene* make it clear that his poem both seeks Queen Elizabeth's grace and graces her. Ben Jonson commonly projects onto James I those virtues he believes the king should have and which, by implication, the humble poet shares. What is different here is the shared identity of an implicitly inferior gender which has been condescendingly exalted by the Petrarchan tradition. The reciprocal grace between poet and patron is in place; so, too, is a new reciprocal grace of lady to lady, in which, as Lynette McGrath has noted, women become "the subjects of the exchange relation," signified in images of mirrors and feasts.[14]

Two further instances will illustrate how Lanyer converts traditional notions of grace into an empowerment of her own agency and the female point of view: her transformation of the contemporary debate between nature and art, and her use of Petrarchan conventions to present (and, at least indirectly, validate) a distinctly female approach to Christ.

The debate between nature and art was a commonplace of Renaissance literary discourse, with nature generally thought to precede art and art to surpass nature.[15] The role of nature, in particular, was the subject of a wide variety of complex arguments. Fallen from its golden age in both classical and Christian mythologies, it was always suspect, untamed, uninformed by law or grace. Natural sons were bastards; a "natural" was an idiot. Yet nature was God's creation, filled with examples of the Divine purpose, good in itself, ordered, mysterious, and fundamental. So Spenser describes Nature in the *Mutabilitie Cantos,* first published in 1609:

> This great Grandmother of all creatures bred
> Great *Nature,* ever young yet full of eld,
> Still mooving, yet unmoved from her sted;
> Unseene of any, yet of all beheld. [vii.xiii][16]

Whatever else she is, Nature is always female. Lanyer claims authority for her own art in part through asserting the traditional primacy of nature, and in part through a vision of nature and art reconciled through the beauty and wisdom of female patrons. The poem to Queen Anne again sets the scene.

Within the first several lines of the volume's first poem, Lanyer petitions for grace, presents her "divinest" subject matter and raises issues of nature and art:

> Renowned Empresse, and great Britaines Queene,
> Most gratious Mother of succeeding Kings;
> Vouchsafe to view that which is seldome seene,
> A Womans writing of divinest things:
>   Reade it faire Queene, though it defective be,
>   Your Excellence can grace both It and Mee.
>
> For you have rifled Nature of her store,
> And all the Goddesses have dispossest
> Of those rich gifts which they enjoy'd before,
> But now great Queene, in you they all doe rest. [ll. 1-10]

Anne as both living patron and Christian queen combines and surpasses the virtues of the three goddesses who strove for Paris's golden apple, and therefore controls both art and nature ("Sylvane Gods, and Satyres"):

> The Muses doe attend upon your Throne,
> With all the Artists at your becke and call;
> The Sylvane Gods, and Satyres every one,
> Before your faire triumphant Chariot fall. [ll. 19-22]

When Lanyer presents herself as author at the end of the poem, she builds from the image of a queen who rules art and nature. While not herself a queen, nor learned nor male, the woman poet is close to the power of Nature and may invite the indulgence of a gracious queen and gracious God ("Jove") as well as the vitalizing attention of Nature herself:

> And pardon me (faire Queene) though I presume,
> To doe that which so many better can;

Not that I Learning to my selfe assume,
Or that I would compare with any man:
    But as they are Scholers, and by Art do write,
    So Nature yeelds my Soule a sad delight.

And since all Arts at first from Nature came,
That goodly Creature, Mother of Perfection,
Whom *Joves* almighty hand at first did frame,
Taking both her and hers in his protection:
    Why should not She now grace my barren Muse,
    And in a Woman all defects excuse. [ll. 145-56]

Within the conventions of patronage the last may be first, and in any case nature precedes art. Traditional hierarchies are turned upside down by traditional arguments. If the woman author is surprisingly assertive, she has nonetheless positioned her stance within a set of well-understood social and literary conventions.

It may not be seriously transgressive to claim that the grace of God and of queens and highborn ladies can enable a lowly and unusual female voice, but the bounds of traditional agency are certainly threatened by a woman who claims an authorial identity. Yet Lanyer does present herself as called to authorship, and to make this more plausible she must bridge the general empowering grace of patronage with a more dedicated picture of a patron who also represents the authority of women who write. This she does in the centering dedicatory piece (the sixth of eleven) to the Countess of Pembroke.

"The Authors Dreame" is a provocative title. The respectable device of the dream, designed to forgive the trespass of fiction, is a mask for "The Author" placing herself in the grandest of authorizing company. Despite the title, the poem begins, interestingly, not with dream but with a contemplative inner vision in which "thought" and "reason" vie with fantasy and fictionalizing:

Me thought I pass'd through th'*Edalyan* Groves,
And askt the Graces, if they could direct
Me to a Lady whom *Minerva* chose,
To live with her in height of all respect.

Yet looking backe into my thoughts againe,
The eie of Reason did behold her there
Fast ti'd unto them in a golden Chaine,
They stood, but she was set in Honors chaire. [ll. 1-8]

Only after this moment of conscious desire and rational vision does the dream take over and appear to lead the dreamer beyond her waking knowledge:

Yet studying, if I were awake, or no,
God *Morphy* came and tooke me by the hand,

And wil'd me not from Slumbers bowre to go,
Till I the summe of all did understand. [ll. 17-20]

The "summe of all" includes a vision of art and nature equitably united under the power of the Countess of Pembroke and her Court of graces, muses, and powerful goddesses. This is a pivotal moment in the poem and in the volume as a whole. Having begun in the poem to Queen Anne with a woman's right to claim the power of nature, Lanyer now uses the model of the perfect woman poet, the Countess of Pembroke, and the goddesses and graces who attend her, to reconcile art and nature in a cooperative gesture reminiscent of Sir Philip Sidney's Arcadian debate between Reason and Passion.[17] The countess and her royal attendants arrive at "A place that yet *Minerva* did not know" (l. 80), where the struggle between art and nature is itself a source of beauty and grace:

That sacred Spring where Art and Nature striv'd
Which should remaine as Sov'raigne of the place;
Whose antient quarrell being new reviv'd,
Added fresh Beauty, gave farre greater Grace. [ll. 81-84]

Although Lanyer's vision began with the "eie of Reason," the ladies who are the "umpiers" of the "delightfull case" between Art and Nature make their judgments based on sensual pleasure, on a knowledge derived from the experience of beauty. Their

    ravisht sences made them quickly know,
T'would be offensive either to displace.

And therefore will'd they should for ever dwell,
In perfit unity by this matchlesse Spring:
Since 'twas impossible either should excell,
Or her faire fellow in subjection bring.

But here in equall sov'raigntie to live,
Equall in state, equall in dignitie,
That unto others they might comfort give,
Rejoycing all with their sweet unitie. [ll. 87-96]

This *locus amoenus* is most certainly a new place, a new *topos,* where all the participants are female and where beauty, delight, and harmony are both the natural and artistic consequences. From this place proceed the countess's psalms, which join art, nature, and the divine harmony, and which also join the attendant ladies with the countess herself:

Those holy Sonnets they did all agree,
With this most lovely Lady here to sing;

That by her noble breasts sweet harmony,
Their musicke might in eares of Angels ring.

While saints like Swans about this silver brook
Should *Hallalu-iah* sing continually,
Writing her praises in th'eternall booke
Of endlesse honour, true fames memorie. [ll. 121-28]

By centering the countess's songs among the muses, graces, goddesses, angels, and saints, and yet affirming them as poetry in a great and recognizable tradition (art and nature conjoined, filled with sensuousness), Lanyer also centers the figure of the divinely ordained woman poet. It comes as no great leap for Lanyer to offer her own work to this paragon of authorizing predecessors:

For to this Lady now I will repaire,
Presenting her the fruits of idle houres;
Thogh many Books she writes that are more rare,
Yet there is hony in the meanest flowres; [ll. 193-96]

Unlike dream allegories that disguise fictions, Lanyer's dream helps her "thought," "Reason," and "waking sprites" to envision an inspiring source and dedicatee for her own work. She is very much awake as she offers her own poetry, both the dedicatory poem and the "feast" of the "Salve Deus" poem, which the countess may read in that new place where women poets dwell, beside the stream where art and nature are united and "saints like Swans" share in the harmony:

And therefore, first here I present my Dreame,
And next, invite her Honour to my feast,
For my cleare reason sees her by that streame,
Where her rare virtues daily are increast. [ll. 205-8]

The poem concludes with the standard language of patronage, suggesting that the grace of the countess's view will make worthy the poem presented. At the same time, Lanyer insists on the worthiness of her subject matter and her own effort as a poet whose "flowres . . . [spring] from virtues ground":

And Madame, if you will vouchsafe that grace,
To grace those flowres that springs from virtues ground;
Though your faire mind on worthier workes is plac'd,
On workes that are more deepe, and more profound;

Yet it is no disparagement to you,
To see your Saviour in a Shepheards weed,
Unworthily presented in your viewe,
Whose worthinesse will grace each line you reade. [ll. 213-20]

The reciprocity of grace takes a familiar turn in this new place: the poem graces the patron, as the patron graces the poem. This is assertive language, but confidently addressed to the most visible model for a Jacobean woman poet.

Authority in the Renaissance can come, ultimately, only from God, and while Lanyer makes much of her patron, Margaret, Countess of Cumberland, the *Salve Deus* presents an image of Christ that underlies the poet's other authorizing strategies. Christ is lowly. He is a friend to the women who surround the Passion story as Lanyer presents it. He is the bridegroom of the Church, explicitly represented by the Countess of Cumberland. The Passion of Christ becomes both the essence and the emblem of glorious humility and the empowering force of grace.

Christ is also very beautiful in Lanyer's vision, as she holds him up to the desiring gaze of women. Unlike epideictic poets such as Jonson and Donne, Lanyer's focus throughout her volume is less on blazoning the beauty and virtues of her dedicatees or vaunting her own eternizing power than it is on pointing toward the portrait of Christ in her narrative, and by situating Christ within the tradition of Petrarchan as well as Christian grace she provides another vehicle for insinuating her own authority. The sacrificial Christ is consistently the "Paschal Lambe," a "feast," and the "Bridegroome."[18] In both the dedications and the main poem Christ is an object of desire to be admired and consumed by appreciative ladies, with his empowering grace a function of both eucharistic and Petrarchan imagery, as in these lines from "To the Ladie *Katherine*":

> No Dove, no Swan, nor Iv'rie could compare
> With this faire corps, when 'twas by death imbrac'd;
> No rose, nor no vermillion halfe so faire
> As was that pretious blood that interlac'd His body . . .
> . . . .
> In whom is all that Ladies can desire;
> If Beauty, who hath bin more faire than he? [ll. 79-83, 85-86]

Red and white and other traditional emblems of courtly beauty pervade Lanyer's description of Christ in his passion. The descriptive language reflects the biblical Canticles, also known as the Song of Songs or Song of Solomon, to which Lanyer explicitly points in a side note near line 1300, but the Petrarchan elements are at least as resonant. Further, as Queen Elizabeth's role as both lady and monarch made literal the feudal conventions of Petrarchism, so Lanyer's portrait of Christ as the beautiful bridegroom and the Countess of Cumberland as the redeemed Christian soul/bride makes visible and explicit a long tradition of Christian interpretation of the Canticles.[19] The language of the two traditions is often very close, here emphasizing the confluence of empowering grace.

An interesting set of parallels with a famous Spenserian text will help to situate Lanyer's Christ in the English Petrarchan tradition.[20] In *Faerie Queene* II.3 Spenser presents a portrait of Belphoebe, the character he describes in his letter to Ralegh as a figure for the queen in her role as "a most vertuous and beautifull Lady." E.C. Wilson calls this depiction "the richest idealization of the royal Laura." Harry Berger observes that it is in "sonneteer's language, the kind of hyperbolic imagery identified with 'Petrarchan,'" which, Kathleen Williams adds, "is interwoven with memories of the sensuous cadences of the Song of Songs."[21] The language Lanyer uses to describe Christ recalls this Spenserian description and, with it, the conflation of Petrarchan, royal, and divine grace that Elizabeth embodied. To describe a queen in terms that invite the male gaze presumes the queen's grace and the poet's right of authorship. Similarly, to describe Christ in terms that invite the female gaze presumes God's grace and the poet's right of authorship. Without that presumption the first case would be treason, the second, blasphemy.

Petrarchan blazon favors red and white, sweet smells, and lively eyes. With these Spenser combines divine powers:

> And in her cheekes the vermeil red did shew
> Like roses in a bed of lillies shed,
> The which ambrosiall odours from them threw,
> And gazers sense with double pleasure fed,
> Hable to heale the sicke, and to revive the ded.
>
> In her faire eyes two living lamps did flame,
> Kindled above at th'Hevenly Makers light.[22]

Lanyer's description makes use of many of the same constituents:

> unto Snowe we may his face compare,
> His cheekes like skarlet, and his eyes so bright
> As purest Doves that in the rivers are,
> Washed with milke, to give the more delight. [ll. 1307-10]
>
> His lips like skarlet threeds, yet much more sweet
> Than is the sweetest hony dropping dew,
> Or hony combes, where all the Bees doe meet;
> Yea, he is constant, and his words are true,
> His cheekes are beds of spices, flowers sweet;
> His lips, like Lillies, dropping downe pure mirrhe,
> Whose love, before all worlds we doe preferre. [ll. 1314-20]

On the beauty of their hair:

> Her Yellow lockes, crisped like golden wyre,
> About her shoulders weren loosely shed. [*FQ,* II.3.30]

His head is likened to the finest gold,
His curled lockes so beauteous to behold. [*SD*, ll. 1311-12]

Gender reversals characterize both portraits. Belphoebe is an armed and powerful hunter; Christ a helpless victim. Perhaps in part as a way to control or mitigate the reversals, both characters are given bodies that invite sexual gaze. Even as Spenser presents her Amazonian power, Belphoebe's sexual effect is paramount:

Below her ham her weed did somewhat trayne,
And her straight legs most bravely were embayld
In gilden buskins. . . .

  a golden bauldricke . . . forelay
Athwart her snowy breast, and did divide
Her daintie paps; which like young fruit in May,
Now little gan to swell, and being tide,
Through her thin weed their places only signifide. [*FQ* II.3.27, 29]

Even in his total humiliation, Christ's beauty dominates the portrait:

His joynts dis-joynted, and his legges hang downe,
His alablaster breast, his bloody side,
His members torne, and on his head a Crowne
Of sharpest Thorns . . . [*SD* ll. 1161-64]

Lanyer offers this beauty, and the contradiction of power from humility ("Griefe and Joy"), directly to the gaze of the Countess of Cumberland:

here both Griefe and Joye thou maist unfold
To view Thy Love in this most heavy plight,
Bowing his head, his bloodlesse body cold;
Those eies waxe dimme that gave us all our light,
    His count'nance pale, yet still continues sweet,
    His blessed blood watring his pierced feet. [*SD* ll. 1171-76]

Finally, both poets insist on their inability to describe such perfect beauty, even as they have spent much ink and many lines doing precisely that. "How shall frayle pen," says Spenser, "descrive her heavenly face, / For fear, through want of skill, her beauty to disgrace" (II.3.25). Lanyer beseeches her countess to

  give me leave (good Lady) now to leave
This taske of Beauty which I tooke in hand,
I cannot wade so deepe, I may deceave
My selfe, before I can attaine the land. [ll. 1321-24]

Both poets dare to describe the dangerous. Both use a writer's epithet for their project: Spenser's "frayle pen" produces here the longest single portrait in *The Faerie Queene*. Lanyer does take "in hand" the task of beauty. Both poets express anxiety in the process ("want of skill," "I may deceave / My selfe").

For both poets, beauty itself is a function of the anxiety. Spenser has "fear" that he may "disgrace" her beauty, and presumably himself as poet and courtier in the process. For Lanyer, herself a woman raised with admonitions against the dangers of beauty, it is a more complex issue.[23] She ignores completely the traditional notion of beauty as a dangerous snare to men, but spends several stanzas on its danger to a woman's virtue. Helen of Troy, Lucrece, Cleopatra, Rosamund, Matilda are all cautionary tales (ll. 209-40). "That outward Beautie which the world commends, / Is not the subject I will write upon" (ll. 185-86), the poet tells her patron and her readers. And she particularly scorns "those matchlesse colours Red and White," which she nonetheless uses with vivid specificity to describe the body of Christ later in the poem. By the end of the poem she has turned those dangerous colors completely around, as they transfer from Christ to the Countess of Cumberland. The countess is described as

> Deckt in those colours which our Saviour chose;
> The purest colours both of White and Red,
> Their freshest beauties would I faine disclose,
> By which our Saviour most was honoured. [ll. 1827-30]

The marginal note describes these as the "Colours of Confessors & Martirs."

Beyond the complexities and anxieties, Lanyer, like Spenser, presumes the game may be played, and that she has a right to try it. Both poets are authors, graced by their divine subjects. While Spenser dedicates the gift of *The Faerie Queene* to the lady he feigns to describe in the person of Belphoebe, Lanyer turns gender around in the languages of Petrarch and the Canticles and, like all Petrarchan poets, she offers the grace of her verse to the lady she serves: the Countess of Cumberland. What is one source of grace for Spenser becomes two for Lanyer, since the beauty she describes, and the primary authority she claims, belong to Christ rather than the countess. This bifurcation of subject and audience is unusual though not unknown in the Petrarchan tradition, but here the gender of the writer gives it some interesting overtones. The poet creates a "beauty" which she then gives to her mistress, but the beauty is of a man on whom both poet and mistress may gaze longingly. And if the Countess of Cumberland is explicitly figured as the bride of this beautiful sacrifical Christ, what is the poet's role in the transaction? Lanyer underscores it without apology: she gives the bridegroom away. She is the author of the pious and sensuous

image, as in traditional weddings the father is the author of the daughter that
he presents to the bridegroom:

> this rich Jewell, which from God was sent,
> To call all those that would in time repent.
>
> Which I present (deare Lady) to your view. [ll. 1263-65]

And again: "Therefore (good Madame) in your heart I leave / His perfect pic-
ture, where it still shall stand" (ll. 1325-26).

In summary, Lanyer derives from several familiar resources the authority
to present Christ's "perfect picture," to offer the Countess of Cumberland (and
all her readers) a feminized Christian view of a world in which the last shall be
first, where Christ's beauty overgoes anything the Petrarchan lover could con-
trive about his mistress, and where the author confidently invites her highborn
patrons to feed on her image of that Christ who himself feeds them with His
grace. She insists that her subject matter demands and justifies her writing:

> [Christ's] high deserts invites my lowly Muse
> To write of Him, and pardon crave of thee,
> For Time so spent, I need make no excuse. [ll. 265-68]

The grace of her patrons makes it possible: "Whose excellence hath rais'd my
sprites to write, / Of what my thoughts could hardly apprehend" (ll. 1833-34).
And even her gender empowers the process: "But yet the Weaker thou doest
seeme to be / In Sexe, or Sence, the more [Christ's] Glory shines" (ll. 289-90).

By embedding her work with models and instruments of grace, Lanyer
needs very little explicit argument to bolster her authority or her right to speak
publicly. When the reader encounters the epithet at the beginning of this pa-
per, which is the first unambiguous claim of personal poetic vocation from a
woman writing in English, and comes well into the volume's main poem, it
provokes no surprise that the speaker presents herself as born to write.

In case we missed it, Lanyer underscores her vocation in the book's final
envoy ("To the doubtfull Reader"): "*Salve Deus Rex Judaeorum* . . . was deliv-
ered unto me in sleepe many yeares before I had any intent to write in this
maner . . . and thinking it a significant token, that I was appointed to performe
this Worke, I gave the very same words I received in sleepe as the fittest Title I
could devise for this Booke." That she is able to speak with such assurance is a
compound of her background, the literary and social conventions of her time,
and her careful choice of subject matter. It is just as certainly a function of
Lanyer's own skill, the product of a strong mind and a vigorous craft. In the
language of her own time, she is the author of the volume, and, through it, she
acts in the world.

NOTES

1. For statements that draw attention to Lanyer as author and giver of the gift of her poetry, see, e.g., "To the Queenes most Excellent Majestie," ll. 3-4, 149-56; "To all vertuous Ladies in generall," ll. 71-72, 89-90; "To the Ladie *Susan*," ll. 43-46; "The Authors Dreame," title, and ll. 193-96, 201-4; "To the Ladie *Margaret*," ll. 27-32; "To the Ladie *Katharine*," ll. 13-22; "To the Ladie *Anne*," ll. 1-2, 57, 85-88; "To the Vertuous Reader," ll. 5-15; "Salve Deus," ll. 9-16, 265-80, 321-28, 1265, 1457-61, 1831-34; "Cooke-ham," ll. 205-06; "To the doubtfull Reader," all.

2. The title page (see frontispiece to this volume) affirms the work to have been "Written by Mistris *Aemilia Lanyer*, Wife to Captaine *Alfonso Lanyer* Servant to the Kings Majestie."

3. *OED* I.571; *Compact OED* 143. The *OED* also defines an obsolete verb sense of the term, with examples all taken from Lanyer's lifetime:: "1. To be the author of an action; to originate, cause, occasion" and "2. To be the author of a statement; to state, declare, say." While one useful tendency of recent Renaissance scholarship has been to stress the extent to which political and economic forces determine cultural products, in this essay my emphasis is on Lanyer's self-conscious claim of authorship/agency in the face of those traditional forces.

4. Thomas Elyot, *Boke Named the Governour* (1531), I.xxi. See also, e.g., Sir Thomas Smith, *Common-welth of England* (1589): the role of the wife is "to save that which is gotten, to tarie at home, to distribute that which commeth of the husbandes labor, for the nutriture of the children, and family of them both, and to keepe all at home neate and cleane" (Sig. C2).

5. Jonson, "On Lucy Countesse of Bedford," in *The Complete Poetry of Ben Jonson*, ed. William B. Hunter, Jr. (New York: Norton, 1968), Epigramme LXXVI, p. 32.

6. Wendy Wall, *The Imprint of Gender: Authorship and Publication in the English Renaissance* (Ithaca and London: Cornell Univ. Press, 1993), p. 338. Wall's book discusses how gender enters into authorial anxiety and the stigma of print, for both men and women, in the Renaissance. For her discussion of Lanyer, see pp. 319-30.

7. On a quick count. By contrast, versions of "disgrace" appear only about fifteen times, and all of these are in the "Salve Deus" poem proper, most related to the Passion itself, where its resonances are sharply literal.

8. The "Eves Apologie" section of the "Salve Deus" poem (ll. 758-832) and the final dedication, "To the Vertuous Reader" are her most extended and direct contributions to the "Woman Controversy" that Linda Woodbridge outlines in *Women and the English Renaissance: Literature and the Nature of Womankind, 1540-1620* (Urbana: Univ. Illinois Press, 1984).

Janel Mueller makes an excellent case for yet another of Lanyer's authorizing strategies, her "feminizing" of Christ, in "The Feminist Poetics of Lanyer's *Salve Deus Rex Judaeorum*," chapter 6, this volume.

9. Forman, Diary BOD MS Ashmole 226 f. 201, cited in Woods, p. xviii.

10. For another discussion of Lanyer's approach to patronage and authority, see Susanne Woods, "Aemilia Lanyer and Ben Jonson: Patronage, Authority and Gender," *Ben Jonson Journal* 1 (1994): 15-30.

11. Daniel cited from *English Sixteenth-Century Verse: An Anthology*, ed. Richard S. Sylvester (New York: Norton, 1984), sonnet 3, p. 578.; Ralegh from "The 11th . . . booke of the Ocean to Scinthia," ll. 196-200, in *The Poems of Sir Walter Ralegh*, ed. Agnes Latham (Cambridge, Mass: Harvard Univ. Press, 1962), p. 32.

12. E.C. Wilson, *England's Eliza* (Cambridge, Mass: Harvard Univ. Press, 1939), esp. ch. 6, "Laura or Idea" (e.g., "If sonneteers were often dazzled by the magnificence of the

sovereign, they were constantly charmed by the beauty and accomplishments of the lady," p. 240). Steven May argues that there were relatively few courtier poets, but that poetry was an activity with consequences in the game of power (*The Elizabethan Courtier Poet* [Columbia: Univ. Missouri Press, 1991], esp. ch. 4, "Utilitarian Poetics, Gorges, Ralegh and Essex"). See also Gary F. Waller, *English Poetry of the Sixteenth Century* (New York: Longman, 1986), p. 79. For the activities and influence of an important woman patron, see Barbara K. Lewalski, "Exercising Power: The Countess of Bedford as Courtier, Patron, and Coterie Poet," in *Writing Women in Jacobean England* (Cambridge, Mass.: Harvard Univ. Press, 1993), pp. 95-123.

13. Susanne Woods, *Lanyer: A Renaissance Woman Poet in Her Context* (New York: Oxford UP, 1998), ch. 1.

14. Lynette McGrath, "Metaphoric Subversions: Feasts and Mirrors in Aemilia Lanier's *Salve Deus Rex Judaeorum,*" *LIT* 3 (1991): 101-13. "The image of the feast and the image of the mirror work well together in association with women, connected by the socially determined position of women as passive consumers/spectators. Lanier's manipulation of these metaphors, however, rescues them from their culturally condoned passive role and encourages them to active agency" (p. 103).

15. Edward W. Tayler, *Nature and Art in Renaissance Literature* (New York: Columbia Univ. Press, 1964), remains the best summary; see also Kitty Scoular, *Natural Magic: Studies in the Presentation of Nature in English Poetry from Spenser to Marvell* (Oxford: Clarendon Press, 1965).

16. Cited from *Spenser's Faerie Queene,* ed. J.C. Smith (Oxford: Clarendon Press, 1909), vol. 2, p. 471.

17. At the beginning of the second group of Eclogues, Reason and Passion debate for dominance, which they in turn give over to the reconciling grace of God: "*R. P.* Then let us both to heavenly rules give place, / Which *Passions* kill, and *Reason* do deface" (ll. 41-42, in William Ringler, ed., *The Poems of Sir Philip Sidney* [Oxford: Clarendon Press, 1962], p. 47). In Lanyer's vision, the reconciliation between the antagonists is more explicit, and more directly presented as a function of the grace of the ladies.

18. E.g., "To the Queenes Most Excellent Majestie," ll. 83, 85; "To the Lady *Elizabeths* Grace," l. 9; "To all vertuous Ladies in generall," l. 9 and *passim;* "To the Ladie *Susan,*" l. 42; "The Authors Dreame," l. 206; "To the Ladie *Katherine,*" l. 51; "Salve Deus," ll. 1305-20, 1777-78, and *passim.*

19. See Barbara K. Lewalski, *Protestant Poetics and the Seventeenth-Century Religious Lyric* (Princeton: Princeton Univ. Press, 1979), pp. 59-69. Lanyer's use of the Song of Songs is further discussed by Kari McBride, this volume, chapter 4.

20. I am not claiming that Lanyer imitated (much less copied) Spenser, though it is quite probable that she read this highly visible poet. I simply use him as an excellent model for Petrarchan imagery dedicated to a figure above the poet's literal reach.

21. Wilson, *England's Eliza,* p. 242. Harry Berger, *The Allegorical Temper* (New Haven: Yale Univ. Press, 1957), p. 137. Kathleen Williams, *Spenser's World of Glass* (Berkeley: Univ. California Press, 1966), pp. 48-49.

22. Spenser, *Faerie Queene,* II.3.22-23, ed. J.C. Smith (Oxford: Clarendon Press, 1909), vol. 1, pp. 199-200. All *FQ* citations are from this edition.

23. The message is clear from the works she alludes to in the "Salve Deus," such as Daniel's *Rosamond* and Drayton's *Matilda.* See Woods, *Lanyer,* ch. 1, and ch. 2, part ii, "'This taske of Beauty.'"

6

The Feminist Poetics of
"Salve Deus Rex Judaeorum"

JANEL MUELLER

Vouchsafe to view that which is seldome seene,
A Womans writing of divinest things
Lanyer, "To the Queenes most Excellent Majestie"

The year 1611 saw the publication, in London, of the first volume of poetry in English written by a woman: *Salve Deus Rex Judaeorum.* Its title page identified the poet as "Mistris *Aemilia Lanyer*, Wife to Captaine *Alfonso Lanyer* Servant to the Kings Majestie." In the expatiating fashion of the time, the title page also highlighted the following portions of the volume's title poem, "1 The Passion of Christ. 2 Eves Apologie in defence of Women. 3 The Teares of the Daughters of Jerusalem. 4 The Salutation and Sorrow of the Virgine Marie," while lumping together its shorter poems as "divers other things not unfit to be read."[1] Who was Aemilia Lanyer, and what was she doing in her *Salve Deus Rex Judaeorum,* thus characterized? Questions like these have proven useful as starting points for interpretation all along the discontinuous time line that charts the history of women's authorship in the West. In historical criticism sensitive to the category of gender it is now regularly accepted that the exercise of authorship, by women no less than by men, requires some empowering sense of authorization, of authority, to write and publish.[2] As applied to Lanyer and her volume, such questions engage the interplay of her social identity with the poetic identity of her work, on the assumption that the two are mutually self-constituting in ways that can be traced, at least to some degree, to recoverable features of text and context.[3]

Who was Aemilia Lanyer? Thanks to the biographical research of Susanne Woods, made conveniently available in the introduction to her recent edition of Lanyer's collected poems, and to David Bevington's wittily incisive review of the evidence in his essay in this volume (chapter 1), the outlines of her life are secure. I will focus on what Lanyer says of herself in her verse epistles. She continued to take pride in the Court connections she contracted as a girl in the milieu of Queen Elizabeth's musicians, and she poetically recast these connections to figure an illustrious society comprised solely of females.[4] The first dedicatory epistle to the *Salve* volume reflects wistfully on that vanished time when "great *Elizaes* favour blest my youth," (l. 110) while another salutes Susan Bertie, Countess of Kent, as "the Mistris of my youth, / The noble guide of my ungovern'd dayes." (ll. 1-2). Lanyer thus signals her adolescent formation under the then widespread practice of being sent from one's family to be trained up in service in an aristocratic household.[5] But she also credits the countess's capacity for moral governance to her mother's influence: "By your most famous Mother so directed, / That noble Dutchesse, who liv'd unsubjected" (ll. 23-24). Susan's mother was Catherine Willoughby Bertie, Duchess of Suffolk, an outspoken Protestant who went into voluntary exile under Mary Tudor, taking her children with her. The duchess had married her former steward, Richard Bertie, in an earlier notable act of self-assertion (and one often invoked as a source-idea for John Webster's tragic heroine in *The Duchess of Malfi*, staged ca. 1614, published in 1624).[6]

On the further testimony of Lanyer's "Description of Cooke-ham," she resided at this royal estate sometime before 1609 in cherished intimacy with Margaret Clifford, Countess of Cumberland, and her daughter, Anne, soon to become Countess of Dorset by marriage. Aemilia's address to

> (sweet *Cooke-ham*) where I first obtain'd
> Grace from that Grace where perfit Grace remain'd;
> And where the Muses gave their full consent,
> I should have powre the virtuous to content. [ll. 1-4]

bespeaks her experience of being called, during her stay there, to a poetic vocation. These enigmatic lines may also intimate that she underwent a conversion; if so, they help to date the onset of the intense religious feeling to which the long title poem of *Salve Deus Rex Judaeorum* bears witness.[7] Aemilia reports nothing else of her doings in the years before her volume of poems appeared. However, inferential links have been drawn between its other contents and the Lanyers' financial situation at the time of publication. Judging from various arrangements of its dedicatory verse epistles to highborn ladies and from presentational inscriptions in its nine extant copies, both she and her husband, Alfonso, used the *Salve* as a means of soliciting patronage.[8]

So much for a basic answer to the question, Who was Aemilia Lanyer? But a no less basic answer is called for when this question is denied the historicizing privilege on which I will be relying in most of my discussion here. The present-day context for asking Who was Aemilia Lanyer? is the happy phenomenon of numbers of women writing poetry that is rich, outrageous, and originary because it is increasingly unfettered and self-assured. Given a contemporary twist by a late twentieth-century, presumably postmodernist, reader the question might run as follows: Who was Aemilia Lanyer, that I should care about poetry written from an outlook almost four hundred years old? Although I am an unabashed enthusiast of her work, I have to concede the datedness of key aspects of Lanyer's outlook.

She holds essentialist ideas of "feminine" and "masculine" as innate features of the female and male sexes. She also makes universalist assumptions about God's purposes both in creating persons whose common humanity is marked by sexual difference and in holding them accountable by a single moral standard for their actions in what simply is for her the course of history. Our current feminist tactics no less than our theories disparage notions that "human nature" has significant traits outside of culture; we emphasize the significance of gender rather than sex as the reciprocal social production and acquisition of a given sexed subject. Relativistic and deterministic implications afford us little basis for moral judgments, but we make these anyway on other terms: our ideological commitments, our best attempts at reasoning, our emotional responses. Emphasizing the cultural embeddedness of humans, we formulate our political, critical, and poetic projects accordingly.

So too, I would urge, does Lanyer, even though her notion of culture is Christian world history and her understanding of embeddedness finds two sexes locked in a domination-subordination relationship that structures the organization of society. Lanyer proves every bit our contemporary in her resolve to locate and articulate transformative possibilities in gender relations that will bear their own urgent imperatives for enactment. For this purpose, which is to say, oddly from a contemporary point of view, she looks to the figure of Christ in history, to divinity humanized or humanity divinized, as she reads the record of Scripture with wholly unconventional eyes. The mystery that explodes into a demonstrated truth in her poem, "Salve Deus Rex Judaeorum," is Lanyer's understanding of Christ's incarnation viewed in light of the Crucifixion as a public, historical action taken by men alone; this vindicates, once and for all, female nature and feminine values and it authorizes gender equality ever after. In her handling, universalism and essentialism directly empower a feminism that proves rich, outrageous, and originary by any present-day standard. Beyond the inherent interest of Lanyer's poem, which I hope to demonstrate, an object lesson emerges for contemporary readers: our best wisdom, our most sophisticated and influential theories, are no *sine qua non* for a feminist poetics. Hers is a striking case in point.

At this point I again take up my historicist approach, to address another continuing need of present-day scholarship, an eventual set of useful generalizations about the conditions that empowered female authorship in preindustrial and pre-Enlightenment Europe. I want to shift from individual biography to a cross-cultural and transhistorical perspective in order to note certain sugges- tive structural similarities between Lanyer's situation and that of Christine de Pizan, the first professional woman of letters in France, despite a divide of two centuries. These structural similarities include expatriate family origins, youthful formation in the inner circle of a major court in close contact with persons of the highest rank, marriage unconstrained by the full force of conventional fe- male subordination and dependency relations, and an extended period of find- ing a living for themselves and their children. They also bear on the second question, about the specially highlighted portions of the title poem of Lanyer's volume, which I began by asking.

In 1369, at the age of four, Christine was brought from Venice with the rest of her immediate family to the court of France by her father, King Charles V's astrologer. Happily married at the age of fifteen to Etienne du Chastel, a court notary ten years her senior, at twenty-five she witnessed within a few short months her father's death and her husband's death, which left her to provide for her three young children and her own mother as well. Converting her grief for her husband into lyric artistry, Christine declined to remarry. In- stead she undertook to make a name for herself, first as a versatile and accom- plished poet, later as an author of prose works, who won herself powerful pa- trons and a position in her own right at Court.[9]

Circumstantial differences aside, a first key homology in Pizan's and Lanyer's accession to female authorship is the double unconventionality of their up- bringings. On the one hand, both were educated to a standard of courtly culti- vation well above their own rank; on the other, both were less than ordinarily bound by social ties and traditional processes of acculturation due to their families' recent relocation out of an ancestral milieu. Again, discounting differ- ences in their marital histories, it seems clear that the exercise of adult female sexuality empowered both Pizan and Lanyer with a conjoint freedom and re- sponsibility to assert their own agency as literary creators and self-providers. Most significantly of all, however, for my purposes, the twofold anomaly of Pizan's and Lanyer's social situations, as insiders to Court circles but outsiders in rank and ethnic descent, positioned them to experience personally but to judge critically the constraints then in effect on female roles as defined in their respective adoptive cultures. The next step—prudential in both cases, but surely not only that—was authorship, and authorship in an otherwise unprecedented feminist vein. By calling both "feminist" I mean that they explicitly confront misogyny and the injustices of male domination and prerogative in their writ- ings, working to counter these with alternative, women-centered constructions.[10] Entering the category of authorship at what, for each, was the present stage of the so-called *querelle de femmes* or controversy about women, Pizan and Lanyer respectively engage as revisionists with vogues in literary practice made current by male writers.

A quantity of recent discussion has documented the extent to which the clashes and aftershocks of the centuries-long, Europe-wide controversy about women served as crucial stimuli for female authorship across several generations and national boundaries. Virtually every explanation of how a premodern woman came to be an author insists on the importance of this controversy.[11] It picks up in 1399 with Pizan's own instigation of the so-called quarrel of the *Romance of the Rose* by attacking this central love allegory of French medieval literature for its general immorality and its particular slanders of women.[12] In Pizan's own reclamation project the central targets were secular works of high repute—Jean de Meun's continuation of the *Roman de la Rose,* Boccaccio's *De mulieribus claris* (*On Illustrious Women*)—which kept in circulation the debased coinage of patristic misogyny long since issued by Tertullian and St. Jerome. In English poetry these antifeminist materials are familiar as the readings that infuriate the Wife of Bath against her scholar-husband, as she vividly relates in her prologue in Chaucer's *Canterbury Tales* (1386-1400).

Preeminently among Pizan's works, her prose *Livre de la cité des dames* or *Book of the City of Ladies* (1405) undertakes to vindicate women's claims to respect and fame by rewriting the tales of their achievements—in the domains of public and cultural life, family relations, and religious sainthood—that have been at best equivocally set down by male authors in secular and ecclesiastical sources. Analogously, Lanyer's *Salve Deus Rex Judaeorum,* an assemblage of shorter poems and two prose pieces around an extended narrative poem on the last events in the life of Christ which gives the volume its title, undertakes to merge the secular genre of verse panegyric addressed to highborn personages— in this case, all females—with the sacred genre of devotional meditation on biblical subjects in verse. Lanyer's increasingly manifest purpose in this generic merger is to articulate the connections she sees as holding in the biblical record between the incarnational theology of Christianity and disclosive truth in speech and action, public as well as private. In her view, these historically concrete connections invest femininity not only with superiority to masculinity but also with mandates for personal and social autonomy that place women in the vanguard of humankind's best accesses to godlikeness. While limitations of space make it unfeasible for me to discuss Lanyer's epistles to noble ladies, these have already drawn some extended critical attention, as I noted above. But not until this present collection has "Salve Deus Rex Judaeorum" received more than brief treatment.[13] Focusing, myself, on this title-poem, I will be arguing the boldness and cogency of Lanyer's feminist theology, language theory, and social theory as well as the expressiveness of the poetic system of equivalences and exchanges by which she forges connections between the feminine and the divine.

To position what may seem, *prima facie,* a somewhat improbable argument for Lanyer as the early seventeenth-century English creator of a fully cognizant feminist poetics, I want to return to considerations of context, this time with a view to further individuating her and her work as subjects of interpretation. While spirited protest against the wholesale denigration of women's bodies and moral character produces the most immediately arresting passages in both Pizan and Lanyer, the differences in the literary forms and the specific inflections that they give their feminism prove at least as significant as the measure of similarity in their situations and writings. These differences arise as functions of the discrete historical and local circumstances of the controversy about women that actuated them, respectively, to write. Lanyer declares as much of her *Salve Deus* in "To the Vertuous Reader":

> I have written this small volume . . . to make knowne to the world, that all women deserve not to be blamed though some forgetting they are women themselves, . . . fall into so great an errour, as to speake unadvisedly against the rest of their sexe . . . which . . . [I] could wish . . . they would referre such points of folly, to be practised by evill disposed men, who . . . doe like Vipers deface the wombes wherein they were bred. . . . It pleased our Lord and Saviour Jesus Christ, . . . to be begotten of a woman, borne of a woman, nourished of a woman, obedient to a woman; and that he healed wom[e]n, pardoned women, comforted women: yea, even when he was in his greatest agonie and bloodie sweat, going to be crucified, and also in the last houre of his death, tooke care to dispose of a woman: after his resurrection, appeared first to a woman, sent a woman to declare his most glorious resurrection to the rest of his Disciples. . . . All which is sufficient to inforce all good Christians and honourable minded men to speak reverently of our sexe, and especially of all virtuous and good women. To the modest sensures of both which, I refer these my imperfect indeavours. [pp. 48-50, ll. 5-58; my textual correction in brackets]

In marked contrast to Pizan, Lanyer locates her own project of defending her female sex squarely in the domain of religious poetry and, beyond that, in a specifically scriptural subject: here, the last events of Christ's life. There are several recoverable reasons for such a choice in a London vernacular publication of 1611. First, in the interval between flare-ups in 1588-97 and 1615-37, the English controversy about women saw a relatively quiescent phase with regard, at least, to the circulation of antifeminist themes in satirical tracts or polemical diatribes.[14] Lanyer had no immediately pressing motive to engage head-on in prose controversy from a feminist position. "To the Vertuous Reader" shows her much more exercised about the bad effects of *both* sexes' speaking ill of women, which undermines not merely women's reputations for virtue but their very capacity and incentive to be virtuous.

While lauding the exemplary virtues of Margaret Clifford, Countess of

Cumberland, in a framing section near the opening of "Salve Deus," Lanyer addresses what she represents as a highly pressing contemporary problem: how female moral agency is represented in recent English secular poetry and drama. She decries portrayals of Lucrece, Cleopatra, Rosamund, and Matilda, alluding perhaps to Shakespeare's *Rape of Lucrece* (1593) and *Antony and Cleopatra* (1606-7) or to Samuel Daniel's *Cleopatra* (1593) and *Complaint of Rosamond* (1592), as well as to Michael Drayton's *Matilda* (1594). The framing section that concludes "Salve Deus" with another celebration of the Countess of Cumberland's active virtue returns once again to the figure of Cleopatra, detailing the fickleness, adultery, cowardice, and treachery of this "blacke Egyptian" as an egregious instance of a woman's loss of moral direction (ll. 1409-32). Lanyer's preoccupation with Cleopatra reads as testimony to a conspicuous development in London stage plays that drama historians regularly note.[15] This is the quite sudden emergence, from a virtual void, of women with the full stature of evil-doing tragic protagonists, such as like Alice Arden in *Arden of Faversham* (1592), Anne Frankford in Thomas Heywood's *A Woman Killed with Kindness* (1603), and Shakespeare's Lady Macbeth (1606). As Lanyer well saw, the moment was ripe for intervening in the discursive construction of women by male authors as (im)moral subjects and entering a counterclaim for them as gender-specific exemplars of virtue.[16]

At just this historical juncture, moreover, calls were sounding for a redirection of poetic energies from secular love to sacred subjects. Probably the best known of these are George Herbert's two sonnets, "My God, where is that ancient heat towards thee" and "Sure Lord, there is enough in thee," sent to his mother as a New Year's gift in 1610.[17] Scriptural subjects, specifically, received fresh validation in the year that Lanyer published the *Salve*. The team of scholars who had been working since 1606 under royal mandate to verify the accuracy of the text of the entire English Bible against its sources in the original languages published their Authorized (or King James) Version in 1611, with an epistle dedicatory offering it "to your MAIESTIE, not onely as to our King and Soveraigne, but as to the principall moover and Author of the Worke: . . . it being brought unto such a conclusion, as that we have great hope that the Church of England shall reape good fruit thereby."[18] Court culture, humanist scholarship, and vernacular biblicism all converge in this milestone event. To lodge a timely challenge to invidious constructions of her sex, onstage and off, by male poets and by her society more broadly, Lanyer considered it necessary not just to contradict standing portrayals or to celebrate actual living women but to develop a new poetic ontology for figuring femininity as worthy, true, and good. This ontology would ground itself in a portrayal of a maligned, about-to-be-murdered Jesus of Nazareth that quite closely follows scriptural sources. It would proceed, however, on Lanyer's own authority in figuring women and women alone as capable of recognizing and receiving the incarnate divine Word aright.

Recent work devoted to Lanyer's poetic development and practice has focused mainly on the two patronesses with whom she represents herself as being most intimate—Margaret Clifford, Countess of Cumberland, and her only child, Anne Clifford, Countess of Dorset—and especially on Lanyer's affectively charged, utopian depiction of her relations with the Cliffords as the source of her personal no less than her poetic *raison d'être* in "A Description of *Cookeham*," written about a year before *Salve Deus Rex Judaeorum* appeared.[19] Nowhere, moreover, does Lanyer say anything explicit about how she positioned herself and her work with respect to contemporary male poets. Yet this question is too significant to leave dangling from lack of direct testimony, for the very reasons that have promoted the advent of gender studies in the second wave of twentieth-century academic feminism. No less than the relational gender categories of femininity and masculinity, women's writing has historically been undertaken and maintained in dynamic relation to men's writing. Differences only register as such, as making a difference, by means of interpretive methods that operate comparatively across both bodies of textual practices.[20]

Regarding Lanyer's literary relations with male poets, there has been the lone opinion voiced by her only modern editor before Susanne Woods's recent edition. A.L. Rowse—better known as a social rather than a literary historian—placed Lanyer "in versification . . . close to Samuel Daniel, and this is natural, for he belonged to the circle of which she became a member. Margaret, Countess of Cumberland was a patroness, with her daughter, Lady Anne Clifford. . . . Daniel was tutor to the daughter."[21] Rowse does not elaborate on the reasons for his judgment. He may have been referring to Daniel's reworking of his four-book historical poem in rime royal, the *Civil Wars between the two Houses of York and Lancaster* (1595); an eight-book version in ottava rima appeared under the same title in 1609. Lanyer's "Salve Deus" is likewise in ottava rima.

But in other respects Lanyer's compositional practices run quite clearly counter to Daniel's. For example, in his *Defence of Rime* (1602) he prided himself on his successful strict avoidance of so-called feminine line endings—final unstressed syllables—especially when rhymed as a pair with a masculine line ending but even, as he insists, in a rhymed pair of their own. Daniel thought feminine endings appropriate only to song lyrics, not to serious narrative poetry:

> To me this change of number in a Poem of one nature sits not so wel, as to mixe uncertainly, feminine Rymes with masculine, which, ever since I was warned of that deformitie by my kinde friend and countriman Maister Hugh Samford, I have alwayes so avoyded it, as there are not above two couplettes in that kinde in all my Poem of the Civill warres: and I would willingly if I coulde, have altered it

in all the rest, holding feminine Rymes to be fittest for Ditties, and either to be
set certaine [i.e., recast as masculine rhymes], or else by themselves."[22]

Lanyer's verses abound in feminine endings across a variety of stanzaic forms in
the *Salve* volume. In larger matters of composition Lanyer also sets herself
against Daniel, not only in what I take above as her aspersions on his tragedy
Cleopatra and his *Complaint of Rosamond* with their sustained studies of the
psychologies of adulterous women, but in the still more fundamental determi-
nant of genre. Lanyer's major poem is religious; all of Daniel's major poems are
on secular subjects.[23]

Although I make no pretense of offering a last word or even a full treat-
ment of this scarcely opened question, my own sense of a suggestively close
antitype in contemporary male-authored poetry for the title poem of Lanyer's
volume is Giles Fletcher's *Christs Victorie and Triumph in Heaven, and Earth,
over and after Death* (1610). His four-part poem in 265 ottava rima stanzas
(with the variant of concluding alexandrines) is framed at its head by prose
epistles to the dedicatee, the scholar-cleric Thomas Neville, and "To the Reader";
these articulate Fletcher's resolve to redeem the poet's role in the common-
wealth by writing verse on a high biblical subject in the line of named illustri-
ous antecedents, climaxing in King James himself. To these are added verses
commending the poet and the poem by Giles's brother and fellow poet, Phineas
Fletcher, and by Sir Francis Nethersole. The last eight stanzas of *Christs Victorie
and Triumph* complete the framing device by entrusting the whole work to the
approbation of King James, hailed for bringing to Britain an earthly peace and
beatitude that are an extension of heaven's, and then by folding this poem's
final religious allegory into that of a poem by Phineas on "faire Egliset," the
Church of England. By comparison, "Salve Deus Rex Judaeorum," in sixty
ottava rima stanzas subdivided by marginal rubrics, has a frame comprised of
opening and concluding celebrations of the surpassing virtues of the closest
noble associates of Lanyer's present adult life: the Cliffords, mother and daughter.
Nearly simultaneous publication, closely similar verse form, framing pieces
that set this scripturally based poetry within a context of relations to influen-
tial patrons (including royalty), and commitment to an affective, strongly rhe-
torical rehearsal of the climactic events in Christ's life comprise the fundamen-
tal resemblances between Fletcher's and Lanyer's poems.

Nevertheless, suggestive differences once again mark Lanyer's feminist
poetics. *Christs Victorie and Triumph* has prominent allegorical dimensions that
are altogether absent from "Salve Deus Rex Judaeorum." In allegory and only
in allegory does Fletcher make place for female personages in sacred story: the
sisters Justice and Mercy of the first part, who dispute in a heavenly council
what dealings fallen, perverse man shall receive at God's hand; the sensual and

seductive Panglorie or Pangloretta, who tempts Jesus in the second part. When
Fletcher first begins to versify biblical material in the third part of his poem, all
of the persons are male. Tracing the events from the evening before the Cruci-
fixion to the entombment of Jesus's body, Fletcher heightens devotional affect
with prolonged evocations of the contrasting psychologies of the betrayer Ju-
das and the loyal, grief-stricken Joseph of Arimathea, but otherwise works his
gospel narrative into a formal rhetorical structure of enumerated topoi (parts,
means, effects) signaled by marginal rubrics.

Lanyer's "Salve Deus" differs strongly from Fletcher's poem in most of
these respects. She discards virtually all allegory: telescoping the debate be-
tween Mercy and Justice, for example, into a single stanza while more nearly
approximating his penchant for embellishment in her set piece on night as the
time when the devil looses evils on the world (ll. 561-68). Most importantly,
her own narrative hews steadily and, for the most part, literally to the compos-
ite account in the gospels, beginning with Christ's agony in Gethsemane and
ending with his expiration on the cross. (The exception to her biblical literal-
ism is "Eves Apologie," which elaborates the message that Pilate's wife is re-
corded as sending to her husband in Matthew 27:19.) Thus, Scripture is in
much firmer ascendancy in Lanyer's poem than in Fletcher's on the same events.

Not only is there this difference within similarity, but Lanyer too is drawn
to study contrasting psychologies for devotional affect. Unlike Fletcher's, how-
ever, her emphasis on spiritual and emotional valence entails that female fig-
ures will come to the fore and assume prominence as actual historical person-
ages from the gospels, not personified abstractions from allegory. At the center
of Lanyer's "Salve Deus" is a highly wrought narration of Jesus's suffering and
abasement, with inset episodes that repeatedly foreground women: Pilate's wife,
the women of Jerusalem, Jesus' mother Mary. That these episodes are crucial to
the design of Lanyer's poem shows in the numbered rubrics of her title page. In
each case, women find means of registering their resistance to the deadly course
of action that the male figures are enforcing as criminal justice. But what the men
treat as criminal justice, the women perceive as the gravest possible injustice to
one who has confounded masculine power and authority by acting and speak-
ing in ways that the women instantly comprehend and appreciate, for the ways
are recognizable as their own. Lanyer's steadily maintained social milieu en-
dows her characters and imagery with the concrete specificity of a seventeenth-
century Dutch genre painting.

A marginal *incipit* opposite stanza 42 of "Salve Deus" signals the onset of
the poem's central narration: "Here begins the Passion of Christ" (p. 65). Lanyer
employs the *in medias res* opening that had become standard in Renaissance
poetic narratives on lofty subjects, secular or sacred. With this she conjoins a
skillful use of temporal and spatial setting for emotive heightening, a conven-

tion shared with such Ovidian poetic narratives as Shakespeare's *Lucrece,* Daniel's *Rosamond,* and Drayton's *Matilda.* It is deep night on the Mount of Olives, in the garden of Gethsemane. Jesus is alone with his fears and forebodings. Behind him is his Last Supper; ahead lies his betrayal by Judas and his forcible seizure by the soldiers of the high priest Caiaphas. The garden's atmospheric darkness is liminal—a space no longer of private familiarity and intimacy, like the meal he has just shared with his twelve disciples, but not quite yet a public space of arrest, interrogation, and judicial sentencing—"That very Night our Saviour was betrayed, / Oh night! exceeding all the nights of sorow" (ll. 329-30).

In this liminal span and place, Lanyer's narration follows the gospel story closely while also furthering her systematic portrayal of a Christ who is not understood for what or who he is by way of any private or public relationships with other men. Peter, James, and John, his favorite disciples, whom he entreats to keep him company while he prays, fall into a sleep which Lanyer feelingly equates with spiritual blindness. They

> . . . could not watch one houre for love of thee,
> Even those three Friends, which on thy Grace depends,
> Yet shut those Eies that should their Maker see;
> What colour, what excuse, or what amends? [ll. 418-21]

Immediately thereafter, Judas leads Christ's enemies to him and betrays him in a far graver perversion of intimacy:

> A trothlesse traytor, and a mortall foe,
> With fained kindnesse seekes thee to imbrace;
> And gives a kisse, whereby he may deceive thee,
> That in the hands of Sinners he might leave thee. [ll. 485-88]

But, as brought out through Lanyer's continuous emotional coloration of her narrative, the public action of arresting Christ also proceeds in total incomprehension and misprision of its subject:

> Now muster forth with Swords, with Staves, with Bils,
> High Priests and Scribes, and Elders of the Land,
> Seeking by force to have their wicked Wils,
> . . . .
> And who they seeke, thou gently doest demand;
>   This didst thou Lord, t'amaze these Fooles the more,
>   T'inquire of that, thou knew'st so well before.
> . . . .
> His name they sought, and found, yet could not know
> *Jesus* of Nazareth. [ll. 489-99]

Incomprehension darkens into wilful misconstrual and perjury as Christ
is brought before Caiaphas to be formally examined. Lanyer's narration tracks
the gradation from abuses of language to abuses of justice that repeatedly leaves
her Christ with the option, only, of keeping silent. "They tell his Words, though
farre from his intent, / And what his Speeches were, not what he meant" (ll.
655-56). In responding to repeated encounters with men who both coerce and
misjudge him—a pattern intensified in his dealings with Caiaphas, Pilate, and
Herod as the legal process runs its course—Lanyer's Christ exhibits perfect
quiescence in both demeanor and language.

> The people wonder how he can forbeare,
> And these great wrongs so patiently can take;
> But yet he answers not. [ll. 667-69]

> Three times thou ask'st, What evill hath he done?
> And saist, thou find'st in him no cause of death,
> Yet wilt thou chasten Gods beloved Sonne,
> Although to thee no word of ill he saith. [ll. 865-68]

> Yet neither thy sterne browe, nor his great place,
> Can draw an answer from the Holy One:
> His false accusers, nor his great disgrace,
> Nor *Herods* scoffes; to him they are all one:
> He neither cares, nor feares his owne ill case. [ll. 881-85]

On those rare occasions when Lanyer's Christ has anything at all to say, the
speech that befits his behavior is correspondingly sparing, yet always transpar-
ent—and true in the strongest sense of truth, self-identity. Every sentence that
Lanyer's scripturally-styled Christ utters under interrogation packs a character-
istic semantic and spiritual force, registering profound self-disclosure in tau-
tology or near-tautology: "I am he," "Thou hast said it."

> For when he spake to this accursed crew,
> And mildely made them know that it was he:
> Presents himselfe, that they might take a view;
> And what they doubted they might cleerely see;
> Nay more, to re-assure that it was true,
> He said: I say unto you, I am hee. [ll. 513-18]

> Beeing charged deeply by his powrefull name,
>   To tell if Christ the Sonne of God he be,
>   Who for our sinnes must die, to set us free.

> To thee O *Caiphas* doth he answere give,
> That thou hast said, what thou desir'st to know. [ll. 702-6]

Where, moreover, Lanyer's Christ proves incomprehensible to the men about him, to her as commentator he remains so continuously readable that she is able to specify the virtues that ground his speech and behavior at each point: "Here faire Obedience shined in his breast, / And did suppresse all feare of future paine" (ll. 529-30); "His paths are Peace, with none he holdes Debate, / His Patience stands upon so sure a ground" (ll. 603-4). One rhetorical and poetic high point takes the form of a bold stanzaic enjambment in which Lanyer asserts herself authorially by interrupting the lying enemies of Christ in Caiaphas's hall. These men call Christ a blasphemer but she can name him truly. And so she does, inserting her catalogue of ascriptions into a sentence that had begun as a description of the men's perjury:

High Priests and Elders, People great and small,
With all reprochfull words about him throng:
   False Witnesses are now call'd in apace,
   Whose trotheless tongues must make pale death imbrace

The beauty of the World, Heavens chiefest Glory;
The mirrour of Martyrs, Crowne of holy Saints;
Love of th'Almighty, blessed Angels story;
Water of Life, which none that drinks it, faints;
Guide of the Just, where all our Light we borrow;
Mercy of Mercies; Hearer of Complaints;
   Triumpher over Death; Ransomer of Sinne;
   Falsely accused: now his paines begin. [ll. 637-48]

As the foregoing quotation clearly indicates, there is nothing explicitly feminist about this poetically striking juncture in Lanyer's narration of the Passion of Christ. Yet here and elsewhere for considerable stretches Lanyer skillfully predisposes her story, description, and commentary to feminist implications. These implications do become remarkably explicit, moreover, when Pilate's wife breaks in upon her husband to remonstrate with him in "Eves Apologie," the second of the subdivisions highlighted on the poem's title-page. I want to work towards a discussion of "Eves Apologie" by tracing the diverse, local feminist predispositions that lead into and away from its unique outspokenness in other parts of Lanyer's "Salve Deus."

Perhaps the most obvious of these predispositions—certainly the first to become conspicuous in the poem—is the pattern of fundamental misprision exhibited by all of the males in the story, friends and foes alike, while the female poet unfailingly understands what and who Jesus is. Although the conventional epic guise of an omniscient narrator serves as Lanyer's vehicle for expressing this understanding, deeper ideological implications remain untouched by this identification of poetic means. As now amply documented in

a range of studies focused on the social construction of femininity in sixteenth-
and earlier seventeenth-century England,[24] it appears scarcely less obvious that
Lanyer understands her Christ because he is thoroughly feminized in demeanor
and language according to the period norms set out in conduct books and
doctrinal tracts, especially those of the late Elizabethan and Jacobean Puritan
divines—John Dod and Robert Cleaver, William Perkins, William Whateley—
who were actively publishing as Lanyer wrote. Her Christ, like the ideal woman
of the Puritan manuals, is silent except when induced to speak, and modest
and taciturn when he does; he is gentle, mild, peaceable, and submissive to
higher male authorities.[25]

    Not only does Lanyer herself appear to understand the traits of her Christ's
character from familiarity with them as the virtues that women were to acquire
and manifest as definitive of their femininity. She also conducts two psycho-
logical studies—of the women of Jerusalem, of Christ's mother Mary—in which
she writes the same process of understanding into her narration of the ostensi-
bly historical events of "Salve Deus." These women empathize with Christ
through their shared affinities in demeanor, language, and feeling. Because his
social identity resonates with their own, they, like Lanyer, can comprehend
him inwardly, from within themselves. And again, on the evidence of the num-
bered subsections of her title page, Lanyer highlighted these instances of recip-
rocal recognition as "The Teares of the Daughters of Jerusalem" and "The Salu-
tation and Sorrow of the Virgine Marie" (p. 1). They are highlighted accord-
ingly in the body of the poem, where schematic gender opposition first links
the women with Christ in action and utterance and then sets them as a group
over against the other males. In a transitional stanza between these two high-
lighted sections, Lanyer's pointed phrases exemplify what I am terming the
feminist predisposition of her commentary:

> When spightfull men with torments did oppresse
> Th'afflicted body of this innocent Dove,
> Poore women seeing how much they did transgresse,
> By teares, by sighes, by cries intreat, [n]ay prove,
> What may be done among the thickest presse,
> They labour still these tyrants hearts to move;
>   In pitie and compassion to forbeare
>   Their whipping, spurning, tearing of his haire.
>   [ll. 993-1000; my correction in brackets]

Thus as Christ sets out toward Calvary, bearing his cross on his scourged and
bleeding shoulders, the executioners and their hangers-on "thinke he answer'd
for some great transgression, / Beeing in such odious sort condemn'd to die"
while the women bystanders see that "his own profession / Was virtue, pa-

tience, grace, love, piety." They weep aloud for Christ as he passes; he in turn pauses and speaks to them consolingly. Lanyer's exactly and multiply repeated nouns—grace, love—affirm the spiritual and ethical oneness of the suffering women with the suffering Christ: "Thrice happy women that obtaind such grace / From him whose worth the world could not containe"; "Your cries inforced mercie, grace, and love / From him, whom greatest Princes could not moove" (ll. 955-76). Although the women of Jerusalem are powerless to affect the outcome of the procession to Calvary in any way, Lanyer nevertheless grants them a clear moral victory by poetic means, as the sound and significance of the men's cries are supplanted by those of the women's cries by stanza's end:

> First went the Crier with open mouth proclayming
> The heavy sentence of Iniquitie,
> The Hangman next, by his base office clayming
> His right in Hell, where sinners never die,
> Carrying the nayles, the people still blaspheming
> Their maker, using all impiety;
> The Thieves attending him on either side,
> The Serjeants watching, while the women cri'd. [ll. 961-68]

Lanyer's section on the salutation and sorrow of the Virgin Mary works a comparable but far more complex and subtle transmutation of tones and themes. The narrative point of departure is a scriptural given, a grief near despair.

> How canst thou choose (faire Virgin) then but mourne,
> When this sweet of-spring of thy body dies,
> When thy faire eies beholds his bodie torne,
> . . . .
> Bleeding and fainting in such wondrous sort,
> As scarce his feeble limbes can him support. [ll. 1129-36]

Lanyer's local poetic objective is to convert this extremity of evil to an assurance of blessedness that the suffering mother will register as immediately and experientially as she does her present grief. To begin this process Lanyer reminds Mary of the greeting pronounced by the angel of the Annunciation and elaborates its significance:

> He thus beganne, Haile *Mary* full of grace,
> Thou freely art beloved of the Lord,
> He is with thee, behold thy happy case; [ll. 1041-43]

> That thou a blessed Virgin shoulst remaine,
> Yea that the holy Ghost should come on thee
> A maiden Mother, subject to no paine,

For highest powre should overshadow thee:
Could thy faire eyes from teares of joy refraine,
When God look'd downe upon thy poore degree?
    Making thee Servant, Mother, Wife, and Nurse
    To Heavens bright King, that freed us from the curse. [ll. 1081-88]

Key to this passage and to Lanyer's broader authority as a religious poet in
"Salve Deus" is the salutation as a locution. A rarely employed poetic resource
in her contemporary English, but a salient feature of spoken dialogue in half a
dozen important gospel episodes,[26] the salutation begins with a special, rever-
ential word of greeting, then adds the name and the significant attributes of
the person being addressed. Its structure here is "Haile *Mary* full of grace, . . .
Servant, Mother, Wife, and Nurse / To Heavens bright King, that freed us
from the curse" (ll. 1041; 1087-88). In Lanyer's poetic, not only does knowing
aright bespeak naming aright, but naming and knowing cast in the form of a
salutation bespeak a direct, intimate encounter with another that authorizes
the salutation itself. What Lanyer does with Mary in this final highlighted
subsection of the poem is to insist on Mary's uniqueness in taking on just those
womanly roles of "Servant, Mother, Wife, and Nurse" that enabled Christ to
incarnate his, correspondingly, as "Her Sonne, her Husband, Father, Saviour,
King, / Whose death killd Death, and tooke away his sting" (ll. 1023-24). If
Mary can sustain her sense of the blessedness of her agency in relation to Christ
as specified in the roles foretold to her by this angel of the Annunciation, even
her present sorrow can be turned into acceptance of Christ's death as a nec-
essary means to the "good" of human redemption. Two remarkable stanzas
narrate Mary's achievement of this delicate spiritual and emotional modula-
tion as she reflects on Christ's gender roles all the while that she performs her
own:

His woeful Mother wayting on her Sonne,
All comfortlesse in depth of sorow drowned;
Her griefes extreame, although but new begun,
To see his bleeding body oft she swouned;
How could she choose but thinke her selfe undone,
He dying, with whose glory shee was crowned?
    None ever lost so great a losse as shee,
    Beeing Sonne, and Father of Eternitie.

Her tears did wash away his pretious blood,
That sinners might not tread it under feet
To worship him, and that[,] it did her good
Upon her knees, although in open street,
Knowing he was the Jessie floure and bud,
That must be gath'red when it smell'd most sweet:

Her Sonne, her Husband, Father, Saviour, King,
Whose death killd Death, and tooke away his sting.
[ll. 1009-24; my bracketed comma]

Lanyer's prose postscript to her volume partially elucidates the vital connotations she attached to the biblical salutation as she lays out her first and only explanation of her title:

> Gentle Reader, if thou desire to be resolved, why I give this Title, *Salve Deus Rex Judaeorum,* know for certaine; that it was delivered unto me in sleepe many yeares before I had any intent to write in this maner, and was quite out of my memory, untill I had written the Passion of Christ, when immediately it came into my remembrance, . . . and thinking it a significant token, that I was appointed to performe this Worke, I gave the very same words I received in sleepe as the fittest Title I could devise for this Booke. [p. 139]

Further elucidation comes at the recurrent junctures where Lanyer as omniscient narrator and commentator reproves Christ's enemies for hailing him by name yet knowing him not at all. Thus she writes of the high priests and scribes who arrest him:

> His name they sought, and found, yet could not know
> *Jesus* of Nazareth . . .
> When Heavenly Wisdome did descend so lowe
> To speake to them: . . .
> . . . .
> Nay, though he said unto them, I am he,
> They could not know him, whom their eyes did see. [ll. 498-504]

And thus she writes, more scathingly, of Christ's interrogation by Caiaphas, who charges him once "in his glorious name" to tell "Whose pleasure 'twas he should endure this shame" and again

>   . . . by his powrefull name,
> To tell if Christ the Sonne of God he be,
> Who for our sinnes must die, to set us free.

Lanyer's Christ returns to Caiaphas the truth of Caiaphas's own linguistic formulation:

> Then with so mild a Majestie he spake,
> As they might easly know from whence he came,
> . . . .
> To thee O *Caiphas* doth he answere give,
> That thou hast said, what thou desir'st to know. [ll. 695-706]

But these words of truth are rejected as blasphemy, and the Word of Truth as a blasphemer. Caiaphas pronounces a sentence of death for blasphemy against this same "Christ the Sonne of God . . . Who for our sinnes must die, to set us free" and sends him to Pilate for its ratification. The soldiers who crucify Christ mock him with a crown of thorns, a reed for a scepter, and the salutation, "Haile king of the Jewes"—in the Latin of the Vulgate, "Salve Rex Judaeorum." Above his head his cross eventually bears a caption—"This is Jesus the king of the Jewes" (Matthew 27:37) or simply "The king of the Jewes" (Mark 15:26, John 19:19)—which the high priests futilely try to have altered to read: "He said, I am King of the Jewes" (John 19:21).[27] These multiplied misprisions that yet vindicate salutation as an acknowledgment of incarnate divinity inscribe the core of Lanyer's poetic and supply the narrative crux of her poem. *Salve Deus Rex Judaeorum.* Hail, God, the king of the Jews. Lanyer's title both opposes and embraces the truth of the gospel narrative that had been uttered uncomprehendingly, as a verbal gesture of mockery, by the soldiers who crucified Christ. By her own addition of just one word in apposition, *Deus,* she makes fully explicit her expression of personal faith in the divinity of one whom the Jews (the people of her own descent on her father's family's side) did not recognize as their king. She does so recognize him, and she salutes him as such.

However, the intricacies that register in "The Salutation and Sorrows of the Virgine Marie" and in the mystique—if I may so call it—of salutation in Lanyer's religious poetics may seem far removed from the feminist predispositions and feminist poetics that I claim for her text. Overall, it may look in this historical narrative of a political and social world as if Christ and the women are the losers, and that the grieving Mary, no less than the women of Jerusalem, must content themselves with either an inward or an otherworldly assurance that this feminized Christ will be victorious over masculinist evil and violence. Despite a sensitive and often perceptive discussion of "Salve Deus," Elaine Beilin comes to adopt this line. As she puts it, "I would not agree . . . that Lanyer was a feminist, because her advocacy for women begins with spiritual power and ends with poetry; and in fact, she assumes that men control society, art, and the worldly destiny of women, including herself."[28] But I in turn cannot agree with Beilin. I read Lanyer's portrayal of the spiritual power of femininity—of Christ and the women—in "Salve Deus" as having extreme revisionary implications for men's control of society, art, and the worldly destiny of women. My reading, apart from the overt declarations of "Eves Apologie" which still await discussion, goes like this.

Lanyer vindicates femininity to male critics and the misogynists of both sexes whom she deplores in her preface, "To the Vertuous Reader," not merely by portraying the closeness of Christ and actual good women. She historicizes her retracing of the gospel account of the Passion. This poetic narrative devolves in a space that is social and political, through and through. Its implications and those of the authorial commentary are social and political as well. More specifically, Lanyer uses her portrayals of Christ and actual good women to trace the impact of feminine or feminized virtue on the masculine side of a range of standing dichotomies that mark conceptions of social and political relations: public/private, mind/body, culture/nature, reason/passion. As narrated, the superiority of feminine virtue is constantly confirmed as it makes its impact in the masculine domain. Christ leaves the privateness of the upper room and the garden to engage the public proceedings of the soldiers, Caiaphas, Pilate, Herod, which the women likewise engage on his behalf. The connection between Christ and the women proves the more effective in that these figures together demonstrate, through what they are made to suffer, the problematic reciprocal relation between political submission and sexual subordination, and they do so more tellingly than almost any other rare sixteenth- and seventeenth-century text that in any way critiques this relation as a problem.[29] The net impact of Christ and the women in the narrative is to leave Jerusalem's public life and its intersecting political and priestly jurisdictions exposed as a sham of justice, as corruption, malignity, and violence.

Similarly, as my account of highlighted sections in "Salve Deus" has already suggested in some measure, Lanyer represents the bodies of Christ and the women as more legible expressions of understanding and morality—the qualities that supposedly make for the mind's superiority—than are the minds of the male figures of authority.

> Here insolent Boldnesse checkt by Love and Grace,
> Retires, and falls before our Makers face. [ll. 511-12]

> Her teares did wash away his pretious blood,
> That sinners might not tread it under feet
> . . . .
> . . . and that[,] it did her good
> Upon her knees, although in open street,
> Knowing he . . .
> . . . must be gather'd. [ll. 1017-22]

In one of several characteristically gendered contrasts, Lanyer authorially reprehends Pilate as he confirms Caiaphas's sentence on Christ. "Art thou a Judge?" she begins.

> The death of Christ wilt thou consent unto,
> Finding no cause, no reason, nor no ground?
> Shall he be scourg'd, and crucified too?
> And must his miseries by thy meanes abound? [ll. 857-62]

Lanyer's Pilate also becomes a prominent locus in the poem for the working out of culture/nature and reason/passion dichotomies that redound to the discredit of male domination. In a stanza that includes both pairs of binaries in its imagery, she demands of him:

> Canst thou be innocent, that gainst all right,
> Wilt yeeld to what thy conscience doth withstand?
> Beeing a man of knowledge, powre, and might,
> To let the wicked carrie such a hand,
> Before thy face to blindfold Heav'ns bright light,
> And thou to yeeld to what they did demand?
>> Washing thy hands, thy conscience cannot cleare,
>> But to all worlds this staine must needs appeare. [ll. 929-36]

Although unanswered, these questions put to Pilate are far from merely rhetorical or, in Beilin's terms, a manifestation—in poetry only—of a woman's spiritual power. The sun attests the innocence of the Son, as a later passage on "The terror of all creatures at that instant when Christ died" will confirm in its evocation of earthquake and other cataclysms—"The Sunne grew darke, and scorn'd to give them light, / Who durst ecclipse a glory farre more bright" (ll. 1191-92). Pilate's handwashing is a sorry irrelevance to the stain of bloodguiltiness incurred through his complicity in putting to death not merely an innocent victim but divinity incarnate. According to Lanyer's "Salve Deus" in the aftermath of Christ's crucifixion read as history, culture must look to nature for moral refounding.

Which is to say that men must look to women for the refounding of existing political and social relations. Exactly thus runs the argument advanced by Pilate's wife in "Eves Apologie" (meaning "Defense"—the sense is clearly that of *apologia*). Lanyer draws the warrant for a spirited portrayal of this figure from the passing notice accorded her in a single biblical verse, Matthew 27:19: "When he [Pilate] was set downe on the Judgement seate, his wife sent unto him, saying, Have thou nothing to doe with that just man [Jesus]: for I have suffered many things this day in a dreame, because of him." In keeping with Lanyer's generic representation of femininity as spiritually superior, Pilate's wife's first utterance discloses her true understanding and faith:

> . . . heare the words of thy most worthy wife,
>> Who sends to thee, to beg her Saviours life.
> . . . .
> Open thine eies, that thou the truth mai'st see,
> . . . .
> Condemne not him that must thy Saviour be. [ll. 751-57]

But she just as directly adds the most ominous pragmatic warning she can give Pilate, one based on the status quo of gender politics: "Let not us Women glory in Mens fall, / Who had power given to over-rule us all" (ll. 759-60). Lanyer's figure starts from a bond to scriptural authority as absolute as Lanyer's own to the Gospels: she acknowledges that men got power over women from the Fall of Adam and Eve. But she goes on to argue that the Gospel as history shatters that power. If men commit the far worse sin of killing Christ, their doing so sets women free from men's rule.

Here Pilate's wife exposes her own author's historicity. With a return to origins that demonstrates typical period procedure for tracing the cause or rationale of current practices, Pilate's wife reflects analytically—which for her and Lanyer means comparatively—on the Fall as narrated in Genesis. She details several considerations and lines of reasoning that work in Eve's favor. First, the serpent lied to Eve only; hence she was deceived into sinning, but Adam was not.

> . . . she (poore soule) by cunning was deceav'd,
> No hurt therein her harmelesse Heart intended:
>   For she alleadg'd Gods word . . .
>   That they should die . . . .
>
> But surely *Adam* can not be excusde,
> .   .   .   .
> Being Lord of all, the greater was his shame:
> Although the Serpents craft had her abusde,
> Gods holy word ought all his actions frame. [ll. 773-82]

The allusion to "Gods holy word" refers to the prohibition against eating the fruit of the tree of knowledge of good and evil that God gave to Adam before Eve was created (Genesis 3:16-18). There is no explicit indication in Scripture that the prohibition was ever transmitted to Eve. This is Pilate's wife's second consideration on Eve's behalf.

> The perfect'st man that ever breath'd on earth
> . . . from Gods mouth receiv'd that strait command,
> The breach whereof he knew was present death:
> .   .   .   .
> Not *Eve* . . . .
> .   .   .   .
> He never sought her weakenesse to reprove,
> With those sharpe words, which he of God did heare. [ll. 786-806]

In the third place, Pilate's wife finds Eve's psychology in sinning far more admirable than Adam's.

We know right well he did discretion lacke,
Beeing not perswaded thereunto at all;
If *Eve* did erre, it was for knowledge sake,

. . . .

Yet Men will boast of Knowledge, which he tooke
From *Eves* faire hand, as from a learned Booke. [ll. 795-808]

Finally, Pilate's wife reasons from Adam's priority in creation to his probable role as source of evil: "If any Evill did in her remaine, / Beeing made of him, he was the ground of all" (ll. 809-10). Her logic infers that an original creature is an originary one also in the case of woman's nature—if not, what is the primacy that is taken to ground male superiority? It will be clear here without further comment how Lanyer lines up the fundamental binaries of culture/nature and reason/passion in this fourfold *apologia* so that Pilate's wife personifies femininity triumphant in masculine terms.

Lanyer's possible antecedents for this passage make a fascinating if necessarily inconclusive subject. So little is known about her education and contacts—for example, whether she might somehow have had knowledge of the disputation conducted in 1451-53 through an exchange of Latin letters by Ludovico Foscarini, a Venetian doctor of canon law, civil law, and medicine, and the learned Veronese noblewoman Isotta Nogarola on the subject *Of the Equal or Unequal Sin of Adam and Eve*. Nogarola argues that Eve's sin was unequal in being less than Adam's, on three counts. First, Eve sinned through ignorance and inconstancy while Adam sinned through a prideful desire for Godlike moral knowledge. Second, in delivering the prohibition, God made Adam responsible for himself and Eve, but Adam did not restrain Eve, hence his guilt was greater. Third, God gave Eve a lesser punishment than Adam: she would bear children in pain, but he was condemned to labor and to death.

Nogarola also rebuts Foscarini's argument that Eve's sin was unequal in being greater than Adam's, again on three counts, in which she undertakes to reconfirm that Adam's sin was greater. To Foscarini's charge that Eve sinned more than Adam by setting him an evil precedent and being, in Aristotle's formulation in the *Posterior Analytics,* "That on account of which any thing exists is that thing and more greatly so," Nogarola responds that Adam's inherent superiority—as God's original creation, as the one to whom dominion over the earth was given—enabled him to resist Eve, and he is responsible for not doing so. To Foscarini's second charge, that Eve's sin was greater than Adam's because she, as an inferior creature, aspired to divinity equally with the superior creature Adam, Nogarola answers shortly with the principle that guilt is never increased by inferiority or weakness but rather the opposite: "In many people it is seen that he who knows less sins less, like a boy who sins less than an old man or a peasant less than a noble."[30] Adam is, therefore, more guilty.

To Foscarini's third charge, that Eve's sin was the greater because her punishment was cumulative—she incurred Adam's punishments of death and labor as well as her own of pain in childbirth—Nogarola retorts that, as opposed to inference, the actual wording of God's pronouncements in Scripture makes Adam's sin look clearly worse. God does not mention Eve's sin at all, only Adam's, in listening to his wife and eating of the tree that he was commanded not to touch (Genesis 3:17). Likewise, God phrases Adam's punishment more harshly than Eve's, for he says to Adam but not to her that he is dust and will return to dust (Genesis 3:19). Nogarola stands fast in her determination that Adam is more guilty than Eve. Hereupon Foscarini moves to close their disputation by admonishing her regarding the fallibility and deceitfulness of the female sex and her possible overconfidence in her own powers of argumentation. Most interestingly for future readers of Lanyer's "Salve Deus", he refers to Pilate's superior moral awareness at the time of Christ's Passion as a matter on which he and Nogarola could agree and thus resolve their differences: "Though I have spoken, you may not hear. You may spurn and disdain my words. . . . Let us read the history of the passion and the dreams of the wife, the words of Pilate, the washing of hands, the avoidance of judgment, and we shall confess that he understood . . . that the sentence was unjust. These things make it quite clear that the force of my arguments has not been weakened."[31]

Whatever she may or may not have known about Nogarola's Veronese-Venetian antecedent, Lanyer unquestionably figures as a feminist innovator within an English vernacular context. Her Pilate's wife prefigures by several years other women authors' analyses of the Fall of Adam and Eve that began to circulate as the English controversy about women entered its earlier seventeenth-century phase with Joseph Swetnam's *Arraignment of Lewde, Idle, Froward and Unconstant Women* (1615). Largely a racy series of anecdotes and denunciations, Swetnam's tract drew fiercest counterfire with its hapless attempts to reason, especially this one:

> Who can but say that women sprung from the Devil? Whose heads, hands, and hearts, minds and souls are evil. . . . For women have a thousand ways to entice thee and ten thousand ways to deceive thee. . . . They are ungrateful, perjured, full of fraud, flouting and deceit, unconstant, waspish, toyish, light, sullen, proud, discourteous, and cruel. And yet they were by God created and by nature formed, and therefore by policy and wisdom to be avoided. For good things abused are to be refused.[32]

Responding in *A Muzzle for Melastomus* (1617), Rachel Speght exclaims against Swetnam's illogic, "An impious conclusion to infer: that because God created, therefore to be avoided. O intolerable absurdity!" and elsewhere argues to exonerate Eve in terms closely resembling Lanyer's:

We shall find the offence of Adam and Eve almost to parallel: . . . Woman sinned, it is true, by her infidelity in not believing the word of God but giving credit to Satan's fair promises that 'she should not die' (Genesis iii.4); but so did the man too. And if Adam had not approved of that deed which Eve had done, and been willing to tread the steps which she had gone, he—being her head—would have reproved her. . . . And he, being better able than the woman to have resisted temptation, because the stronger vessel, was first called to account: to show that to whom much is given, of them much is required.[33]

Later in 1617 Speght is followed by another, tartly self-styled opponent of Swetnam, "Esther Sowernam," who in *Esther Hath Hang'd Haman* commends and sharpens Speght's detection of multiple fallacies in Swetnam's gloss on the Genesis account of the Fall. But Sowernam reserves her chiefest triumph for her exposure of Swetnam's mistaking of an echo of Euripides for a verse of Scripture, "If God had not made them only to be a plague to a man, he would never have called them necessary evils." "Out of what scripture, out of what record, can he prove these impious and impudent speeches? . . . If he had cited Euripides for his author, he had had some colour. . . . Thus a pagan writeth profanely, but for a Christian to say that God calleth women 'necessary evils' is most intolerable and shameful to be written and published."[34]

Not only does Pilate's wife in Lanyer's "Salve Deus" reason her way to a defense of Eve without explicitly presupposing what Nogarola, Speght, and Sowernam all do, that Eve by nature is inferior to Adam. She also takes the controversy about women two steps further. Both of these, as far as I know, are completely unprecedented and original. Granting for the purposes of argument that Eve deserved to be subjugated to Adam for having been the first to fall, Pilate's wife challenges Pilate on the relative blameworthiness of the Fall and the Crucifixion, in which, she charges, "you in malice Gods deare Sonne betray":

Whom, if unjustly you condemne to die,
Her sinne was small, to what you doe commit;
All mortall sinnes that doe for vengeance crie,
Are not to be compared unto it:
If many worlds would altogether trie,
By all their sinnes the wrath of God to get;
    This sinne of yours, surmounts them all as farre
    As doth the Sunne, another little starre. [ll. 817-24]

Sardonically invoking the superiority of the sun's light to image the greater male culpability of the Crucifixion in her female eyes, Pilate's wife inverts the culture/nature and reason/passion dichotomies to explicit female advantage once again in Lanyer's poem. The Crucifixion is worse than the Fall because malice is worse than ignorance as the state of mind in which evil is done. Moreover, by the implicit standards of the long-traditional conception of sin as self-murder, killing oneself is far less culpable than killing the son of God. Finally, no woman wants the Crucifixion; it is only men who do. Pilate's wife now spells out to Pilate the implications she sees her relative assessment of the Crucifixion and the Fall as having for gender relations in the social and political spheres:

> Then let us have our Libertie againe,
> And challendge to your selves no Sov'raigntie;
> . . . .
> Your fault being greater, why should you disdaine
> Our beeing your equals, free from tyranny?
> . . . .
> This sinne of yours, hath no excuse, nor end.
>
> To which (poore soules) we never gave consent,
> Witnesse thy wife (O *Pilate*) speakes for all. [ll. 825-34]

Foscarini's complacent hunch to the contrary, an intelligent woman of the Renaissance, reflecting on Pilate, Pilate's wife, and Christ's Crucifixion, would not easily find for the superiority of Pilate's moral understanding and thus confirm the subjection of females to males ordained by God after the Fall. These two personages are styled to enforce exactly the opposite finding in Lanyer's feminist poetics while a fully reasoned claim—no mere yearning—issues for sexual equality in the aftermath of the Crucifixion. Interestingly, the lack of punctuation marks to enclose reported speech in early seventeenth-century texts makes it impossible to determine whether the last two lines of the foregoing quotation are spoken by Pilate's wife or by Lanyer as omniscient narrator. No less interestingly, the indeterminacy does not affect the interpretation or the prescient feminism of "Salve Deus Rex Judaeorum," because a brief for an end to male domination, thus historicized, holds for any date subsequent to the Crucifixion and for any nominally Christian place. In this poem Aemilia Lanyer takes more seriously—that is to say, more historically—the radical social and political implications of the new order broached in the gospel narrative of primitive Christianity than would any other English thinker or writer of either sex until a quarter century later, in the mid-century ferment of revolution and interregnum.[35] Even in that later company, she and her Pilate's wife sound voices of the utmost immediacy and cogency as they lay claim to what has long since remained for women the receding future of gender equality.

NOTES

1. The title page of the 1611 edition is reproduced as the frontispiece of the present volume.

2. Examples of this critical approach abound. See, variously, Natalie Zemon Davis, "Gender and Genre: Women as Historical Writers, 1400-1820," in *Beyond Their Sex: Learned Women of the European Past*, ed. Patricia H. LaBalme (New York and London: New York University Press, 1980), pp. 153-82; Susan Gubar, "'The Blank Page' and the Issues of Female Creativity," in *Writing and Sexual Difference*, ed. Elizabeth Abel as a special issue of *Critical Inquiry* 8.2 (winter 1981): 243-64; Gary F. Waller, "Struggling into Discourse: The Emergence of Renaissance Women's Writing," in *Silent But for the Word: Tudor Women as Patrons, Translators, and Writers of Religious Works*, ed. Margaret Patterson Hannay (Kent, Oh.: Kent State University Press, 1985), pp. 238-56.

3. On relevant theory and methodology, see Dominick LaCapra, *Rethinking Intellectual History: Texts, Contexts, Language* (Ithaca, N.Y.: Cornell University Press, 1983), pp. 13-71.

4. See chap. 8, "Imagining Female Community: Aemilia Lanyer's Poems," in Barbara K. Lewalski, *Writing Women in Jacobean England* (Cambridge, Mass.: Harvard University Press, 1993).

5. See Ralph Houlbrooke, *The English Family, 1450-1700* (London: Longmans, 1984), p. 147; and Peter Laslett, *The World We Have Lost: England before the Industrial Age*, 3d ed. (New York: Scribner's, 1984), p. 13.

6. For details on Susan Bertie's marriage and her possible relation to Lanyer, see Leeds Barroll's essay in this volume (chapter 2).

7. See Lewalski, *Writing Women in Jacobean England*, pp. 216-18; Louise Schleiner, *Tudor and Stuart Women Writers* (Bloomington and Indianapolis: Indiana University Press, 1994), pp. 23-24.

8. See discussions in A.R. Rowse, ed. *The Poems of Shakespeare's Dark Lady* (London: Jonathan Cape, 1978), pp. 11-16; Germaine Greer, Susan Hastings, Jeslyn Medoff, and Melinda Sansone, eds., *Kissing the Rod: An Anthology of Seventeenth-Century Women's Verse* (New York: Noonday Press, 1989), pp. 44-46; Woods, ed., *Poems of Aemilia Lanyer*, pp. xlvii-l; and Schleiner, *Tudor and Stuart Women Writers*, pp. 24-25.

9. Christine de Pizan, *The Book of the City of Ladies [Livre de la Cité des Dames]*, trans. and intro. Earl Jeffrey Richards (New York: Persea Books, 1982), pp. ix-xx; Maureen Quilligan, *The Allegory of Female Authority: Christine de Pizan's Cité des Dames* (Ithaca and London: Cornell University Press, 1991), pp. 1-2.

10. Constance Jordan thoughtfully considers the pitfalls of possible anachronism but finds it possible to define "the feminism of Renaissance texts" as "a theory of a point of view, by which to justify feminist assumptions of the virtue of women and, conversely, to call into question patriarchal assumptions of their inferiority" which, for its own part, presumes that "a representation of the world from a woman's point of view has validity, and that such a representation entails an understanding of the assumptions held by the various participants in the debate on the woman question" (*Renaissance Feminism: Literary Texts and Political Models* [Ithaca and London: Cornell University Press, 1990], pp. 6-7).

11. See, variously, Joan Kelly, "Early Feminist Theory and the *Querelle des Femmes*," in *Women, History, and Theory: The Essays of Joan Kelly* (Chicago and London: University of Chicago Press, 1984), pp. 65-109; Introduction, Katherine U. Henderson and Barbara F.

McManus, eds., *Half Humankind: Contexts and Texts of the Controversy about Women in England, 1540-1640* (Urbana and Chicago: University of Illinois Press, 1985), pp. 3-184; Ann Rosalind Jones, *The Currency of Eros: Women's Love Lyric in Europe, 1540-1620* (Bloomington: Indiana University Press, 1990), pp. 1-35; and Simon Shepherd, ed., *The Women's Sharp Revenge: Five Women's Pamphlets from the Renaissance* (New York: St. Martin's, 1985), pp. 9-23. For an alternative formulation that builds upon Jürgen Habermas's concept of "consensual discourse," see Schleiner, *Tudor and Stuart Women Writers,* pp. 31-33, 193-94.

12. Pizan, *Book of the City of Ladies,* ed. Richards, pp. xxi-xlvi.

13. Earlier treatments include Elaine V. Beilin, *Redeeming Eve: Women Writers of the English Renaissance* (Princeton: Princeton University Press, 1987), pp. 191, 193-99; Lynette McGrath, "Metaphoric Subversions: Feasts and Mirrors in Amelia Lanier's *Salve Deus Rex Judaeorum,*" *Literature Interpretation Theory* 3.2 (1991): 101-13; and Schleiner, *Tudor and Stuart Women Writers,* pp. 26-29.

14. See Henderson and McManus, *Half Humankind,* pp. 14-19.

15. E.g., Mary Beth Rose, *The Expense of Spirit: Love and Sexuality in English Renaissance Drama* (Ithaca and London: Cornell University Press, 1988), p. 95.

16. So, too, John Donne appears to have thought at the same date in writing his extravagantly hyperbolical meditative elegies, the two *Anniversaries* (1610-11), on the deceased fifteen-year-old heiress Elizabeth Drury, only child of his patron, the then prominent courtier-diplomat Sir Robert Drury. Louise Schleiner (*Tudor and Stuart Women Writers,* pp. 166-74) has ascribed a similar significance to Donne's "First Anniversary." Nonetheless, there are basic aspects of Donne's representation that would surely have failed to satisfy Lanyer: his only supremely good woman, the source of all cosmic vitality and value, is a girl who dies of a fever in her virginal adolescence.

17. *The English Poems of George Herbert,* ed. C. A. Patrides, Everyman's University Library (London: J.M. Dent & Sons, 1974), p. 205.

18. *The Holy Bible: A Facsimile . . . of the Authorized Version Published in the Year 1611,* ed. A.W. Pollard (Oxford: Oxford University Press, 1911), fol. A2v.

19. This especially has been the focus of three discussions by Barbara K. Lewalski: "Of God and Good Women: The Poems of Aemilia Lanier," in Hannay, *Silent But for the Word,* pp. 203-24; "Re-writing Patriarchy and Patronage: Margaret Clifford, Anne Clifford, and Aemilia Lanier," *Yearbook of English Studies* 21 (1991): 87-106; and *Writing Women in Jacobean England,* pp. 213-42. Lanyer's other major witness to poetic inspiration from a female source is her evocative vision-poem, "The Authors Dreame to the Ladie *Marie,* the Countesse Dowager of *Pembrooke,*" which extols the moral, spiritual, and creative power manifested in Mary Sidney's psalm translations and declares them the "faire impression" that "Seales her pure soule unto the Deitie" (Woods ed., p. 29).

20. See Gayle Greene and Coppélia Kahn, "Feminist Scholarship and the Social Construction of Woman," in *Making a Difference: Feminist Literary Criticism,* ed. Greene and Kahn (London: Methuen, 1985), pp. 1-36; Joan Scott, "Gender: A Useful Category of Analysis," *Gender and the Politics of History* (New York: Columbia University Press, 1988), pp. 28-56; Judith Lowder Newton, "History as Usual? Feminism and the 'New Historicism,'" in *The New Historicism,* ed. H. Aram Veeser (New York and London: Routledge, 1989), pp. 152-67; Carolyn Porter, "History and Literature: 'After the New Historicism,'" *New Literary History* 21.2 (1990): 253-72.

21. Rowse ed., p. 18.

22. Samuel Daniel, *Poems and A Defence of Ryme,* ed. Arthur Colby Sprague (London: Routledge and Kegan Paul, 1950), pp. 156-57.

23. Further discrepancies emerge where Lanyer and Daniel write in the same genre, as they do in both addressing laudatory verse epistles to Anne Clifford and to Lucy, Countess of Bedford. Daniel's "To the Lady Anne Clifford," in terza rima set in block form, praises a girl of "tender youth" for her virtuous self-containment in demure silence and stoic circumspection (Daniel, *Poems and A Defence of Ryme,* pp. 119-21); Lanyer's "To the Ladie Anne, Countesse of Dorcet," in ottava rima stanzas, hails a young woman for a virtue so surpassingly potent that it dissolves social hierarchy and becomes the standard and repository ("steward") of all human worth, not excluding Lanyer's own moral perceptions and the poetry praising Anne that she writes in the light of them (Woods ed., pp. 41-47). Daniel's "To the Lady Lucie, Countesse of Bedford," in cross-rhymed iambic pentameter, hails its subject for studiousness in virtue so exalted and retired, and for happiness so perfected, that she is now positioned as arbiter of all the moral efforts and aspirations of her fellow mortals (*Poems and A Defence of Ryme,* pp. 116-18); in sharp contrast, Lanyer's four stanzas of rime royal addressed "To the Ladie Lucie, Countesse of Bedford" envisage her spiritualized erotic intimacy in her heart's loving embrace of Christ (Woods ed., pp. 32-33).

24. Formative contributions to this still growing field of studies include Ruth Kelso, *Doctrine for the Lady of the Renaissance* (Urbana: University of Illinois Press, 1956); Suzanne W. Hull, *Chaste, Silent and Obedient: English Books for Women, 1475-1640* (San Marino, Calif.: The Huntington Library, 1982); Lisa Jardine, *Still Harping on Daughters: Women and Drama in the Age of Shakespeare* (Sussex, Eng.: Harvester Press, 1983); Linda Woodbridge, *Women and the English Renaissance: Literature and the Nature of Womankind, 1540-1620* (Urbana and Chicago: University of Illinois Press, 1984).

25. I am not by any means implying that Lanyer is the first, or even the first female, author in English to feminize a portrayal of Christ. There is a rich earlier meditative tradition to this effect, which Caroline Walker Bynum has studied for the thirteenth century in *Jesus as Mother: Studies in the Spirituality of the High Middle Ages* (Berkeley and Los Angeles: University of California Press, 1982) and which Julian of Norwich applies in chapters 59-61 of her *Showings* (or *Revelations*) *of Divine Love* (ca. 1393) on Jesus as mother, after having unprecedentedly broached a conception of God as mother in chapter 58. Lanyer, however, does not feminize her Christ in a medieval fashion as maternal. He has, rather, the cultivated graces and virtuous bearing associated with marriageable women of rank in the Renaissance, a type that Lanyer could draw from life through her familiarity with the Elizabethan Court.

26. On the rarity of even poetic usage, see *OED,* "hail," vb. The angel of the Annunciation greets Mary with "Haile thou that art highly favoured" (Luke 1:28). Judas betrays Christ in the garden with "Haile master" and a kiss (Matthew 26:49). The soldiers who put a crown of thorns on Jesus's head and a reed in his hand shortly before they crucify him mock him with "Haile king of the Jewes" (Matthew 27:29, Mark 15:18, John 19:3). This exhaustive listing gives the readings of the King James Version; see Pollard, *The Holy Bible.*

27. Biblical citations here and subsequently are from the King James Version in Pollard's facsimile.

28. Beilin, p. 320.

29. Indeed I would say that a recognition of this problem should qualify a text of any

era as feminist, not only in such clear cases as Mary Wollstonecraft's *Vindication of the Rights of Women* or John Stuart Mill's *On the Subjection of Women,* but also in Elizabeth Cary, Lady Falkland's *Tragedy of Mariam, Fair Queen of Jewry* (published 1613), a work nearly contemporaneous with Lanyer's *Salve Deus Rex Judaeorum.*

30. Margaret L. King and Albert Rabil, Jr., eds. and trans. *Her Immaculate Hand: Selected Works by and about the Women Humanists of Quattrocento Italy* (Binghamton, N.Y.: Medieval and Renaissance Texts and Studies, 1983), pp. 62-63.

31. Ibid., p. 68.

32. Joseph Swetnam's *Arraignment* is excerpted in Henderson and McManus, *Half Humankind,* p. 201.

33. Rachel Speght's *Muzzle for Melastomus* is reprinted in Shepherd, ed., *The Women's Sharp Revenge;* pp. 77, 66.

34. Esther Sowernam's tract is also reprinted in Shepherd, ed., and in Barbara Kiefer Lewalski, ed., *The Polemics and Poems of Rachel Speght* (Oxford: Oxford Univ. Press, 1996), pp. 94-95 pp. 14-15, 26.

35. See Elaine Hobby, *Virtue of Necessity: English Women's Writing, 1649-88* (Ann Arbor: University of Michigan Press, 1989), and Keith Thomas, "Women and the Civil War Sects," *Past & Present* 13 (1958): 42-62.

7

The Gendering of Genre:
Literary History and the Canon

~

Marshall Grossman

In what ways does Aemilia Lanyer solicit us to think about the theory and practice of literary history? In general, when we write the history of literature we construct a variety of narratives to connect events, works, styles, writers, genres—what have you—over time. The narratives so constructed serve not only to represent the past, but to represent it to the present, and, the past being past, it is in the present that these narratives must have their effect. The very small number of surviving copies of the *Salve Deus Rex Judaeorum* and the lack of contemporary reference to it or to any other literary works by Lanyer argue against her having participated in any great way in the construction of English literature. Perhaps something of hers was in some manner appropriated by writers the impact of whose work is easier to trace. Ben Jonson comes to mind as someone she might have influenced, and though the evidence does not support A.L. Rowse's contention that she was Shakespeare's "dark lady," her connections to the court music as well as to the Lord Chamberlain may well have placed her on occasion in the milieux of Court and theater inhabited by Jonson, Shakespeare, and other familiar literary names of the period. We cannot rule out the possibility of her direct influence in literary history, but neither can we adduce any positive evidence for it. The question, then, arises: if, as appears to be the case, Lanyer's publication had, in fact, no historical consequence, failed to *cause* anything at all, in what sense (if any) was it a literary historical event? What does it mean—now—for Lanyer so belatedly to enter literary history?

As is typically true of historical questions, we can project possible answers to this question on two scenes: the past and the present. The *Salve Deus Rex Judaeorum* is a historical document. Its existence tells us that a woman did, in fact, publish a work of this genre in 1611 (or 1610) and that it was possible for her to address a particular group of aristocratic women in this way, although we cannot say whether the address succeeded.

Physical differences among the extant copies suggest some things about how presentation copies were prepared and patronage sought.[1] Specific references in the poems may illuminate specific historical events (in, for example, the family histories of the Russells and the Cliffords) and general trends (like that toward litigiousness regarding the heritability of land holdings). Moving a bit closer to literary history, we can also see Lanyer's book as a moment in the *querelle des femmes* and deduce from it interesting facts about the lives of noble and middle-class women in the early seventeenth century.[2]

In respect of what it suggests about life in the early seventeenth century, we might say that whether or not the *Salve* was, in itself, a literary historical event, it is for us a historical document. My present interest, however, is to emphasize the specifically literary historical implications of the *Salve* as they might come to be played out on the other scene, that of the present. I want to consider how Lanyer's addition to the canon might change the way we read other more familiar poets so as to recreate the narrative of our literary history in its relation to the present, and I want briefly to reflect on what that revision or reconstruction of the familiar might more generally indicate about the sort of knowledge literary history affords.

To illustrate the potential power of Lanyer's work as an intervention in the present construction of a literary historical narrative, I think it useful to begin with a small example: some familiar lines by a poet whose settled familiarity Lanyer disturbs:

> The Sun is lost, and th'earth, and no mans wit
> Can well direct him, where to look for it.
> And freely men confesse, that this world's spent,
> When in the Planets, and the Firmament
> They seeke so many new; they see that this
> Is crumbled out againe to his Atomis.
> 'Tis all in pieces, all cohaerence gone;
> All just supply, and all Relation:
> Prince, Subiect, Father, Sonne, are things forgot,
> For euery man alone thinkes he hath got
> To be a Phoenix, and that there can bee
> None of that kinde, of which he is, but hee.[3]

In these lines, published in the same year as the *Salve Deus Rex Judaeorum*, John Donne laments the contemporary reduction of the world to its "atomies" by the death of Elizabeth Drury, a young girl he never met and whose most salient feature in the poem is her indistinction as an individual.[4]

Now the very fact that these lines are quoted in an essay about Aemilia Lanyer suffices to call attention to what in other circumstances has gone unnoted: that when Donne enumerates the relations "all forgot," in 1611, he forgets to forget relations among women. Moreover, Donne evokes not just the loss of patrilineal relations but also a series of analogous disorientations. These disorientations progress upward through the loss of fealty between sovereign and subject, the order of the planets and stars and the relation of the sun to the earth. The poem thus implies the existence of a previously homogenous and integrated cosmic order, of which the "idea of a Woman" served as a symbolic representative. This order produces Woman as idea, or concept, while silently erasing the relations of actually existing mothers, daughters, and sisters, which would tend in every case to disable the concept by making it more concrete. Donne's substitution of the "idea of a woman" for the material existence of the girl whose death he commemorates shifts the focus of the poem from the loss of Elizabeth Drury, the *daughter* he has been commissioned to memorialize, to the failure of the cosmic order as traditionally represented. The "death" of the idealized figure of Woman is used to represent the death of a certain way of representing the world. In his reduction of (lost) relation to the parallel and inclusive sets of prince-subject, father-son, "shee," whose death is represented in the poem as the death of the world, dies twice: once as an individual human being and a second time as the generalized holder of symbolic place in the universal order.[5]

Yet, insofar as "Her Ghost doth walke" in a "kind of world remaining still" (ll. 67-70), the world of dead male relations is haunted by another, in which the relevant relations are the unspoken ones of queen and subject, mother and daughter.[6] It is in the interest of literary history to consider Lanyer's peculiar ability to make us aware of what we might not otherwise notice, to recall what we have been in fact trained to forget, giving voice to the maternal ghost necessarily inhabiting and perhaps outliving a patriarchal genre. I have just invoked Donne's lamentation, in the *Anniversaries,* for the loss of "the idea of a woman" from whom all relation stems and to whom no relation is necessary, and I will soon advert to Jonson, because I want to begin to see what, if anything, happens, in a literary historical sense, when *her* voice, Aemilia Lanyer's voice, the voice of a woman who, like her contemporaries Donne and Jonson, needs financial means and seeks patronage through the poetry of praise, is (re)placed in dialogue with the voices of the two male poets whose names have, again, in a literary historical sense, served alternatively as ways to name seventeenth-century verse: for example, in university courses with names like "Age of Jonson" or "Donne and the Metaphysicals" and enduringly useful books like Joseph Summers's *The Heirs of Donne and Jonson.*[7]

Therefore, in addition to its intrinsic poetic interest, which is considerable, the *Salve Deus Rex Judaeorum,* by virtue of its early date and the example it affords of a feminine voice speaking in the genres of the poetry of praise, presents an opportunity to consider in a concrete way issues central to our understanding of the interrelationship of material history and literary form. I am thinking in particular of two large questions: (1) What is the relationship between the ideological work performed by seventeenth-century epideictic poetry and the becoming canonical of certain generic conventions? and (2) In what ways do generic conventions function as protocols of reading, and, conversely, to what extent and in what ways are noncanonical poems rendered opaque by these protocols? Gaining access to the intrinsic poetic interest of Lanyer's poems is, I want to suggest, not just a matter of learning to value the conventions and figures of *her* poetry as we have been taught to value those of (generically speaking) *his*, but of learning to read otherwise, a process of dialectical negation in which the "natural" is converted to the "historical" through an active consideration of the genders of genre.

Choosing the most obvious generic parallel, I want to consider how a comparison of Lanyer's "The Description of Cooke-ham" and Jonson's "To Penshurst" helps to make visible how deeply implicated Jonson's poem is in assumptions about land tenure and inheritance from which Lanyer is excluded by gender.[8] Lanyer's poem allows us to stand at a key distance from Jonson's poem and the rhetorical norms established in it. While "The Description of Cooke-ham" may well be the first English country-house poem, by virtue of its feminine origin and address it cannot sensibly engage what will become the canonical metaphors of the English country-house genre. Thus the comparison illuminates the facts that the country-house genre was gendered at its inception, and that, unsurprisingly, in literary historical as in material historical terms, the male form engendered a self-conscious lineage beneath which the female genealogy becomes difficult to read. The material ways in which the male country-house poem and the legal system of patrilineal descent reinforce each other at the expense of the female country-house poem and female genealogy are obvious, but the details of this interaction between literary and material history can be illuminating.

Jonson's poem does its ideological work by identifying land and lord as earth and fruit, mother and father; these metaphors, like Donne's summary of relation "all forgot," use the commonplace assumption that the microcosm will reproduce the macrocosm to assert a relation not between nature and humankind but between natural *order* and *man*: the rhetorical formalization of this analogy as at once metaphor and mimesis—comparison and imitative representation—posits an immanent reduplication between *logos* and maleness, constituting and establishing precisely what we might today call *phallogocentricity*.[9]

The gendered distinction between nature and natural order for which I am reaching here is aptly characterized in Luce Irigaray's recent *je, tu, nous: Toward a Culture of Difference* (1993). In order to illuminate the deployment of nature and order within the broad context of discursive phallogocentricity I am going to quote at some length from an essay, "On Women's Discourse and Men's Discourse," included in that book. Asserting, a very generalized difference between masculine and feminine discourse, Irigaray characterizes men's discourse as distinctly mediated by culture:

> Most of the time, in *men's discourse,* the world is designated as inanimate abstractions integral to the subject's world. Reality appears as an always already cultural reality, linked to the individual and collective history of the masculine subject. It's always a matter of a secondary nature, cut off from its corporeal roots, its cosmic environment, its relation to life. This relation is only ever mentioned to be denied, and is perpetually passing into uncultured behavior. The forms may change, but the blind immediacy of the behavior stays the same. The male subject's relations to his body, to what it has given him, to nature, to the bodies of others, including those of his sexual partners, are yet to be developed. In the meantime, the realities of which his discourse speaks are artificial, mediated to such an extent by one subject and one culture that it's not really possible to share them.[10]

Now it is necessary to be careful and precise about this assertion. I would want, at some point, to meditate on the doubly paradoxical situation of (1) Irigaray's reliance on this highly conceptualized language to make the point that a discourse mediated by the concept is characteristically masculinist and (2) the decorum of my situation as a man appropriating her distinction for the traditionally masculine demands of literary *history.* More importantly, I think, we would do better to think of what Irigaray describes as a style of discourse identified as masculine within a certain historically occurring patriarchal configuration rather than as "men's discourse." Many men may be quite comfortable in "women's discourse," which by implication we may characterize as less culturally mediated—more "natural" in the sense of being more in touch with the body, its senses, and their more or less immediate objects—as some women are surely quite comfortable in "men's discourse." A fully theorized use of Irigaray's gendered discourses would thus require a careful consideration of the (at least quasi-) essentialist tendencies of the broad distinctions she makes, and an emphasis on the fact that insofar as we are talking about discourse, we are not talking about unmediated nature at all, but about a cultural ideal of nature, a distinction not between nature and culture but between cultural attitudes toward nature and culture.

For now, however, I have the more modest aim of noting the admirable specificity of Irigaray's formulation in relation to the seventeenth-century poems I have been discussing. It is not, then, a question of women actually or *essentially* having an unmediated relation to nature—an assertion I would deny on the grounds I have just suggested—but of the fact that, when seen in their difference from Lanyer's poems, Jonson's "To Penshurst" and Donne's *Anniversaries* (to take just the two examples I have discussed) answer as well as they do to Irigaray's description of "men's discourse." Both Irigaray and Lanyer use the same opposition between culturally mediated and naturally immediate discourse as a way of figuring difference; that is, of figuring the feminine as difference, as that which remains outside or beyond the conceptual frame.

One might, after all, think that the language system formed around the expected repetition of the same divinely instituted structure in microcosm and macrocosm is precisely and historically a mediation of world by body.[11] Hegel thought it such when he labelled such rhetorical tools image thinking. To become fully patriarchal such figures need to be negated as image and incorporated in the more general and abstract form of concept. But in the dialectic of patriarchal practice it tended to be also the body which was mediated by the world—that is, by the world experienced in accord with a highly determined idea of cosmic design. Within this idealization the immediacy of *things* was sacrificed to a reassuring sense of the immediately significant. The suppression of women under the figure of a generic and idealized Woman who functions as the focal point around which male (conceptual) discourse may be constituted was one important symptom of this displacement. Beatrice and Laura are two of the better known names of the generic "she," who functions, in this way, as the support of a conceptual discourse from which she is, herself, excluded.

The putative subject of Donne's *Anniversaries*, Elizabeth Drury, fulfills a similar function.[12] Donne's 1611 poem is, however, more reflexively diagnostic than its predecessors, representing the death of Drury as marking precisely the end of the effectiveness of the figure of idealized femininity as the constitutive other of "men's discourse." In the *First Anniversary*, "her" disappearance is identified with the inviability, in 1611, of a cosmology that organized *vision* around "natural" forms that offer themselves *immediately* as also symbolic representations. Thus Donne identifies and records a historical moment in which the figure of the idealized woman is itself lost to a conceptual mediation of the cosmos. The circular orbits of the Ptolemaic planets traced real lines in real space to outline the abstract conceptual being of a God whose center is everywhere and circumference nowhere. This visual world organized *relation,* made the world cohere. "Shee" then, as the conventional and visual embodiment of a sublimed and subjected desire is also this sign of significance:

> She that was best and first originall
> Of all faire copies; and the generall
> Steward to Fate . . .
> . . . .
> She to whom this world must itselfe refer,
> As Suburbs, or the Microcosme of her [ll. 222-36]

Donne's lament gives us some idea of what is at stake in appropriating the figure of Woman as the emptied center around which a patriarchal conceptual economy circles, or, to put it another way, of foreclosing the space in which something other than that idealized figure might be maintained. The unspoken dialogue between the country-house poems of Lanyer and Jonson tells us something of what might happen if that space, which threatens to become silent and disorganized for Donne, were actually to be filled with the sound of women's voices.

The implicit or explicit claim that these voices would, if they could be heard, paradoxically speak a relation to nature unmediated by the logos—that is, according to the categories, compartments, and polarities of a conceptual order—takes on a particular potency in this dialogue because it poses a very specific threat to the work of the Jonsonian poem. This work, in the case of "To Penshurst" at least, is rhetorically to assimilate patrilinearity to nature—to unify the origin of the logocentric and the phallocentric by representing a particular and historically determined set of laws and customs as expressing a divinely designed natural order.

The seventeenth century was aware of and sensitive to a crucial point of resistance inherent in this naturalizing arrangement. Take, for example, the following exchange between Miranda and Prospero:

> MIR. Sir, are not you my father?
> PROS. Thy mother was a piece of vertue, and
> she said thou wast my daughter; and thy father
> Was Duke of Milan; and his only heir
> And princess, no worse issued.[13]

Prospero's rejoinder evinces both the system of patrilineal descent that makes Miranda *his* heir and the word of the silenced mother on which that system depends.

Whatever status we might want finally to assign to Irigaray's (and Lanyer's) claims for a distinctively feminine access to a material reality unmediated by discursive culture, I think we can acknowledge that maternity is a position that can be established on empirical grounds. It is written visibly on the mother's body and witnessed visually at birth. Paternity, on the contrary, is not only necessarily mediated by the word; it is, in fact, necessarily mediated precisely by the mother's word. As we see in Prospero's exchange with Miranda, this is a word that cannot be spoken without paradoxically evoking the scandal of its potential falsity. This scandal in the structure of patrilinearity itself is acknowledged in Jonson's penultimate compliment to Penshurst, when, like Prospero, the poet presumes to speak the mother's word: "Thy lady's noble, fruitful, chaste withal. / His children thy great lord may call his own" (ll. 90-91).[14] The serious tension that underlies these lines is betrayed by the poet's attempt to relieve it with the wry addition of "A fortune in this age but rarely known" (l. 92). The relation of dialectical negation between male and female genres comes into view in these lines. In the very moment that Lady Sidney's word is made good, generic woman must be denigrated, her word made nought. The individual is praised at the expense of the genus.

In Jonson's "To Penshurst" the assertion of an autochthonous link between the Sidney family and the Kentish land covers over two ideologically less convenient possible accounts of the Sidney estate: the relatively recent, Henrician origins of the family's landed status in Kent and Robert Sidney's financial dependence on Barbara Gammage's legacy to replenish family fortunes depleted by his illustrious brother Philip.[15]

Moreover, the presentation of the Sidneys as cultivating and cultivated by the land covers over this political and economic history in a way that exemplifies Irigaray's remark that

> Although our societies, made up half by men, half by women, stem from two genealogies and not one, patriarchal power is organized by submitting one genealogy to the other. Thus, what is now termed the oedipal structure as access to the cultural order is already structured within a single, masculine line of filiation which doesn't symbolize the woman's relation to her mother. Mother-daughter relationships in patrilinear societies are subordinated to relationships between men. [16]

This subordination is not news, but there is, I believe, value—for literary history and, perhaps, for contemporary feminism—in tracing out in concrete cases some of the specific ways in which patrilineal succession is expressed in the legal system on the one hand and validated or resisted by generic conventions on the other. The way in which Jonson substitutes the land for women as the womb from which succeeding generations of Sidney heirs are produced is all the more exemplary when contrasted with Lanyer's country-house poem in the feminine voice.

Lanyer's poem attacks (possibly preemptively, as it may have preceded Jonson's) the substitution of land (wealth-patrimony) for woman (mother) that characterizes the rhetoric of patrilinearity. Thus, to exemplify what I propose to call, after Adorno, the negative dialectics of the canon, the comparison of our two earliest examples of the English country-house poem makes visible the way in which "To Penshurst" significantly excludes female descent by metaphorically assimilating the Sidney women to the land from which the Sidney men descend.[16] Just as Prospero's "so thy mother told me," the "ghost" of Elizabeth Drury haunting Donne's dead world and the references to Barbara Gammage in "To Penshurst" represent remainders of the feminine genealogy negated by patriarchal practice, Lanyer's encoding of a feminine poetic subject persists as a remainder with which to confront the patrilinear literary history whose generic conventions tended to negate it.

Margaret Russell, Countess of Cumberland, and her daughter Anne Clifford, later Countess of Dorset, appear to have retreated to Cookham, a royal estate in the Russell family's holding, during the countess' estrangement from the errant Clifford in the years before his death in 1605. Jonson celebrates (or, more correctly, recommends) Robert Sidney's dwelling on the Kentish land. Lanyer, on the contrary, recalls the moment of a leave taking that probably occurred when the dowager countess moved to a Russell estate before beginning the epic litigation by which she and her daughter—the remarkable diarist—struggled to enforce an entail from the time of Edward II that would allow the property to descend through the female line and thus prevent the customary passage of her *husband's* estates to collateral male heirs.[17] As Barbara Lewalski has noted, Lanyer portrays Cookham as a place without men, a sort of feminine academy, and evokes the departure of the spirit of the place, when the women disperse, Margaret to one of her dowager holdings and Anne to the estate of her new husband, Robert Sackville, the Earl of Dorset.[18]

The implications for the poems of the very different legal relations to landed property experienced by men and women within a system governed by the principle of patrilineal primogeniture may be exemplified by the gender specific ways in which trees are used to figure the relation of land to lord and lady respectively in "To Penshurst" and "The Description of Cooke-ham." In "To Penshurst" Jonson evokes trees: Philip's Oak, "That taller tree, which of a nut was set, / At his great birth, where all the muses met," "thy lady's oak," under which Barbara Gammage is said to have gone into labor, producing a new Sidney, as it were fruit of the land, and, acknowledging in a cleverly repressed form her necessary financial contribution, the copse

> named of Gammage, . . .
> That never fails to serve thee seasoned deer,
> When thou would'st feast, or exercise thy friends. [ll. 13-21]

These arboreal associations serve to develop a picture of the Sidneys' *rootedness* in the Kentish land, which brings forth trees and Sidneys with equal fecundity.

Lanyer, on the contrary, combines the image of an oak and a strategically motivated pathetic fallacy to figure the experience of virilocality and patrilinear descent in the feminine community as a disruption, not of the logocentric order in which men read a self-validating design, but of an immediate identification of woman and nature itself. Thus the poet coming to "That Oake that

did in height his fellowes passe, / As much as lofty trees, low growing grasse"
(ll. 55-56), remarks:

> How often did you visite this faire tree,
> Which seeming joyfull in receiving thee,
> Would like a Palme tree spread his armes abroad,
> Desirous that you there should make abode. [ll. 59-62]

Seated not under but in the tree, Lady Margaret "might plainly see,"

> Hills, vales, and woods, as if on bended knee
> They had appeard, your honour to salute,
> Or to preferre some strange unlook'd for sute:
> All interlac'd with brookes and christall springs,
> A Prospect fit to please the eyes of Kings. [ll. 68-72]

It is striking here that Lanyer does not simply oppose the figure of woman-in-nature in contradistinction to Jonson's assimilation of man to natural order; rather, she posits a distinctly alternative mode of reading the logos. Reversing Jonson's metaphoric transfer of the qualities of permanence, stability, and rootedness from tree to man, Lanyer's pathetic fallacy transfers human attributes to the landscape, which appears "as if on bended knee." Where the trees at Penshurst knit the Sidneys to a land that willingly provides for their needs, the tree at Cookham affords a "Prospect" from which the landscape appears to want something of the ladies: "some strange unlook'd for sute." Finally, where Jonson's construction emphasizes the expanse of time—the Sidney line reaching backward to the immemorial time measured by the slow growth of trees and forward to the horizon of anticipation, the view from Lanyer's poem collapses time to a visual prospect that mediates an eternal moment beyond anticipation or retrospection:

> What was there then but gave you all content,
> While you the time in meditation spent,
> Of their Creators powre, which there you saw,
> In all his Creatures held a perfit Law;
> And in their beauties did you plaine descrie,
> His beauty, wisdome, grace, love, majestie.
> In these sweet woods how often did you walke,
> With Christ and his Apostles there to talke;
> Placing his holy Writ in some faire tree,
> To meditate what you therin did see:
> With *Moyses* you did mount his holy Hill,
> To know his pleasure, and performe his Will. [ll. 75-86]

With subtle irony this evocation of the logos read in rather than out of the trees (in contrast to Sir Philip's Oak, where "in the writhèd bark, are cut the names / Of many a Sylvan, taken with his flames" ["To Penshurst," ll. 15-16]) abridges the law of primogeniture that governs Jonson's figures and evokes instead a divine first genesis that envelopes and subsumes man's phallocentric law.[19] An alternative to this law appears when the "prospect" of a divine communion beyond time gives way to a vision of female descent and timely communion in the praise of Anne Clifford:

> And that sweet Lady sprung from *Cliffords* race,
> Of noble *Bedfords* blood, faire, streame of Grace;
> To honourable *Dorset* now espows'd,
> In whose faire breast true virtue then was hous'd:
> Oh what delight did my weake spirits find
> In those pure parts of her well framed mind. [ll. 93-98]

In sharp contrast to Jonson's stress on Sidney's dwelling, Lanyer, evoking the futility of feminine attachments, astutely connects the demands of virilocality—which disrupt female community and make impossible the ideological identification of land and lady that Jonson makes of land and lord—to the demands of hereditary degree:

> And yet it grieves me that I cannot be
> Neere unto her, whose virtues did agree
> With those faire ornaments of outward beauty,
> Which did enforce from all both love and dutie.
> Unconstant Fortune, thou art most too blame,
> Who casts us downe into so lowe a frame:
> Where our great friends we cannot dayly see,
> So great a difference is there in degree. [ll. 99-106][20]

In contrast to Jonson's slyly muted presentation of the movement of Barbara Gammage from her late father to her new husband, which served to replenish Penshurst with wealth and a continuing supply of Sidneys with which to ensure the historical perpetuity of her lord's dwelling, Lanyer represents the movement of Anne Clifford from Cookham to Dorset's Kentish estate, Knole, as the disruption of a community that, because it lacks a locus of perpetual descent, must be retained and preserved in the perpetual present of inward recollection: "Therefore sweet Memorie doe thou retaine / Those pleasures past, which will not turne againe" (ll. 117-18).

The force of the structural and thematic differences between the male and female country-house poems may be appreciated in relation to J.G.A. Pocock's argument locating the English discovery of *history* in common-law debates about the "ancient constitution."[21] These debates, which become crucial in the 1640s as arguments about the priority of king or parliament, begin in land use and inheritance cases—like the lengthy litigation in which Margaret tried to retain the Clifford estates for her daughter Anne.

The urgent litigation of the Cliffords, to which Lanyer alludes in the *Salve Deus Rex Judaeorum,* was unusual in its scope and duration, and in the difficulties and the opportunities of defiance it would later present to Anne, but the necessity of litigation to preserve rights of descent through the female line seems to have been a definite feature in the landscape of feminine experience referenced in Lanyer's work: witness the fact that the poet herself would, within a few years, enter her own bitter and protracted efforts to enforce on her brothers-in-law an agreement concerning the proceeds of her late husband's hay- and straw-weighing patent. Although this litigation was in Lanyer's future when she wrote "The Description of Cooke-ham," Simon Forman's records suggest that she already brought to the poem her own experience of her husband's misappropriation of funds she derived from the Lord Chamberlain, and, of course, the anomalous experience of having been cast off as Hunsdon's acknowledged mistress in consequence of producing a son who could not also be an heir.

Excluded by gender from the glorification (and mystification) of patrilinear descent that structures Jonson's poem, Lanyer develops the alternative notion of a lateral or synchronic community of women.[22] This community is at once the product and the audience of the *Salve Deus Rex Judaeorum.* In the title poem, Lanyer underlines the tension that exists between this community and the patriarchal and virilocal culture which is its host. Setting the temporal arrangements of patrilineal descent against an eternal arrangement that both precedes and succeeds it, she subsumes Margaret Russell's temporal passage to widowhood—a passage through which her husband's estates and titles passed to his brothers, leaving her with the dubious title dowager countess—in the comprehensive and eternal legacy of Christ:

> Still reckoning him, the Husband of they Soule,
> Which is most pretious in his glorious sight:
>> Because the Worlds delights shee doth denie
>> For him, who for her sake vouchsaf'd to die.
>
> And dying made her Dowager of all;
> Nay more, Co-heire of that eternall blisse
> That Angels lost, and We by *Adams* fall. ["Salve Deus," ll. 253-59]

Once again Jonson's use of trees to figure aristocratic continuity over time may be contrasted with Lanyer's use of the two trees, by tradition one and the same, to which she alludes in this astonishing passage. To figure the divine abridgment of time, Lanyer represents the tree of knowledge, as a gift of Eve misused by men, and the tree of the Passion, through which this ambiguous gift of "blisse" returns.

The "Description of Cooke-ham" is necessarily gendered in its dissent from the Jonsonian celebration of patrilineal dynastics. Take for example the very different rhetorical uses of trees in "To Penshurst," where they bind the generations to the soil and mark the passage of time, and of the tree in "Cooke-ham," which serves as a focal point for feminine companionship and endeavor during the stay of Margaret and Anne, but becomes *insignificant* in their absence, because, in the absence of the women who grasp its significance, its function as a meditative lever out of time lies dormant. As in winter:

> Each arbour, banke, each seate, each stately tree,
> Lookes bare and desolate now for want of thee;
> Turning greene tresses into frostie gray,
> While in cold griefe they wither all away. ["Cooke-ham," ll. 191-94]

The *Salve Deus Rex Judaeorum,* in general, and "To Cooke-ham," in particular, present a specific resistance to the recollection of the past as *history.* Attending to this model provides a better understanding of the ideological work performed by its canonical alternative and perhaps allows us to hear differently and for the first time the heretical voice that the canonical form suppresses. Ironically, this voice, when it is heard, has the potential precisely to restore *history,* by opening a dialogue in which can be traced that history's formulation in and as ideology. From the point of view of literary history, and that is the point of view I have been trying to establish, the canon cannot be simply opened through addition, nor paralleled by another canon, nor can it be discarded. Like patriarchy itself, the canon is a historical fact, which must be submitted to dialectical negation, a practice which reinscribes canonicity as a temporal performance by a historically situated work. This negation is, for the moment, the positive task of the literary historian.

NOTES

1. For a discussion of the different forms of extant presentation copies of the *Salve* for Prince Henry and Thomas Jones, Archbishop of London, see Woods, *Poems,* "Textual Introduction," pp. xlviii-xlix. See also, Leeds Barroll, this volume, chapter 2.

2. See, for example, Ann Baynes Coiro, "Writing in Service: Sexual Politics and Class Position in the Poetry of Aemilia Lanyer and Ben Jonson," *Criticism* 35 (1993): 357-76; Lorna Hutson, "Why the Lady's Eyes Are Nothing Like the Sun," in *Women, Texts and*

Histories, 1575-1760, ed. Clare Brant and Diane Purkiss (London and New York: Routledge, 1992), pp. 13-38; and Barbara K. Lewalski, *Writing Women in Jacobean England* (Cambridge: Harvard University Press, 1993), pp. 213-41.

3. John Donne, *An Anatomy of the World,* in *John Donne: The Anniversaries,* ed. with an intro. and commentary, Frank Manley (Baltimore: Johns Hopkins University Press, 1963), ll. 206-18.

4. Donne, of course, is reported to have told Ben Jonson that he described "the idea of a woman, and not as she was." "Conversations with William Drummond," in *Ben Jonson: The Complete Poems,* ed. George Parfitt (New Haven and London: Yale University Press, 1975), p. 462.

5. For a cogent discussion of Donne's "Idea of a Woman," see, Edward W. Tayler, *Donne's Idea of a Woman: Structure and Meaning in The Anniversaries* (New York: Columbia University Press, 1991). The argument about *The Anniversaries* here summarized is developed at length in my *The Story of All Things: Writing the Self in English Renaissance Narrative Poetry* (Durham, N.C.: Duke University Press, 1998), chapter 5.

6. The ghost may be discerned, for example, when Donne alludes to the matrilineal relationship in the passage just before the one quoted: "The euening was the beginning of the day, / And now the Springs and Sommers which we see, / Like sonnes of women after fifty bee" (202-4). So, the loss of patriarchal relation ("Prince, Subiect, Father, Sonne") coincides with the inherited exhaustion and weakness of superannuated mothers, whose spectral presence nevertheless persists.

7. Joseph Summers, *The Heirs of Donne and Jonson* (London: Chatto and Windus, 1970).

8. My comparison of Lanyer and Jonson will be confined to the two country-house poems. For broader discussion of the two poets see Susanne Woods, "Aemilia Lanyer and Ben Jonson: Patronage, Authority, and Gender," *Ben Jonson Journal* 1 (1994): 15-27, and Coiro, "Writing in Service."

9. On the coming together of metaphor and mimesis in seventeenth-century epideictic poetry, see Joel Fineman, *Shakespeare's Perjured Eye: The Invention of Poetic Subjectivity in the Sonnets* (Berkeley: University of California Press, 1985).

10. Luce Irigaray, *je, tu, nous: Toward a Culture of Difference,* trans. Alison Martin (New York: Routledge, 1993), p. 35.

11. For further discussion of the mediations accomplished by the microcosm/macrocosm analogy, see my *The Story of All Things,* chapter 5.

12. As Joseph Hall astutely notices in a commendatory poem, "The Harbinger to the Progres," included in the 1612 *Anniversaries:* "Still vpwards mount; and let thy makers praise / Honor thy Laura, and adorne thy laies" (ll. 35-36; quoted in Manley ed., pp. 89-90).

13. William Shakespeare, *The Tempest,* ed. Frank Kermode, The Arden Edition of the Works of William Shakespeare (London: Methuen, 1954), I,ii,55-59.

14. All citations of "To Penshurst" are from *Ben Jonson: The Complete Poems,* ed. Georges Parfitt (London: Penguin, 1988).

15. Both aspects of the Sidney family history are documented by Don E. Wayne, *Penshurst: The Semiotics of Place and the Poetics of History* (Madison: University of Wisconsin Press, 1984). See also Kari Boyd McBride, "Gender and Class in the Country House Poem," *SEL* 38 (1998): "[T]he Sidneys, social arrivistes who were granted Penshurst only under Henry VIII, needed both to link themselves to the history of the house and to dis-

count the unique valorization implicit in the estate. They needed both to pretend they had always lived there and pretend it didn't matter that they hadn't."

16. Theodor Adorno, *Negative Dialectics,* trans. E. B. Ashton (New York: Continuum, 1987): "The critique of every self-absolutizing particular is a critique of the shadow which absoluteness casts upon the critique; it is a critique of the fact that critique itself, contrary to its own tendency, must remain within the medium of the concept. It destroys the claim of identity by testing and honoring it; therefore, it can reach no farther than that claim. The claim is a magic circle that stamps critique with the appearance of absolute knowledge" (p. 406).

17. See Barbara K. Lewalski, "Re-writing Patriarchy and Patronage: Margaret Clifford, Anne Clifford, and Aemilia Lanyer," *The Yearbook of English Studies* 21 (1991): 104-6.

18. Ibid. See also Barbara K. Lewalski, "The Lady of the Country-House Poem," in *The Fashioning and Functioning of the British Country House,* ed. Gervase Jackson-Stops, Gordon J. Schochet, Lena Cowen Orlin, and Elisabeth Blair MacDougall, Studies in the History of Art, no. 25 (Hanover and London: National Gallery of Art, 1989), pp. 261-75.

19. For an intriguing development of the differing functions of the "Sidney oak" and the oak at Cookham in their respective poems, see Coiro, "Writing in Service": 374.

20. Cf. Lewalski, *Writing Women,* p. 225: "Alluding both to Anne's loss of her lands and to her own loss of contact with Anne, now Countess of Dorset, Lanyer contrasts male succession through aristocratic titles with a female succession grounded on virtue and holiness, drawing radical egalitarian conclusions."

21. J.G.A. Pocock, *The Ancient Constitution and the Feudal Law: A Study of English Historical Thought in the Seventeenth Century* (Cambridge: Cambridge University Press, 1957), pp. 30-55.

22. For a dissenting view on the presence of feminine commonality in "The Description of Cooke-ham," see Lisa Schnell, "'So Great a Difference Is There in Degree': Aemilia Lanyer and the Aims of Feminist Criticism," *MLQ* 57 (1996): 23-35.

8

(M)other Tongues:
Maternity and Subjectivity

Naomi J. Miller

In the present essay, I have chosen to focus upon Aemilia Lanyer's representations of women as at once mothers and others in the *Salve Deus Rex Judaeorum,* in order to consider the complex dynamic linking maternity and subjectivity in early modern England. Given that married women who remained childless were considered to be biological failures, bereft of the defining role of motherhood,[1] the early modern emphasis upon women's reproductive functions quite evidently had implications not only for women's bodies, but also for their selves. Furthermore, connections between maternity and subjectivity can be seen to have relevance not simply for women who claimed the actual title of mother, but also for all those women who found their speaking positions (pre)determined by masculine judgments of their (pro)creative capabilities. My use of the term "(m)other tongues," then, refers to the voices of women—both mothers and mothers' daughters—who struggle to give birth to speech in the face of cultural prescriptions which would restrict them to an otherness defined primarily in relation to constructions of masculinity.

While a number of valuable studies from historians of early modern women have focused on the physical activities of childbirth and nursing associated with the mother's body, recent literary studies have explored myths and fantasy associated with representations of mothers primarily in male-authored works, particularly when concerned with suffocating powers or malevolent witchcraft, with a predominant focus on the drama of the period.[2] In this essay, I am interested in actual as well as mythic mothers, and in the cultural undercurrents, encompassing both norms and aberrations, which can be glimpsed when some of the tensions between literary myths and social practices are scrutinized. While canonical male-authored texts have tended to shape much of our understanding of early modern maternity, it is equally important to explore the variety of ways in which some early modern women authors set out to justify their transgressive voices on the basis of perceived as well as actual maternal authority, while others utilized mother-daughter bonds to license a space for representing women's speech.

In a number of female-authored texts, for example, ranging from unpublished letters and diaries, mother's advice books and polemical pamphlets, to the published literary works of women writers such as Aemilia Lanyer, the voices of mothers and daughters serve at crucial moments to define the "otherness" of female subjectivity not simply in contrast to men, but also among women. Certainly the potentially multiple conflicts between the voices and concerns of mothers and mothers' daughters—even in a single author—may be seen to encompass competing and sometimes widely divergent conceptions of women as mothers. Furthermore, when mothers begin to claim positions for themselves not simply as reproductive bodies, but as generators of their own words and images, issues of authority and authorship collide. Such collisions indicate at once the presence of deep-seated ambivalence regarding the implications of maternal power, as well as the emergence of strategies of female self-assertion both inside and outside the patriarchal family. The intimate connections between mothers and female "others" in the social body as well as in the writings of female authors testify to the potential significance of female homosocial bonds in enabling women to speak as (m)others not simply to men, but also to each other.

Aemilia Lanyer was one of the first women in early modern England to claim a professional poetic voice for herself, by publishing her collection of poems, *Salve Deus Rex Judaeorum,* in 1611.[3] Although she is often compared to male contemporaries such as Ben Jonson (whose well-known country-house poem, "To Penshurst," was published five years after Lanyer's country-house poem, "A Description of Cooke-ham"), Lanyer, unlike Jonson, constructs her writings with specific reference to other women: her female friends, acquaintances, and patrons. According to the testimony of her poems, the patrons who influenced her own life most deeply were a mother-daughter pair, Margaret, Countess of Cumberland, and her daughter, Anne Clifford, with whom she spent some time at the country house estate of Cookham. Recognizing her social and artistic position on the margins of court and literary circles, Lanyer deliberately claims a legitimized space for her voice by identifying the countess and Anne Clifford as powerful figures whose example spurred her poetic inspiration. Yet given that Anne Clifford and her mother spent many years engaged publicly in the attempt to secure Clifford's inheritance of land, in direct defiance of King James's attempted arbitration as well as in conflict with Clifford's husband and uncle, their significance as models of inspiration for Lanyer extends beyond their upper-class social standing to their defiance of patriarchal directives and traditions. Lanyer's own lyric attacks on unwarranted masculine privilege, from the time of Christ to the present, thus acquire added depth through her identification with the resolute voices of other women.

In fact, Lanyer's volume of poetry is both dedicated and addressed only to women, a remarkable choice at a time when the few women who published tended either to apologize for their effrontery in presuming to use their voices, or to discount the value of their words. While the popular mothers' advice books of the period justified their female authorship with reference to the primary audience of their children, who might be expected to appreciate a mother's words, Lanyer's volume might seem to have little to do with actual motherhood on her own part. And yet Susanne Woods points to the birth of Lanyer's first and only daughter, Odillya, who died in 1599 at nine months old, as a significant event in her life, suggesting that her daughter's name might even derive from combining "ode" with her own name, "Aemilia," thus reflecting a possible intersection of her identities as mother and poet. Furthermore, Woods calls attention to Lanyer's involvement with the family of her only son, Henry, which extended to an active role in raising her grandchildren after Henry's death, again indicating Lanyer's ongoing engagement with maternal responsibilities even as she forged her voice as a writer.[4]

Previous critics, including Elaine Beilin and Susanne Woods, Barbara Lewalski and Ann Coiro, have already attended usefully to Lanyer's biographical background in more detail than the scope of the present essay will allow.[5] While not attempting to claim a transparent relation between the biographical details of Lanyer's life and her poetic strategies and concerns, I nevertheless cite the presence of details regarding Lanyer's maternity as useful insofar as they shed additional light upon her experience, complementing the often-quoted facts regarding her connections with men, which include her descent from an Italian musician named Baptist Bassano, her affair with Queen Elizabeth's Lord Chamberlain, Henry Cary, her marriage to Captain Alfonso Lanyer, and her recorded sessions with Simon Forman (which arguably indicate more about his preoccupations than hers).

The recent critical attention to Lanyer's life and works has served to identify a number of the challenges and resultant choices facing both early modern women authors in general and Lanyer in particular. Along these lines, Elaine Beilin and Barbara Lewalski have analyzed the complex subject matter of Lanyer's eloquent celebrations of good women, relating her protofeminist position to the varying stances adopted by other women writers in the period.[6] Attending more specifically to the implications of publication, Wendy Wall has examined the strategies which enabled Lanyer to create an authorial role as a woman in print. In reviewing Lanyer's reversal of the dynamics of the blazon and her simultaneous deconstruction of its relationship between subject and object, Wall, for example, maintains that by associating women's struggle against misogynist traditions with Christ's entrapment by male authorities, Lanyer feminizes Christ and renders women holy.[7] Adopting another tack, Ann Coiro and Kari McBride have explored some of the tensions and ambivalences associated with Lanyer's lower social status in relation to the aristocratic female patrons whom she praises. Coiro argues that Lanyer's service to the women whom she hopes to win as patrons is complicated by an underlying anger against both gender and class roles which reveals the strain of that service upon her writing.[8] With a slightly different emphasis, McBride suggests that Lanyer ultimately displaces the aristocratic female contemporaries whom she addresses in her poems, by shifting her praise to biblical models of heroism, so that her own voice finally is seen to govern all the constructions within her poetic world.[9]

My concern in the present essay is not so much with Lanyer's celebration of a community of good women as "other" than men, or with Lanyer's representation of Christ as the "erotic Other" on display before women as desiring subjects, as with Lanyer's strategic constructions of women as (m)others *to each other* as well as men. Instead of discounting maternity in favor of femininity as a driving force in Lanyer's poetry, I would like to reevaluate the polyvocal connections between (m)other tongues in her text. In addition, by attending to social and familial bonds and tensions among the women whom Lanyer chooses to represent, I hope to complement the already detailed analyses of social status offered by critics such as Coiro and McBride. I find that the *Salve Deus Rex Judaeorum* at once explores the implications of such socially acceptable roles for women as those of mother and daughter, and exposes the inadequacy of that cocoon of social acceptability for women who must learn to define themselves not simply according to patriarchal constructs, but both through and against one another as well.

In *This Sex Which Is Not One,* Luce Irigaray observes that female sexuality has always been conceptualized on the basis of masculine parameters, and proposes a redefinition of "woman" as *"neither one nor two."* In Irigaray's terms, "woman" can be viewed as "indefinitely other in herself."[10] More recently, in several essays concerned with maternity and "the maternal order," Irigaray points out that "the female body engenders with respect for difference,"[11] and she calls attention to distinctions marking men's and women's relations to "the mother tongue."[12] Early modern women were faced on all sides with "masculine parameters" and with definitions of female sexuality and subjectivity as "other" in mirror-image relation to masculine standards and assumptions, within male-authored texts ranging from handbooks for women to Petrarchan sonnet sequences. Yet in many instances their own discourse, in letters and diaries, poems and plays, works both to expose the difficulties of attempting to voice divided "selves," and to uncover the potential power of female subjectivity conceived in multiple rather than singular terms. Instead of accepting masculine definitions of "woman" simply as "other" in relation to "man"—however divided those definitions of man might be—some early modern women authors were able to explore versions of the "otherness in themselves" (to borrow Irigaray's language), through their use of (m)other tongues.

Notions of "difference" can be seen to structure both male-authored representations of subjectivity in which "woman" stands for "other," for the "object" of a masculine "subject," and the constructions of each female author/ other who seeks to define an/other subject for herself. Along these lines, Rosi Braidotti explores the significance for a female subject of "the presence of the other woman, of *the other as woman,*" and consequently posits "the recognition of the otherness of the other woman" as the first step towards redefining women's identities.[13] Although in some circumstances this notion of "the other woman" might reinscribe a victim's discourse, still in many cases the recognition of otherness in homosocial terms can prove to undermine binary constructions of female subjectivity as the inverse of a masculine model. Rather than deriving models of female subjectivity solely from the otherness of sexual *difference,* then, we can explore the otherness of sexual *identity* for a range of women, both written by and writing against the gendered preoccupations of their culture.

As feminist literary critics—including Virginia Woolf and Adrienne Rich, Margaret Homans and Mary Beth Rose—have observed, on the one hand the death or absence of the mother has been treated by male authors as a founding condition of the construction of language and culture, while on the other hand the remembered presence of the mother has provided women authors with an alternative experiential and sometimes even discursive framework for their own authorship.[14] Furthermore, although women writers have often been read as daughters in relation to actual or literary "fathers" (as seems implicitly to be the case in some of the readings which pair Aemilia Lanyer with the canonized Ben Jonson, despite the later publication date of his country-house poem), when the women authors are mothers as well as mothers' daughters themselves, their written relation to their own female forebears, contemporaries, and successors acquires new resonances of authority and subjectivity. The figure of the mother then can no longer be relegated to the position of the essential but silent other, the passive mirror in which the child searches for (his) reflection, the prediscursive body written by the language (and governed by the "Law") of the father. Thus Susan Suleiman, for example, analyzes the problematic dynamic distinguishing "the-mother-as-she-is-written" from "the-mother-as-she writes," and Daly and Reddy emphasize the importance of resisting the binary logic opposing motherhood and authorship, in order to assert "the value of both procreation and creation."[15] When both mother and daughter speak with the voice of the author, the otherness of female subjectivity can be defined not simply against men, but among women.

Feminists have exposed the tendency of traditional psychoanalytic criticism to construct the mother always as other to the infant subject, typically gendered male, without allowing the mother herself the status of a speaking subject or "author."[16] At the same time, even feminist psychoanalysts who privilege the role of the mother tend to focus on the effects of maternal behavior more consistently than on the implications of maternal subjectivity. In early modern England, tensions between tropes of sexual reproduction and discursive production mark the texts of female authors in particular, revealing the strains as well as the challenges facing women who attempted to establish positions for themselves as speaking subjects within the familial structures of the culture. Whereas many early modern treatises on the nature of women were written by men and addressed to men in their roles as fathers and husbands, the feminist pamphlets in defense of women, as well as the popular mothers' advice books, provided a counter-discourse which often attempted to reclaim publicly the mother's importance in the patriarchal structures of family and society.[17]

Aemilia Lanyer chooses to write not a prose polemical pamphlet or a mother's advice book, however, but a long sequence of lyric poems. Within the majority of Renaissance lyrics, moreoever, the figure of the woman is represented as consistently other than man, while the figure of the mother is noticeably absent. The Petrarchan objectification of the beloved which recurs in many Renaissance sonnet sequences, for example, figures forth a "dark lady" in more senses than one, a distant and unattainable object of desire—beautiful and virtuous on the one hand but proud and cruel on the other—whose very elusiveness serves both to perpetuate male desire and to allow masculine figurations of her identity not bound by the limitations of any professed subjectivity on her part. While the recipient of voluble praise from the sonneteer, the sonnet lady often remains voiceless herself within the poems, her description serving more to indicate the exclusive nature of the sonneteer's passion and ingenuity in love than to reveal her own character.[18] Such literary inscriptions of the sexual difference of the beloved are not far removed, in cultural terms, from the anxieties and prohibitions on women's behavior inscribed in the conduct manuals and sermons on marriage, linking the otherness of the apparently unattainable beloved and the seemingly attained wife and mother after all.

Although lyric forms in early modern England often seem configured primarily to lament or celebrate the progression of heterosexual love relations, whether in sonnet form or not, Eve Sedgwick's discussion of how male homosocial desire can be located within the context of triangular, heterosexual desire indicates the potential for a consideration of alternate triangulations of desire which encompass female homosocial relations as well.[19] While the religious translations of the Countess of Pembroke seemingly sublimate heterosexual relations to spiritual concerns, for example, the original poetry of Lanyer's *Salve* represents religious devotion not so much in "asexual" terms as specifically in relation to female homosocial bonds. In the revised triangulation of desire in Lanyer's sequence of poems, Christ provides a divine focal point around whom women can join with one another in a worship that excludes all earthly men, from Adam to Pilate. Rather than remaining fixed in the male gaze as objects of desire, then, the community of women in Lanyer's poem functions as worshipping subjects, as discussed by Wendy Wall. Furthermore, their passion for Christ exhibits the potential not only to liberate them from the sexualized foreclosure of female subjectivity implicit in earthly heterosexual relations, but also to connect them with one another in spiritual homosocial bonding.

Publishing the *Salve* under her own name in 1611, Lanyer dared to author a narrative of female experience in which gender makes not only a difference, but all the difference. With eleven dedications to women, a title poem on Christ's Passion and death which includes subsections for "Eves Apologie in defence of Women," "The Teares of the Daughters of Jerusalem," and "The Salutation and Sorrow of the Virgine Marie," and a final country-house poem, "The Description of Cooke-ham," which celebrates the Countess of Cumberland's estate as a female Eden, the *Salve* establishes not only the range but also the authority of women's voices in a religious context.

Furthermore, even as female-authored tracts such as the mothers' advice books work to inscribe maternal authority within a social framework, so Aemilia Lanyer situates her volume of religious poems within an explicit framework of matriarchal authority. The *Salve* opens with a dedicatory poem to Queen Anne, "most gratious Mother of succeeding Kings" ("To the Queenes most Excellent Majestie," l. 1), and concludes with a country-house poem which celebrates the feminine power encoded in the relationship between the Countess of Cumberland and her daughter, Anne Clifford. In light of this matriarchal emphasis, proceeding from maternal authority over men to mother-daughter bonding, it becomes possible to view the volume not simply as a "Book of Good Women" in the tradition of Christine de Pizan, but even more particularly as a lyric commemoration of the polyvocality of (m)other tongues.

The very first dedicatory poem opens with acclaim for the queen's sovereign maternity. Addressing Anne of Denmark as "Renowned Empresse, and great Britaines Queene" ("To the Queenes most Excellent Majestie," l. 1), Lanyer loses no time in indicating that the power of maternity defines Britain's future, given that all "succeeding Kings" must originate from this "most gratious Mother." Moving from motherhood to the mother tongue, Lanyer immediately proceeds to call attention to the gendered significance of her own authorship, in inviting the queen "to view that which is seldome seene, / A Womans writing of divinest things" ("To the Queenes most Excellent Majestie," ll. 3-4).

Even while praising the queen, the poem constantly calls attention to its own "lines" and "Text," and establishes its general audience as well, in professing to be written not simply in honor of the queen, but in honor of the queen's "sexe" (ll. 35, 74, 76). Furthermore, Lanyer reconfigures the mirroring potential of verse, traditionally claimed by male Renaissance poets to depict women as objects in mirrored opposition to their own subjectivity, in the service of constructing femininity in female-authored terms. Thus she urges Queen Anne to "Looke in this Mirrour of a worthy Mind, / Where some of your faire Virtues will appeare" (ll. 37-38), and subsequently urges "all vertuous Ladies in generall" to "Let this faire Queene not unattended bee, / When in my Glasse she daines her selfe to see" ("To all vertuous Ladies in generall," ll. 6-7). The "mirror" of Lanyer's verse can reflect the potential multiplicity of female subjectivity, when women "read" each other rather than suffering themselves to be written and read by men.

The poem concludes with the hope that Nature, the originator of "all Arts," might inspire Lanyer's tongue, "And in a Woman all defects excuse" ("To the Queenes most Excellent Majestie," ll. 151, 156). The trials of female authorship thus surface at the beginning of the volume, in the poet's apparent desire to seek "excuse" for her "defects" (discursive transgressions?) as a woman. Moreover, the poem's opening praise of Queen Anne as once and future queen-mother modulates by its conclusion into a celebration of Nature as "that goodly Creature, Mother of Perfection," who is able to grace the poet's "barren Muse" (ll. 152, 155). Here Lanyer constructs a direct link between the procreative powers of Nature and the creative potential of the Muse, whose temporary barrenness may be transformed into fertile speech as a result of explicitly female ties.

The second dedicatory poem, to Princess Elizabeth, looks backward to the "*Phoenix* of her age," Queen Elizabeth herself. Once again, the opening stanza constructs female sovereignty in unequivocally matriarchal terms, naming Elizabeth I "that deare Mother of our Common-weale," a title which the queen herself had claimed publicly on a number of occasions during her reign ("To the Lady *Elizabeths* Grace," ll. 4, 7). The poet's seemingly defensive position on the issue of female authorship appears when she asks the princess to accept "the first fruits of a womans wit," despite having seen "farre better Bookes" (ll. 13, 12). And yet already, by contrast to the "defects" cited in the preceding poem, the speaker refers to the written products of her wit as "fruits," suggesting that her previously "barren Muse" has acquired the capacity to (re)produce, as a result of the inspiring maternal triumvirate of Queen Anne, Queen Elizabeth, and Nature, that "Mother of perfection."

In the following dedicatory poem, "To all vertuous Ladies in generall," Lanyer specifically enjoins her fellow women to embrace each other in the service of Christ, in language which celebrates the female subject. Her exhortation to her listeners to adorn their temples "with faire *Daphnes* crowne / The never changing Laurel, alwaies greene" (ll. 22-23), manages to appropriate in the service of religious worship a myth of female escape from the prospect of male sexual abuse. The transformed body of Daphne, liberated from rape and represented by the laurel wreath, is reconceived not as a symbol of masculine accomplishment, but rather as a crown for the spiritual heroism of women. Through her "reincorporation" of the myth of Daphne, Lanyer succeeds implicitly in contrasting the "never changing" fidelity of women (l. 23) with the contrasting behavior of the other sex—all without yielding any space in her verse to the male perpetrator implicated by the myth. In urging self-definition in relation not to men, but rather to *the other as woman,* Lanyer signals the potential for women to affirm their own affinity for their mother tongue.

In a further extension of the community of women to whom her poem is addressed, Lanyer urges her audience to "let the Muses your companions be, / Those sacred sisters that on *Pallas* wait" ("To all vertuous Ladies," ll. 29-30). Once again, Lanyer revises the conventional male-authored literary subordination of feminine figures, representing the Muses here not as objects of inspiration for male poets, but rather as a sisterly community attendant upon the specifically female authority of Pallas Athena. Interestingly, Lanyer does not direct her advice regarding the sororal companionship of the Muses to fellow women writers in particular. Instead, her address suggests that "*all* vertuous Ladies in generall" (italics mine) may strive to claim voices for themselves, worthy of the assistance of the Muses.

In subsequent dedications, such as those addressed to "the Ladie *Susan,* Countesse Dowager of Kent, and Daughter to the Duchesse of Suffolke," to "the Ladie *Katherine* Countesse of Suffolke" and mother to "noble daughters," and to "the Ladie *Anne,* Countesse of Dorcet" and daughter to the Countess of Cumberland (the principal patron of the volume), Lanyer repeatedly constructs the mother-daughter bond as a prime source not only of female security, but also of women's subjectivity. In this maternal line of descent, it is not the Law of the Father, but rather (m)other tongues which authorize women's voices and identities. Indeed, Lanyer's construction of the mother's part can be linked to the "mother's advice book" proclamations of Dorothy Leigh, which locate both wisdom and authority in maternal affection, by contrast to the more characteristic paternal critiques, during this period, of excessive fondness on the part of mothers toward their children.[20]

Dorothy Leigh, for example, explains in the preface to her advice book that she could conceive of no better way of directing her children than "to write them the right way."[21] While acknowledging that writing is considered "a thing so unusual" among women, Leigh locates the origins of her authorship in her "motherly affection," and asserts the authority of her words over her offspring. Furthermore, Leigh links her status as a speaking subject with her written authorship, claiming that "my mind will continue long after me in writing."[22] At several moments in her text, Leigh even associates the power of her written words with the text of the Bible, which her children may learn to read "in their own mother tongue."[23] Under the direction of their mother's "many words," then, Leigh's children may gather food for the soul "out of the word as the children of Israel gathered manna in the wilderness."[24] While Leigh takes care never to substitute the authority of her text for that of the Bible, the conflation of her maternal words with the "mother tongue" of the Bible suggests her power as a mother to provide verbal and spiritual nourishment for her children.

Furthermore, although Leigh addresses her book to her three sons, Joan Larsen Klein has argued that the very fact that she caused her book to be published reveals a conscious intention to reach a wider audience which was clearly intended to be women, particularly given that she addresses women directly (speaking, as does Lanyer, throughout her book of "we women"), and counsels her sons concerning matters that involve women and children.[25] Leigh unabashedly presumes upon her authority as a mother in assuring her sons that "if you get wives that be godly and you love them, you shall not need to forsake me," whereas "if you have wives that you love not, I am sure I will forsake you."[26] Leigh thus uses her maternal authority to safeguard the marital positions not of her sons, but rather of her future daughters-in-law, suggesting her solidarity with her potential audience of other women. Significantly, Leigh's *The Mother's Blessing* went through sixteen editions between 1616 and 1640, indicating that her stance as a mother proved of interest to a sizeable portion of the populace.

Where the mothers' advice books in general address relations between mothers and children of both sexes, however, Aemilia Lanyer elects to focus in her patronage poems specifically on mother-daughter bonds, both literal and figurative. Lanyer hails Susan Bertie, Countess Dowager of Kent, for instance, as "the Mistris of my youth, / The noble guide of my ungovern'd dayes," whose example of "those gifts that grace the mind" was in turn inherited from her "most famous Mother . . . who liv'd unsubjected" ("To the Ladie *Susan*," ll. 1-2, 11, 23-24). The mirroring function of "other" women reappears in Lanyer's address to the Lady Susan, this time in reverse, when the poet observes that the Countess Dowager's "rare Perfections shew'd the Glasse / Wherein I saw each wrinckle of a fault" (ll. 7-8). Rather than always constructing her dedicatees as "other" to the mirror of her own voice, Lanyer professes to see herself more clearly, faults and all, in the mirror of another woman's figure. Reflection, then, can be mutually illuminating. Once again attributing the power of her voice to a maternal other, Lanyer asserts in conclusion that the Lady Susan's "Virtues do incite / My Pen, they are the ground I write upon" (ll. 45-46). At once model and mirror, figure and ground, this dedicatee serves to enable the poet's authorship, not through the traditional (male) venue of monetary patronage ("no former gaine hath made me write" [l. 43]), but rather through the past distinction of her example. In this, as in many other instances in the *Salve,* the gap between a past connection and a present separation of circumstances seems to suggest that while social ties themselves may not endure, the memory of homosocial bonds, often represented by Lanyer in maternal terms, may sustain a narrative connection across distance.

Lanyer contextualizes her earlier reference to other "farre better Bookes," from the dedicatory poem to the Princess Elizabeth, in her dream poem addressed to "the Countesse Dowager of *Pembroke,*" where she compares her own written "fruits" directly with the "many Books" written by Mary Sidney ("The Authors Dreame," ll. 194-95). Even as she finds the countess's books to be "more rare" than her own, she maintains the value of her own authorship, observing that "Yet there is hony in the meanest flowres: / Which is both wholesome, and delights the taste" (ll. 195-97). Far from comparing herself unfavorably with male authors, then, Lanyer situates herself in a literary community of women who compose both authors and audience, where even "the meanest flowers" can coexist harmoniously with "farre better Bookes" when produced by and for other women. The dream context of this particular poem further develops the sense of connection across distance, where it is precisely the distance itself which makes visible the "golden Chaine" binding the countess to the Graces (l. 7), and the poet to her female literary forebear.

From one dedicatory poem to the next, Lanyer returns repeatedly to women not simply as others, but also as (m)others, representing maternal bonds both inside and outside familial boundaries. The significance of maternity in these poems begins to emerge not in necessarily, or even primarily, literal or physical terms, given that mothers or mother-figures can nourish their daughters not simply with milk, but with the white ink (to paraphrase Helene Cixous) of a woman's writing voice. Indeed, Elizabeth, Countess of Lincoln, constructs a contemporary version of that connection when she offers to her daughter-in-law, Bridget, "the first worke of mine that ever came in Print; because your rare example, hath given an excellent approbation to the matter contained in this Booke; for you have passed By all excuses, and have ventured upon, and doe goe on with that loving act of a loving mother; in giving the sweete milke of your owne breasts, to your owne child."[27] In *The Countesse of Lincolnes Nurserie* (1622), mother's milk and maternal advice share the capability to provide nourishment.

Along similar lines, in the example of the dedicatory poem "To the Ladie *Katherine* Countesse of Suffolke," Lanyer urges the mother to "let your noble daughters likewise reade / This little Booke that I present to you," adding: "On heavenly food let them vouchsafe to feede" (ll. 49-51). In this case, Lanyer proffers her own words as food, "heavenly" because of her subject matter. From "defects" to "fruits" to "heavenly food," Lanyer's writing voice has been transformed both by and for the benefit of her fellow women. Justifying this transformation, she proclaims boldly that she has been "guided" to "frame this worke of grace, / Not of it selfe, but by celestiall powres" (ll. 7-8). Lanyer concludes that "Gods powre" has given her "powre to write," so that in turn she may offer "these lines" to figures of female authority such as the Lady Katherine (ll. 13, 19), establishing in the process the enabling powers of her mother tongue for other women.

In the dedicatory poem to Anne Clifford, Lanyer disparages men who have proven unworthy of their responsibilities as "Gods Stewards," and in their stead praises Anne "as Gods Steward," "In whom the seeds of virtue have bin sowne, / By your most worthy mother" ("To the Ladie *Anne,*" ll. 55, 57-59). Maternity and sovereignty are conjoined once more, this time in symbolic rather than literal terms, when Lanyer proclaims Anne Clifford to be "the Heire apparant of this Crowne," advising her that "by birth its yours, then keepe it as your owne," and concluding: "The right your Mother hath to it, is knowne / Best unto you, who reapt such fruit thereby" (ll. 65, 67, 69-80). The fruit of the mother is the empowerment of the daughter. Lanyer's emphasis on maternal rather than paternal legacies extends from the "seeds of virtue" to the more explicit education provided by the mother, who has "So well instructed" her daughter "to such faire designes," that no further "art" is necessary to complete her education (ll. 93-94).

Interestingly, the actual legacies bestowed by early modern women favored daughters over sons in no uncertain terms. Susan Amussen's examination of wills for both women and men in the early modern period indicates that more than twice as many women as men left land to one daughter, and of those with more than one child mentioned in their wills, women were more likely to leave land to one daughter than to one son. Furthermore, not only did early modern women give more authority and power in the form of land to their daughters than did their husbands, but they were also far more likely to choose daughters, or indeed other women, as executors of their wills than were men.[28] Maternal legacies, then, existed not only in fiction, but also in fact.

Lanyer's celebration of Anne Clifford's empowering inheritance from her mother is borne out by Clifford's own writing voice, in the pages of her diary. Clifford herself lived to see the birth of seventeen grandchildren and nineteen great-grandchildren, in the process laying claim to a role, as matriarch, far more enabling as well as challenging than the initial role of wife detailed in her description of her first marriage. At the same time, Clifford's narration of her close relation to her own mother illumines her identity as a daughter, and suggests that her assumption of matriarchal authority may have been empowered as much by daughterly loyalty as by her own maternal responsibilities. Given that both Anne Clifford and her mother, the Countess of Cumberland, strove over their lifetimes toward the goal of enabling landed inheritance to be passed down through the female line, while affirming lasting legacies of maternal affection toward their daughters, it seems appropriate that Lanyer's attention to their bond literally frames the significance of maternity in the *Salve*, from dedication to closing poem. Women's diaries, wills, mothers' advice books, and the examples of Lanyer's patronage poems, then, share in many instances one notable attribute in common: mothers and mother-figures who dare to assert their authority through their legacies, whether of land or of language, to their daughters and to other women.

At the same time, some of the homosocial ties between women within Lanyer's poem can be seen to involve a dynamic of competition as well as cooperation, whether between mothers and daughters or others. Instead of simply glossing over the potential for competition, Lanyer builds it into her constructions of female connection across distance, whether that distance is represented in relation to biographical, historical, or (as in "Cooke-ham") geographical contexts. Along biographical lines, for example, the mother/daughter relations in many of the dedicatory poems are represented in comparative terms which place the burden of achievement on the daughter who must live up to her mother's example. Thus in the dedicatory poem to Anne Clifford, discussed above, there is an admonitory as well as exhortative tone to the speaker's warning to the daughter regarding the maternal crown: "By birth its yours, then keepe it as your owne, / Defend it from all base indignitie" ("To the Ladie Anne," ll. 67-68). Given the constant threat of defamation of "poore Women" by "more faultie Men," cited in the opening poem ("To the Queenes most Excellent Majestie," ll. 77-78), daughters quite evidently must never take their inheritance of maternal sovereignty for granted. Only by moving beyond patriarchal constructs of maternal duties and capabilities, conceived in primarily physical terms, to potentially enabling maternal legacies of speech and female authority, can the daughters whom Lanyer addresses hope to pass on their own legacies free from the constraints of male defamation.

Lanyer's own relation to the historical women whom she addresses as patrons can be viewed as occasionally ambivalent as well as celebratory, competitive as well as cooperative. As McBride points out, while the patrons Lanyer addresses are important to her own program of self-fashioning, their superior social status can be read as a threat to her authority as well. Thus McBride argues that Lanyer's contemporaries are "both empowered and then displaced in her poems," most particularly in the central portion of the *Salve* by her "semi-mythical" catalogue of biblical heroines, whose virtue serves as model rather than threat.[29] This competitive relation can be identified in the dedicatory poems as well, where an undercurrent of comparative evaluation coexists with the most fulsome strains of praise.

In her dream poem to the Countess of Pembroke, for example, that "golden Chaine" binding the countess to the Graces connotes a certain constraint as well as closeness, which receives further illumination in the subsequent description of the "quarrell" between Art and Nature regarding "which should remaine as Sov'raigne of the place" ("The Authors Dreame," l. 82). Brought into close proximity, competition is inevitable between such powerful female figures, both represented elsewhere in the *Salve* in maternal terms. The judgment of the female Muses, however, identifies in the very balance of the competition the seeds for enduring cooperation:

> And therefore will'd they should for ever dwell,
> In perfit unity by this matchlesse Spring:
> Since 'twas impossible either should excell,
> Or her faire fellow in subjection bring.
>
> But here in equall sov'raigntie to live,
> Equall in state, equall in dignitie,
> That unto others they might comfort give,
> Rejoycing all with their sweet unitie. [ll. 89-96]

Lanyer's emphasis upon "equall sovraigntie" between these female figures, which benefits not only themselves but also those around them, contrasts starkly with her earlier articulation of the subjection imposed upon women by "more faultie men." Furthermore, in the context of her address to the Countess of Pembroke, her dream of equal sovereignty extends from the relation between the Graces and the countess to the connection between the countess and herself, whose "meanest flowres" can be adjudged equal in value to the countess's "many Books" (ll. 195-96).[30]

McBride suggests perceptively that the patronage poems themselves serve ultimately to limit all other women's power in relation to Lanyer, because her voice "is finally the only one authorized to speak within her poetic world."[31] On the other hand, it is necessary to remember that Lanyer's decision to claim the authority of her writing voice specifically in relation to a community of women, however ambivalently constructed, is in itself a daring move which insists upon the enabling potential of female homosocial bonds, not only in "gossips'" conversations focused upon marriage or childbirth, but also in feminine praise of divine authority. Thus in her dedicatory poem "To all vertuous Ladies in generall," as well as in her epistle "To the Vertuous Reader," Lanyer explicitly addresses her volume to "all virtuous Ladies and Gentlewomen of this kingdome; and in commendation of some particular persons of our own sexe" (p. 48). For Lanyer, writing openly as a woman on women to women, in a society marked by numerous strictures against female speech, the engendering of discourse for female author and female audience go hand in hand.

Following upon the dedicatory poems, Lanyer's prose epistle "To the Vertuous Reader" anticipates Constantia Munda's attack on Joseph Swetnam for denigrating his "mother's sex," when she berates "evill disposed men, who forgetting they were borne of women, nourished of women . . . doe like Vipers deface the wombes wherein they were bred" ("Vertuous Reader," p. 48). Instead of reducing women to the sum of their domestic responsibilities, however, Lanyer underscores the spiritual as well as physical significance of the mother's role by reminding her readers that "our Lord and Saviour Jesus Christ" was "begotten of a woman, borne of a woman, nourished of a woman, obedient to a woman" ("Vertuous Reader," p. 49). In emphasizing the necessity of a woman's presence for Christ's conception and birth, Lanyer links the divine power of God with the female authority of maternity. Even as the Countess of Lincoln calls attention to the importance of nursing mothers by describing the example "of the *blessed Virgin:* as her womb bare our *blessed Saviour,* so her papps gave him sucke,"[32] so Lanyer refers to the nourishment which Christ could receive only from a woman. Appropriately enough, the breast milk of the Virgin Mary served in the Christian tradition as a maternal image of infinitely divisible grace. Lanyer thus chooses to celebrate Christ's origins not as the "son of man" so much as the son of God and a woman, while men are portrayed in the body of her poem as sinners and crucifiers of Christ. Finally, Lanyer's bold assertion that Christ was not simply "borne of a woman," but also "obedient to a woman"—submitting not simply to the divine direction of God but also to the maternal direction of Mary—expands the significance of women's maternal authority from purely physical to spiritual terms.

In the title poem and main body of the *Salve Deus Rex Judaeorum,* Lanyer expands her representation of (m)other tongues from her female contemporaries in early modern England to the women of biblical times. In the process, she at once constructs a range of powerful women's voices and works to re-form the historical and social contexts within which they may be heard. While Renaissance authorship commonly is represented as a male-centered concept in the writings of men, with the Muse often configured as a mistress or female beloved answerable to the entreaties or commands of men's voices, Lanyer addresses her Muse as mother to her "Infant Verse," thus calling upon the potentially empowering force of maternity to liberate her voice even as did the contemporary authors of the mothers' advice books ("Salve Deus," ll. 273, 279). Although on the one hand she deplores the "poore barren Braine" of her Muse, recalling the reference to her "barren Muse" in the opening poem of the volume ("To the Queenes most Excellent Majestie," l. 155), in the same breath she celebrates the confidence which impels the "forward Mind" of her Muse beyond any "restrain[t]" ("Salve Deus," ll. 276, 278).

Furthermore, even as Lanyer details the dangers confronting her fledgling verse, she transforms the trials of her authorship into evidence of the power of God, for whom "the Weaker thou doest seeme to be / In Sexe, or Sence, the more his Glory shines" ("Salve Deus," ll. 289-90). Openly acknowledging the vulnerabilities of "Sexe, or Sence" associated with her female authorship in a patriarchal culture, Lanyer identifies her words with "the Widowes Myte," whose "little All" proved "more worth than golden mynes" in the eyes of the Lord ("Salve Deus," ll. 293-94). Just as the treasures of wealthy men seem as nothing by comparison to the widow's "All" in the eyes of Christ, so the abundant production of male authors in Lanyer's culture may yet, Lanyer warns, be found insignificant by comparison to her "plainest Words" ("Salve Deus," l. 311). Empowered by the illumination of the Holy Spirit, who may "vouchsafe to guide my Hand and Quill" ("Salve Deus," l. 324), Lanyer thus embarks upon her extended narration of the Passion of Christ with a fertile rather than barren tongue after all.

Lanyer's long poem on Christ's Passion develops her focus on (m)other tongues with a detailed defense of "our Mother *Eve*," whom Lanyer represents as accepting the fruit from the serpent "for knowledge sake," while Adam was simply beguiled by its "faire" appearance ("Salve Deus," ll. 763, 797-8). Again expanding her consideration of maternal authority beyond merely physical limits, Lanyer asserts that men, despite their boasting, owe not only their bodily lives ("You came not in the world without our paine") but also their very knowledge to the first mother: "Yet Men will boast of Knowledge, which [Adam] tooke / From *Eves* faire hand, as from a learned Booke" ("Salve Deus," ll. 827, 807-8). This particular identification, with its implication that what comes from the hand of a woman—indeed, the Mother of us all—may not only be compared to a learned book, but may even prove a source for learned books, further underscores the latent power in Lanyer's own "Hand and Quill" ("Salve Deus," l. 324), an image at once female and authorial.

Subsequently, Lanyer moves from Eve, the mother of all mankind, to Mary, "Deere Mother of our Lord," whose maternity elevates her to the position of "most beauteous Queene of Woman-kind" ("Salve Deus," ll. 1031, 1039). Lanyer's select choice of titles for Mary succeeds in conjoining maternity and sovereignty in the context of divinity. Writing in Protestant terms, Lanyer finds a way to appropriate the Virgin Mary as a model, not as Catholic intercessor but as exemplary mother. Developing the significance of Mary's position beyond the condensed reference in her prose epistle "To the Vertuous Reader," discussed above, Lanyer represents Mary's maternal sorrow at Christ's death as the greatest grief ever suffered—"None ever lost so great a losse as shee" ("Salve

Deus," l. 1015)—thus claiming the primacy of a mother's bond with her child even as she underscores the exclusive nature of Christ's relation to his mother. Lanyer's emphasis, indeed, rests with Christ's identity as the son of Mary and the son of God, in that order, as when she recounts Gabriel's message that "this blessed Infant borne of thee, / Thy Sonne, The onely Sonne of God should be" ("Salve Deus," ll. 1071-72). Born of a woman and of God, Christ emerges as a figure whose divinity quite evidently comes from his heavenly Father, but whose humanity is directly attributable not to "more faultie Men," but rather to the woman who is his mother.

While Dorothy Leigh asserts that "man can claim no part in" Mary's redemption of all women from the shame of the Fall,[33] Aemilia Lanyer goes even further in maintaining both the originary innocence of Eve and the power of Mary's position, not only as unsubordinate to any man but as bearing the authority of a mother over Christ as well. Maternal subjectivity within the poem on Christ's Passion, then, manifests itself both within Eve as seeker and source of knowledge and within Mary as queen-mother of "Heavens bright King" ("Salve Deus," l. 1088). From Athena, the mythic embodiment of all human wisdom, to Eve, the mother of all humankind, to Mary, the mother of "our Lord," Lanyer identifies women throughout "Salve Deus" as the shaping forces within society at large, and calls upon her female listeners—both mothers and others—to recognize that power within one another as well. In observing that Mary is "from all men free," being "farre from desire of any man" ("Salve Deus," ll. 1077-78), Lanyer deconstructs the conventional dynamic of heterosexual desire in the service of liberating women to bond with one another in religious devotion instead. The effect of her repeated invocations of a community of female believers who can understand and identify with Christ's sufferings far more effectively than the men who were responsible for Christ's death is to dignify female homosocial bonds in a religious context which excludes deleterious bonds with men.

Bringing to fruition the feminized authorial promise of her "little All" as the title poem attains its climax, Lanyer recontextualizes the conventional Petrarchan blazon for her praise of Christ as more "true a Lover" than any man ("Salve Deus," l. 672). She conjoins Petrarchism with the biblical imagery of the Song of Songs in an address to the Countess of Cumberland:

> His lips like skarlet threeds, yet much more sweet
> Than is the sweetest hony dropping dew,
> Or hony combes, where all the Bees doe meete;
> Yea, he is constant, and his words are true,
> His cheekes are beds of spices, flowers sweet;
> His lips like Lillies, dropping downe pure mirrhe,
> Whose love, before all worlds we doe preferre. ["Salve Deus," ll. 1314-20]

By choosing the same technique of praise used by male poets to construct their mistresses, Lanyer turns the blazon convention inside out, empowering women (in this case herself and her female mentor, the Countess of Cumberland) as active contemplators rather than passive objects of contemplation.[34] Unlike the figure of the Petrarchan mistress, Christ is also present to his admirers rather than absent, and thus the poet's expression of loving praise can be predicated on achieved rather than forever deferred union, between two subjects (bride and groom) rather than subject and object.

On the one hand, Lanyer's sexualization of Christ as bridegroom can be compared to Donne's rhetoric in the *Holy Sonnets,* yet Donne could never this comfortably conjoin the erotic and the spiritual—his address to Christ as bridegroom focuses upon the troublingly sexualized role of Christ's spouse, "Who is most true and pleasing to Thee then / When she is embraced and open to most men" (*Holy Sonnet* XVIII).[35] For a woman poet, the spousal relation to Christ is naturally gendered female, and thus Lanyer can speak with a woman's authority in identifying Christ as the only "constant" and "true" lover and beloved in one, "whose love, before all worlds we doe preferre." Furthermore, embedded within her praise of the countess is a catalogue of famous biblical heroines who triumphed over "more faultie Men," and whose past examples serve literally to mirror the present range of the countess's virtues, allowing Lanyer to shape her alternative narrative of the countess in relation to stories of other women.

Lanyer reconfigures the conventional container/contained metaphor, so favored by male Petrarchan poets, in feminine terms, describing the Countess of Cumberland not as a hollowed-out receptacle for masculine desire, but rather as a vessel for her own love for God:

> You loving God, live in your selfe confind
> From unpure Love . . .
> Your perfit sight could never be so blind,
> To entertaine the old or yong desires
>   Of idle Lovers. ["Salve Deus," ll. 1547-51]

Recalling the ever-green laurel of the dedicatory poem "To all vertuous Ladies," with its connotations of female spiritual heroism and fidelity, Lanyer locates the sovereign authority of the countess in a parallel comparison here between "the constant Lawrell, always greene," and the countess's position "still . . . as Queene" ("Salve Deus," ll. 1553, 1557). Finally, it is as women unencumbered by the constraints of masculine desire that she and the Countess of Cumberland ("we") choose to "preferre" Christ, and thus it is as a woman poet that Lanyer is able to adapt Petrarchan discourse to a feminine mode of praise.[36]

At the close of her long poem on Christ's Passion, Lanyer hails the Countess Dowager of Cumberland as her earthly inspiration for authorship, thus positioning the countess, as Elaine Beilin points out, in the role of "a mother-figure, giving birth and nurture to poetry itself."[37] Lanyer further characterizes the countess as "the Articke Starre that guides my hand" (l. 1839), indicating the enabling power of this homosocial bond for her writing voice. Guided by both divine and female authority and illumined by female affection, Lanyer's "Hand and Quill" produce a text which confronts the patriarchal exclusions of her society, and works to deconstruct the social codes which authorized the marginalization of the female subject, both as mother and other.

In the final poem in the volume, "The Description of Cooke-ham," Lanyer represents a female Eden in which the mother-daughter bond between the Countess of Cumberland and Anne Clifford simultaneously embraces Lanyer and empowers her to assert her own subjectivity in discursive terms.[38] Unmarked by the presence of men, Cookham emerges at once as a locus of female authority and a vision of female community. Lanyer celebrates the countess's powers of both governance and learning, addressing her as "(great Lady) Mistris of that Place," and praising her use of the estate as a site for the transmission of knowledge from mother to daughter, "Where many a learned Booke was read and skand" ("Cooke-ham," ll. 11, 161). By contrast to Eve's expulsion from Eden after her initial pursuit of knowledge, the already learned Countess of Cumberland departs Cookham of her own accord upon the occasion of her daughter's marriage, to carry out her ongoing responsibilities as a figure of female authority, including the litigation in support of her daughter's inheritance. Even as the poet is left to lament the loss of female companionship, Lanyer transforms that separation into grounds for establishing a voice of her own, thus articulating her authorial connection with the maternal inspiration of the countess.

Lanyer's erasure of the masculine presence from her revised triangulation of desire in "Cooke-ham" allows her to position herself as the "other woman" in a potentially cooperative rather than conventionally competitive triangular bond, which includes the Countess of Cumberland and her daughter, Anne Clifford. No longer situating her narrative in a primarily religious context, Lanyer crafts an explicitly female version of the heterosexual family state and estate subsequently idealized by such male poets as Jonson in "To Penshurst." While Jonson's poem extols the virtues of a procreative fertility which encompasses fish and fruits, "better cheeses" and "ripe daughters," all cultivated apparently for the purposes of consumption, and culminating in the lord's "fruitful" lady and his children ("Penshurst," ll. 53-54, 90), Lanyer's poem celebrates a bond among three women, made visible at once in the beauty of the landscape and in the "first fruits of a womans wit" ("To the Lady *Elizabeths* Grace," l. 13). Cookham emerges as an estate and a family state informed by female subjectivity, as well as by maternal authority conceived in intellectual and spiritual rather than merely physical terms.

As Lewalski has observed in relation to the biblical subject matter of the *Salve* as a whole, Cookham takes on the appearance of a ravaged Eden after the expulsion of the first human couple, with the difference that in Lanyer's poem it is not a heterosexual couple but rather a female trio who depart.[39] The female poet's sojourn in this Edenic community, governed by a "Mistris" rather than a master, enables her participation in that sisterhood of "the Muses" to which she first refers in her dedicatory poem to "all vertuous Ladies," so that here, at the end of the *Salve,* she is able to claim "powre" for her verse from those very same Muses ("Cooke-ham," ll. 3-4, 11). Although the dispersal of the Countess of Cumberland, her daughter, and Aemilia Lanyer from Cookham results, according to the poet, in the disintegration of the beauty of the estate, it also produces the music of the poem itself, whose lament offers a visible and lasting memorial to bonds among women which otherwise can prove neither visible nor lasting within a society dominated by masculine subjects. Significantly, then, in Lanyer's alternative narrative of an ideal family state, the effects of both presence and absence, separation and ultimate connection, are defined solely in relation to female subjects.

Near the end of "Cooke-ham," Lanyer describes a kiss bestowed by the Countess of Cumberland upon "that stately Tree" which figures so importantly in the poem as a haven for feminine communion with "Christ and his Apostles" (ll. 53, 82). Immediately thereafter, Lanyer claims that she herself takes back the kiss from the tree, "Scorning a sencelesse creature should possesse / So rare a favour, so great happinesse" (ll. 167-68). This kiss-once-removed epitomizes the displaced homosocial bonding which informs the *Salve* from the very beginning, where Lanyer concludes her opening dedicatory poem with an expression of desire that her written words might be "kisse[d]" and "imbrace[d]" by the hands of her queen ("To the Queenes most Excellent Majestie," ll. 142, 144). Through her verbal recounting in "Cooke-ham" of the mute kiss of the "Mistris," at once deflected and redirected through the body of the tree, the female poet finally constructs a position for herself as author outside the realm of potential threat or competition. Within the elegiac frame not only of "Cooke-ham," but also of the *Salve* as a whole, pervaded by an awareness of women's precarious yet precious bonds, connection occurs most clearly across social and physical distance.

Lanyer offers her poem not as a static monument to the estate, which itself is "deface[d]" by dust and desolation once the women depart (l. 202), but rather as a living testament to the female ties which have informed a single location with such communicative vitality. Asserting that "When I am dead thy name in this may live" (l. 206), the poet secures life for the memory of Cookham through her (mother) tongue. In closing, Lanyer declares that the virtues of the countess lodge within her, "Tying my heart to her by those rich chaines" (l. 210). Just as the "golden Chaine" binding the Countess of Pembroke to the Graces established not simply closeness, but also connection across distance ("Authors Dreame," l. 7), so the "rich chaines" here at the end of "Cooke-ham" represent ties that bind, even in separation. At the same time, the implicit connotations of constraint as well as intimacy attest to the tensions which mark homosocial bonding between women, in the face of the divisive constructions attached to women's relations by "more faultie Men."[40]

Ultimately, Lanyer's poetry speaks with the tongues of women, if not angels, in order to enable her female audience to glimpse for themselves the potential to see other women no longer as in a (male-constructed) glass darkly, but face to face. A mirror itself is necessarily a separating as well as connecting medium—one cannot dwell within a mirror, only gaze into it. The narratives of female bonding in the *Salve* reflect back to the viewer a framed version of the audience whom Lanyer has identified as a community of "vertuous Ladies." Significantly, when Lanyer uses the metaphor of a mirror in her verse, as discussed earlier, she does not stop at providing a reflection of the multiplicity of female subjectivity, but instead urges women to proceed further to read each other rather than suffering themselves to be read and written by men. When the mirroring surface of Lanyer's poetry literally "defaces" itself at the conclusion of "To Cooke-ham," deconstructing its own interpretive frame, all that is left is the continuing communication of (m)other tongues outside the frame of the poem.

Taken as a whole, Lanyer's volume of poems shares with the female-authored social treatises a concern with attending to the relation between mothers and other women, while extending even further the grounds for discourse outlined by the mothers' advice books, in which maternal authority is represented as an important context for female subjectivity. Lanyer's "last farewell" (l. 205) to the departed female inhabitants of the estate, as well as to the readers of *Salve Deus Rex Judaeorum*, can be viewed, finally, as a proactive strategy predicated on "both the sameness and the otherness of the other woman, her symbolic function as agent of change,"[41] which allows her to appropriate the absence of those "other" women as the authorization for the emergent subjectivity of her own valedictory voice. At the same time, as the author of a poem in which the names of other women, from Eve to Mary, Queen Anne to the Countess of Cumberland, "may live," Lanyer positions herself as both mother and other to her addressees, even as she locates the inspiration for her lyric authority in the very polyvocality of (m)other tongues which forms her subject matter. Writing on the margins of a male-dominated lyric tradition and yet celebrating women's presence at the center of her spiritual narrative, Lanyer works to reframe the (pro)creative authority of women, both mothers and others, during the early modern period. By representing simultaneously competitive and cooperative bonds among women across biographical and historical, generational and geographical lines, *Salve Deus Rex Judaeorum* offers the possibility for a range of female readers to claim (m)other tongues of their own.

Notes

1. Retha Warnicke, presentation in workshop on Maternal Bodies in Early Modern Society, for symposium on Attending to Early Modern Women: Crossing Boundaries, University of Maryland, College Park, November 1997.

2. Examples of historical studies include Renate Blumenfeld-Kosinski, *Not of Woman Born: Representations of Caesarean Birth in Medieval and Renaissance Culture* (Ithaca: Cornell Univ. Press, 1990); Valerie Fildes, ed., *Women as Mothers in Pre-Industrial England* (London: Routledge, 1990); and Merry Weisner, *Women and Gender in Early Modern Europe* (Cambridge: Cambridge Univ. Press, 1993). Literary studies include Janet Adelman, *Suffocating Mothers: Fantasies of Maternal Origins in Shakespeare's Plays* (London: Routledge, 1992); Gail Kern Paster, *The Body Embarrassed: Drama and the Disciplines of Shame in Early Modern England* (Ithaca: Cornell Univ. Press, 1993); and Deborah Willis, *Malevolent Nurture: Witch-Hunting and Maternal Power in Early Modern England* (Ithaca: Cornell Univ. Press, 1995).

3. For a detailed account of Lanyer's life and literary background, see Susanne Woods' introduction to *The Poems of Aemilia Lanyer: Salve Deus Rex Judaeorum*, pp. xv-xlii.

4. Woods, *Poems*, Introduction, pp. xxv, xxix-xxx.

5. See Elaine Beilin, "The Feminization of Praise: Aemilia Lanyer," chapter 7 in *Redeeming Eve: Women Writers of the English Renaissance* (Princeton: Princeton Univ. Press, 1987), pp. 177-207; Woods, introd. to *Poems*; Barbara K. Lewalski, "Imagining Female Community: Aemilia Lanyer's Poems," chapter 8 in *Writing Women in Jacobean England* (Cambridge: Harvard Univ. Press, 1993), esp. pp. 213-42; and Ann Baynes Coiro, "Writing in Service: Sexual Politics and Class Position in the Poetry of Aemilia Lanyer and Ben Jonson," *Criticism* 35, no. 3 (1993): 357-76.

6. Beilin, *Redeeming Eve*, pp. 177-207; Lewalski, *Writing Women*, pp. 213-42.

7. Wendy Wall, "The Body of Christ: Aemilia Lanyer's Passion," in *The Imprint of Gender: Authorship and Publication in the English Renaissance* (Ithaca: Cornell Univ. Press, 1993), pp. 319-30, and "Our Bodies/Our Texts?: Renaissance Women and the Trials of Authorship," in *Anxious Power: Reading, Writing, and Ambivalence in Narrative by Women*, ed. Carol Singley and Susan Sweeney (New York: SUNY Press, 1993), pp. 51-72, esp. pp. 64-67.

8. See Coiro, "Writing in Service," esp. pp. 365-69.

9. Kari Boyd McBride, "Engendering Authority in Aemilia Lanyer's *Salve Deus Rex Judaeorum*," Ph.D. dissertation, Univ. of Arizona, 1994; see esp. "Redeeming the Daughters of Eve," pp. 27-74, and "Self-Fashioning in the Patronage Poem," pp. 75-107.

10. Luce Irigaray, "This Sex Which Is Not One," in *This Sex Which Is Not One,* trans. Catherine Porter (Ithaca: Cornell Univ. Press, 1985), pp. 26, 28-29.

11. Irigaray, "The Culture of Difference," in *je, tu, nous: Toward a Culture of Difference,* trans. Alison Martin (London: Routledge, 1993), p. 45.

12. Irigaray, "On the Maternal Order," in *je, tu, nous,* pp. 42-43.

13. Rosi Braidotti, "The Politics of Ontological Difference," in *Between Feminism and Psychoanalysis,* ed. Teresa Brennan (London: Routledge, 1989), p. 98.

14. See Virginia Woolf, *A Room of One's Own* (New York: Harcourt Brace Jovanovich, 1957), pp. 51, 61, 86-87, 117-18; Adrienne Rich, "Motherhood and Daughterhood," in *Of Woman Born: Motherhood as Experience and Institution* (New York: W.W. Norton, 1986), pp. 218-55; Margaret Homans, "Representation, Reproduction, and Women's Place in Language," chapter 1 in *Bearing the Word: Language and Female Experience in Nineteenth-Century Women's Writing* (Chicago: Univ. of Chicago Press, 1986), pp. 1-39; Mary Beth Rose, "Where Are the Mothers in Shakespeare? Options for Gender Representation in the English Renaissance," *Shakespeare Quarterly* 42 (fall 1991): 291-314.

15. Susan Rubin Suleiman, "Writing and Motherhood," in *The (M)other Tongue: Essays in Feminist Psychoanalytic Interpretation,* ed. Shirley Nelson Garner, Claire Kahane, and Madelon Sprengnether (Ithaca: Cornell Univ. Press, 1985), pp. 352-77, focuses the latter portion of her discussion on the positions of Kristeva, Cixous, and Irigaray; see also Brenda O. Daly and Maureen Reddy, "Narrating Mothers," in *Narrating Mothers: Theorizing Maternal Subjectivities,* ed. Daly and Reddy (Knoxville: Univ. of Tennessee Press, 1991), p. 5.

16. See Garner, Kahane, and Sprengnether, eds., introd. to *The (M)other Tongue,* pp. 24-25; Valerie Traub, "Prince Hal's Falstaff: Positioning Psychoanalysis and the Female Reproductive Body," *Shakespeare Quarterly* 40 (winter 1989): 456-58, 470.

17. See for example, Jane Anger, *Her Protection for Women* (1589), reprinted in *Half Humankind: Contexts and Texts of the Controversy about Women in England, 1540-1640,* ed. Katherine Usher Henderson and Barbara F. McManus (Urbana: Univ. of Illinois Press, 1985), pp. 172-86; Joseph Swetnam, *The Arraignment of Lewd, idle, froward, and unconstant women* (1615), in *Half Humankind,* pp. 189-216; Esther Sowernam, *Esther hath hanged Haman* (1617), in *Half Humankind,* pp. 217-243; Constantia Munda, *The Worming of a mad Dog* (1617), in *Half Humankind,* pp. 244-63; *Hic Mulier: or, The Man-Woman and Haec-Vir: or, the Womanish-Man* (1620), in *Half Humankind,* pp. 264-89; Dorothy Leigh, *The Mother's Blessing* (1618), reprinted in *Daughters, Wives, and Widows: Writings by Men about Women and Marriage in England, 1500-1640,* ed. Joan Larsen Klein (Urbana: Univ. of Illinois Press, 1992), pp. 287-302; and Elizabeth Joceline, *The Mothers Legacie to her Unborne Childe* (1622), reprinted in *A Lasting Relationship: Parents and Children over Three Centuries,* by Linda Pollock (London: Fourth Estate, 1987).

18. For much more detailed analysis of these tensions, see Nancy J. Vickers' well-known essay, "Diana Described: Scattered Woman and Scattered Rhyme," *Critical Inquiry* 8 (1981): 265-79, and Louis Montrose, "The Elizabethan Subject and the Spenserian Text," in *Literary Theory/Renaissance Texts,* ed. Patricia Parker and David Quint (Baltimore: Johns Hopkins Univ. Press, 1986), pp. 303-40.

19. Eve Kosofsky Sedgwick, *Between Men: English Literature and Male Homosocial Desire* (New York: Columbia University Press, 1985), pp. 16, 18.

20. See, for example, the letters of Robert Sidney (father to another early modern woman author, Mary Wroth), who warns his wife, Barbara, regarding her otherwise exemplary

care of their children: "I doe not feare anything so much as your to much fondnes" (20 April 1596, De L'Isle MS, U1475, Z53/49, Kent County Archives Office, Maidstone, England).

21. Dorothy Leigh, *The Mother's Blessing* (London, 1618), prefatory material reprinted in Linda Pollock, *A Lasting Relationship*, p. 174.

22. Leigh, *The Mother's Blessing*, reprinted in Klein, ed., *Daughters, Wives and Widows*, pp. 293-94. All subsequent citations of *The Mother's Blessing* will be taken from Klein's edition.

23. Ibid., p. 295.

24. Ibid., p. 292.

25. See Klein, ed., *Daughters, Wives and Widows*, p. 289.

26. Leigh, *Mother's Blessing*, p. 301-2.

27. Elizabeth, Countess of Lincoln, *The Countesse of Lincolnes Nurserie* (Oxford, 1622), transcription reproduced by the Brown University Women Writers Project (1993), 3. All subsequent citations of this work will be taken from the WWP transcription.

28. See Susan Dwyer Amussen, *An Ordered Society: Gender and Class in Early Modern England* (Oxford: Basil Blackwell, 1988), pp. 34, 38, 91-94.

29. McBride, "Engendering Authority," pp. 27-28, 41.

30. For more detailed analysis of the countess's praise and subsequent "displacement" in Lanyer's poem, see McBride, "Engendering Authority," pp. 127-30.

31. McBride, "Engendering Authority," p. 75. See also Coiro, "Writing in Service," pp. 365-66, on Lanyer's deployment of "sophisticated irony about her position in a world where she is dependent on a matriarchy she often resents."

32. *The Countess of Lincolnes Nurserie*, p. 7.

33. Leigh, *Mother's Blessing*, pp. 297-98.

34. McBride, "Engendering Authority," pp. 56-57, points out that by assigning to Christ the traits and characteristics of both lovers of the Canticles, Lanyer merges male and female, implicitly calling into question the way Petrarchan conventions of love poetry appropriated the descriptive materials of the Old Testament poems.

35. John Donne, *Poetical Works*, ed. Sir Herbert Grierson (Oxford: Oxford Univ. Press, 1977), p. 301.

36. For a perceptive analysis of Lanyer's vision of female community, see Lewalski, *Writing Women in Jacobean England*, pp. 213-42.

37. Beilin, *Redeeming Eve*, p. 201.

38. Lewalski, "Of God and Good Women: The Poems of Aemilia Lanyer," in *Silent But for the Word: Tudor Women as Patrons, Translators, and Writers of Religious Works*, ed. Margaret P. Hannay (Kent, Oh.: Kent State Univ. Press, 1985), pp. 203-24, analyzes Lanyer's "Edenic myth" in careful detail; see also Lewalski, *Writing Women in Jacobean England*, pp. 213-42.

39. Lewalski, "Of God and Good Women," p. 224.

40. See Coiro, "Writing in Service," p. 373, for an analysis of "the chains of obligation, need, love, and sometimes humiliation which bind [Lanyer] to the women above her."

41. See Braidotti, "The Politics of Ontological Difference," pp. 93-95, 100-2.

9

The Love of Other Women: Rich Chains and Sweet Kisses

Michael Morgan Holmes

Aemilia Lanyer devoted herself to God and other women. Her visions of past and future utopian worlds consistently place love of the deity in and through a community of women at the center of social order. Scholars such as Barbara Lewalski, Lynette McGrath, and Janel Mueller have discussed the importance of female association to Lanyer's *Salve Deus Rex Judaeorum.*[1] In general, though, they have not considered the relations between Lanyer's poetry and other seventeenth-century contemplations of love among women or the ways in which homoeroticism figures in her routings of desire. Like John Donne, Lanyer paints the loneliness brought about by the disappearance of affective bonds between women; like Andrew Marvell, she questions the exclusive virtue of cross-gender couplings and depicts the destruction of women's collective happiness at the hands of men.[2] Lanyer goes beyond both poets, however, in detailing the intersections between survival and homoerotic desire. Indeed, prior to the writings of Katherine Philips in the 1650s and '60s, Lanyer's poems include some of the imagistically richest and most sympathetic early modern conceptualizations of women's homoerotic companionship.[3] In this essay I hope to show that, by drawing together religious devotion, artistry, friendship, and homoeroticism in ways that Marvell glimpsed but did not fully explore, Lanyer presents homoerotic affection as a way for women to overcome the ravages of men's proprietary claims and as a positive ground for real-world communities.

In his discussion of early modern England, Keith Wrightson observes that community "is not a thing; it is a quality in social relations which is, in some respects, occasional and temporary, and which needs periodic stimulation and reaffirmation if it is to survive the centrifugal forces of the inevitable tensions which arise in local society."[4] While Wrightson is primarily interested in large-scale threats to ideological norms of "order, harmony and subordination," his understanding of community in terms of social relations and tensions also allows room to consider the actions of particular human agents. Texts by early modern women are ripe for analysis along such lines. As Lewalski observes, much of seventeenth-century women's writings in England possessed an "oppositional nature"; that is, texts by Lanyer, Rachel Speght, Arabella Stuart, and others testify to "inner resistance and a critical consciousness" capable not only of criticizing the status quo but also of effecting social transformations.[5]

These women's insights and reformulations coincide with the various expressions of dissidence that Alan Sinfield finds characteristic of many other early modern texts. Rather than looking for subversion, Sinfield advocates reading for perspectives that contest received norms by producing "alternative, potentially rival, subjectivities."[6] As I hope to show, in the *Salve* Lanyer does more than merely oppose misogynist norms that picture women as weak and corrupt, and that mandate their subordination to men. Lanyer's dissidence also involves—to a significant degree through homoerotic desire—the prioritization of women's spiritual experience and affective women's communities. Piety, a defense of women, and a celebration of their mutual passion and devotion provocatively commingle in the *Salve*. By facilitating a recognition of the contingency of cultural norms, and by suggesting new ways of viewing such phenomena as class divisions, gender identity, and erotic desire, Lanyer's poems not only make a claim for one person's liberty of conscience but also encourage alternative configurations of human relations.[7]

My study begins with a brief outline of the cultural and significatory space that same-gender desire occupied for early modern women. Following that, I discuss Donne's "Sapho to Philaenis" and Marvell's "Upon Appleton House," the poems in which these writers most cogently explore the limitations of heteronormative convention in contrast to the beauty of women's loving communities. The major part of this essay then investigates Lanyer's representation of love between women as a stabilizing (albeit threatened) phenomenon and basis for psychosocial well-being.

Alan Bray, Bruce Smith, and others have pointed out that the literary and historical records of "lesbian" desire in early modern England differ from those that depict love between men because, in Smith's words, "women lived in such a different relationship to the ideology and the power structure of Elizabethan and Jacobean society."[8] As a result of women's marginality and the absence of a reified "lesbian" identity in the modern sense, theorists and historians have noted that an archeology of same-gender female desire confronts deep obscurity. At the outset of her study of "woman-identified women" in medieval Christianity, E. Ann Matter confesses that hers is "by no means a statistically valid study; it is rather a venture into a realm of silence and contradiction."[9] Valerie Traub reaches a similar conclusion regarding the early modern research terrain.

In an essay discussing "lesbian" desire on the English stage, Traub "extrapolates a cultural *presence* from a discursive *silence*."[10] To a great extent because of prejudice and women's sociocultural marginality, readers of Lanyer's work ought not to expect any blazing declarations of embodied homoeroticism such as one finds in, for example, Richard Barnfield's *The Affectionate Shepheard* or Christopher Marlowe's *Edward II*. Although I am in general agreement with Matter and Traub on the subject of "lesbian" invisibility, I believe that Lanyer's writings in particular afford an opportunity to see that, despite the difficulties faced by women who wished to write about their desires for other women, there were certain avenues of expression that could be turned to engaging use.[11] In addition, Lanyer dedicated her work to some of the nation's most powerful individuals who also, as it happened, were women. This political positioning of the text suggests that, if we accept that same-gender desire plays a vital role in the *Salve Deus,* female homoeroticism could play a role nearer to the center of official ideology than is commonly thought.[12]

Turning our attention to Donne and Marvell should help to broaden understanding of early modern homoeroticism and clarify the originality of Lanyer's volume. In "Sapho to Philaenis," Donne poignantly represents Sapho's laments and pleas to her former partner, Philaenis, to give up the love of men and resume their relationship. Claude Summers notes that Donne "pointedly fails to represent lesbianism as sodomitical"; in fact, as Janel Mueller observes, Donne's Sapho is "an ardent, active lesbian in full experiential and emotional career." Although one might quarrel with Mueller's unqualified application of a modern identity category, she aptly characterizes the poem's figuration of same-gender desire as powerfully moving.[13]

Sapho's strongest argument as to why Philaenis ought to abandon cross-gender eroticism rests on a defense of mutuality and likeness.[14] Begging Philaenis to "restore / Me to mee; thee, my *halfe,* my *all,* my *more*" (ll. 57-58), Sapho draws on the Aristophanic myth (expressed in Plato's *Symposium*) that sexual history involves the attempt of divinely-bifurcated same-gender and cross-gender couples to reunite. Sapho can claim that "touching my selfe, all seemes done to thee" (l. 52), because of the notion that, at one time, they *were* the same person. Being with "some soft boy," contrariwise, "wants yet / A mutuall feeling which should sweeten it" (ll. 31-32). A boy's body is subject to daily changes such as the "thorny hairy" growth of a beard (l. 33); Philaenis's body, though, is an immutable "naturall *Paradise*" (l. 35). The georgic "tillage of a harsh rough man" (l. 38) contrasts starkly with Philaenis's golden-age pastoral gentleness and fecundity.

In his country-house poem "Upon Appleton House," Andrew Marvell explored the possibility of a same-gender *locus amoenus* in a community of religious women. Ostensibly a celebration of the Fairfax family's martial heroism,

Marvell's text also investigates the weak points of the aristocratic chivalric ethos, queries the violent means men use to bring about social order, and suggests that humans possess options other than conjugal domesticity. Neither the natural landscape nor human lives, Marvell reminds his readers, need to be cultivated in only one way. As John Dixon Hunt remarks, "the poet who invented the Mower was also ready to scoff at absurd 'enforcements' either of garden art or of personality." Although Hunt's comment refers specifically to Marvell's support of his patron Thomas "Black Tom" Fairfax's controversial decision to follow his conscience rather than public pressure when he retired as leader of the Commonwealth army, "Upon Appleton House" also demonstrates the absurdity and even cruelty of "enforcement" in defining and persecuting non-normative erotic desires and behaviors.[15]

Marvell's problematization of various cultural orthodoxies is most cogently detailed in the narration of events leading up to the 1518 marriage of Isabel Thwaites and William Fairfax of Steeton (Thomas Fairfax's ancestors) and in the forest sequence in which the poem's narrator abandons human society for erotic, dreamlike solitude. Stanzas XI through XXXV detail Isabel's seduction by the nuns who inhabited the Cistercian convent of Nun Appleton before it became a noble estate, and William's capture of his fiancée from them. On the surface, Marvell's representation of the nuns' homoerotic enticements might appear to be merely anti-Catholic propaganda. The "*Suttle Nunns*" (l. 94) weave a spell of words, telling Isabel that she "'resembles much'" the Virgin Mary (l. 132) and that they "'see the *Angels* in a Crown / On you the Lillies show'ring down'" (ll. 141-42). In addition, the sisters promise Isabella command over a world of mystical sensuality in which she and a "'fresh and Virgin Bride'" chosen from among the nuns will repose "'All Night embracing Arm in Arm, / Like Chrystal pure with Cotton warm'" (ll. 186, 191-92). These promises are never given a chance to materialize, however, because Fairfax seizes Isabel by using brute force against the sisters, whose only weapons are "*Wooden Saints,*" an "old *Holy-Water Brush,*" and the crying of their voices (ll. 249-72).

On its own, Marvell's description of Fairfax's victory over a group of defenseless women would be enough to render the narrative bathetic. However, as the lines I have quoted indicate, the nuns' offers *are* genuinely seductive and call into question Fairfax's strict delineation between true and false desires and ways of life. Most significantly, the nuns' promises mirror the narrator's own alluring religio-erotic fantasies articulated later in the poem:

Bind me ye *Woodbines* in your twines,
Curle me about ye gadding *Vines*,
And Oh so close your Circles lace,
That I may never leave this Place:

But, lest your Fetters prove too weak,
Ere I your Silken Bondage break,
Do you, O *Brambles,* chain me too,
And courteous *Briars* nail me through. [ll. 609-16]

The appeal of these reveries (and others like them in Marvell's "The Garden") contests Michael Wilding's claim that both the enticements of the nunnery and the wood are "rejected counter-retirements" because "neither of them represents the virtues of the family." "Upon Appleton House," however, is far from dogmatic on the superiority of "family" life. As Lee Erickson notes, Marvell's narrator is not "willing to be tied down to fretful parenthood"; he wants to be "safe from the demands love and marriage would bring."[16] In this poem, Marvell gives us the opportunity to see that the narrator's and the nuns' sensual pleasures are not by nature perverse, but only become defined as such when contrasted with other social imperatives, especially marriage, procreation, and inheritance.

Anna K. Nardo perceptively comments that the Appleton convent threatens patriarchal culture because it is an all-female place of work and cooperation set apart from men.[17] Textual evidence abounds for this reading of the Appleton community's independence. The nuns, for instance, label men "'wild Creatures'" (l. 102); one nun asks: "'What need is here of Man? unless / These as sweet Sins we should confess'" (ll. 183-84). At Nun Appleton, a man's only use would be as an erotic stimulator; however, as the lines quoted above show, women are abundantly able to satisfy for each other cravings of both the body and the soul. Such estimations of men's low value and women's ability to find solace and pleasure in each other's company runs dangerously counter to patriarchal gender ideology as embodied in the Fairfax dynasty. This is especially so when one takes into account the fact that the whole episode involving Isabel's seduction and capture is, as Erickson notes, a dynastic "founder's myth" intended to justify "the great Race," a fact that the poem's early readers would have easily recognized.[18] Marvell's rendering of William's supposed heroism supplied the Fairfaxes with a cover for the fact that their family fortune depended on the dowry Isabel brought with her. Indeed, as Erickson remarks, from that Fairfax union on, "there was little romance or grandeur in their shrewd marriages and careful acquisition of property for the historian or the poet to celebrate." Adding to the historiographic pressures, Marvell also had to find a way to smooth over the ungentle fact that, at the time of the poem's composition, his pupil's parents were busy angling to secure their only child a wealthy, titled husband by investing upon her several large estates.[19]

"Upon Appleton House" looks in two directions in its treatment of same-gender female attraction. On the one hand, homoeroticism is depicted as a sensual state of grace; on the other, it is a manifestation of iniquity. The Appleton nuns are only sodomitical, however, from the point of view of marital and pro-creational imperatives that have been imposed figuratively and even literally[20] over the top of other desires and types of relationships that have little or nothing to do with conventional marriage, family life, genealogical continuity, and in-heritance. Fairfaxian heteronormativity constituted an ideological as well as material palimpsest; ingeniously, Marvell ensures that just as the dwelling's foun-dational architecture can still be glimpsed, so too can its original erotic fabric.

Women's relationships with one another are not oppositional per se, Traub remarks, but only become so when they are thought to threaten reproduction within a heterosexual marriage.[21] Religious sisterhoods were ideal targets for such attacks because, as Lyndal Roper observes, nuns used "the language of kinship" but formed relationships that were "at odds with civic kin structures"; in addition, nuns inverted normal gender roles by owning and administering property.[22] In "Upon Appleton House," William Fairfax responds to the gen-der and sexuality trouble that conventual life potentially sparks when he gives a sodomitical reading of the nuns as women who "'alter all,'" and the convent as a place where "'vice infects the very Wall'" (ll. 215-216). This evaluation, though, is voiced as Fairfax's opinion, one that is not necessarily shared by readers or (even less likely) the narrator. In addition, Marvell qualifies Fairfax's sentiments through a manipulation of readerly sympathy brought about by first presenting the convent's seductive allure and then echoing it in the narrator's own green world fantasies. Perhaps the most dissident aspect of Marvell's poem is the fact that Isabel is never given a voice. As Fairfax comes crashing in, "truly bright and holy *Thwaites* / . . . weeping at the *Altar* waites" (ll. 263-64); wait-ing for what, or whom, is never clear.

Although I agree with Holstun that Isabel is treated as aristocratic "prop-erty," I dissent from his view that Marvell depicts lesbianism solely as "a crea-ture of the papist past and possibly no more than a self-interested economic fiction."[23] Holstun accords finality to Fairfaxian domestic ideology without considering the ways in which the narrator's own sceptical regard for norma-tive values influences a reader's interpretation not only of depicted events but also of the production and naturalization of certain desires. While not subver-sive of Fairfaxian hegemony, Marvell's treatment of the Appleton nuns and their conquest by a violent man illuminates the contingent nature of erotic moral standards, thereby enabling readers to re-evaluate non-heteronormative (especially same-gender female) desire as capable of sustaining and enriching personal and community life.

John Dixon Hunt contends that Marvell's poems on a nymph's loss (in "The Nymph complaining for the death of her Faun") and a storm-tossed lover (in

"The unfortunate Lover") pivot on "the recognition of a love larger than the earth allows."[24] This suggestive remark applies as well, I believe, to numerous other of Marvell's texts. Nevertheless, the recognition of "larger" loves rarely engenders extended, affirmative illustrations of how such desires might circulate in actual society. With regard to female-female eroticism and companionship, however, Aemilia Lanyer gave voice to dreams of solidarity among women that are very much oriented towards present and future aspirations. The differences between their two approaches likely tells us much about historical transformations occurring in evaluations of same-gender female desire and interaction. Writing forty years after Lanyer, Marvell incorporates into his poem what Traub has identified in other texts as an increasing ideological "perversion" of "lesbian" desire as the seventeenth-century wore on. Earlier in the century, though, Lanyer was less constrained by cultural prejudice. Her *Salve Deus Rex Judaeorum* prompts a modification of Traub's suggestion that early modern English writers (all Traub's examples are male) imagined eroticism between women as either tribadic or as a past, temporary stage on the way to normative heterosexual closure.[25] Differing from Marvell (although somewhat like Donne), Lanyer resists the tendency to depict female-female love in entirely elegiac terms. In actuality, we know that Lanyer was unsuccessful in her bid to establish an enduring community of supportive female friends.[26] Her *Salve* presents proof, though, that it was possible at least to *imagine* a loving, companionate future.

Similar to "Upon Appleton House," Lanyer's book primarily uses spiritual erotics to address love between women. Classical references gave Lanyer literate and culturally-sanctioned expressions of same-gender desire in the same way that male writers could draw on figures such as Ganymede and Apollo to express love for other men. Meanwhile, Christianity's antiworldly orientation empowered her to think beyond immediate social and ideological restrictions to a condition such as Saint Paul describes when he says that all sex and gender identities vanish in Christ (Gal. 3:28). Lanyer's decision to employ a discourse of Christian devotion makes sense, given that religion was one of the few areas of artistic endeavor open to early modern women.[27] In addition, as Barbara Lewalski observes, because of their emphasis on adhering to the dictates of conscience and on believers' personal relationships with God, Christianity and, in particular, Protestantism, possessed a significant potential for dissidence and destabilization.[28] When, for instance, Lanyer eulogizes Margaret Russell, Countess of Cumberland, as one whose "chaste breast, guarded with strength of mind, / Hates the imbracements of unchaste desires" (SD, ll. 1545-46), she puts forward her friend as a model of conscientious liberty derived from having lead a godly life.

Lanyer's vision of an ideal female community is, like that of Donne's Sapho, predicated on mutuality. Describing the actions of a powerful woman of the past, Lanyer reasons that

> Spirits affect where they doe sympathize,
> Wisdom desires Wisdome to embrace,
> Virtue covets her like, and doth devize
> How she her friends may entertaine with grace;
> Beauty sometime is pleas'd to feed her eyes,
> With viewing Beautie in anothers face:
>> Both good and bad in this point doe agree,
>> That each desireth with his like to be. [SD, ll. 1593-1600]

This stanza ostensibly reveals the Queen of Sheba's motivation to journey to King Solomon's court. On a more symbolic level, Lanyer's Neoplatonic lexicon of sympathy and embraces contributes to the *Salve's* investment in spiritual and physical sameness as the grounds of affection between women. In Sheba's case, the desire to be with another person who was "like" herself prompted her to transgress the conventional "nicenesse and respect Of woman-kind" (ll. 1603-4). As a ground for the rejection of normative gender behavior, the aspiration to coexist with a wise, virtuous, and beautiful friend serves as a paradigm for Lanyer's independent-minded quest for emotional and spiritual fulfillment, not in the usual environment of female-male domesticity, but in the potentially homoerotic company of other women.

Lanyer's "extraordinary, and unprecedented"[29] step in turning from men to a community of women within which to find inspiration and to fashion an identity is based on a belief that, with men, mutuality and peace are impossible. She takes it as a given that many men want to strip women of their liberty:

> greatest perills do attend the faire,
> When men do seeke, attempt, plot and devise,
> How they may overthrow the chastest Dame,
> Whose Beautie is the White whereat they aime. [SD, ll. 205-8]

Lanyer suggests that by objectifying women, courtly and Petrarchan social and literary conventions can naturalize violent attitudes and behaviors (e.g., SD, ll. 825-32); she, meanwhile, is interested in likeness and equality. In a sense, she concurs with attitudes such as Michel de Montaigne expressed when he claimed that women and men could never be true friends because genuine amity can only be achieved between equals. As Lanyer and Montaigne knew it, the world showed few signs of developing parity between the sexes. Lanyer, though, clearly rejects the frequently coordinate position that women can never attain true friendship (even with each other) because they possess "a rash and wavering fire, waving and divers," when what is needed is "a generall and universall heat."[30] Friendship among women is not only possible, according to Lanyer, but also spiritually laudable.

In an oddly underexamined dedicatory poem, "The Authors Dreame to the Ladie *Marie,* the Countesse Dowager of *Pembrooke,*" Lanyer draws on an ancient cultural reservoir to depict the enchantment of women's community. The text's length (it runs fourteen lines longer than "The Description of Cooke-ham"), structural centrality, and unique verse-form all suggest its thematic weight. It is therefore no surprise that the poem opens by expressing an aspiration germane to much of Lanyer's work:[31]

> Me thought I pass'd through th' *Edalyan* Groves,
> And askt the Graces, if they could direct
> Me to a Lady whom *Minerva* chose,
> To live with her in height of all respect. [ll. 1-4]

Dissidently reinscribing the practice of fathers who assign husbands to their daughters with no regard for emotional complementarity, Lanyer turns to Minerva as a better guardian who will find for her a more agreeable, female partner.[31] In "The Authors Dreame," the lady of whom Lanyer dreams (i.e., Mary Sidney, Countess of Pembroke) is "ti'd" to her "thoughts" by "a golden Chaine" of Platonic love. This beautiful woman is encircled by "nine faire Virgins . . . / With Harps and Vialls in their lilly hands" (ll. 9-10), a scenographic indication of the poet's ideal sisterhood and an evocation of the lyrical charm Lanyer associates with homoerotic desire.

The events that transpire in "The Authors Dreame" bear out this promise of tranquillity and affection among women. First to arrive on the scene is the goddess Bellona, "A manly mayd which was both faire and tall," in whom, Lanyer writes, "I tooke no small delight" (ll. 35, 40). Soon after, "faire *Dictina* by the breake of Day, / With all her Damsels round about her came" (ll. 45-46). Dictina, otherwise known in the poem as Diana, Phoebe, and Cynthia, is invited by the lady to take her hand and "keepe with them continually" (ll. 60), aspirations that Lanyer herself claims to share. Aurora, goddess of the morning, arrives next and competes successfully with the male god Phoebus for the assembled ladies' "favours" (ll. 61-76). With women now fully in charge of all aspects of the pastoral landscape, Lanyer recounts that the group moved on to a secret bower with which even Minerva was not familiar, "a place full of all rare delights . . . where Art and Nature striv'd / Which should remaine as Sov'raigne of the place" (ll. 79, 81-82). Enacting principles of peace and equality, the ladies quickly decide that "T'would be offensive either to displace" and therefore decree that Art and Nature "should for ever dwell, / In perfit unity" together (ll. 88-90). The "sweet unitie" (l. 96) of these two female creative forces, recognized and affirmed by women, parallels an observation Sapho makes to Philaenis in Donne's poem, that "betweene us all sweetnesse may be had; / All, all that *Nature* yields, or *Art* can adde" (ll. 43-44). In each case, the perfect,

holistic balance between Art and Nature represents a vision of creative mutual-
ity that ideally characterizes women's relationships with each other. In confir-
mation of this harmony, the sweet sounds of women singing Mary Sidney's
"holy hymnes" (l. 116) aurally affirm women's sublime emotional and spiritual
unions.

Diana—the goddess invited to hold the lady's hand—is the classical figure
who most clearly represents Lanyer's dual investment in solidarity and eroti-
cism between women. In the poem dedicated "To all vertuous Ladies in
generall," Lanyer counsels women to "In wise *Minerva's* paths be alwaies seene; /
Or with bright *Cynthia,* thogh faire *Venus* frown" (ll. 25-26). As McGrath
observes, here and elsewhere in Lanyer's book Venus is the goddess of "hetero-
sexual passion," whereas Cynthia is "specifically woman-identified."[32] While
McGrath is probably not using the term "woman-identified" in the eroticized
sense Matter does, the contrast she draws between Dianic and Venerian pas-
sion interfaces with my own exploration of desire in Lanyer's book. "Of all the
goddesses," Christine Downing notes, Diana "is most evidently one who mod-
els women's love of women" in spiritual and potentially sexual terms. Traub's
commentary on "lesbian" desire in Thomas Heywood's play *The Golden Age*
(which appeared the same year as Lanyer's *Salve*) demonstrates how "the loving
ministrations of Diana's circle" could signify homoerotic desire, especially when
contrasted with harsh acts of "heterosexual" coercion of women by men. Pri-
marily surveying art historical sources, Patricia Simons likewise finds abun-
dant evidence that visual images of Diana and her nymphs could, in certain
circumstances, offer early modern women images of same-gender erotic and
spiritual bonds.[33]

As in other dream visions, such as Chaucer's *Booke of the Duchesse,* the
dreamer must awake and bring to the quotidian world the lessons that have
been learned. In fact, Lanyer claims that the *Salve Deus Rex Judaeorum* is itself
the fruit of a divinely inspired dream (see "To the doubtfull Reader"). Yet this
book is not the product of a Miltonic holy spirit writing through a human
amanuensis. Instead, Lanyer takes full responsibility for her dream vision, claim-
ing that "what *my* heart desir'd, *mine* eies had seene" ("Authors Dreame," l.
174; emphasis added). By taking seriously the enthusiasm and longing that
Lanyer conveys in her depictions of female community in a mythic garden of
beautiful women, we are better positioned to comprehend the ways in which
her panegyrics to Christ and Cookeham also embody homoerotic desire as a
key to spiritual and social happiness. Referring to her entire book, Lanyer in-
forms the Countess of Pembroke that "I here present my mirrour to [your]
view, . . . My Glasse beeing steele, declares them to be true" (ll. 210-12). If
"Salve Deus" and "Cooke-ham" mirror the poet's mind, then they also reflect
the desires that inform the visions in "The Authors Dreame."[34]

Difference of social rank is the only stumbling block that Lanyer sees to friendship with other women. She does away with class hierarchies, though, by arguing that they are merely products of "Unconstant Fortune" (CH, l. 103) and are therefore not essential.[35] Love and solidarity between women is possible if one circumvents Fortune by routing desire through Christ. Whereas Montaigne felt compelled to attempt to sublimate the erotic component of his friendship with Étienne de la Boétie so as to avoid accusations of "Greek licence," by turning to love of Christ Lanyer engaged a discourse that came with its own protective warrant.[36] Because affection for Christ was expected of all true believers, if challenged Lanyer could always fall back on traditional piety as an excuse for her utterances. In her own view, however, love of Christ and other women go hand in hand.

As "The Authors Dreame" leads one to suspect, the close-knit society of women that Lanyer imagines in "Salve Deus Rex Judaeorum" and "The Description of Cooke-ham" is foreshadowed throughout the series of nine dedicatory poems. In a number of these prefatory texts, Lanyer evokes a world of quasi-Catholic devotion not unlike that which Marvell imagined in "Upon Appleton House." Commenting on early modern women's opportunities, Retha Warnicke observes that "young Protestant females had their future mapped out for them in the words, 'women to be married,' for no other occupation was possible for them, the last of the English nunneries having been dissolved at the accession of Elizabeth." Warnicke's positing of convents as valuable refuges for women whose desires ran counter to domestic ideology highlights a possible cultural source in Roman Catholic devotion and, especially, religious sisterhood for the kind of resistance Lanyer (and later Marvell) imagined.[37]

Drawing on imagery associated with convent life, Lanyer depicts herself as piously meditating in what sounds like a nun's chamber when she writes to Queen Anne (a devout Roman Catholic) that she has been living "clos'd up in Sorrowes Cell, / Since great *Elizaes* favour blest my youth" (ll. 109-10). The queen herself functions as a kind of mother superior for the poet's devotions; Lanyer describes her as a woman who has always taken a "holy habite" in order "Still to remaine *the same,* and still her owne" (ll. 117-18). With a quite likely allusion to Protestant pressures on the queen to convert, Lanyer finds in Anne's Catholicism evidence of women's ability to remain true to themselves. Similarly, although Lucy, Countess of Bedford, was a Protestant, Lanyer deploys Catholic (rather Crashavian) imagery when she imagines "the closet of your lovely breast" and "that Cabbine where your selfe doth rest" ("To the Ladie *Lucie*," ll. 2, 4). Striking a similar note, in "To the Ladie *Susan*" Lanyer asks her dedicatee to "grace" Christ's Passion, which she describes as "this holy feast" (l. 6), a term reminiscent of Roman devotion. Most Catholic of all, the numerous references to Christ as spouse scattered throughout Lanyer's texts suggest nuns' marriages to Jesus (see SD, ll. 77, 253, 1170), while her baroque descriptions of Christ's both horrifying and beauteous body have a long history in Catholic poetry and visual art (see "To the Ladie *Lucie*," ll. 13-14; SD, ll. 1332-36, 1724-40). I do not want to imply that Lanyer was a closet Roman Catholic; my point is that Catholic devotional and symbolic traditions, especially as they relate to conventual companionship, likely appealed to her because they offered a way to imagine happiness with other women devoted to Christ. Given what we have seen of Marvell's later practice, it was certainly possible in the seventeenth century to paint a literary picture of the intersection between homoerotic desire, Catholicism, and *clausura*.[38]

Love of Christ is at the heart of Christian sisterhood as well as Lanyer's vision of female companionship. Even a cursory examination of her meditations on Christ confirms McGrath's point that the "erotic implications of these images are not accidental" (p. 342). In keeping with conventional language drawn from allegorical readings of the *Song of Songs,* Christ is repeatedly termed "Bridegroome" and "Husband" to the various women Lanyer addresses (e.g., "Ladie *Anne*" l. 15; "To all vertuous Ladies" l. 9; SD, ll. 77, 253). More erotically, Lanyer often calls Christ a "lover" (e.g., "To the Ladie *Lucie*," l. 16; SD, ll. 982, 1358, 1398). Lanyer even observes that Christ is a better lover than earthly men; for instance, when she describes the Passion so that Margaret may "judge if ever Lover were so true" (SD, l. 1267), and writes to Lady Katherine, Countess of Suffolk, that her *Salve* is intended so that readers "may see a Lover much more true / Than ever was since first the world began" (ll. 52-53).

The image of Christ as lover is enriched by noting (as a number of critics have done) Lanyer's sustained representation of Christ as feminine.[39] In the devotional tradition outlined by Caroline Walker Bynum in her study *Jesus as Mother,* Lanyer feminizes Christ, Lynette McGrath contends, in order to strengthen women's sense of themselves as "active subjects of their own religious experience."[40] While McGrath's observations are valid so far as they go, they ultimately limit the resonance of Lanyer's poetics by strangely separating an erotic from a feminine Christ. McGrath argues that, in the *Salve* "gender relationships between Christ and His female followers are slipperily problematized. Christ is an androgynous figure, at once both male lover-Bridegroom and feminine in character." In terms of McGrath's conceptualization of Lanyer's or a reader's desire for Christ, however, her sense of conflation vanishes; as she sees it, as a lover Christ can only be male. Yet, Christ's androgynous nature defies simple gender ascription and opens the possibility that "he" may be interpreted and loved as a "she." After all, as Diane Purkiss points out, the *Salve* is a "rhetorical project of considerable complexity," one that consistently problematizes normative "protocols" of interpretation. Wendy Wall comments that Lanyer represents Christ "in the socially inscribed female position as well as the eroticized position of Otherness."[41] I would like to take another step and suggest that Lanyer combines the female and the erotic in Christ as a valid way for women to satisfy their spiritual needs, relate to one another, and dissent from misogynist gender ideology. Meanwhile, through the insertion of a supposedly essential boundary between sexuality and religion, McGrath erases the possibility that a woman might find a feminine Christ erotically engaging.[42] No such duality, however, exists in Lanyer's poems; in fact, they forthrightly draw eroticism and religion together in such a way as to emphasize the homoeroticism involved in women's love of Christ.[43]

Lanyer searches the canon of Petrarchan and Christian *ars amatoria* to describe Christ's infinite desirability, finding some of her most potent images in the *Song of Songs*. A sensual blazon based on the Canticles captures the fervor of her devotion:

> unto Snowe we may his face compare,
> His cheekes like skarlet, and his eyes so bright
> As purest Doves that in the rivers are,
> Washed with milke, to give the more delight. [SD, ll. 1307-10]

In the next stanza, the erotic implications of the imagery intensify; Christ's hair is described as being

> Blacke as a Raven in her blackest hew;
> His lips like skarlet threeds, yet much more sweet
> Than is the sweetest hony dropping dew,
> Or hony combes, where all the Bees doe meet;
> . . . .
> His lips, like Lillies, dropping downe pure mirrhe,
> Whose love, before all worlds we doe preferre. [SD, ll. 1313-16, 1319-20]

Like the Canticles themselves, Lanyer's descriptions generally defy strict gender classification; yet, as Susanne Woods remarks, at one point Lanyer deploys an image that, in the Bible, is used specifically of a female figure: by portraying Christ's lips as "skarlet threeds" (cf. Song 4:3), Lanyer draws attention to the femininity of Christ's mouth.[44] This reinscription carries special weight when one notices (as in the above passage) the persistently oral quality of Lanyerian spirituality. Elsewhere, Lanyer writes that Christ's blood and tears are "Sweet Nectar and Ambrosia," as well as (again) "hony dropping dew of holy love, / [and] Sweet milke" to be ingested by devoted lovers (SD, ll. 1735, 1737-38). Christ and his female devotees are thus linked through a mutual feminizing of the orifice responsible for the numerous ingestions of salvific and erotic spice, milk, honey, nectar, and dew that flow throughout the text and lubricate women's bonds.[45]

For Lanyer, it is only a small step from an erotic appreciation of Christ to imagining him as the locus of triangulated eroticism between women themselves. Susanne Woods comes closest to acknowledging the point I want to make here when she observes that Margaret Russell is "the location for Lanyer's sensuous vision of Christ."[46] Woods quotes the following quatrain in support of her statement:

> in your heart I leave
> His perfect picture, where it still shall stand,
>   Deepely engraved in that holy shrine,
>   Environed with Love and Thoughts divine. [SD, ll. 1325-28; cf. l. 180]

Margaret is no mere passive vessel, however; the following stanzas indicate that Lanyer imagines her as an active lover:

> There may you reade his true and perfect storie,
> His bleeding body there you may embrace,
> And kisse his dying cheekes with teares of sorrow,
> With joyfull griefe, you may intreat for grace;
> . . . .
> Oft times hath he made triall of your love,
> And in your Faith hath tooke no small delight,
> . . . .
>   Your constant soule doth lodge betweene her brests,
>   This Sweet of sweets, in which all glory rests. [SD, ll. 1331-34, 1337-38, 1343-44]

Such encounters with Jesus are not limited to the Countess of Cumberland. Throughout "Salve Deus" Lanyer deploys imagery of internalization and privacy to express the most intimate moments of devotion and erotic engagement between Christ and *her* female lovers. By routing desire through Christ, women's mutual love acquires a truthfulness and profundity that is unavailable in conventional female-male relations.[47]

As the focal point of various women's religio-erotic desires, Christ is the *locus amoenus* in which they can all share love for one another. Lanyer's undertaking is not without precedent in Western spirituality. One of the most engaging examples of coordinate human-divine love from the Middle Ages is also homoerotic, although in this case desire circulates between men. In his treatise *Spiritual Friendship*, the twelfth-century Cistercian abbot, Aelred of Rievaulx writes that "friend cleaving to friend in the spirit of Christ, is made with Christ but one heart and one soul, and so mounting aloft through degrees of love to friendship with Christ, he is made one spirit with him in one kiss. Aspiring to this kiss the saintly soul cries out: 'Let him kiss me with the kiss of his mouth.'"[48] In heavily eroticized language also drawn from the *Song of Songs* (1:2), Aelred

celebrates ecstatic unity between two friends in and through Christ, under-
mining as he does so the heteronormative exegesis commonly afforded the
Canticles. Not a whit less fervent, Lanyer also imagines herself and her female
companions on a "friendly" progress to God. While Christ is in Margaret's
heart, in a loving *envoi* to "Salve Deus" Lanyer speaks of the countess as inside
of her. "Your rarest virtues did my soule delight, / Great Ladie of my heart,"
writes Lanyer in Petrarchan language. Not unlike Philip Sidney's Astrophel,
who eulogizes his beloved as the "star of heavenly fire, / Stella, lodestar of de-
sire" ("Eighth Song," ll. 31-32),[49] Lanyer celebrates Margaret as the "Great
Ladie of my heart" and "the Articke Starre that guides my hand," assuring her
that "All what I am, I rest at your command" (SD, ll. 1836, 1839-40). Like
Russian dolls, Aemilia, as poet and lover, contains her friend Margaret who, in
turn, houses Christ. The trio are now primed to discover and enjoy the fruits of
homoerotic love and devotion.

The final portion of Lanyer's book that I want to discuss is "The Descrip-
tion of Cooke-ham," the first country-house poem published in England. In
this text Lanyer explores most incisively the fissures between ideals and reality,
at the same time as she makes explicit that the ideal real-world fulfillment of
her spiritual reveries would be mutually respectful cohabitation with one or
more women. Because her poem contemplates the harsh realities of life for
women who are dependent on men's economic favor, it comes closest to em-
bodying the elegiac strain Traub notes in early modern female-female homo-
eroticism. Lanyer attests to "Memorie . . . [of] / Those pleasures past, which
will not turne againe" (ll. 117-18), and she describes Anne Clifford's "preserva-
tion" of the natural world's affection as taking place through "noble Memory"
(ll. 155-56). Whereas the examples Traub cites, however, exist irrecoverably in
the past and give way to heteronormative closure, Lanyer draws on the mind's
power to overcome loss by presenting comforting remembrances of former
happiness between women.[50] As she makes clear in "Cooke-ham," remember-
ing is not about repeating the past in exactly the same forms as it was once
known. Rather, Lanyer undertakes a creative manipulation as, for instance, in
her description of Anne in terms of Neoplatonic perfection: her "virtues did
agree / With those faire ornaments of outward beauty, / Which did enforce
from all both love and dutie" (ll. 100-2). Lanyer also requests her Memory to
"Remember beauteous *Dorsets* [i.e., Anne's] former sports" and informs the
reader that, in these recreations, "my selfe did alwaies beare a part, / While
reverend Love presented my true heart" (ll. 119, 121-22). As Barbara Lewalski
notes, because of differences in age and social rank, it is unlikely that Lanyer
actually ever participated in her noble friend's "sports." Yet, this is an "egalitar-
ian" fantasy of love that, through the ameliorative power of nostalgia, can eas-
ily mingle aristocratic and common hearts in a garden of pleasure.[51]

In "The Description of Cooke-ham," Lanyer's deepest sympathies are for Anne's mother, Margaret, a woman only nine years older than herself who had also experienced less than full happiness in her married life. Lanyer paints a reverent but fanciful portrait of Margaret as a goddess of Nature for whom "The very Hills right humbly did descend, / When you to tread upon them did intend" (CH, ll. 35-36). As a part of this idealization process, Margaret acquires a distinctly Dianic identity; for example, when Lanyer addresses her as holding a "Bowe in your faire Hand" (l. 51).[52] The former dream-state figure of a divine huntress who protects other women resurfaces in Lanyer's imagination at a moment when, attempting to ease the pain of real-life separation, such a woman-identified deity is needed most.

One scene in particular captures the erotic element of Lanyer's devotion to Margaret. Returning to the tree, "Whose faire greene leaves much like a comely vaile" (l. 63) had so often sheltered her from the sun when she had walked abroad as Dianic mistress of the park, Margaret guides Lanyer to the site of her former happiness:

> To this faire tree, taking me by the hand,
> You did repeat the pleasures which had past,
> Seeming to grieve they could no longer last.
> And with a chaste, yet loving kisse tooke leave,
> Of which sweet kisse I did it soone bereave:
> Scorning a sencelesse creature should possesse
> So rare a favour, so great happinesse. [ll. 162-68][53]

In this episode, which Elaine Beilin notes is "the single dramatic event of the poem," Lanyer posits her own belief in the worthiness of homoerotic love and companionship. Lewalski comments, however, that, with the theft of the kiss "the scene turns sentimental"; Coiro, meanwhile, suggests that, while readers "are moved by the act of sisterhood" that the theft entails, Lanyer's story of Lady Margaret kissing a tree is "gaspingly funny" and a "ludicrous joke."[54] Despite their differences, these two responses characterize the majority of critics' reluctance to consider seriously the genuine eroticism of Lanyer's act. This evasion contrasts with, as noted above, their willingness to address the erotic (albeit supposedly hetero) component of Lanyer's portrayals of Christ. It is not coincidental, however, that Lanyer's stealing of the kiss, her fantasies of Christ's embrace and oral delectableness, and her dream of a woman-only pastoral bower, all pivot on homoerotic intimacy. Her actions and vision, in fact, involve a recognition that not all women's desires are exclusively heteroerotic or are oriented toward marriage and procreation.

To label Lanyer's action as merely "sentimental" misconstrues her earnest expression of friendship as well as her rebuttal of patriarchal ideology. The "faire tree," after all, had been the site where Margaret and her daughter had gone to "take the ayre" and read books together (ll. 157, 159). In her memory, Margaret "repeat[s]" those past "pleasures" and bestows a kiss on the tree as a sign of nostalgic affection. However much sympathy Lanyer may have for melancholic plants, she places her own desires first when she steals Margaret's "sweet kisse." As Lanyer admits, her action has brought about a participation in Fortune; yet, in a larger scheme, she has also triumphed over Fortune's habit of using class divisions and prescriptive gender norms to separate women from one another. "[N]othing's free from Fortunes scorne" (CH, l. 176), Lanyer attests; by imagining an egalitarian community of loving women free of men, she nevertheless strives to make Fortune survivable.

The sestet that concludes "The Description of Cooke-ham" intertwines the *Salve*'s various strands of desire:

> This last farewell to *Cooke-ham* here I give,
> When I am dead thy name in this may live,
> Wherein I have perform'd her noble hest,
> Whose virtues lodge in my unworthy breast,
> And ever shall, so long as life remaines,
> Tying my heart to her by those rich chaines. [ll. 205-10]

While Lanyer draws on the familiar conceit of poetry's ability to effect immortality for its subject, her more pressing concern is to testify to Margaret's continued presence in her living "breast." At the end of "Cooke-ham," Lanyer looks back to "Salve Deus" and echoes her own earlier figuration of desire and mutuality: Christ is inside Margaret who is again thought of as within Aemilia. The "rich chaines" of love that unite Margaret and Aemilia's hearts echo the "golden Chaine" of Platonic love that joins together the poet and Mary Sidney in "The Authors Dreame" (l. 7). Whereas in her dream world Lanyer sought to live with Mary Sidney "in height of all respect," in the real world she articulates her wish to remain with women whom she actually knows.

It has not been my purpose in this essay to argue that Aemilia Lanyer was a "lesbian." Although I would not want to rule out the possibility that, at the time she composed the *Salve*, Lanyer's principal erotic desires were for other women, that is not my interest here. I hope instead to have shown that, like John Donne and Andrew Marvell, Lanyer found images of same-gender desire to be useful and emotionally engaging vehicles through which to express religious devotion, as well as to explore and document solidarity and love between women as a remedy for worldly vicissitudes brought about by people of both genders. Homoeroticism enabled Lanyer to negotiate the complex relations between social hierarchies and gender identities; it also assisted her in moving beyond mere rebuttal of patriarchal ideology to envision the psychological groundwork for a classless community of women. Finally, homoeroticism provided Lanyer with a symbolic repertoire with which to intervene in the production of gender norms by positing the agency of desires that do not conform to normative definitions of female identity and destiny. As Montaigne remarks in his essay on friendship: "our genuine libertie hath no production more properly her owne, than that of affection and amitie."[55] *Salve Deus Rex Judaeorum* reveals that this ancient association between freedom and homoerotic friendship was not lost on Aemilia Lanyer.

NOTES

I would like to thank Michael Bristol and Bruce Smith for their good will and ideas, Dennis Denisoff for his partnership and insights, and Doris Zibauer for her stories of women's communities. I also gratefully acknowledge support from the Social Sciences and Humanities Research Council of Canada.

1. See Barbara K. Lewalski, *Writing Women in Jacobean England* (Cambridge: Harvard Univ. Press, 1993), pp. 213-41; Lynette McGrath, "'Let Us Have Our Libertie Againe': Aemilia Lanier's Seventeenth-Century Feminist Voice," *Women's Studies* 20 (1992): 331-48; Janel Mueller, "The Feminist Poetics of Aemilia Lanyer's 'Salve Deus Rex Judaeorum,'" in *Feminist Measures: Soundings in Poetry and Theory,* ed. Lynn Keller and Cristanne Miller (Ann Arbor: Univ. of Michigan Press, 1994), pp. 208-36, rev. and rpt. in the present volume as chapter 6.

2. Unless otherwise stated, the poetry of John Donne is quoted from *The Complete English Poems,* ed. C.A. Patrides (New York: Knopf-Everyman, 1985), that of Andrew Marvell from *The Complete Poems,* ed. George deF. Lord (New York: Knopf-Everyman, 1993). If it is unclear from the context which of Lanyer's poems I am quoting, I parenthetically give before the line numbers either the abbreviation SD for "Salve Deus Rex Judaeorum," CH for "The Description of Cooke-ham," or a shortened title, such as "To the Ladie *Lucie.*"

3. For a discussion of Philips's homoeroticism, see Arlene Stiebel, "Not Since Sappho: The Erotic in Poems of Katherine Phillips and Aphra Behn," in *Homosexuality in Renaissance and Enlightenment England: Literary Representations in Historical Context,* ed. Claude J. Summers (New York: Haworth Press, 1992), pp. 153-71.

4. Keith Wrightson, *English Society: 1580-1680* (New Brunswick: Rutgers Univ. Press, 1982), p. 62.

5. Lewalski, *Writing,* p. 3. Merry E. Wiesner's international and interdisciplinary survey of women and gender in early modern Europe discusses at length women's opportunities to achieve self-expression and to question prevailing norms. See esp. her chapters on "Women and the Creation of Culture," and "Gender and Power" in *Women and Gender in Early Modern Europe* (Cambridge: Cambridge Univ. Press, 1993), pp. 146-75, 239-58. Hilda Smith's *Reason's Disciples: Seventeenth-Century English Feminists* (Urbana: Univ. of Illinois Press, 1982) usefully complements Wiesner's work.

6. Alan Sinfield, *Faultlines: Cultural Materialism and the Politics of Dissident Reading* (Berkeley: Univ. of California Press, 1991), pp. 49, 174-75.

7. Ross Chambers's theory of textual seduction has also influenced my understanding

of oppositionality, cultural change, and the importance of desire in producing "room to maneuver"; see esp. his introduction and chapter 1 in *Room to Maneuver: Reading (the) Oppositional (in) Narrative* (Chicago: Univ. of Chicago Press, 1991). Anthony Giddens's remarks on the inherence of change to social reproduction also inform my thinking; see his *Central Problems in Social Theory: Action, Structure and Contradiction in Social Analysis* (Berkeley: Univ. of California Press, 1979).

8. Bruce R. Smith, *Homosexual Desire in Shakespeare's England: A Cultural Poetics* (Chicago: Univ. of Chicago Press, 1991), p. 28. See also Alan Bray, *Homosexuality in Renaissance England* (London: Gay Men's Press, 1982), p. 17.

9. E. Ann Matter, "My Sister, My Spouse: Woman-Identified Women in Medieval Christianity," *Journal of Feminist Studies in Religion* 2.2 (fall 1986): 81.

10. Valerie Traub, "The (In)significance of 'Lesbian' Desire in Early Modern England," in *Erotic Politics: Desire on the Renaissance Stage*, ed. Susan Zimmerman (New York: Routledge, 1992), p. 164. In a subsequent essay, "The Perversion of 'Lesbian' Desire," *History Workshop Journal* 41 (spring 1996): 19-49, Traub elaborates on seventeenth-century "lesbian" invisibility (in particular the "femme" role) and relates it to heteronormative strategies of abjection.

11. Although it discusses the cultural and political history of same-gender female desire at a slightly later date than the poems I examine, Emma Donoghue's *Passions between Women: British Lesbian Culture, 1668-1801* (New York: HarperCollins, 1993), complements my own work by dispelling "the myth that seventeenth- and eighteenth-century lesbian culture was rarely registered in language" (3). Similarly, in her study of female same-gender desire in history and literature from the eighteenth through the twentieth centuries, Terry Castle effectively rebuts what she calls "the no-lesbians-before-1900 myth"; see *The Apparitional Lesbian: Female Homosexuality and Modern Culture* (New York: Columbia Univ. Press, 1993), p. 96. Castle's argument against imagining "romantic friendship" between women to have been at all times devoid of sexual content and/or intention (see esp. pp. 10-11, 92-106) encourages one to pose questions of (as well as of how one thinks about) women's identities and avenues of pleasure and self-expression in earlier periods.

12. Lanyer provides dedicatory poems to Queen Anne; Princess Elizabeth; Lady Arabella Stuart; Lady Susan, Dowager Countess of Kent; Lady Mary, Countess of Pembroke; Lady Lucy, Countess of Bedford; Lady Margaret, Countess Dowager of Cumberland; Lady Katherine, Countess of Suffolk; and Lady Anne, Countess of Dorset. These dedications should not be construed as unproblematic assertions of the middle-class poet's comfort with a hereditary social hierarchy. As Ann Baynes Coiro shows, Lanyer numerous times questions the privileges and authority of a matriarchy that she, in part, resents; see "Writing in Service: Sexual Politics and Class Position in the Poetry of Aemilia Lanyer and Ben Jonson," *Criticism* 35 (1993): 365, 369-73. Coiro overstates the case, though, when she claims that because of Lanyer's criticisms the *Salve* is a "subversive" (p. 372; see also p. 369) "radical manifesto" (p. 370; see also p. 365). The complex mediations of class operating in Lanyer's relationship to her dedicatees is further discussed by Kari Boyd McBride in chapter 4 of this volume.

13. Claude J. Summers, "Marlowe and Constructions of Renaissance Homosexuality," *Canadian Review of Comparative Literature* 21 (1994): 31; Janel Mueller, "Troping Utopia: Donne's Brief for Lesbianism," in *Sexuality and Gender in Early Modern Europe: Institutions, Texts, Images*, ed. James Grantham Turner (Cambridge: Cambridge Univ. Press,

1993), p. 183. Mueller's discussion is one of the most historically and textually informative readings of "Sapho to Philaenis." As Mueller points out, the interpretations given by Elizabeth Harvey and James Holstun, though sensitive to same-gender desire, tend to limit Donne's sympathy with Sapho and the poem's ability to critique patriarchal norms (pp. 203-4, n. 5). In "'Will you rent our ancient love asunder?': Lesbian Elegy in Donne, Marvell, and Milton," *ELH* 54 (1987): 835-67, for example, Holstun views Donne's poem as an example of "a repressive patriarchal periodization of lesbian desire" (845); cf. Elizabeth Harvey, "Ventriloquizing Sappho: Ovid, Donne, and the Erotics of the Feminine Voice," *Criticism* 31 (1989): 115-38. My reading of "Sapho to Philaenis" departs from Holstun's "elegiac" interpretation of the text and of early modern literary lesbianism in general (see Holstun, 838-47). I believe that Donne leaves the outcome of Sapho's pleas undetermined in order to make space for readers' various responses.

14. Paula Blank's illumination of the ways in which Donne's poem "exposes sameness as rhetorical rather than material" (p. 359) demonstrates that mutuality is a culturally constructed way of understanding and expressing homosexual desire and identity; see her "Comparing Sappho to Philaenis: John Donne's 'Homopoetics,'" *PMLA* 110 (1995): 358-68. Nevertheless, in the poetry of Donne, Marvell, and Lanyer, homoerotic mutuality is strategically essentialized so as emphatically to contrast the perceived fragmentary and oppressive nature of heterosexual unions with the kinder, equitable bonds of female companionship.

15. John Dixon Hunt, *Andrew Marvell: His Life and Writings* (Ithaca: Cornell Univ. Press, 1978), p. 100. Between 1650 and 1652 Marvell resided at Fairfax's Nun Appleton House, tutoring his patron's daughter Mary (Maria in the poem) and writing some of his best-known poetry, including his panegyric on the estate. For more biographical details, see Hunt and Pierre Legouis, *Andrew Marvell: Poet, Puritan, Patriot* (rev. ed., London: Clarendon Press, 1970).

16. Michael Wilding, *Dragons Teeth: Literature in the English Revolution* (Oxford: Clarendon Press, 1987), 166; Lee Erickson, "Marvell's *Upon Appleton House* and the Fairfax Family," *English Literary Renaissance* 9 (1979): 167. Recent critics' unwillingness to consider the pleasurable and positive side of the nuns' offers appears to be linked to a refusal to consider as real or worthy any desires other than cross-gender. For example, instead of using the term homoeroticism A.D. Cousins refers to the sisters' "sexual unnaturalness" (p. 68); see "Marvell's 'Upon Appleton House, to my Lord Fairfax' and the Regaining of Paradise," in *The Political Identity of Andrew Marvell*, ed. Conal Condren and A.D. Cousins (Aldershot, UK: Scolar Press, 1990), 53-84. Similarly, Wilding writes euphemistically of the nuns' "sensual misbehaviour" (p. 148) and "protected intensification" of "worldly ambitions and corruptions" (p. 164).

17. Anna K. Nardo, *The Ludic Self in Seventeenth-Century English Literature* (Albany: SUNY Press, 1991), p. 125. Despite her numerous insights, Nardo exceeds textual evidence when she claims that Marvell shows cloistered life to be "a narcissist's paradise, where infantile fantasies of grandiosity can come true" (p. 125). Her reading derives from a psychoanalytic *telos* of personality "maturity" that informs virtually her entire study, and which she bases strictly on cross-gender paradigms of erotic desire (see e.g., pp. 119, 130).

18. Erickson, 160. In mythic fashion, Marvell telescopes history (ll. 269-72) by merging together the dates of Isabel's marriage (1518) and the convent's dissolution (1542). Barbara Lewalski suggests that Marvell's treatment even echoes the Fall in the Garden of Eden and Christ's salvific agency; see "The Lady of the Country-House Poem," in *The*

Fashioning and Functioning of the British Country House, ed. Gervase Jackson-Stops, Gordon J. Schochet, Lena Cowen Orlin, and Elisabeth Blair MacDougall (Hanover, N.H.: Univ. Press of New England, 1989), p. 271.

19. Erickson, pp. 159, 161. Erickson also points out that Lord Fairfax's entailment provoked considerable controversy within the family (p. 161), and notes the "hard historical irony" that Mary and her husband George Villiers, Second Duke of Buckingham—a "scheming dissolute philanderer, and the epitome of the Restoration rake"—were miserable together, lost a great deal of money, and died childless (p. 163).

20. Surveying the many shapes that Appleton House took over the years, Hunt reports that when Marvell sojourned with them the Fairfaxes were "living 'in a modest house cobbled up out of part of the nunnery'" (p. 83).

21. Traub, "(In)significance," p. 164. As Jody Greene observes, in the early modern period the meanings attached to sodomy "always operated by an analogy, however distant, to the original notion of the sodomite as a destroyer of that most basic unit of the social fabric, the procreative, married, heterosexual couple"; see "'You Must Eat Men': The Sodomitic Economy of Renaissance Patronage," *GLQ: A Journal of Lesbian and Gay Studies* 1 (1994): 166.

22. Lyndal Roper, *The Holy Household: Women and Morals in Reformation Augsburg* (Oxford: Clarendon Press, 1989), pp. 206, 216. Conventual homoeroticism as a sign of iniquity has numerous literary and historical manifestations. See, for example, Erasmus's colloquy "The Girl with No Interest in Marriage" (*Virgo μισόγαμος*), in *The Colloquies of Erasmus,* trans. Craig R. Thompson (Chicago: Univ. of Chicago Press, 1965), and Clément Marot's lively French translation, "La vierge mesprisant mariage," in *Oeuvres* (1911, rpt., Geneva: Slatkine, 1969). For literary contextualizations of these men's opinions, see Graciella Daichman's *Wayward Nuns in Medieval Literature* (Syracuse: Syracuse Univ. Press, 1986), and Lillian Faderman's *Surpassing the Love of Men: Romantic Friendship and Love between Women from the Renaissance to the Present* (New York: William Morrow, 1981); on a later but related treatment, see the discussion of Denis Diderot's novel *La Religieuse* in Donoghue, pp. 190-97. Judith Brown's study of the sixteenth-century "lesbian" nun, Sister Benedetta Carlini, provides useful historical information on the topic; see *Immodest Acts: The Life of a Lesbian Nun in Renaissance Italy* (New York: Oxford Univ. Press, 1986).

23. Holstun, 851.

24. Hunt, p. 67.

25. Traub, "Perversion," 25, 39-43; "(In)significance," pp. 158-59.

26. Susanne Woods argues that through the *Salve* Lanyer attempted "to make a bid for restoration of her place, however peripheral, among the great" (p. xxvii); see Woods's introduction to *The Poems of Amelia Lanyer,* esp. pp. xxv-xxvii.

27. On religion's special role in women's lives, see McGrath, 341; Mueller, "Feminist Poetics," pp. 222-23, 228; Roper, *passim;* Woods, p. xxxi; and Retha Warnicke, "Private and Public: The Boundaries of Women's Lives in Early Stuart England," in *Privileging Gender in Early Modern England,* ed. Jean R. Brink, Sixteenth Century Essays & Studies, vol. 23 (Kirksville, Mo.: Sixteenth Century Journal, 1993), p. 140.

28. Lewalski, *Writing,* 8.

29. McGrath, 337.

30. Michel de Montaigne, *Montaigne's Essays,* vol. 1, trans. John Florio (1910, rpt., London: J.M. Dent & Sons, 1965), pp. 199, 198. Bruce Smith gives an excellent overview

of the classical background of Montaigne's celebration of male-male bonds and his rejection of friendship between the sexes (Smith, pp. 33-41).

31. Minerva, the goddess of wisdom, is an apt guide for women who seek other women's love through contemplation, study, and art. In Jorge de Montemayor's romance *La Diana,* for instance, the temple of Minerva near the river Duerus is the site of a yearly celebration in which young "Shepherdesses" and "faire Nymphes" from the neighborhood gather, free from men, "to celebrate the feast, and to make merry with one another"; see *Diana,* trans. Bartholomew Yong, ed. Judith M. Kennedy (Oxford: Clarendon Press, 1968), p. 33. De Montemayor's depiction of the complicated relations between Selvagia and Ismenia, which involve "mutuall imbracings" and "loving speeches to one another," brings to the fore the homoeroticism of Minerva's shrine and festival.

32. McGrath, p. 339. In his continuation of Marlowe's *Hero and Leander,* George Chapman makes a similar distinction between the two goddesses; see his "Continuation of 'Hero and Leander,'" in *Christopher Marlowe: The Complete Poems and Translations,* ed. Stephen Orgel (Harmondsworth: Penguin Books), IV.315-344. I am indebted to Claude Summers for this observation.

33. Christine Downing, *Myths and Mysteries of Same-Sex Love* (New York: Continuum, 1989), pp. 210-11; Traub, "(In)significance," p. 161; Patricia Simons, "Lesbian (In)visibility in Italian Renaissance Culture: Diana and Other Cases of *donna con donna," Journal of Homosexuality* 27 (1994): 81-122.

34. Lanyer also describes her work as "this Mirrour of a worthy Mind" in her poem to Queen Anne (l. 37; see also ll. 90, 97).

35. Lanyer makes a similar complaint about social rank in her dedicatory poem "To the Ladie *Anne,* Countesse of Dorcet" (ll. 33-40). For the view that institutional constraints beyond class resist Lanyer's female community and are recognized in her poems, see Grossman, chapter 7 in this volume.

36. Montaigne, p. 199.

37. Warnicke, p. 133. Wiesner discusses at length the appeal of convents (as well as less-structured religious communities and anchoritic conditions) for women during and after the Reformation and the Tridentine reforms (see pp. 192-201); see also Roper, *passim.* Since, as Wiesner points out, the relative openness to women's writings and political involvement during the early years of the Protestant Reformation contrasted with a rapid shutting-down of opportunities to publish and speak (pp. 186-89), it is not surprising that Lanyer turned to Catholic-inspired imagery as a way to express women's solidarity and power.

38. The fact that Lanyer's father, Baptist Bassano, was a Venetian (Woods, p. xv) and her husband, Alfonso Lanyer, a Roman Catholic (Coiro, p. 362), might suggest the poet's awareness of, and interest in, Catholic devotion. Lanyer's portrayal of the Virgin Mary—a figure possessing particular resonance in Roman Catholicism—in the polyvalent roles of mother, wife, daughter, subject, servant, and nurse (SD, ll. 1023, 1087) may also indicate a fascination with opportunities to use religion in order to unsettle women's traditional, unitary identifications and desires. It is quite clear from "Salve Deus" that Mary's lack of "desire" for "any man" symbolized for Lanyer the coupling of perfect virtue and absolute freedom from male tyranny (see SD, ll. 1077-78). The prose and poetry of the Dutch Beguine, Hadewijch, and the anonymous voice recorded in a twelfth-century Bavarian manuscript, add historical precedents for Lanyer's spiritual homoeroticism; see Matter, "My Sister."

39. On Lanyer's Christ as feminine, see McGrath, pp. 342-43, and Mueller, "Feminist," p. 222.

40. See Caroline Walker Bynum, *Jesus as Mother: Studies in the Spirituality of the High Middle Ages* (Berkeley: Univ. of California Press, 1982); McGrath, p. 344.

41. McGrath, p. 343; Diane Purkiss, Introduction to *Renaissance Women: The Plays of Elizabeth Cary, The Poems of Aemilia Lanyer* (London: William Pickering, 1994), p. xxxiv; Wendy Wall, "Our Bodies/Our Texts?: Renaissance Women and the Trials of Authorship," in *Anxious Power: Reading, Writing, and Ambivalence in Narrative by Women,* ed. Carol J. Singley and Susan Elizabeth Sweeney (Albany: SUNY Press, 1993), p. 67.

42. Richard Rambuss explores a similar bifurcation in critical responses to the poetry of seventeenth-century men such as John Donne, Richard Crashaw, and George Herbert; see his "Pleasure and Devotion: The Body of Jesus and Seventeenth-Century Religious Lyric," in *Queering the Renaissance,* ed. Jonathan Goldberg (Durham, N.C.: Duke Univ. Press, 1994), pp. 253-79. Rambuss problematizes Bynum's work which has encouraged critics to oppose "the vivid corporealities of pre- and early modern devotional practices" and the erotic (especially homoerotic) implications of that corporeality (p. 268). My reading of Lanyer's work accords with Rambuss's contention that readers should not "turn away from regarding the body as always at least potentially sexualized, as a truly polysemous surface where various significances and expressions—including a variety of erotic ones—compete and collude with each other in making the body *meaningful.*" Although Michael C. Schoenfeldt reads all eroticism in Donne and Herbert as heteroerotic, he also contributes to an understanding of how these poets meld the erotic and the religious; see his "'That Ancient Heat': Sexuality and Spirituality in *The Temple,*" in *Soliciting Interpretation: Literary Theory and Seventeenth-Century English Poetry,* ed. Elizabeth D. Harvey and Katharine Eisaman Maus (Chicago: Univ. of Chicago Press, 1990), pp. 273-306.

43. Christ, of course, also appears in the *Salve Deus* as a humanized "man" (e.g., the "good old man," SD, l. 1347). I am not arguing for the exclusivity of Christ's effeminization or homoerotic appreciation; Lanyer's spiritual homoerotics are but one significant way to love God and other women.

44. Woods, in Lanyer, p. 107. Lanyer's feminization of the ungendered biblical raven (Song 5:11) also contributes to her portrayal of Christ.

45. A similar homoerotic orality occurs in a later, Italian text. Traub has recently noted that in Pier Francesco Cavilli's opera *La Calisto* (1651), a sensual "oral economy of desire" between women displaces a "conventional phallic economy" ("Perversion," 31).

46. Woods in Lanyer, p. xxxviii.

47. See, for example, "To the Ladie *Susan,*" l. 42, "To the Ladie *Lucie,*" *passim,* and "To the Ladie *Anne,* ll. 118-20, 143. Though she does not note its erotic component, Mueller points to internalization as fundamental to Lanyer's religious devotion ("Feminist," p. 222).

48. Saint Aelred of Rievaulx, *Spiritual Friendship,* trans. Mary Laker, Cistercian Fathers Series, no. 5 (Washington, D.C.: Cistercian Fathers, 1974), 2:21. John Boswell offers the best analysis of Aelred's homoerotic writings in the context of late-medieval culture; see his *Christianity, Social Tolerance, and Homosexuality* (Chicago: Univ. of Chicago Press, 1980), pp. 221-226. E. Ann Matter's work on countering claims that the *Song of Songs* dispenses with the body also offers valuable sidelights to Lanyer's own body-soul integration; see her *The Voice of My Beloved: The Song of Songs in Western Medieval Christianity* (Philadelphia: Univ. of Pennsylvania Press, 1990), esp. pp. 139-142.

49. Philip Sidney, "Astrophel and Stella," in *Selected Poetry and Prose,* ed. Robert Kimbrough (1969, 2d ed., Madison: Univ. of Wisconsin Press, 1983), pp. 163-240.

50. Achsah Guibbory's discussion of Donne's use of memory in *The Anniversaries* to "counter[] the degenerative process of time" helps one to understand Lanyer's own use of memory as an important restorative and, paradoxically, future-oriented faculty; see Guibbory, *The Map of Time* (Urbana: Univ. of Illinois Press, 1986), pp. 88-95.

51. Lewalski, *Writing,* pp. 239, 241. Discussing late-seventeenth and eighteenth-century passions between women, Donoghue adduces other examples of spiritual friendship that override distinctions imposed by social rank (pp. 154-57).

52. Woods, in Lanyer, p. 132, notes Margaret's Dianic appearance.

53. The fact that Margaret takes Lanyer's hand when she guides her to the tree may echo Mary Sidney's offer to take Diana's hand in "The Authors Dreame," a parallel that, by turning the poet into a Dianic figure, would similarly make her an eroticized protector of women.

54. Elaine V. Beilin, *Redeeming Eve: Women Writers of the English Renaissance* (Princeton: Princeton Univ. Press, 1987), p. 205; Lewalski, *Writing,* p. 240; Coiro, 372-73.

55. Montaigne, p. 198.

10
The Gospel According to Aemilia: Women and the Sacred

Achsah Guibbory

In the history of Western religion, women have had a far more ambiguous relation to the sacred than men. Although women were celebrated in the Hebrew Bible for their heroism and devotion to God, it was men, we are told, who were the priests and prophets chosen for God's service. With the destruction of the temple in 70 C.E., the study of the sacred Torah became exclusively the province of males, and the rabbis replaced the priests, while women engaged in practical, domestic roles supporting the spirituality of the male scholars. In some ways, the advent of Christianity might have marked a change in women's relation to the sacred, for Christ's teachings could be seen as giving women equal access to the divine—"there is neither male nor female: for ye are all one in Christ Jesus" (Gal. 3:28); the fact that all believers, male and female, are "sonnes" of Christ (e.g., Gal. 4:6-7) and strive to be his "spouse" (e.g., Matt. 25:1-13) might minimize gender as well as class differences.[1] But there were other passages in the New Testament that implicitly placed women at a farther remove from the sacred than men. Paul in 1 Corinthians 11:4-8 insists that women in church must be "covered" as a sign of their inferiority and subjection.[2] Whereas men can freely "prophecy" in the church, Paul orders women to "keepe silence" there, instead asking their husbands "at home" about spiritual matters, over which men are presumed to have more authority (1 Cor. 14:34-35).

As the work of Elaine Pagels, Peter Brown, and Caroline Bynum has shown, the growth of the church as an institution reveals both the importance of women's devotion and the ways in which women were distanced from authoritative, direct contact with the divine. The early centuries of the church saw women martyrs, patrons of the church, and ascetics, though the church fathers encouraged a sense of women's remove from the sacred by associating woman and the feminine with the body or "flesh," and by presenting marriage as a model of Christian order in which women's "subjection" to their husbands mirrors both the hierarchical order of society and the body's proper subjection to the rule of the soul.[3] From the late twelfth through the fourteenth century, women saints and mystics cultivated and displayed their spirituality, insisting on women's special, intimate connection with God.[4] But as the church grew, so did the power of the priests and bishops, and restrictions were placed on women's activities within the sacred church.[5]

In some ways, the Protestant Reformation actually deepened the distance between women and the sacred. In getting rid of monastic orders and religious houses, it deprived women of a special form of sacred experience. In rejecting the adoration of the Virgin Mary and the female saints, it eliminated important models as well as objects for women's devotion. Moreover, Protestantism associated the "feminine" with the supposed "carnal idolatry" of Roman Catholicism.[6] But Protestantism also had the potential to give women equal access with men to the sacred.[7] All were "brethren" in God, all people could know God through reading the Scriptures, and women as well as men could be touched by God's grace.

Aemilia Lanyer's own relation to the sacred has seemed particularly ambiguous. In 1611, she published a single volume of poetry which presented itself as sacred verse, but our contemporary source of information about Lanyer, Simon Forman, presents her in his diary entries as a woman very much of the world—the mistress of Lord Hunsdon, who married Alfonso Lanyer to cover an illegitimate pregnancy, who sought a knighthood for her husband and took her brothers-in-law to court to secure her late husband's custom patent. Her reputation for holiness has not been helped by A.L. Rowse's inference from Forman's diary that she was promiscuous, or his speculation that she was Shakespeare's "dark lady."[8] Even Barbara Lewalski has questioned the appropriateness of calling Lanyer's poetry religious, for she finds the poems notably worldly in their concern with patronage.[9] I would argue, however, that, for all its concern with patronage, *Salve Deus Rex Judaeorum* asks to be taken seriously as religious poetry that adopts Christ's message to give a special place to women in devotion. *Salve Deus Rex Judaeorum* has a claim to our interest, not only as one of the first substantial volumes of poetry published by a woman in England, but also because it is a significant cultural document expanding our understanding of women's religious roles. In her poetry, Lanyer is a biblical interpreter who claims the status of a true apostle of Christ and even assumes a quasi-priestly role. The importance of the *Salve* becomes clearer when read within the broad historical context of woman's vexed relation with the sacred as well as within the specific historical context of the Protestant culture of early Jacobean England—a culture that assumed women did not have as privileged a connection with God as men, but that also sanctioned the individual reader's authority to interpret the Bible.

With the accession of James I in 1603, the dominant structure of power shaping English culture and society became more distinctly patriarchal than it had been in Elizabeth's reign. As a female ruler, Queen Elizabeth had violated the traditional assumption that women were subject to men. Though it has been argued that Elizabeth's example was the exception that proved the rule of patriarchy, the very existence of a woman monarch destabilized the traditional gender hierarchy. Moreover, in constructing her monarchical authority, Elizabeth appropriated the symbols and imagery of the Virgin Mary, attempting to give religious sanction to her political rule and also implicitly preserving a powerful role for female spirituality. During her long reign, she served as head of the English Church as well as the state, thus assuming a spiritual authority that had been presumed to belong only to Protestant kings. But with the death of Elizabeth, a male figure of monarchical power replaced that of the Virgin Queen, and James promoted a rigorously patriarchal authority in both church and state. Whereas the English Church had followed the Catholic practice of allowing women as well as lay men to baptize in an emergency, James insisted in 1604 that only ministers could baptize, thus restricting women's role in the Church as he reinforced the distance between clery and laity (Crawford, p. 56). Masculine authority was also emphasized in the king's writings and speeches, as James figured himself as husband and father of the realm. Clearly preferring the company and advice of men, he created a court with a strongly homosocial and patriarchal ethos.[10] But as Leeds Barroll and Barbara Lewalski have shown, this patriarchal ethos did not go unchallenged. James's wife, Queen Anne, established a separate court, which "provided a locus, unstable yet influential, of female resistance" to the ethos and policies of James's court.[11] This sense of a female alternative to the male nexus of power—both secular and sacred—informs Lanyer's poem. In her prefatory poems, Lanyer looks back nostalgically to the reign of Elizabeth but in dedicating the volume to Queen Anne and the powerful noblewomen associated with her, Lanyer attempts to attach herself to Anne's court as it provided a female-centered alternative to James's.

Salve Deus Rex Judaeorum appeared in 1611, the same year as the King James Bible, the work of Launcelot Andrewes and a group of distinguished divines commissioned by James to provide "an exact Translation of the holy Scriptures into the *English Tongue.*"[12] In the very year that the "Authorized Version" of the Bible was published, founded on the Protestant belief that every Christian should be able to read the Bible in the vernacular, and dedicated to King James as "the principall moover and Author of the Worke" (sig. A2v), Aemelia Lanyer published her version of the Passion, proclaimed her authority as a woman to read and interpret the Bible, and asked for the queen's patronage of her work. Might we not, then, see the *Salve* as in some sense constituting an oppositional alternative to the monumental biblical project of James?

Though, as Lewalski observes, religious poetry was considered more appropriate than secular verse for women (Lewalski, "Re-writing Patriarchy,"

p. 98), "Salve Deus" is hardly a conventional, modestly pious poem for a woman. Whereas the institution of the Church had increasingly restricted women's roles, "Salve Deus" places women at the heart of the sacred: it is introduced by ten dedicatory pieces to prospective or actual women patronesses and a prose address to her "Virtuous Readers" (defined as exclusively female), which defends the special affection and distinction Christ showed to women. The principal poem is a narrative of Christ's Passion that also contains a lengthy panegyric frame praising Margaret Clifford, Countess of Cumberland, as a virtuous woman and spouse of Christ, a catalogue of good women in biblical and classical history, and a description of the Queen of Sheba as exemplary of female spiritual devotion. As an epilogue, the country-house poem "The Description of Cookeham" presents the estate where Margaret Clifford lived as a spiritual retreat where women had a special connection with the holy. Though, as Elaine Beilin recognizes, women's relation with the sacred pervades the entire volume (*Redeeming Eve,* pp. 177-207), it is particularly striking in Lanyer's bold version of Christ's Passion that literally forms the center of the *Salve.* I will argue that, defying powerful cultural restrictions, Lanyer presents her poem as a true gospel, inspired and authorized by God, offering a distinctive version of the significance of Christ's Passion, bearing a message for social as well as spiritual change, and founded on a critical and independent reading of the Scriptures that recognizes the New Testament as not simply the Word of God but a series of texts, written by men, in which all parts are not equally authoritative. In reading the Bible, she discovers a disturbing discontinuity between Christ's teachings and those of his disciples.

Paul's advice that women remain "silent" in the church not only discouraged women's speaking publicly about religious matters but also suggested that men possessed greater authority about spiritual concerns—hence their freedom to prophecy and the subsequent selection of men as priests in the church. Paul's comments about women's "place" would be radically challenged in the foment of the Civil War years, when radical women of the 1640s and '50s took it upon themselves to preach or prophecy, claiming special inspiration from God. But the conduct books of the early seventeenth century and the "Homilie of the state of Matrimonie," read regularly in every church during Elizabeth's and James's reigns, encouraged the silence of women, not only in the church but even within the home. Women's silence was a mark of their subjection, a subjection which confirmed the order of society as founded on the obedience of people to their superiors.[13]

Lanyer's "preamble" before the Passion makes clear her awareness that she is violating the social codes sanctioned by these books and by Paul's foundational verses that women be "covered" and "silent" in the church.

But my deare Muse, now whither wouldst thou flie,
Above the pitch of thy appointed straine?
With *Icarus* thou seekest now to trie,
Not waxen wings, but thy poore barren Braine,
Which farre too weake, these siely lines descrie. [ll. 273-77]

Aware that in seeking to narrate and interpret Christ's Passion she is transgressing the "appointed" boundaries for a woman (her insistent consciousness of gender makes these lines more than the conventional humility topos), she prays for God's "Grace":

Therefore I humbly for his Grace will pray,
That he will give me Power and Strength to Write,
That what I have begun, so end I may,
As his great Glory may appeare more bright;
Yea in these Lines I may no further stray,
Than his most holy Spirit shall give me Light:
    That blindest Weakenesse be not over-bold,
    The manner of his Passion to unfold.
  · · · · · · · · · · ·

Yet if he please t'illuminate my Spirit,
And give me Wisdom from his holy Hill,
That I may Write part of his glorious Merit,
If he vouchsafe to guide my Hand and Quill,
To shew his Death, by which we doe inherit
Those endlesse Joyes that all our hearts doe fill
    Then will I tell of that sad blacke fac'd Night,
    Whose mourning Mantle covered Heavenly Light. [ll. 297-304, 321-28]

Like the women prophets during the English Revolution and like Milton in *Paradise Lost* and *Paradise Regained,* Lanyer invokes divine inspiration, hence insisting on divine authority for what she will speak. Her prayer recalls Matthew's and Mark's accounts in the New Testament that when Christ sent out his Apostles to preach the Gospel, he told them: "take no thought how or what ye shall speake: for it shal be given you in that houre, what yee shall say. For it is not yee that speake, but the spirit of your father which speaketh in you" (Matt. 10:19-20; cf. Mark 13:11). She extends the argument still further, suggesting that her very "Weakeness" makes God's glory shine more fully, as if she is simply a medium for transmitting God's truth. But by publishing her interpretation of the Passion and its significance for humanity—a version which, like Milton's versions of biblical truth in his epics, will include significant departures from tradition and original additions—she defies Paul's prohibition against women's speaking publicly about religion, suggesting, as she will do later in the poem, that women are more qualified than men since in their weakness and humility they are closer to God and more open to his grace:

> But yet the Weaker thou doest seeme to be
> In Sexe, or Sence, the more his Glory shines,
> That doth infuze such powerfull Grace in thee,
> To shew thy Love in these few humble Lines. [ll. 289-92]

Echoing Christ's privileging of the poor, humble, and weak, Lanyer suggests that the traditionally masculine faculty of reason ("Sence"), like the masculine "Sexe," in its supposed strength competes with and hence may exclude divine illumination. If she is led by God's spirit and his hand guides her "Quill," then her poem will be "true," even perhaps in the sense that the Gospels, written by men visited by the spirit of God, are "true."[14] Like Milton, later she implies that biblical truth is not "fixed" but that God may grant later, additional revelations. Lanyer cites evidence of being favored by divine illumination when she claims in a final note "To the doubtfull Reader" that she received the title for the work "in sleepe many yeares before" (p. 139). In the prayer for divine inspiration, which introduces her narrative of Christ's Passion, she not only follows in the footsteps of those holy women of early Christianity and of the later Middle Ages who claimed to be filled by the spirit of God, but also raises the possibility that a woman could be chosen to be a true witness of God, a belated "author" of the Gospel of Christ. As she says with a simplicity born of confidence: "I was appointed to performe this Worke" (p. 139)—not by men but by God. Like the Gospels the male disciples wrote after the death of Christ, Aemilia Lanyer's, as we shall see, bears revolutionary messages radically at odds with the dominant values of the contemporary society and the institution of the church.[15] Using the gospel form, she revives the gospel tradition of subverting worldly authority.

Lanyer's version of the Passion of Christ is a mixture of the conventional and the original. All the "facts" and incidents are taken from the New Testament; her language is often close to the Bible—both when she describes the key events and when she praises Christ in terms taken from the *Song of Songs,* which had for centuries of Christian exegesis been understood to describe the reciprocal love between Christ and the Church. She draws her narrative of the Passion from the accounts in the Gospels of Matthew, Mark, Luke, and John, but she takes on herself the ability to *interpret* the Bible, guided by grace, and emphasizes the distinctive roles that women and men played in their relations to Christ. Her confidence that she has interpreted the Bible correctly is evident in her challenge to Queene Anne: "judge if it agree not with the Text" ("To the Queenes most Excellent Majestie," l. 76).

The story she tells is one of men's betrayal and women's faith. Following Matthew and Mark closely, she recounts how on "That very Night our Saviour was betrayed," Christ "told his deere Disciples that they all / Should be offended by him" and forsake him (ll. 329, 337-38; cf. Matt. 26:31-33, Mark 14: 27-29), how Peter who "thought his Faith could never fall" and protested his constancy would before morning "deny" Christ three times (ll. 341, 345-46; cf. Matt. 26:34-35, Mark 14:30-31, Luke 22:33-34, John 13:37-38), and how Christ in Gethsemane told Peter and "the sonnes of *Zebed'us*" (James and John) of his sorrows (ll. 369-76) only to have them fall asleep rather than watch through the night (Matt. 26:40-45, Mark 14:37-38, Luke 22:45). While Matthew, Mark, and Luke (but not John) mention the sleeping apostles, Lanyer gives far more attention to this detail, drawing out its symbolic and spiritual significance:

> But now returning to thy sleeping Friends,
> That could not watch one houre for love of thee,
> Even those three Friends, which on thy Grace depends,
> Yet shut those Eies that should their Maker see;
> What colour, what excuse, or what amends,
> From thy Displeasure now can set them free?
>   Yet thy pure Pietie bids them Watch and Pray,
>   Lest in Temptation they be led away.
>
> Although the Spirit was willing to obay,
> Yet what great weakenesse in the Flesh was found!
> They slept in Ease, whilst thou in Paine didst pray;
> Loe, they in Sleepe, and thou in Sorrow drown'd. [ll. 417-28; cf. Mark 13:38]

But the sleep of the apostles signifies not just the inescapable weakness of the body—it is a defect of the heart: "Their eyes were heavie, and their hearts asleepe" (l. 465). The ominous sleeping, the fatal inattentiveness to Christ, anticipates their disloyalty when Christ's "foes" come to seize him: "all his deere Disciples do forsake him" (ll. 623-24).

> Those deare Disciples that he most did love,
> And were attendant at his becke and call,
> When triall of affliction came to prove,
> They first left him, who now must leave them all:
> For they were earth, and he came from above,
> Which made them apt to flie, and fit to fall:
>   Though they protest they never will forsake him,
>   They do like men, when dangers overtake them. [ll. 625-32]

If Christ's apostles, his closest friends, "forsake" him, what can one expect of his enemies? Lanyer makes explicit what is implicit in the biblical accounts, that those responsible for Christ's death were all men: the Jewish high priest Caiaphas; the witnesses who make false charges; Judas, whose example shows that only "faithlesse dealing" "can be expected / From wicked Man" (ll. 737-39); Pontius Pilate, who consents to Christ's death and frees Barrabas; King Herod; the "Crier" and the "Hangman" (ll. 961, 963); and the "spightfull men [who] with torments did oppresse / Th'afflicted body" of Christ (ll. 993-94).

In sharp contrast to these men—who are guilty of contributing to Christ's death through evil, cowardice, or (in the case of Pilate) the desire to please Caesar (ll. 919-20)—are the women. Again relying closely on the New Testament Gospels for her evidence, but particularly on Luke, who distinctly emphasizes the importance of women in Christ's life, Lanyer presents women as the only ones to recognize Christ's innocence, remain constant in their devotion, and be moved by compassion.[16] The tears of the Jewish women of Jerusalem elicit Christ's "grace" as he comforts them (Luke 23:27), though they cannot touch the men, whose "hearts [are] more hard than flint, or marble stone" (ll. 975, 1002). Elaborating on John's remark that Mary "stood by the cross of Jesus" (John 19:25), the poem describes the sorrows of the Virgin Mary, presenting her as a model of devotion (ll. 1009-1104, 1129-36). Lanyer's extended attention to this "Blessed" "Mother of our Lord" (ll. 1032, 1031) recalls and perhaps revives the devotion to the Virgin Mary that blossomed in medieval Catholicism but withered with Protestantism.[17] But it is Pilate's wife who drives home Lanyer's point that the women are the true believers and who articulates the significance of Christ's Passion, a significance Lanyer finds implicit in the New Testament accounts but either unobserved or suppressed by male writers who have interpreted the Passion.

The role of Pilate's wife is her most original and startling addition to the narrative of the Crucifixion. The Gospel according to Matthew mentions in passing, "Also when hee [Pilate] was set downe upon the judgement seate, his wife sent to him, saying, Have thou nothing to doe with that just man: for I have suffered many things this day in a dreame by reason of him" (Matt. 27:19). But Lanyer expands the episode, giving the wife a ten-stanza speech that defends Jesus, offers an "Apologie" for Eve, and asserts women's rightful liberty. It is this speech that has struck her readers as most radical. Lanyer's earlier claim that she receives "divine illumination" in writing her poem sanctions her invention of this speech, authorizing her version, which adds to the known Gospels of the New Testament, much as Milton later in *Paradise Regained* will invoke God's special inspiration in order to write what had been "unrecorded left through many an Age" about the temptations of Christ.[18] The argument of Pilate's wife's speech deserves further attention for its centrality in Lanyer's interpretation of the Crucifixion's significance.

The section begins as Lanyer, addressing Pilate, who is about to judge "faultlesse *Jesus*" (l. 746), tells him in close paraphrase of Matthew 27:19 to "heare the words of thy most worthy wife, / Who sends to thee, to beg her Saviours life" (ll. 751-52). It ends ten stanzas later as Lanyer paraphrases the last part of Matthew's verse:

> Witnesse thy wife (O *Pilate*) speakes for all;
> Who did but dreame, and yet a message sent,
> That thou should'st have nothing to doe at all
> With that just man. [ll. 834-37]

The stanzas in between are the "message" or "words" that Pilate's wife sent, though a certain indeterminacy of voice has led some critics to suggest this is Lanyer's speech rather than that of Pilate's wife (Hutson, p. 170; Lewalski, "Rewriting Patriarchy," p. 103). The confusion of voice is significant, for the poet's identification with Pilate's wife—a woman who also had a dream, whose knowledge came from divine illumination—allows her to speak with and for her. The implication is that both women have not only interpretive power but the right and responsibility to speak publicly. The words of both women violate the codes of their respective societies that encourage the silence of women and their subordination to the authority of husbands. Far from yielding to her husband, Pilate's wife advises him, judges Jesus more justly, and makes her "words" public, sending them to him. Thus in her intervention, Pilate's wife provides Lanyer with an example for the role she herself assumes in publishing her devotional poem. That the wife's words went unrecorded in Matthew (and Matthew is the only apostle to mention her) may suggest the silencing of women's words by the men who wrote the Gospels, or their blindness to their importance—an omission Lanyer is out to correct.

The warning to Pilate to "open thine eyes" yields to a defense of Eve contrasting her small, innocent sin with the sin Pilate commits in condemning Jesus. In Lanyer's reading of the brief narrative of the Fall in Genesis—the text that, subjected to the exegesis of men throughout history, had been used to sanction the authority of men and the inferiority and submission of women to their husbands—Eve appears "simply good" (l. 765), possessing an "undiscerning Ignorance" that allowed her to be "deceav'd" by the "cunning" of the "subtile Serpent" (ll. 769, 773, 769). Though Lanyer's indictment of Adam as "most too blame" (l. 778) because he was stronger and "Lord and King of all" (l. 783) may seem sophistical, her emphasis on Eve's simplicity and on her generous nature (her "fault was onely too much love, / Which made her give this present to her Deare," ll. 801-2) could be considered a plausible interpretation of the biblical account (Gen. 3:1-6). Even more important, however, in a single move that overturns centuries of exegesis, Lanyer turns Eve's credulity into a *virtue,* much as she had turned her own weakness of "Sexe" and "Sense" into a strength. For Eve's credulity is presented as an innate tendency to believe and trust, that is, a disposition to faith—and thus her simple credulity links her to the receptive, humble faith that the Virgin Mary shows in receiving the visitation from God (she "could hardly apprehend" Gabriel's "salutation," "Nor couldst [she] judge, whereto those words did tend," ll. 1058-60) and to the faith of all the women who believe in Christ and instinctively acknowledge his innocence and divinity. The credulity and gullibility of Eve is but the reverse side of the faith that sustains these women and distinguishes them from the men who, either weak in faith or moved by hate rather than love, are complicit in the Crucifixion.

Because Pilate's act is far worse than Eve's sin, it lessens her guilt: Eve's "weakenesse did the Serpents words obay; / But you in malice Gods deare Sonne betray" (ll. 815-16). While Lanyer follows Genesis in acknowledging that men "had power given to over-rule us all" (l. 760; cf. Gen. 3:16), she argues that Pilate's sin—and by extension men's role in crucifying Christ—invalidates and revokes God's sentence subjecting Eve and her female descendents to their husbands' authority. If Pilate condemns Jesus to die,

> Her sinne was small, to what you doe commit;
> All mortall sinnes that doe for vengeance crie,
> Are not to be compared unto it.
> . . . .
>   This sinne of yours, surmounts them all as farre
>   As doth the Sunne, another little starre.
> Then let us have our Libertie againe,
> And challendge to your selves no Sov'raigntie;
> You came not in the world without our paine,
> Make that a barre against your crueltie;
> Your fault beeing greater, why should you disdaine
> Our beeing your equals, free from tyranny?
>   If one weake woman simply did offend,
>   This sinne of yours, hath no excuse, nor end. [ll. 818-20, 823-32]

Here in this crucial passage, Lanyer offers a new understanding of the significance of Christ's crucifixion. Rather than simply following the tradition from Paul and Augustine through Luther and Calvin that interprets the Crucifixion as generally abrogating the human bondage to sin, to the flesh, and to the Mosaic laws that Christians believed were the mark of human bondage to sin, Lanyer sees it as, in addition, specifically redeeming *women,* liberating them from their subjection to men under the Law.[19] Just as the "sleeping" apostles and the otherwise treacherous men failed to see what the women saw in Christ, so Lanyer implies that throughout the history of Christianity the male apostles who interpreted the events of the Passion and, after them, the male interpreters of the Bible have failed not only to recognize women's devotion to the sacred but also to understand the full significance of the events surrounding the Crucifixion. Though her version of the Passion is closely based on the "facts" and words of the New Testament, her interpretation is independent of church tradition. Identifying with the women who from the beginning accepted Jesus, and especially with Pilate's wife, Lanyer claims the authority to interpret the Bible and the meaning of Christ's Crucifixion for humankind. In her Gospel, Christ's Passion reverses the order that gave men "power . . . to over-rule us all," undoing the punishment that God placed on Eve and cancelling the bondage of women. Speaking through and with Pilate's wife, as if she were present at Christ's Passion, Lanyer insists that now—with Pilate's condemnation of Jesus—there is a new dispensation that should make women the "equals" of men, "free" from their "tyranny." But the fact that she is also writing in seventeenth-century England and protesting the continued subjection of women suggests that Christ's redemption, which should have changed the social order, has yet to be enacted on earth.

For Lanyer, Christ's Passion and his teachings bear significance for transforming the secular order of society as well as humans' spiritual relation with God. Recalling the early Christians and anticipating the radical Protestants of the mid-seventeenth-century English Civil War, Lanyer recognizes the radical message of Christ's life and death for reordering society. Many of the teachings of Jesus were socially revolutionary. The pronouncements that the last shall be first, and that the meek shall inherit the earth, inverted the social and economic orders of secular society and thus were considered dangerously subversive in the centuries before Christianity became the established religion of Rome. Similarly defiant of the contemporary social order were Christ's teachings suggesting that the true Christian should cast off the bonds of marriage and family to follow Christ: "if any man come to me, and hate not his father, and mother, and wife, and children, and brethren, and sisters, yea, and his own life also, he cannot be my disciple" (Luke 14:26); "He that is unmarried careth for the things that belong to the Lord, how he may please the Lord: But he that is married careth for the things that are of the world, how he may please his wife" (1 Cor. 7:32-33). For all the seeming worldliness of Lanyer's concern for patronage, she recaptures something of the revolutionary spirit of Christianity in her interpretation of the Passion as calling for a radical reordering of society even in her own time. Properly understood, Lanyer suggests, Christianity undoes not only the power hierarchy in which the strong dominate the weak, but also the socially constructed gender hierarchy in which men rule over women— an order that characterized early seventeenth-century England much as it did Roman and Jewish societies in the time of Christ, and that was inscribed in the social codes of marriage that were understood to uphold the larger social order.

In early seventeenth-century England, marriage, far from circumscribing a fully private sphere, was part of the public world. Like the homily on marriage, the numerous marriage conduct books, with their various prescriptions for women's obedience, all assume the value of marriage in sustaining the order of society. While it is often mentioned that the marital conduct books of this period show the Puritan valuing of companionate marriage (in contrast to the supposed Catholic privileging of celibacy and virginity), in Protestant England in the late sixteenth and early seventeenth centuries marriage was particularly valued because it was understood to embody, encourage, and preserve a hierarchical social order. Domestic order mirrors and breeds order within the church and state. As Robert Cleaver puts it in *A Godly Forme of Houshold Government,* "a Household is as it were a little Common-wealth."[20] Given this close connection between marriage and the social order, it is far from coincidental that Aemelia Lanyer's poem, with its socially radical interpretation of the Passion as offering a new liberty to women, also implicitly rejects the institution of marriage.

Lanyer praises those women whose devotion to Christ has taken the place of earthly, human marriages: the Virgin Mary, who is "Farre from desire of any man" (l. 1077, her marriage to Joseph is erased from Lanyer's text), and Margaret Clifford, who as a widow refuses to entertain the "desires / Of idle Lovers" (ll. 1550-51) and is completely faithful to Christ, whom she has chosen to be her sole "Lord" and "Lover" (ll. 1705, 1398). Her prefatory poems encourage women to take Christ as their bridegroom, to put on "wedding garments" ("To all vertuous Ladies in generall," l. 8) and take him into "your soules pure bed" ("To the Ladie *Susan,*" l. 42). In "Salve Deus," she tells Margaret Clifford that Christ is the "Bridegroome" from whom she "shalt never be estrang'd" (ll. 77, 60)— a phrase that evokes the countess's former unhappy marriage, in which for a number of years she lived apart from her philandering husband. Drawing on the familiar biblical analogy between human marriage and the relation between the individual believer (or the Church) and Christ, particularly as developed in centuries of Christian interpretations of the *Song of Songs,* Lanyer presents Christ as the only "true" "Lover" (l. 1267), the only husband a woman needs.

> This is that Bridegroome that appeares so faire,
> So sweet, so lovely in his Spouses sight,
> That unto Snowe we may his face compare,
> His cheekes like skarlet, and his eyes so bright
> As purest Doves that in the rivers are,
> Washed with milke, to give the more delight;
>   His head is likened to the finest gold,
>   His curled lockes so beauteous to behold;
>
> Blacke as a Raven in her blackest hew;
> His lips like skarlet threeds, yet much more sweet

Than is the sweetest hony dropping dew,
Or hony combes, where all the Bees doe meete;
Yea, he is constant, and his words are true,
His cheekes are beds of spices, flowers sweet;
    His lips, like Lillies, dropping downe pure mirrhe,
    Whose love, before all worlds we doe preferre. [ll. 1305-20]

In a sense, this appropriation of the *Song of Songs* is conventional, as is her eroticization of the relationship between the countess and Christ: the language of human, erotic love is the only language we have for apprehending divine, spiritual love. But rather than emphasizing the congruence between secular and sacred love, Lanyer draws the analogy only to reject secular love, arguing that Christ is the only true object of our love and fulfills all our desires. Whereas the interpretations of the *Song of Songs* in the Middle Ages saw Solomon and Sheba's marriage not only as describing the relation between Christ and the Church but as validating or sacramentalizing human marriage and thus supporting the social order (Astell, pp. 31, 63, 179), Lanyer's reading of the Song of Songs ultimately points to a rejection of earthly marriage. Although Lanyer's praise of the Queen of Sheba might initially seem to validate a reordered human marriage in emphasizing the equality between Solomon and Sheba ("Here Majestie with Majestie did meete, / Wisdome to Wisdome yeelded true content," ll. 1585-86) and celebrating female agency (she fearlessly travels over "sea and land" to pursue her "Desire," ll. 1604-1601), the example of Solomon and Sheba actually yields to the greater example of Margaret's passion for Christ, which leaves actual, secular marriage behind as something no longer necessary for the fulfilment of Christian women:

Yet this rare Phoenix of that worne-out age,
This great majesticke Queene comes short of thee,
Who to an earthly Prince did then ingage
Her hearts desires, her love, her libertie,
Acting her glorious part upon a Stage
Of weaknesse, frailtie, and infirmity:
    Giving all honour to a Creature, due
    To her Creator, whom shee never knew.

But loe, a greater thou hast sought and found
Than *Salomon* in all his royaltie;
And unto him thy faith most firmely bound
To serve and honour him continually. [ll. 1689-1700]

Ultimately, the *Salve* uses the language of love and marriage to reject marriage in favour of a celibacy that recalls not so much the Catholic privileging of virginity as the socially revolutionary stance of those women and men in the early centuries of Christianity who, following Christ's teachings, chose virginity, repudiating the institution of marriage that was the foundation of their society, and disdaining to perpetuate that society by producing offspring.[21] The rejection of secular marriage in the *Salve* may also recall Queen Elizabeth's refusal to marry so as not to compromise her authority by having a man "over" her. Whatever one makes of Lanyer's position as mistress of Lord Hunsdon in the early 1590s, her 1611 poem, with its revolutionary gospel spirit, its sense of exclusive devotion to Christ, its sense that earthly loves and marriages conflict with marriage to God, aligns itself with those passages in the New Testament in which Christ teaches that "The children of this world marrie and are married. But they which shalbe counted worthy to enjoy that world, and the resurrection from the dead, neither marrie wives, nor are married" (Luke 20:34-35; cf. Matt. 22:30). It is notable that many of the women she dedicated her poetry to were in some sense independent of, or in conflict with, the authority of husbands.[22] Moreover, while her inclusion of mothers and daughters seems to emphasize family and lineage, sons and husbands are conspicuously absent in her addresses to contemporary women—almost as if these women, as she says of Christ, exist "without the assistance of man" ("To the Vertuous Reader," p. 49).

The rejection of marriage in the *Salve* is an integral part of Aemilia Lanyer's socially radical understanding of the meaning of Christ's Passion. To reject marriage is to undo the hierarchical social order in which men rule over women, thus freeing women from bondage to men and thus fulfilling the redemptive significance of Christ's Passion. If the goal of life is union with Christ in heaven at the end of the world, then marriage, with its commitment to reproduction, only delays that goal. Moreover, for a woman to choose Christ as her only Spouse, her true lover, is not just to be devoted to God but to reject the authority of any earthly husband, an authority understood in early seventeenth-century England to be representative of the authority of all earthly magistrates, particularly the king. Hence her argument has strongly subversive implications. King James well expressed this notion of the symbolic authority of husbands when, in his speech to his first English Parliament (19 March 1603), he compared the union between the monarch and his subjects to marriage: "I am the Husband, and all the whole Isle is my lawfull Wife. I am the Head, and it is my Body" (*Political Works,* p. 272).

James's comment here, which genders the notion of obedience as it insists on the interconnection between marital and political order, echoes Paul's comments in Ephesians comparing a well-ordered marriage to the relation between Christ and the Church:

> Wives, submit your selves unto your husbands, as unto the Lord. For the husband is the wives head, even as Christ is the head of the Church, and the same is

the saviour of his body. Therefore as the Church is in subjection to Christ, even so let the wives bee to their husbands in every thing. . . . So ought men to love their wives, as their owne bodies: he that loveth his wife, loveth himselfe. . . . This is a great secret, but I speak concerning Christ, and concerning the Church. Therefore every one of you, doe yee so: let every one love his wife, even as himselfe, and let the wife see that shee feare her husband. [Ephesians 5:22-24, 28, 32-33]

Paul's analogy identifies the husband with Christ and the head, the wife with the Church and the body, defining a mutual dependence and "love" based on woman's "subjection" and "submission," which is seen as necessary for a well-ordered society. These foundational verses from Ephesians, as well as other New Testament verses on marriage in which the apostles gave prescriptions for women's behavior, were enormously influential in Lanyer's time.[23] Cited in the "Homilie on . . . Matrimonie" and marital conduct treatises, they were used to give religious sanction to the established social and political order. Frances Dillingham's *Christian Oeconomy* opens with the passage from Colossians 3:18, "wives subject yourselves to your husbands, as it is meete in the Lord," and quotes Paul's advice in 1 Timothy 2:12 ("I permit not a woman to teach, neither to usurpe authoritie over the man, but to be in silence"). Robert Cleaver's *A Godly Forme of Household Government,* the most popular of these books (it went through nine editions between 1598 and 1624), repeatedly cites Ephesians 5:22-27 to encourage wives' obedience to their husbands, sometimes invoking a number of biblical passages in powerful combination: "wives [should] submit themselves, and be obedient to their owne husbands, as to the Lord, because the husband is by Gods ordinance, the wives head, . . . and therefore she oweth her subjection to him, like as the Church doth to Christ; and because [of] the example of *Sarah,* the mother of the faithfull, which obeyed *Abraham* and called him Lord" (Ephes. 5:22, 1 Cor. 11:3, 1 Pet. 3:6, Ephes. 5:24, cited in margin).[24]

Perhaps these conduct books, with all their emphasis on women's subjection, described an ideal at odds with actual practice. The point I wish to make, however, is that in all these treatises the apostles, particularly Paul and Peter, are understood to provide unshakeable biblical authority for prescriptions about domestic order, seen as the basis of all order in society. These apostolic verses are precisely the ones Lanyer so insistently defies in the *Salve,* as she gives women a public voice, insists on their equality or even superiority, and argues against the authority of men to rule them.[25] The argument of the entire poem, as well as of "Eves Apologie," constitutes a firm rejection of those New Testament verses in which the apostles rigorously prescribed wives' submission to the authority of their husbands. The evidence of Lanyer's poem thus suggests her recognition of a fundamental contradiction or discontinuity between Christ's teachings, which subverted the social order of Roman and Jewish society and emphasized the equality of the sexes, and those interpretations of Christ's message by his disciples that perpetuated the subjection of women.

The *Salve* reveals a surprisingly sophisticated hermeneutics, touched by a skepticism about the Bible one would not expect to find in the seventeenth century, for she clearly distinguishes between, on the one hand, Jesus's words and the "facts" of the Gospels and, on the other, the moral, domestic, and social prescriptions concerning women made by the male disciples and authors of the books of the New Testament. In a fundamentally Protestant move, Lanyer returns to the words of Christ, rejecting later human interpretations and accretions. But she goes considerably further than most of her Protestant contemporaries, for she rejects many of the apostolic texts themselves as corruptions of Christ's teachings. A discriminating reader of the text of the Bible, she suggests that all of its words are not equally inspired and authoritative. For Lanyer, the prescriptions of Paul and the other disciples for ordering/subjecting women and for silencing them in the Church—principles at odds with the teachings and actions of Christ as recorded in the Bible—prove to be misinterpretations of Christ's message that, supported by centuries of Christian commentary, have perpetuated the very bondage the Crucifixion was to have abrogated.

Finally, it is not only confidence in divine inspiration that allows Lanyer to claim religious authority; it is also her identification with a uniquely privileged woman, the Virgin Mary. Her description of the "blessed Virgin" (l. 1025)—of "meane estate" and "lowly mind," "hardly [able to] apprehend" Gabriel's salutation, yet deserving that "the Holy Ghost should . . . overshadow thee" (ll. 1034-35, 1058-59, 1082-84)—mirrors Lanyer's sense of herself as lowly ("To the Queenes most Excellent Majestie," ll. 109-14, 127-28), "Weake" in "Sexe" and "Sense," and fully receptive to God's grace and illumination (ll. 289-302). In what is perhaps a Protestant revision of Catholic mariolatry, the Virgin Mary becomes a pattern for the individual woman's unmediated connection with the divine. Like the Virgin Mary, Lanyer has been "chosen" to be a vessel for Christ ("To the doubtfull Reader"; cf. "Salve Deus," l. 1030). Thus her poem contains Christ. She presents his "picture" as something the Countess of Cumberland can keep in her "heart" and draw spiritual nourishment from (ll. 1325-28). But her prose dedication to the countess insists she is offering not simply an image or picture, but God himself: "Right Honourable and Excellent Lady . . . I present unto you even *our Lord Jesus himselfe.* . . . Therefore good Madame, to the most perfect eyes of your understanding, I deliver the inestimable treasure of all elected soules, to bee perused at convenient times" (pp. 34-35; italics mine).[26] The language here suggests that she is like the priests of the church who in celebrating Holy Communion offer Christ to the congregation.[27] Finding in Mary a precedent for a female priesthood, for woman's worthiness to contain and offer up God for human salvation, Lanyer thus assumes for herself something like the public, priestly power denied to women within the institution of the Christian church. In this assumption of a priestly function, she turns to women's advantage the Protestant emphasis on the priesthood of all believers. But she is also a true descendent of the early Christian women who believed they had the right to preach and even baptize, and of the medieval holy women who, as Bynum says, "saw themselves as authorized to teach, counsel, serve, and heal by mystical experience rather than by office" (*Holy Feast*, p. 235) and thus challenged the exclusive, intimate connection with God enjoyed by the priest.[28] Lanyer's presumption of this authority was certainly radical in 1611. But even today, the idea that women might bear priestly authority remains intensely controversial—witness the furor over the decision to allow the ordination of women in the Church of England, a decision prompting clergy as well lay Anglicans to consider conversion to Roman Catholicism. Claiming the authority to reinterpret the Bible and the significance of the Crucifixion, joining the ranks of the (male) apostles and correcting their prescriptions for human behavior where they diverge from what seems to her the message of Jesus, Aemilia Lanyer takes the next logical step and defies the assumption that the priesthood is an exclusively male privilege.

NOTES

1. Peter Brown, *The Body and Society: Men, Women, and Sexual Renunciation in Early Christianity* (New York: Columbia University Press, 1988), esp. ch. 1 (pp. 5-32), discusses Christianity within the cultural context not only of Rome but of the first-century Jews. See also Elaine Pagels, *Adam, Eve, and the Serpent* (New York: Random House, 1988). On women's roles in early Judaism and early Christianity, see Elisabeth Schussler Fiorenza, *In Memory of Her: A Feminist Theological Reconstruction of Christian Origins* (New York: Crossroad, 1983). On the discontinuities about woman implicit in the two creation stories in Genesis, and their complex development through centuries of Christian tradition, see James Grantham Turner, *One Flesh: Paradisal Marriage and Sexual Relations in the Age of Milton* (Oxford: Clarendon, 1987). New Testament references are to the Geneva Bible (1602 ed.); i/j and u/v have been modernized.

2. The marginal annotations on these passages in the 1607 printing of the third (1602) ed. of the "Geneva" New Testament, based on Beza, point out that the "covering" of women "declareth that the woman is one degree beneath the man by the ordinance of God," and that "having their heades covered . . . was then [in Paul's time] a signe of subjection." *The Geneva Bible (The Annotated New Testament, 1602 Edition)*, ed. Gerald T. Sheppard, Pilgrim Classic Commentaries, vol. 1 (New York: The Pilgrim Press, 1989), p. 85r.

3. See Pagels's account of the heroism of Thecla and Perpetua (ch. 1-2). Brown (p. 145) notes the important role of women in the church by 200 C.E., though Pagels implies that as early as the deutero-Pauline letters of the New Testament (particularly Timothy 1 and 2, and Ephesians) there was an attempt to suppress the empowering of women evident in the case of Thecla, who claimed that women could teach and baptize (ch. 1, esp. pp. 24-26).

See Augustine, *The City of God,* trans. Marcus Dods, 2 vols. (New York: Hafner Publising Co., 1948), Bk. 14 ch.7 (II, 10-12), Bk. 15 ch. 20, and Bk. 15 ch. 22-23 (II, 84-89, 91-97) on the association of woman with flesh, which tempts man from God. On subjection in marriage as the model of order, see Augustine, *City of God,* Bk. 14. ch. 7 (II, 10-12), Bk. 19 ch. 14 and 16 (II, 322-23, 325-26) and Pagel's discussion of Augustine (p. 114). On the association of woman with the flesh, see also Brown's discussion of Ambrose (pp. 348-49) and Jerome (pp. 375-77), Pagel's discussion of Augustine, esp. pp. 113-14, and Ann W. Astell's discussion of Origen in *The Song of Songs in the Middle Ages* (Ithaca: Cornell University Press, 1990), esp. pp. 2-5. Brown and Pagels emphasize the powerful influence of Augustine on Christianity and, indeed, Western values (Brown, ch. 19; Pagels, ch. 5).

4. Caroline Walker Bynum, *Holy Feast and Holy Fast: The Religious Significance of Food to Medieval Women* (Berkeley and Los Angeles: University of California Press, 1987).

5. Caroline Walker Bynum, *Jesus as Mother: Studies in the Spirituality of the High Middle Ages* (Berkeley and Los Angeles: University of California Press, 1982), esp. Introduction (pp. 1-21), and "Women Mystics in the Thirteenth Century: The Case of the Nuns of Helfta" (pp. 170-262). Bynum (*Holy Feast*) argues that the increased power of the clergy was related to the late medieval proliferation of holy women, for these women claimed an immediate, intimate experience of God that was similar to that enjoyed by the priest. Astell sees a distinctly positive valuing of the feminine in religious experience in medieval interpretations of *Canticles.*

6. On the Protestant suppression of the feminine aspect of Catholic spirituality, see Maureen Sabine, *Feminine Engendered Faith: The Poetry of John Donne and Richard Crashaw* (London: Macmillan, 1992), pp. 1-42, and Patricia Crawford, *Women and Religion in England, 1500-1720* (London: Routledge, 1993), pp. 21-37.

7. Elaine V. Beilin, *Redeeming Eve: Women Writers of the English Renaissance* (Princeton: Princeton University Press, 1987), discusses the Reformist women prose writers and poets, some of whom contributed to religious polemic (see esp. pp. 48-150). On women's status as defined in English Protestant writings, particularly in relation to Roman Catholicism, see also Charles H. George and Katherine George, *The Protestant Mind of the English Reformation, 1570-1640* (Princeton: Princeton University Press, 1961), pp. 258-65, 275-89.

8. A.L. Rowse, *Sex and Society in Shakespeare's Age: Simon Forman the Astrologer* (New York: Scribners, 1974); Rowse, "Introduction: Shakespeare's Dark Lady," in *The Poems of Shakespeare's Dark Lady* (New York: Clarkson N. Potter, 1979), pp. 1-37.

9. Barbara K. Lewalski observes: "The title of Lanyer's volume promises, somewhat misleadingly, a collection of religious poetry" ("Re-writing Patriarchy and Patronage: Margaret Clifford, Anne Clifford, and Aemilia Lanyer," *Yearbook of English Studies* 21 [1991]: 98). See also Lewalski, *Writing Women in Jacobean England* (Cambridge, Mass.: Harvard University Press, 1993), pp. 213-41. Lewalski stresses the secular aspect of the volume as a "defense and celebration of the enduring community of good women" (*Writing Women,* p. 213).

10. On Elizabeth, see Sabine, p. 13; Roy Strong, *The Cult of Elizabeth:Elizabethan Portraiture and Pageantry* (London: Thames and Hudson, 1977), pp. 117-28, esp. p. 126, and Phillippa Berry, *Of Chastity and Power: Elizabethan Literature and the Unmarried Queen* (London: Routledge, 1989), who emphasizes the importance of Elizabeth's spiritual authority, noting also that the queen assumed the title "supreme governor" of the Church rather than "supreme head," the title of Henry VIII (pp. 65-66). On James, see Sabine (p.

25) and Jonathan Goldberg, "Fatherly Authority: The Politics of Stuart Family Images," in Margaret W. Ferguson, Maureen Quilligan, and Nancy J. Vickers, ed., *Rewriting the Renaissance: The Discourse of Sexual Difference in Early Modern Europe* (Chicago: University of Chicago Press, 1986), pp. 3-32. For James's writings, see *The Trew Law of Free Monarchies* and his first speech to the English Parliament, in *The Political Works of James I,* intro. Charles Howard McIlwain (New York: Russell and Russell, 1965), pp. 55, 273.

11. Lewalski, *Writing Women,* p. 18. See also Leeds Barroll, "The Court of the First Stuart Queen," in Linda Levy Peck, ed., *The Mental World of the Jacobean Court* (Cambridge: Cambridge University Press, 1991), pp. 191-208.

12. *Holy Bible* [King James Authorized Version] (London, 1611), dedicatory epistle "To the Most High and Mightie Prince James," sig. A2v. Janel Mueller, "The Feminist Poetics of Aemilia Lanyer's 'Salve Deus Rex Judaeorum,'" in *Feminist Measures: Soundings in Poetry and Theory,* ed. Lynn Keller and Christanne Miller (Ann Arbor: University of Michigan Press, 1994), pp. 208-36—and in the revised version of this essay that appears in this volume—mentions the publication of the King James Bible as part of the context for the *Salve* (Keller and Miller, p. 215; and see above, chapter 6).

13. *An Homilie of the State of Matrimonie* insists wives should suffer in silence and "be quiet," for they will get their reward hereafter; in *Certaine Sermons or Homilies Appointed to be Read in Churches in the Time of Queen Elizabeth I (1547-1571),* Facsimile Reprod. of the Edition of 1623, intro. Mary Ellen Rickey and Thomas B. Stroup, 2 vols. in one (Gainesville, Fla.: Scholars' Facsimiles and Reprints, 1968), II, 245. On women's silence, see William Whately, *A Bride-Bush. Or, A Direction for Married Persons* (London, 1623), pp. 200-1; Robert Cleaver, *A Godly Forme of Houshold Government* (London, 1603), p. 230: "The best meanes therefore that a wife can use to obtaine, and maintaine the love and good liking of her husband, is to be silent, obedient, peaceable."

14. In her emphasis on the role of women, Lanyer is closest to Luke, the one gospel written by someone who did not claim to have witnessed the Crucifixion.

15. The question of whether a woman could have written one of the Gospels is intriguing. Among the Gnostic Gospels purporting to be the secret teachings of Jesus condemned as heretical (most of which were discovered at Nag Hammadi in 1945) is a Gospel supposedly by Mary Magdalen. On the *Gospel of Mary,* see Pagels, *Adam, Eve, and the Serpent,* p. 61, and Pagels, *The Gnostic Gospels* (New York: Random House, 1979), pp. 11-14, 64-65. Fiorenza, *In Memory of Her,* argues for the importance of recovering "the women disciples and what they have done" (p. xiv).

16. Lorna Hutson, "Why the Lady's Eyes Are Nothing Like the Sun," in Isobel Armstrong, ed., *New Feminist Discourses: Critical Essays on Theories and Texts* (London: Routledge, 1992), pp. 154-75, aptly observes: "Lanyer figures the climax of the narrative as a drama of interpretation, in which women elicit radiance and meaning from the event which had remained mute and indecipherable to masculine exegesis" (p. 170). Mueller, "Feminist Poetics," notes the "pattern of fundamental misprision exhibited by all of the males in the story . . . while the female poet unfailingly understands what and who Jesus is" (p. 222).

17. Beilin (p. 198) observes Lanyer's emphasis on Mary but does not see the possible Catholic significance of this. Instead, she sees Lanyer's poetry as "ardently Protestant" (p. 182). Lewalski observes that many of the dedications are to women "linked through kinship or marriage with the Sidney-Leicester faction," which was strongly Protestant (*Writing*

Women, p. 221). However, two of Lanyer's dedicatees—Queen Anne and Lady Arabella Stuart—had Roman Catholic connections; Anne may even have converted. Certain aspects of her poem (particularly the attention to the Virgin Mary, who has thirteen stanzas devoted to her) make the label "Protestant" problematic.

18. John Milton, *Paradise Regained,* in *Complete Poems and Major Prose,* ed. Merritt Y. Hughes (New York: Odyssey, 1957), 1.16.

19. See Augustine, *City of God,* Bk. 15 ch. 2-3 (II, 51-53), Luther, *Treatise on Christian Liberty,* in *Works of Martin Luther,* vol. 2 (Philadelphia: A.J. Holman, 1916), pp. 312-48, and John Calvin, *Institutes of the Christian Religion,* trans. John Allen, 5th American edition, 2 vols. (Philadelphia: Presbyterian Board of Publication, n.d.), Bk. 2, ch. 11 (I, 405-19), Bk. 3, ch. 19 (II, 62-76).

20. Cleaver, *A Godly Forme of Houshold Government,* p. 13. See also William Gouge, *Of Domesticall Duties* (London, 1623), "the family is a seminary of the Church and common-wealth" (p. 17); and *An Homilie of the State of Matrimonie.* On the analogy of family and politics, particularly in the Stuart period, see Gordon Schochet, *Patriarchalism in Political Thought: The Authoritarian Family and Political Speculation and Attitudes especially in Seventeenth Century England* (New York: Basic Books, 1975), pp. 54-84, and Lawrence Stone, *The Family, Sex and Marriage in England, 1500-1800* (New York: Harper and Row, 1977), pp. 152-54.

21. Brown (esp. pp. 1-4, 5-102) gives an eloquent, sympathetic explanation of the socially revolutionary significance of sexual renunciation for the early ascetic Christians. See also Pagels, *Adam, Eve, and the Serpent,* esp. ch. 1, 2, 4. Brown points out the social usefulness of Augustine's later defense of marriage in a society where "the security of the Catholic church depended on the authority of male heads of households" (p. 404).

22. Queen Anne had a separate court as well as a relatively separate life from her husband, King James, who was known for his homoerotic attachments to male favorites. (See Lewalski, *Writing Women,* pp. 15-43, on Anne's "oppositional politics"). The queen's daughter, Elizabeth, was as yet unmarried; the Dowager Countess of Kent and Margaret Clifford, Countess of Cumberland, were both widows; Margaret's daughter, Anne Clifford, was to be in conflict for many years with her husband as she struggled to gain legal rights to her inheritance from her father.

23. As Pagels (*Adam, Eve, and the Serpent,* pp. 23-26) and Brown (p. 57) have shown, the deutero-Pauline writings, which include Ephesians, Colossians, and 1 Timothy, endorse marriage and thus "correct" the preference for celibacy and sexual renunciation in Paul's first epistle to the Corinthians (1 Cor. 7:1, 7-8), though the sense of gender hierarchy remains generally consistent throughout the Pauline epistles.

24. *An Homilie of the State of Matrimonie,* esp. p. 242; Francis Dillingham, *Christian Oeconomy: or Houshold Government* (London, 1609), pp. 1, 11; Cleaver, p. 224. For further examples of reliance on these biblical verses, see also Whately and Gouge. 1 Peter 3:1, 5-6 ("let the wives bee subiect to their husbandes. . . . For even after this maner in time past did the holy women, which trusted in God tire themselves, & were subject to their husbands. As Sara obeyed Abraham, and called him Sir"), which Cleaver paraphrases, was regularly invoked to encourage women's proper "reverence." See *An Homilie . . . of Matrimonie,* pp. 242-43; Whately, p. 203; Gouge, p. 283.

25. On the differences between the Pauline and deutero-Pauline texts on women and sexuality, see Pagels, *Adam, Eve, and the Serpent,* pp. 23-25; on the differences between these

texts concerning marriage, see Brown, pp. 44-58; and on the contradictions in Paul concerning gender, see Daniel Boyarin, "Paul and the Genealogy of Gender," *Representations* 41 (winter 1993): 1-33.

26. Wendy Wall, *The Imprint of Gender: Authorship and Publication in the English Renaissance* (Ithaca: Cornell University Press, 1993), points out that Lanyer creates her authorial role as "her text becomes the Word Incarnate"; "her published text becomes Christ" (pp. 324-25).

27. Cf. 1 Peter 2:5, 9 on the faithful as a holy priesthood. But Peter implies it is men who speak God's words and minister (4:10-11). In her claims for being able to "present" Christ, Lanyer recalls the medieval holy women who, Bynum has argued, were assuming the power of priests to handle and enjoy God ("Women Mystics in the Thirteenth Century: The Case of the Nuns of Helfta," in *Jesus as Mother,* pp. 170-262).

28. Pagels, *Adam, Eve, and the Serpent,* p. 24, observes that early Christian women claimed the right to preach and baptize.

11
"Pardon . . . though I have digrest": Digression as Style in "Salve Deus Rex Judaeorum"

Boyd Berry

Despite Barbara Lewalski's outline of Aemilia Lanyer's *Salve Deus Rex Judaeorum*,[1] there has been little work on the rhetorical textures of the central poem of the volume. In particular, little attention has been paid to the opening and closing sections of that poem—those which frame the much discussed narrative of the Crucifixion. Indeed, I wish here to follow up on Elaine Beilin's suggestion that, while undertaking "to redeem women" and "to alter the traditional separation between woman and God," the poem is "superficially digressive" and that it "mixed genres, interrupted sequence, and juxtaposed high matter with low."[2] Attention has been focused not on the opening and closing movements but primarily on the obviously insubordinate features of the volume, especially "Eves Apologie in defence of Women" at the heart of the Crucifixion narrative.[3] In form, the "Apologie" can be read as a digression or intrusion into the narrative, that is, as a rhetorical movement that is subversive of some set of expectations about how a narrative will or should proceed. The basic premise of this essay is that that sort of digression is the most obvious, frequent, and fundamental rhetorical strategy of the poem; that is, that the formal features which Lewalski outlined and Beilin sketched constitute a pervasive, sly, insubordinate verbal texture—not "superficial" but essential to the whole performance—which enacts upon the reader a series of subversive disorientations in addition to that overtly articulated in the preface and in "Eves Apologie in defence of Women."[4] In short, I argue that the poem *also* opens and closes with a sense of mischief, perhaps, of satire, of invective, or even of hard-headed complaint at work in language which questions and subverts important formal features of male discourse of the age.[5]

I choose the term "digression" rather than "dilation," which Patricia Parker has so memorably explored because, while both function somewhat negatively in a male verbal economy which sets a premium on "point," digression seems a bit more negative; Parker reminds us, for example, how dilation figured in the generation of male orations and sermons and was associated with the exclusively male activity of "preaching of the Word," however effeminate it could appear to be. Still another way of putting my point would be to suggest that, in her own way, Lanyer's mimesis of the Crucifixion story is not unlike Parker's own project. Both re-present important features of male discourse—about the Crucifixion, about fat women and fat texts—in order, perhaps, to recast them slightly, although one might argue that Lanyer's intrusion into the story of Jesus, "Eves Apologie," is more overtly a recasting than Parker's discussion of dilation.[6] Moreover, while the central movement of the poem is mimetic, the opening and closing movements dilate the text through continual refocusing of attention—between the deity and the Countess of Cumberland, most simply—which are basic to digression.

Most obviously (from a religious point of view) there is a great discrepancy between the language used to re-present the deity in the central narrative of the Crucifixion and the language used of the deity in the opening and closing movements. Jesus, in the narrative of the Crucifixion—a narrative which proceeds in strict chronological step with the account of the Gospels (excepting, obviously, the "Apologie")—might be said to re-present a "woman's deity."[7] He pointedly refrains from speaking publicly to patriarchal authority, he is largely acted upon rather than acting, he is the object of adoration and even an anatomy and blazon echoing to male amatory verse of the age. This presentation of the deity at the center of the poem contrasts sharply with the language used of the deity in the opening and closing sections, where God is all-powerful, male, controlling, judgmental. Indeed, these opening and closing sections may gain much of their digressive force from this powerful contrast.

To illustrate the "womanly" features of Jesus, let me begin with his talking. With his lowly disciples, Jesus "opened all his woe" in Gethsemane, and "gave them leave his sorows to discusse," which seems so striking as to puzzle the narrative "I": "Sweet Lord, how couldst thou thus to flesh and blood / Communicate thy griefe? tell of thy woes?" ("Salve Deus," ll. 371-78). In contrast, when he is apprehended, Jesus acknowledges his identity, yet his efforts to communicate fail.

When Heavenly Wisdome did descend so lowe
To speake to them: they knew they did not well,
Their great amazement made them backward goe:
    Nay, though he said unto them, I am he,
    They could not know him, whom their eyes did see. [ll. 500-4]

Again, before Caiaphas, his accusers "tell his Words, though farre from his intent, / And what his Speeches were, not what he meant" (ll. 655-56). More pointedly, Jesus more than once withholds speech, as before Caiaphas, when

> they all doe give attentive eare,
> To heare the answere, which he will not make;
> The people wonder how he can forbeare,
> And these great wrongs so patiently can take;
> But yet he answers not. [ll. 665-69]

Eventually, he does reply to Caiaphas, and communication again fails. He answers fully and "Nor Priests, nor People, meanes he now to blame; / But answers Folly, for true Wisdomes sake" (ll. 700-701). But, "I" points out to Caiaphas, "Though he expresse his Glory unto thee, / Thy Owly eies are blind, and cannot see" (ll. 711-12). Perhaps the greatest failure of communication occurs in the passage about Pilate, since "I" intervenes, seemingly to record Pilate's wife's comments, the two female voices blending in "Eves Apologie." After Pilate fails to respond to "thy wife (O *Pilate*) [who] speakes for all," Jesus is constructed as noncommunicative, when "I" addresses Pilate finally: "Yet neither thy sterne browe, nor his [Herod's] great place, / Can draw an answer from the Holy One" (ll. 834, 881-82).

This strand of the narrative, focussed on Jesus's withholding of speech before male authority, culminates, on the way to the cross, in Jesus's response to the tears of the "Daughters of Jerusalem," whose

> cries inforced mercie, grace, and love
> From him, whom greatest Princes could not moove:
>
> To speake one word, nor once to lift his eyes
> Unto proud *Pilate*, no nor *Herod,* king;
> By all the Questions that they could devise,
> Could make him answere to no manner of thing;
> Yet these poore women, by their pitious cries
> Did moove their Lord, their Lover, and their King,
>   To take compassion, turne about, and speake
>   To them whose hearts were ready now to breake. [ll. 975-84]

That is, Jesus is caught in a time-centered rhetorical structure, within which he behaves in precisely the ways which male-authored conduct books proposed virtuous women should act.[8] Further, his suffering culminates in a blazon from *Canticles:*

> This is that Bridegroome that appeares so faire,
> So sweet, so lovely in his Spouses sight,

That unto Snowe we may his face compare,
His cheekes like skarlet, and his eyes so bright
As purest Doves that in the rivers are,
Washed with milke, to give the more delight;
    His head is likened to the finest gold,
    His curled lockes so beauteous to behold;

Blacke as a Raven in her blackest hew;
His lips like skarlet threeds, yet much more sweet
Than is the sweetest hony dropping dew,
Or hony combes, where all the Bees doe meet. . . .
His cheekes are beds of spices, flowers sweet;
    His lips, like Lillies, dropping downe pure mirrhe,
    Whose love, before all worlds we doe preferre. [ll. 1305-20]

Moreover, his passivity in suffering is emphasized in his execution:

His harmelesse hands unto the Crosse they nailde,
And feet that never trode in sinners trace,

. . . .

With sharpest pangs and terrors thus appailde,
Sterne Death makes way, that Life might give him place:
    His eyes with teares, his body full of wounds,
    Death last of paines his sorrows all confounds.

His joynts dis-joynted, and his legges hang downe,
His alablaster breast, his bloody side,
His members torne, and on his head a Crowne
Of sharpest Thorns, to satisfie for pride. [ll. 1153-64][9]

In contrast to this representation of the hero-deity as publicly silent before authority, as passive, as cruelly beautiful, and as anatomized or verbally dis-membered, the language used to present the deity in the opening and closing sections of the poem focusses our attention on the timeless, potent, authoritarian, and judgmental aspects of "great *Jehova* King of heav'n and earth" (l. 137). These sections speak of how

With Majestie and Honour is He clad,
And deck'd with light, as with a garment faire;

. . . .

He rides upon the wings of all the windes,
And spreads the heav'ns with all powrefull hand;
Oh! who can loose when the Almightie bindes?
Or in his angry presence dares to stand? [ll. 73-74; 81-84]

Again, at the close of the poem, in a passage praising the Countess of Cumberland, we read:

> This is that great almightie Lord that made
> Both heaven and earth, and lives for evermore;
> By him the worlds foundation first was laid:
> He fram'd the things that never were before:
> The Sea within his bounds by him is staid,
> He judgeth all alike, both rich and poore:
>   All might, all majestie, all love, all lawe
>   Remaines in him that keepes all worlds in awe. [ll. 1641-48]

Moreover, this talk of first creation flows conventionally into talk of the final millennium, when time shall be shut up.

> This is Gods Sonne, in whom he is well pleased,
> His deere beloved, that his wrath appeased.

> He that had powre to open all the Seales,
> And summon up our sinnes of blood and wrong,
> He unto whom the righteous soules appeales,
> That have bin martyrd, and doe think it long. [ll. 1663-68]

The discrepancy between these two sorts of representation of deity is, to be sure, a common feature of Christian language.[10] Yet the strong verbal marking of that discrepancy provides perhaps the most obvious example of the essentially digressive structure of the poem, since a sense of verbal discrepancy is precisely what leads a reader to label a passage digressive.

Briefly let me reinforce my point that the sense of discrepancy, essential to the reader's feeling of digression at points where language has subverted his/her expectations, pervades the poem. Let me do so by noting two salient features, first of the central tale of the Crucifixion, then of the opening and closing movements. First, then, "Eves Apologie in defence of Women" not only breaks the flow of the chronological narrative of the central section but also disrupts our sense of the narrator's voice, while it is perhaps the most extensive embroidery upon the Gospel account. Arrived at the trial before Pilate, the narrative "I" exhorts Pilate to attend to his wife's advice; what follows then may be Pilate's wife's report of her dream, mentioned in the Gospels, yet it is also a continuation of the narrative. That is, the voice of the narrative "I" and the voice of Pilate's wife fuse. Moreover, this is "Eves Apologie," both in the positive and the humble sense, and while the sentences are about Eve—take Eve as their subject—in one sense they may be thought of as Eve's anachronistic words as well. That is, one could argue that the narrator, Pilate's wife, and Eve fuse verbally at this point, problematizing the narrative structure in a host of ways. But, regardless of whether two or three voices fuse, these female voices not only utter subversive claims on behalf of women, they do so publicly, directly addressing patriarchal authority. That is, they refuse to behave verbally in the ways in which the publicly silent Jesus behaves; they refuse to be silent in the ways which male writing shaped for "virtuous" women.

Turning to the opening and closing movements of the poem, we note perhaps most obviously how the narrator's attention repeatedly swings back and forth between biblical and religious matters on the one hand and adoration, perhaps sycophantic flattery of the Countess of Cumberland on the other.[11] Here one's sense of digression is most pronounced, as is the narrative "I" in her frequent comments about her ability/inability to write. Consider the opening movement of forty-one stanzas, which (evoking the timeless, male deity) focusses upon varieties of talking and indulges in what "I" labels a series of digressions. Initially it appears that "I" will praise the Countess of Cumberland "Sith *Cynthia* is ascended to that rest / Of endlesse joy and true Eternitie." Immediately, contradictions pop up. "I" must immediately seek pardon for not writing what the countess has "commaunded." Cynthia is enthroned in "That glorious place that cannot be exprest / By any wight clad in mortalitie" and is so far exalted that "she gives glorie unto God alone." Yet the countess commanded "I" to write "When shining *Phoebe* gave so great a grace, / Presenting *Paradice* to your sweet sight." So, one manifestation of the moon resides in an inexpressible place; almost certainly "Cynthia" refers to the dead Elizabeth I, and one implication is that, with the demise of one powerful woman, the countess must take her place. Clearly the other lunar manifestation, Phoebe, does not reside in the inexpressible.[12] At the same time, "I" voices her problems as writer, since "wanting skill I shall but purchase blame." Indeed, she requires two sorts of pardon, first for "want of womans wit / To pen thy praise, when few can equall it" and then for not writing as she has been instructed (ll. 1-24).

Indeed, the early stanzas of this initial section repeatedly raise the question whether "I" can write with authority when limited by her "womans wit"; they also evoke the powerful male deity, arriving there through further sycophantic address to the countess,

> [God's] all-reviving beautie, yeelds such joyes
> To thy sad Soule, plunged in waves of woe,
> That worldly pleasures seemes to thee as toyes,
> Onely thou seek'st Eternitie to know. [ll. 33-36]

Further, the construction of the judgmental prowess of "great *Jehova* King of heav'n and earth" is tied to a construction of good and evil, both of which are defined exclusively in terms of verbal behavior. On the one hand, there are evil-talking persons.

> But woe to them that double-hearted bee,
> Who with their tongues the righteous Soules do slay;

. . . .

> The Lord wil roote them out that speake prowd things,
> Deceitfull tongues are but false Slanders wings. [ll.105-6; 111-12]

Indeed, "As venemous as Serpents" is the "breath" of the ungodly, "With poysned lies to hurt in what they may / The innocent" (ll. 117-19). On the other hand, the virtuous person, whom the powerful deity protects, "no untrueths of Innocents doth tell, / Nor wrongs his neighbour, nor in deed, nor word" and never "whets his tongue more sharper than a sword, / To wound the reputation of the Just" (ll. 131-35).

But, this evocation of Jehovah punishing bad talk and protecting good talk has been a digression, we suddenly learn:

> Pardon (good Madame) though I have digrest
> From what I doe intend to write of thee,
> To set his glorie forth whom thou lov'st best. [ll. 145-47]

And, as attention swings back to the Countess of Cumberland, for the first time extensively, she is constructed as virtuous because she has left the Court and shunned physical beauty. She is, presumably, thus free from the force of slanderous talkers (commonly associated with Court life) as well as the perils which the Court could (and, likely in the case of Lanyer, did) hold for a beautiful and powerless woman. Indeed, the hazards of female beauty require seven (or perhaps ten) stanzas and the tales of Helen, Lucrece, Cleopatra, Rosamond, and Matilda to explore. Oddly enough, "I" does not label these stanzas a digression, perhaps because the list parodies or inverts the standard, male-authored lists of wicked women (and their mirror image, lists of the virtuous in praise of women). Clearly, the women are a foil to the countess, who "from the Court to the Countrie art retir'd" and, "the wonder of our wanton age / Leav'st all delights to serve a heav'nly King" (ll. 161, 169-70). Christ's death has

> made her Dowager of all;
> Nay more, Co-heire of that eternall blisse
> That Angels lost, and We by *Adams* fall;
> Meere Cast-awaies, rais'd by a *Judas* kisse,
> Christs bloody sweat, the Vineger, and Gall,
> The Speare, Sponge, Nailes, his buffeting with Fists,
>   His bitter Passion, Agony, and Death,
>   Did gaine us Heaven when He did loose his breath. [ll. 257-64]

It would seem, at this point, as the countess is severed from the slanderous tongues (which no doubt would have wagged about the pregnant mistress of Lord Hunsdon) as well as from these beauties, while a male and powerful deity is set in judgment on those bad talkers, and as the connection between the dowager countess and her true Bridegroom seems about to yield to the violent apparatus of the Crucifixion, that "I" will take up the narrative. However, eight additional stanzas, addressed to the Muse and raising further questions about "I"'s authority to use language, intervene. "I" initially claims that "These high deserts invites my lowely Muse," though it remains unclear whether those merits be Jesus' or the dowager's—since the dowager remains on "I"'s mind and requires a second, self-contradictory and potentially insubordinate apology. "I" craves pardon of the countess,

> For time so spent, I need make no excuse,
> Knowing it doth with thy faire Minde agree
> So well, as thou no Labour wilt refuse. [ll. 267-69]

The phrasing is seriously ambiguous, the "time so spent" *either* requiring "pardon" or needing "no excuse." And this turnabout provokes "I" to address the Muse, asking where it hopes to "flie," raising the possibility of Icarus' "waxen wings," noting the limitations of "thy poore barren Braine," yet asserting the Muse will, despite all, fly;

> Yet cannot this thy forward Mind resraine,
>> But thy poore Infant Verse must soare aloft,
>> Not fearing threat'ning dangers, happening oft. [ll. 278-80]

Repeatedly "I" harps on these limitations as well as the impulse to ignore them and press forward, aided by the deity.

> But yet the Weaker thou doest seeme to be
> In Sexe, or Sence, the more his Glory shines,
> That doth infuze such powerfull Grace in thee,
> To shew thy Love in these few humble Lines;
> The Widowes Myte, with this may well agree. [ll. 289-93]

"I" wishes to write only what agrees with "pure Doctrine, and most holy Writ," lest "blindest Weakenesse" err, become "over-bold," and employ "other Phrases than may well agree" with truth. "I" does not seek worldly fame, "The Vulgars breath, the seed of Vanitie." Further, this is "A Matter farre beyond my barren skill," "Yet if he please t'illuminate my Spirit. . . . Then will I tell of that sad blacke fac'd Night, / Whose mourning Mantle covered Heavenly Light" (ll. 305-28). That is, "I" will not write in a slanderous or "vain" way; presumably she can both please the countess and become exempt from carping critics if she is able as an author to fly, and indeed will and does fly, buoyed (she claims at times) by the male, paternal deity. More generally, in this first movement of the poem, only slowly or hesitantly turning its attention to the Crucifixion of the contrasting "womanish" deity, there is repeated submission, admission of incapacity, and as well discrepant assertions of power and ability, while "I" shifts her attention between "great *Jehova* King" and the dowager.

This initial movement of the poem (and the closing section) problematizes the narrative voice an additional way, because it echoes to the nine ingratiating dedications addressed to the queen and other powerful women (as well as to the brief "Description of Cooke-ham" with which the volume closes), all of which have given rise to the view that Lanyer's volume was put together for "profit."[13] Readers commonly assume there is a discrepancy between religious sentiment and an interest in patronage, hence are confused about how to "take" the rhetorical "I" of this volume.[14]

To be sure, if we admit the generally accepted understanding of Lanyer's biography, the poem may be read as querying that easy dichotomy.[15] What was a woman to do? What was she to do with religious sentiments *and* the perception that she needed patronage? In particular, what was a woman—daughter of an alien (and Jew), unprotected first by her father (who died when she was young), then by her husband (who lost the money Hunsdon apparently paid at her pregnancy and subsequent marriage), born into the functionary stratum of the Court, physically (perhaps incarnately) aware (in her pregnancy by Hunsdon) of the potency of male and elite privilege (which fobbed her off into what must have been a most uncomfortable marriage with Lanyer)—what was such a woman to do?

If we read the poem in the light of these biographical considerations— which in my view is not necessary—we may first note that this particular woman produced and published this volume (with her name and marital status on the title page) at a time when women found it difficult to do so. More particularly, we may be led to focus more acutely on the way the opening and closing movements *combine* adulation of the countess with insubordinate comments, beginning with the following aside:

> pardon (Madame) though I do not write
> Those praisefull lines of that delightful place,
> As you commaunded me . . . [ll. 17-19]

The issue of subordination/insubordination similarly arises in the concluding couplet: "You are the Articke Starre that guides my hand, / All what I am, I rest at your command." These lines may be read as the culmination of a process of religious consolation, achieved over the course of the entire rhetorical production, for the plight of the seriously vulnerable or they may be read as expressing quite human, secular complaints about inferior social status and that vulnerability.

It seems appropriate, before I turn to the closing movement of the poem and the way it problematizes religious consolation and secular complaint, to digress on my own—to a markedly disruptive, central outburst in "The Description of Cooke-ham"—the shorter poem which concludes the volume. Briefly, that poem opens and closes with symmetric movements in which the estate of Cookham is first constructed as welcoming the countess in a spring-like advent and then finally as lamenting in a wintry way her departure from the estate. Between these two movements occurs a passage in which so many rhetorical moves are made so quickly it is difficult to explain them briefly. The narrative "I" has been praising the countess's almost utopian, Christian existence. From her reading of "holy Writ," the countess has imitated first Moses—"to know his pleasure, and performe his Will"—then David—"to sound his prayses, morning, noone, and night"—and finally Joseph in acts of charity:

> With blessed *Joseph* you did often feed
> Your pined brethren, when they stood in need.
> And that sweet Lady sprung from *Cliffords* race,
> Of noble *Bedfords* blood, faire steame of Grace;
> To honourable *Dorset* now espows'd,
> In whose faire breast true virtue then was hous'd:
> Oh what delight did my weake spirits find
> In those pure parts of her well framed mind. ["The Description of Cooke-ham,"
>   ll. 91-98]

The abrupt disruption of syntax and narrative focus occasioned by the reference to "that sweet Lady," triggers a host of other discrepant moments. The poem only obliquely shows that that lady was Anne Clifford, daughter of the Countess of Cumberland, who in February, 1609, was married to Richard Sackville, subsequently Earl of Dorset. Hence, her "well framed mind" is absent from "I," which provokes the lament "that I cannot be / Neere unto her." As the focus, upon the natural features of the estate, is disrupted, "I" rails at "Unconstant Fortune":

>   thou art most too blame,
> Who casts us downe into so lowe a frame:
> Where our great friends we cannot dayly see,
> So great a difference is there in degree. ["Cooke-ham," ll. 103-6]

Not only does "I" lose sight of the countess, of Anne Clifford, and of Cookham, but she also apparently loses interest in the religious virtues she has been extolling, turning attention instead to "Fortune" and to "degree." Indeed, "I" pursues the issue of social rank while admitting that her writing has apparently veered away from its prior progress.

Many are placed in those Orbes of state,
Parters in honour, so ordain'd by Fate;
Neerer in show, yet farther off in love,
In which, the lowest always are above.
But whither am I carried in conceit?
My Wit too weake to conster of the great.
Why not? although we are but borne of earth,
We may behold the Heavens, despising death;
And loving heaven that is so farre above,
May in the end vouchsafe us entire love. ["Cooke-ham," ll. 107-16]

It is hard to "conster"—that is, interpret or impose a framework on—the curious syntax of this passage. Who or what is "so ordain'd [to what] by Fate"? Perhaps it is social status, the result of birth, which apparently serves to part persons "in honour." And perhaps those born high are "near" (what?) in seeming or "appearance" yet distant in "love" while "the lowest" are superior in love. Despite the doubts, it does seem fairly clear that the "lowest" are being privileged in some way insubordinate to hierarchy, as the focus moves to secular, social rather than spiritual considerations.

In the midst of this small moment of social disequilibrium, "I" points to her own verbal disruption—"But whither am I carried in conceit?"—while claiming provisionally she cannot "conster" the great. Just as suddenly, "I" questions her own submission ("Why not?"). Yet, instead of going on to "conster" the "great," "I" effectively revokes that insubordinate thought. We are "but borne of earth" yet we (presumably "the lowest") "may behold the Heavens." "We" are, suddenly, not socially but religiously defined persons. "We, "borne of earth," are capable of "loving" not Anne Clifford and her elite crowd but "heaven" and thereby, presumably, receive a condescending, heavenly reward. The process of valorizing lowliness transmutes it back from a social to a religious term, and from thence the spiritually focused narrative of the estate can again flow smoothly, albeit with increasing lament for absence.

In short, one could see the poem, overall, as first evoking a *locus amoenus,* next, as puncturing that pleasure with the marriage of Anne Clifford, with consciousness of inferior social status, with abuse of "Fortune," and with insubordination and social disequilibrium, and finally as transmuting that social note back into religious language, social acquiescence, and the symmetry of the concluding movement. Religion, in such a view, opiates the "lowest." The moment of social insubordination is, as it were, self-corrected by "I," who reasserts her lowliness while reconverting "lowliness" into a spiritual term leading to a renewed, ascending, spiritual narrative. In such a reading, then, almost exactly at the center of the "Description of Cooke-ham," there is an act of insubordination which is focused not on spiritual but on social distinction and

on "fortune" or, perhaps, simply birth and lineage, and that act is then spiritu-
alized out of existence.[16]

Or is it? The poem can also be read, I suggest, as never fully "recovering"
from that insubordinate moment.[17] For one thing, the lament becomes more
dire, verbally, as wintry and seemingly killing language is applied, in this sec-
ond description, to the natural features of the estate. The trees, for example,
suffered a withering of leaves; they wept in vain, and finally "cast their leaves
away, / Hoping that pitie would have made" the countess "stay." And then
there is a strange tale told of how the countess, in bidding a much-favored oak
tree farewell, kissed it. "I" reports that she stole the kiss and remains unrepen-
tant of the theft.

> To this faire tree, taking me by the hand,
> You did repeat the pleasures which had past,
> Seeming to grieve they could no longer last.
> And with a chaste, yet loving kisse tooke leave,
> Of which sweet kisse I did it soone bereave:
> Scorning a sencelesse creature should possesse
> So rare a favour, so great happinesse. ["Cooke-ham," ll. 162-68]

Nor is "I" willing to recompense the tree for her theft.

> No other kisse it could receive from me,
> For fear to give backe what it tooke of thee:
> So I ingratefull Creature did deceive it,
> Of that which you vouchsaft in love to leave it.
> And though it oft had giv'n me much content,
> Yet this great wrong I never could repent:
> But of the happiest made it most forlorne,
> To shew that nothing's free from Fortunes scorne. ["Cooke-ham," ll. 169-76]

Fortune, "thou-ed" in the central passage, returns with "I"'s expression of scorn
and lack of repentance. Indeed, "I," formerly victim of scornful "fortune," now
has become the self-appointed and scornful agent of fortune, stealing from the
tree as, in a sense she had earlier been stolen from. This odd tale, then, might
be thought to unravel much of the religious verbiage of the entire poem. "I"
feels "scorn" that a "senceless creature" should receive this token of the countess's
love, though admittedly, "I" then claims, the tree goes right back to feeling—
albeit "forlorne."

Taking "I" to be basically unrepentant makes sense if we consider what
would have happened had "I" more extensively "conster[ed] of the great." Why
did the countess leave Cookham? On the one hand, the insubordinate out-
break in the center of the poem suggests the cause was either the marriage of

Anne Clifford or Fortuna, and that the problem each posed was one of birth. And that seems to be the only cause the text even suggests. On the other hand, Barbara Lewalski believes the countess resided at Cookham during 1604-5, four to five years before the marriage of Anne Clifford (and the drafting of the poem), as a function of her estrangement from her wretched husband;[18] his treatment of the countess and of his daughter is well known. In either case, male intrusion into the lives of women appears to operate, since, with the exception of Dorset, who comes in as an appendage of the description of Anne Clifford, the cast is wholly female. Hence, the rhetoric of the poem can be seen in two opposed ways—either as evading or smoothing over secular and gendered concerns (by not "constering" the great), and thereby proposing symmetry, balance, and control of language, or else as constructing an exclusively female-oriented tale in which only women (the countess, Anne Clifford, mother nature, Fortuna, and "I") act, a tale which remains asymmetric and unrepentant, a tale which breaks down spiritual language with nearly crass and scornful considerations of theft and possession.[19]

One could fault the language here for lack of syntactic control. But one might more usefully consider that the language, generating two feasible readings at least, enacts an interrogation of gendered issues of power and control, that it provokes discrepant readings in a multiply digressive moment as a way of marking both female powerlessness (consoled by religious sentiment) and an almost scornful sense of unrepentant female power. Even the concluding lines, addressed to the countess, partake of this ambiguous doubleness.

> All desolation then there did appear,
> When you were going whom they [parts of the estate] held so deare.
> This last farewell to *Cooke-ham* here I give,
> When I am dead thy name in this may live,
> Wherein I have perform'd her noble hest,
> Whose virtues lodge in my unworthy breast,
> And ever shall, so long as life remaines,
> Tying my heart to her by those rich chaines. ["Cooke-ham," ll. 203-10]

"I" claims to have fulfilled the countess' behest, yet also claims to have immortalized the estate; submission balances with deific authority. Are the ultimate "rich chaines" binding and constricting or spiritually elevating and enriching, "rich" or valuable only "so long as life remaines" or beyond this life? Is the motive heaven or profit? Must we or can we choose?

Returning from my digression, I will point out that much the same doubleness seems to obtain in "Salve Deus Rex Judaeorum." Not only is there the appearance of symmetry between the opening and closing sections (as in "The Description of Cooke-ham")—symmetry marked particularly by evoking the male, timeless, creative, judgmental deity as well as by frequent departures in praise of the countess. Further, the third movement of the "Salve" can be read as achieving consolation after the disruptive central *agon* or, again, can be read as failing to achieve consolation. The timeless deity reappears, after the narrative of the Crucifixion, as "I" also imagines a potent, regal, wise queen, the Queen of Sheba, encountering Solomon in verbal equality. That perhaps utopian vision climaxes extensive praise of the countess; she surpasses a second list of prominent women, a list which is symmetrical to the list in the opening section. Yet, the situation of the Queen of Sheba is not matched in the opening movement, and neither is the strong note of martyrdom with which the poem concludes. In short, there are thematic symmetries—the potent deity, the praise of the countess—and asymmetries—the figure of the Queen of Sheba and the martyrs. The asymmetries may undermine the sense of control and consolation.

Praise of the countess, which allows "I" to break off from the blazon of Jesus's beauty, basically takes the form of showing she is greater than other great women. The breaking off is clearly marked—"Ah! give me leave (good Lady) now to leave / This taske of Beauty . . . / I cannot wade so deepe" (ll. 1321-23). The countess is then represented as having obtained almost pontifical keys as a result of her "workes of mercy" in relieving the poor and sick.

> These are those Keyes Saint *Peter* did possesse,
> Which with a Spirituall powre are giv'n to thee,
> To heale the soules of those that doe transgresse,
> By thy fair virtues . . . [ll.1369-71][20]

The countess is also represented as eschewing "fowle disorder, or licentiousness," and the sexual note struck in the first movement is loosely elaborated by comparisons which show how the countess surpasses Cleopatra, the Scythian women, Deborah, Judith, Hester, and Susanna.

Culminating this section are seventeen stanzas focused on the Queen of Sheba, perhaps the most powerful female subject to appear in the poem; hence praise of the countess, who surpasses her, is very strong here. The queen is constructed as talking back and forth with Solomon, while grammatical parallelism establishes social, intellectual, and moral equality. The conversational tone is set, for example, in the following:

> Yea many strange hard questions did shee frame,
> All which were answer'd by this famous King:
> > Nothing was hid that in her heart did rest,
> > And all to proove this King so highly blest. [ll. 1581-84]

The next two stanzas extensively parallel male and female:

Here Majestie with Majestie did meete,
Wisedome to Wisedome yeelded true content,
One Beauty did another Beauty greet,
Bounty to Bountie never could repent;
Here all distaste is troden under feet,
No losse of time, where time was so well spent
  In vertuous exercises of the minde,
  In which this Queene did much contentment finde.

Spirits affect where they doe sympathize,
Wisdom desires Wisdome to embrace,
Virtue covets her like, and doth devize
How she her friends may entertaine with grace;
Beauty sometimes is pleas'd to feed her eyes,
With viewing Beautie in anothers face. [ll. 1585-98]

In short, we have here a utopian vision of a fully empowered female, active (since *she* travelled to meet Solomon) and not limited, "Not yeelding to the nicenesse and respect / Of woman-kind" as she was drawn "forth of her native Land" and "past both sea and land." "All feare of dangers shee did quite neglect" in order to find the male reflection of her superlative gifts and abilities. The queen might be thought of as a foil to Eve, since she seems the opposite of blameable, "weak" or "simple"—key terms in "Eves Apologie."

Yet, the queen is "but a figure" and her love but the "shadow" of the countess's religiosity (ll. 1610, 1682). And between the two assertions of the countess's supremacy, "I" reconstructs the powerful male deity she evoked in the opening section of the poem. And, as I noted, motifs of the original Creation flow into motifs of the final un-creation:

He that had powre to open all the Seales,
And summon up our sinnes of blood and wrong,
He unto whom the righteous soules appeales,
That have bin martyrd, and doe thinke it long,
To whom in mercie he his will reveales,
That they should rest a little in their wrong,
  Untill their fellow servants should be killed,
  Even as they were, and that they were fulfilled. [ll. 1665-72]

It is not, of course, surprising that a passage focused on the Creation will recapitulate itself by focusing on the ultimate, glorious un-creation—"New Heav'n and Earth, wherein the Just shall dwell" as *Paradise Lost* phrases it. Here, one might argue, the millennial note suggests a dynamic of the poem as a whole. The basic "sandwich"—"Jehovah," Crucifixion, "Jehovah"—can be read as a static three-part structure, in which the tale of the woman's deity, Jesus, in time, is as it were enclosed by talk of the very male deity who is creator and eternal and judge and defender at the shutting up of time. To the extent that that latter construct is extended (conventionally, to be sure) to the millennium, one might suppose that the Jehovah is constructed in more forward-looking, less punitive terms. Perhaps, one might argue in this view, the intervention of the figure of a woman's deity alters "I"'s perspective so as to take in this future vision so important to a poet like Milton. Perhaps "Eves Apologie," interwoven into the story of the woman's deity has also helped emotionally to "set things right" as they will perfectly be in the Day of Judgment.[21]

Yet, dilation, in the sense of deferral, must eventually give over to an ending, and these stanzas on this judging deity also introduce the focus of the concluding twelve stanzas of this final section—on martyrdom. The section commences with Stephen, then moves on to Saint Lawrence, Andrew and "the Princes of th'Apostles," the final figure being John the Baptist.[22] In two final stanzas, the countess regards these martyrs at the same time that "I" resubmits herself to the countess. Insubordination is over then, perhaps, and the third movement of the poem, concluding with the submission of the martyrs and of the countess, closes with the submission of "I," especially in the final couplet to the countess: "You are the Articke Starre that guides my hand, / All what I am, I rest at your command."

This final, martyr-strewn note might well suggest, again, that the structure of the poem is not static, simply beginning and ending with the male controller. Rather, one could see it as closing on a prolonged note of intense vulnerability which echoes to the vulnerability of Jesus. Despite the figure of the Queen of Sheba, or perhaps because she is a utopian figure in her relationship of balanced equality with Solomon, the final passage, in this view, sounds again a note of ultimate submission.

That is, one can read the poem as spiritualizing the predicament of women blamed and vulnerable and forced into submission; God's benevolent control counterbalances the wrongs of such a world. Or one can see the poem as confronting hardheadedly the suffering of the vulnerable while only seeming to spiritualize it.

Indeed, it is possible that the poem—despite its sustained religious note—slyly contests social inequality based on birth in the way "The Description of Cooke-ham" does, however briefly. To get at that, let me recall that throughout, the distinction between virtuous and evil-doers seems absolute. What is the basis of that difference? A few passages in the "Salve Deus" suggest that it is a matter of birth, much as differences of birth caused pain and rhetorical havoc in "The Description of Cooke-ham." "Froward are the ungodly from their berth, / No sooner borne, but they doe goe astray," comments the narrator when first presenting the evil-speakers (ll. 113-14). Again, concerning physical, female beauty, we encounter a suggestion that evil is a person's fate as well.

That pride of Nature which adornes the faire,
Like blasing Comets to allure all eies,
Is but the thred, that weaves their web of Care. [ll. 201-3]

And, as Lanyer turns to the martyrs at the end of the poem, there may be echoes of this suggestion that the distinction begins at birth. Stephen was "sweetened" by the "sweetness" of a vision of Christ in heaven, a vision "whose sweetnesse sweet'ned that short sowre of Life" (l. 1769). It seems arguable that the poem is commenting on the "short sowre of life" for those who are not of great or good birth, in which case, the mischievous social disruptions of the Cookham poem may here reappear in what otherwise might seem a wholly religious piece of writing. Perhaps the lines, already quoted, which introduce the section on the martyrs could be considered a test case of the two readings.

He unto whom the righteous soules appeales,
That have bin martyrd, and doe thinke it long,
To whom in mercie he his will reveales,
That they should rest a little in their wrong,
    Untill their fellow servants should be killed,
    Even as they were, and that they were fulfilled. [ll. 1667-72]

Are we to take comfort from the fact that the martyrs must "rest a litle in their wrong" because they will ultimately be "fulfilled," or are we to take the martyrs as human, almost vindictive, "fulfilled" when fellow martyrs "should be killed." As with the end of "The Description of Cooke-ham," where the question arose how to take the phrase "so long as life remaines," the question here might be how one feels the martyrs are "fulfilled"—by the spiritual assurances of Jesus or by the prospect that their fellows will be killed as well? Is there consolation or complaint? Surely, one might exclaim, the latter cannot be intended here! Yet we have seen several examples where complaint appears as a prominent mode, and insofar as one considers the effort here to achieve consolation, one cannot escape the fact that that effort can always sound like complaint. Does the final couplet, addressed perhaps for profit to the countess, show consolation? "You are the Articke Starre that guides my hand, / All what I am, I rest at your command." Or do the lines describe the situation of an author who, in important and to her starkly visible ways, lacks authority?

    Taken together, these discrepancies in the language of *Salve Deus Rex Judaeorum*—which seem to me tightly interrelated—can be read as formally interrogating a series of easy, dichotomous assumptions: about narrative chronology versus digressive, chronologic intrusion; about adherence to Scripture versus fanciful elaboration; about the hero-deity as timebound, suffering, passive, publicly silent versus the hero-deity as timeless, potent, judicial; about the consolation derived from contemplating the suffering of Jesus (and the martyrs) versus the hope that the punitive, male deity will (vindictively, perhaps) set social inequality aright; about fears of verbal inadequacy or "want of womans wit / To pen thy praise" versus a sense that "If he please t'illuminate my Spirit . . . then will I tell of that sad black fac'd Night"; about an overall, rhetorical "opiating" of the speaker versus persistently strident assertions of human worth in the face of social injustice. If the opening and closing movements of the poem repeatedly interrogate the virtue and effectiveness of woman speaking, they also problematize a host of assumptions about women, hierarchy, the deity, narrative, and language that were central to the male discourse of the age.

NOTES

1. Barbara K. Lewalski, "Of God and Good Women: The Poems of Aemilia Lanyer," in *Silent But for the Word: Tudor Women as Patrons, Translaters and Writers of Religious Works* ed. Margaret Patterson Hannay (Kent, Oh.: Kent State University Press, 1985), pp. 203-24.

2. Elaine V. Beilin, *Redeeming Eve: Women Writers of the English Renaissance* (Princeton: Princeton University Press, 1987), pp. 183, 207.

3. Tina Krontiris, *Oppositional Voices: Women as Writers and Translators of Literature in the English Renaissance* (London and New York: Routledge, 1992), in her section on Lanyer (pp. 103-20), is a recent case in point.

4. That is, my project here is largely explicatory. Clearly, however, since I shall be showing how rhetoric opens itself to multiple readings rather than a single, unified reading, while stressing verbal discrepancies and disjunctions—that verbal texture which can lead a reader to dismiss some utterance as a "digression"—my aim is not "New Critical." It seems to me important to show how in sentence after sentence, in passage after passage, the poem enacts verbally a sort of sly insubordination. Rhetoric I here define as the manner in which persons treat persons (including themselves in self-fashioning) with words—a definition informed by an acute sense of the *polysemous* nature of language and hence of all rhetorical performance.

5. "Digression" can be said to reside in the eye of the beholder—that is, what we label as digression is writing which does not conform to expectations about how discourse will unfold or unroll. Luce Irigaray, *Speculum of the Other Woman,* trans. Gillian C. Gill (Ithaca: Cornell University Press, 1985), and more directly Helene Cixous in Cixous and Catherine Clement, *The Newly Born Woman,* trans. Betsy Wing, Foreword by Sandra M. Gilbert (Minneapolis: University of Minnesota Press, 1986) suggests that formal features like digression may be essential to female interrogation of male discourse.

6. Patricia Parker, *Literary Fat Ladies: Rhetoric, Gender, Property* (London and New York: Methuen, 1987). In the title chapter, Parker takes as her epigraph some remarks by Luce Irigaray concerning female mimesis which leads a woman to "resubmit herself—inasmuch as she is on the side of the 'perceptible,' of 'matter'—to 'ideas,' in particular to ideas about herself that are elaborated in/by a masculine logic, but so as to make 'visible,' by an effect of playful repetition, what was supposed to remain invisible."

7. For male formulations of "virtuous" female behavior, see Suzanne Hull, *Chaste,*

Silent, and Obedient (San Marino: Huntington Library, 1982). I have deliberately chosen "Woman's" (later, "womanish"), avoiding the term "feminized" with its diminutive connotations and adopting the language of the value judgments of male authors in that culture concerning appropriate feminine behavior rather than in any "universal" scheme of things. Tina Krontiris, has noted, briefly, "female characteristics" attributed to Jesus in the poem—passivity being her prime point (see note 3 above). For other approaches to the "female characteristics" Lanyer ascribes to Christ, see the essays by McBride and Holmes in this volume, chapters 4 and 9, respectively.

8. To be sure, male writers could, as Milton did in his extraordinarily different *Paradise Lost,* seek an alternative to male heroism in heroic, religious figures. For example, Milton's narrator pursued an

> argument
> Not less but more Heroic than the wrath
> Of stern *Achilles* on his Foe pursu'd
> Thrice Fugitive around *Troy* Wall [*Paradise Lost,* 9.13-15]

One of the great differences between Milton's poem and Lanyer's is the fascination with the Crucifixion in the one and the apparent distaste for and diminution of the Crucifixion story in the other. That difference has the effect that Jesus in Milton's poem is represented as active on the cross;

> But to the Cross he nails thy Enemies,
> The Law that is against thee, and the sins
> Of all mankind, with him there crucifi'd. . . .
> . . . so he dies
> But soon revives. [*Paradise Lost,* 12.415-20]

Lanyer's Jesus, at the center of her poem, is simply the vulnerable object of physical violence. Milton quoted from *Complete Poems and Major Prose,* ed. Merritt Y. Hughes (Indianapolis, New York: Odyssey Press, 1957).

9. Amatory anatomy was common, particularly in the Petrarchan laments of Elizabeth's reign. An incisive contemporary comment on this *topos* occurs in Spenser's grim parody of male, amatory "anatomy" in the tale of Sirena, who was discovered sleeping by cannibals.

> So round about her they them selues did place
> Vpon the grasse, and diuersely dispose,
> As each thought best to spend the lingring space.
> Some with their eyes the daintiest morsels chose;
> Some praise her paps, some praise her lips and nose;
> Some whet their kniues, and strip their elboes bare:
> The Priest him selfe a garland doth compose
> Of finest flowres, and with full busie care
> His bloudy vessels wash; and holy fire prepare. [Edmund Spenser, *The Faerie Queene,* ed. Thomas P. Roche (Harmondsworth: Penguin, 1978), Book VI, Canto viii, stanza 39, p. 972]

10. Again, compare *Paradise Lost,* and the marked segregation, in language, of the voices of "Father" and "Son" as well as the contrasting verbal manifestations of deity in

books 6 and 7 (or 3 and 10). To be sure, Mercy and Justice are at times "colleague" verbally, yet the voices of the persons of the Trinity are more strikingly *different* than unified in the poem. The paradox of the Trinity is difficult to represent. It is worth remarking that the separateness of the persons, in Lanyer's poem, is constructed not primarily in terms of justice and mercy (though some language suggests that) but rather in terms of power and vulnerability, as it is not in *Paradise Lost.*

11. I use the term sycophantic advisedly. Betty Travitsky, *A Paradise of Women: Writings by Englishwomen of the Renaissance* (Westport, Conn.: Greenwood Press, 1981) is troubled that Lanyer wrote "for profit." There seems no reason to doubt that Aemilia Lanyer was heavily exploited in a host of ways, and the clear effort to curry favor with the countess and eight other powerful women (in verse dedications) can certainly be seen as a function of that exploitation. Moreover, as any sampling of dedications will show, Lanyer's are not unusual in soliciting the well-to-do, though the number of dedications is striking. However, additionally, the Greek word sycophant—meaning one who shows figs—remains a mystery, one possible etymology being a reference to a person who "makes the sign of the fig"; the possibility that sycophancy originally involved a gesture of sexual insubordination appeals to me in this instance.

12. Virginia Beauchamp initially pointed out in conversation that Cynthia refers to Elizabeth. In another conversation, Marshall Grossman suggests that, as the estate of Cookham was a Crown estate, Phoebe may also point in that way to Elizabeth and royal permission for the countess to reside on the estate. I shall later point out how the passage may be read as referring to Cookham.

13. Travitsky, *A Paradise of Women.*

14. Surely, the assumption can be challenged. Joseph Loewenstein, "The Jonsonian Corpulence: Or, The Poet as Mouthpiece," *ELH* 53 (1986): 491-518, and Bruce Thomas Boehrer, "Renaissance Overeating: The Sad Case of Ben Jonson," *PMLA* 105 (1990), 1071-82, both frolic with the profit motive in Jonson's writing, and given the similarity between Jonson's "Penshurst" and Lanyer's "Description of Cooke-ham," their remarks are germane here. To be sure, most male writers more effectively sublimated or shrouded the issue of patronage in their writing. *Paradise Lost* sounds, as much as anything, like the pursuit of "fame," that "last infirmity of noble minds" (Milton, "Lycidas," l. 71, in *Complete Works*).

15. Skeptical of biographical interpretations generally, I am loath to entertain them here, since the source of much I will comment upon derives from Simon Forman's journal—which Rowse used in quite unsatisfactory ways. However, both the careful Barbara K. Lewalski and Germaine Greer et al., *Kissing the Rod: An Anthology of Seventeenth-Century Women's Verse* (New York: Farrar, Straus, Giroux, 1988) quote or use Forman to comment on Lanyer's hardships, the death of her father and failure of his estate, her pregnancy by Lord Hunsdon, master of the revels, her marriage (presumably as a buy-out), her former opulence, her beauty in youth, her miscarriages, etc. Lewalski concludes that "it seems clear from this that Lanyer had enjoyed some access to the life of the Court as a young girl by reasons of the Hunsdon connection, and that she had obtained an estate in money and jewels which her husband squandered" (p. 205). If we accept this view, we might further consider that Lanyer was keenly aware of the operations of power and exploitation—sexual and financial—as she lived at the edges of the Court and was herself affected by them. Her family and her husband's were foreign, servitors of the Court and yet presumably clearly not of the Court elite; that seems likely her role as well. Both the issue of vulnerability and the

sense I have of sly insubordination work in tandem with this proposed biography. (For more detailed discussion of Lanyer's life, see the essays by Bevington and Barroll in this volume, chapters 1 and 2, respectively.)

16. In his generally aggravating chapter, "Poetry by Women" in *English Poetry of the Seventeenth Century,* 2d ed. (London and New York: Longman, 1992), George Parfitt urges that "Description of Cooke-ham" is basically apolitical. Parfitt seems not to have read *Salve Deus Rex Judaeorum,* does not appear to recognize the figure of Anne Clifford in "Description," and hence, while his view may coincide with the reading just proposed, it also opens the way for the reading which follows. Additionally, it is worth noting that the dedication to Anne Clifford harps on the issue of birth in such a way as to be almost insulting to Anne, until the voice pulls abruptly back; that is the only dedication in which birth is so negatively handled, and reinforces the view that Anne figured as a sort of nexus for thoughts of social inequality.

17. In proposing, here, opposed readings of "The Description of Cooke-ham" (and later, of the "Salve"), I do not mean to suggest one is better than another or that they are exhaustive readings. My aim here is primarily to show that this writing (like all writing) opens itself to multiple interpretations. To the *belle-lettristic,* that means it could enter the canon. However, since in my anti-*belle-lettristic* view, all writing opens itself to multiple readings, simply as a consequence of the nature of language and of interpretation, my point here *au fond* is that Lanyer's writing, like that vast treasure trove of "nonliterary" writing of the English Renaissance, merits serious and careful attention—a view which the practice (although, clearly, not the theoretical bases) of the present "new historicism" commonly does not enact.

18. Barbara Lewalski, *Writing Women in Jacobean England* (Cambridge: Harvard University Press, 1993), pp. 212-41, n. 11.

19. Krontiris comes at the matter in a useful, third way, arguing that Lanyer repressed feminist sentiments in "Description" as part of her pursuit of patronage, arguing that Lanyer may have felt "the feminist sentiments of the principal potential patronesses of the book could not be taken as granted or used in public. Although these two women had grudges against men that Lanyer could appreciate and exploit, she could not with certainty enlarge them into a public castigation of the male sex" (p. 119).

20. It is an odd passage, which might be said to praise the countess by likening her positively to the pope (not commonly a positive role model in England at the time, to be sure) or which could be said to spiritualize and dismiss the power of the pontiff, showing how it is not special but rather something any holy woman could exercise through acts of charity. Or, perhaps, since the surpassing force of the countess's virtue will be elaborated at length, we may take it to show she surpasses the pope. However we take them, the lines could certainly invite controversy—something one would not expect in such a piece of writing "for profit."

21. Tina Krontiris, noting inconsistencies in Lanyer's feminist stance, focuses particularly on the ending of the title poem as an attempt at offering a counterweight to the earlier unflattering picture of men, a point Lewalski had made, and turns it neatly to suggest Lanyer could not count on public support from her patronesses for feminist sentiments (pp. 119-20). Krontiris has an agenda different from my own, yet we seem to be talking about the same features of the poem.

22. Here remains a small mystery. John the Baptist seems to be one of two "Princes of the Apostles." Of the two, we are told, "One chose the Gallowes, that unseemely death, / The other by the Sword did loose his breath." The second, it subsequently emerges, is clearly John the Baptist, not customarily thought of as an apostle though plausibly thought of as a martyr. It is then a question which is the other prince. Lewalski sensibly opts for Peter (p. 220), though the phrase "Princes of the Apostles" suggests, if anything, Peter and Paul and certainly not John the Baptist.

12
Annotated Bibliography:
Texts and Criticism of
Aemilia Bassano Lanyer

KAREN L. NELSON

This bibliography is designed as an aid to scholars and teachers of Aemilia Lanyer's life and work. It includes general references in literary dictionaries as well as full-length studies of Lanyer's texts, and refers to anthologies in which Lanyer's writing is excerpted as well as to more complete editions of her work. My goal is to offer a resource for someone approaching Lanyer's poems for the first time as well as for someone trying to teach Lanyer's texts. The recovery efforts and scholarship surrounding Lanyer reveal that her writing is important in a variety of contexts: critical, historical, aesthetic, and pedagogic. Her poetry can take its rightful place in a syllabus for a seventeenth-century literature class, or for a poetry survey, or for a course on women's writing. For those with a more narrowly defined interest in the writing of early modern women, this bibliography collects in one place as much of the work on Lanyer as possible and offers a useful checklist. The sheer quantity of material reveals the importance of Lanyer's writing to contemporary critics and suggests that she is earning a place in the canon of seventeenth-century literature.

I have modeled this bibliography on single-author bibliographies such as *John Donne: An Annotated Bibliography of Modern Criticism, 1912-1967,* by John R. Roberts (Columbia: University of Missouri Press, 1973), and *Sir Philip Sidney: An Annotated Bibliography of Texts and Criticism (1554-1984),* edited by Donald V. Stump et al. (New York: G.K. Hall & Co., 1994). Like those compilers, I have tried to be thorough and inclusive, although a completely exhaustive list is probably already impossible. Elizabeth H. Hageman's "Recent Studies in Women Writers of the English Seventeenth Century, 1604-1674," in *Women in the Renaissance: Selections from English Literary Renaissance,* edited by Kirby Farrell, Elizabeth H. Hageman, and Arthur Kinney (Amherst: University of Massachusetts Press, 1990), was an important resource for critical works to 1990. In addition, computerized databases helped my efforts enormously, and I relied most heavily on the OCLC FirstSearch; the OCLC WorldCat; the OCLC Article1st; the MLA Bibliography; the University of Maryland's VICTOR; the Music Index 1981-1992 on CD-ROM; Dissertation Abstracts OnDisc; and RILM Abstracts of Music Literature.

ORIGINAL EDITIONS

The Short Title Catalogue (STC) offers two listings for Aemilia Lanyer's *Salve Deus Rex Judaeorum:*

15227. Lanyer, Æmilia, Mrs. Salve deus rex Judæorum. Containing, the passion of Christ . . . [In verse.] 4°. V. Simmes for R. Bonian, 1611. Entered in the Stationer's Register on two occasions in 1610. Held at the Huntington Library. Imprint in four lines.

15227.5. ———. [Another edition with imprint in 5 lines.] Held at: the British Library, London; the Dyce Collection, Victoria & Albert Museum (variant not determined); the Bodleian Library, Oxford; the Municipal Libraries, Bath; the Folger Library (imperfect); the Chapin Library, Williams College, Williamstown, Mass.; the Huntington Library.

MODERN EDITIONS

Lanyer, Aemilia. *The Poems of Shakespeare's Dark Lady: "Salve Deus Rex Judaeorum" by Emilia Lanier,* A.L. Rowse, ed. London: Jonathan Cape, 1978.
  Lengthy introduction (1-37) uses Simon Forman's diaries to suggest that Lanyer is Shakespeare's "dark lady." Reprints complete poems with original spelling, punctuation, and layout; also includes portraits of dedicatees: Queen Anne; Lady Arabella Stuart; Susan Bertie, Countess of Kent; Mary Sidney, Countess of Pembroke; Lucy Harington, Countess of Bedford; Margaret Russell, Countess of Cumberland; Katherine Knevet, Countess of Suffolk; and Anne Clifford, Countess of Dorset.

———. *The Poems of Aemilia Lanyer: Salve Deus Rex Judaeorum,* Susanne Woods, ed. Women Writers in English, 1350-1850. Oxford: Oxford University Press, 1993.
  Contains the complete poems; reproduces original spelling, punctuation, and orthography with the exception of i, j, s, u, v, w, which it regularizes. Also includes extensive biography and excerpts from primary material: the will of Baptista Bassano, Lanyer's father; Simon Forman's manuscript; *Calendar of State Papers;* maps of St. Botolph's, Bishopsgate; Westminster; St. Giles in the Fields; St. James, Clerkenwell. Thorough textual introduction which offers reading of "To Cooke-ham" in relation to Lanyer's connection with Anne Clifford; describes "Salve Deus Rex Judaeorum," which Woods situates within the context of middle-class authors and complicates with Lanyer's position as a woman; analyzes dedicatory and prefatory poems; contrasts "Salve Deus Rex Judaeorum" with Katherine Parr's *The Lamentacion of a Sinner* (1547); discusses Lanyer's feminist revision of the Gospels.

————. *Salve Deus Rex Judaeorum*. In *Renaissance Women: The Plays of Elizabeth Cary; the Poems of Aemilia Lanyer,* Diane Purkiss, ed. London: William Pickering, 1994.

Counters Joan Kelly's question, "Did women have a Renaissance?" with this publication of three texts by two early modern women: the complete text of *Salve Deus Rex Judaeorum* by Aemilia Lanyer; and *The Tragedy of Mariam* and *The History of the Life, Reign, and Death of Edward II,* two works attributed to Elizabeth Cary. Modernizes spelling, punctuation; explanatory endnotes. Prefaces texts with biography of each woman and reviews their texts' appropriation by feminist scholars. Emphasizes aspects of "its generic and discursive experimentation" and suggests that "*Salve Deus Rex Judaeorum* is a carefully-structured and organised attempt to put together the discourses of patronage, encomium, religious verse, defences of women, and the evocation of nature in a new way to create a new means of praising women and a new system of interpretation" (pp. xxiii-xxiv).

ANTHOLOGIES

Aughterson, Kate, ed. *Renaissance Women: Constructions of Femininity in England.* London and New York: Routledge, 1995.

This collection of source materials on the construction of gender in early modern England includes the preface from *Salve Deus Rex Judaeorum* in a section on protofeminisms (pp. 268-69). Other subject headings include: Theology; Physiology; Sexuality and Motherhood; Politics and Law; Education; Work; and Writing and Speaking.

Abrams, M.H., ed. *The Norton Anthology of English Literature.* 6th ed. New York: W.W. Norton, 1993.

This two-volume survey of literature in English includes, in the first volume, two selections from *Salve Deus Rex Judaeorum:* "Eves Apologie in defence of women" excerpted from the title poem (pp. 1059-62) and "The Description of Cooke-ham" (pp. 1062-67).

Barnstone, Aliki, and Willis Barnstone, eds. *A Book of Women Poets from Antiquity to Now.* Rev. ed. New York: Schocken Books, 1992.

An extensive anthology of poetry by women from around the world translated into English; entries are sorted by language and geographical region. For example, the Spanish section includes poems from Spain, Mexico, Puerto Rico, El Salvador, Peru, Argentina, and Chile. The English section includes a brief biography of Lanyer (p. 435) and "Eves Apologie" (pp. 436-38).

Dawson, Terence, and Robert Scott Dupree, eds. *Seventeenth-Century Poetry: The Annotated Anthology.* New York: Harvester Wheatsheaf, 1994.

Introduces Lanyer and other poets it anthologizes with brief discussions of biography, context, genre, critical reception, further reading, editions, and critical studies. Includes "The Description of Cooke-ham" (pp. 154-59), which it connects to the tradition of country-house poems in analysis following the poem (pp. 159-60). Includes extensive annotations (pp. 160-65).

Fowler, Alastair. *The Country House Poem: A Cabinet of Seventeenth-Century Estate Poems and Related Items.* Edinburgh: Edinburgh University Press, 1994.
Throughout the "Introduction" (pp. 1-29) to this collection of country-house poems, Fowler offers an overview of the genre and refers to Lanyer's *Salve Deus Rex Judaeorum* in discussions of "Topics," "Hospitality," "Sources and Genres," and "Phases." Includes "The Description of Cookeham" (pp. 45-52) with extensive annotations.

———, ed. *The New Oxford Book of Seventeenth Century Verse.* Oxford: Oxford University Press, 1991.
Lanyer entry features "To the Lady Arabella," an excerpt from "To the Lady Anne, Countess of Dorset," and a lengthy passage from "Salve Deus" (from "Now Pontius Pilate is to judge the cause" to "For thy soul's health to shed his dearest blood" ll. 745-840).

Gilbert, Sandra M., and Susan Gubar, eds. *The Norton Anthology of Literature by Women.* New York: W.W. Norton & Company, 1985.
An anthology that "[gathers] in a single volume a range of literary works in which women writers have expressed their sometimes problematic, sometimes triumphant relationship to culture and society" (p. xxvii). Includes two-paragraph introduction to Lanyer and her works; reprints "Eves Apologie in defence of women" from *Salve Deus* (pp. 35-38).

Greer, Germaine, Susan Hastings, Jeslyn Medoff, and Melinda Sansone, eds. *Kissing the Rod: An Anthology of Seventeenth-Century Women's Verse,* pp. 44-53. London: Virago Press, 1988.
Survey of fifty women poets of the seventeenth century, with emphasis on the latter half of the period. Biographical introduction to Aemilia Lanyer (pp. 44-46); "The Description of Cooke-ham" (pp. 46-51), with explanatory notes.

Mahl, Mary R., and Helene Kohn, eds. *The Female Spectator: English Women Writers before 1800.* Bloomington: Indiana University Press, 1977.
Entry for Lanyer includes biographical introduction (pp. 73-74); bibliographical references (p. 75); "The Authors Dreame to the Lady Marie, the Countess Dowager of *Pembrooke*" (pp. 75-83), and an excerpt from "Salve Deus," from "Now when the dawn of day gins to appear" to "purchase shame, which all true worth defaceth" (pp. 83-87).

Norbrook, David, and H.R. Woudhuysen, eds. *The Penguin Book of Renaissance Verse 1509-1659.* London and New York: Penguin Books, 1992.
Anthology of sixteenth- and seventeenth-century English poetry, organized into categories of "The Public World"; "Images of Love"; "Topographies," including Lanyer's "The Description of Cooke-ham" (pp. 414-20); "Friends, Patrons and the Good Life"; "Church, State and Belief," including an excerpt from Lanyer's "Salve Deus" (pp. 556-58); "Elegy and Epitaph"; "Translation"; "Writer, Language and Public."

Otten, Charlotte F., ed. *English Women's Voices, 1540-1700.* Miami: Florida International University Press, 1992.
This anthology of sixteenth- and seventeenth-century women's nonfiction writing focuses on genres reflecting eight categories of women's lives, including: abuse;

persecution; political statements and petitions; love and marriage; health care; child-birth, sickness, and death; meditation and prayer; preaching. Briefly mentions Lanyer's "survey of biblical women and their contributions to the life of the church" in intro-duction to "Part Seven: Women Meditating and Praying" (pp. 281-82).

Pritchard, R.E., ed. *English Women's Poetry: Elizabethan to Victorian.* Manchester: Carcanet Press, 1990.

Gathers recently recovered poems as well as more canonical works by women authors such as Isabella Whitney; Anne Finch, Countess of Winchelsea; Hannah More; Elizabeth Barrett Browning; and Edith Nesbit. Entry for Lanyer includes brief biogra-phy (p. 39), "The Description of Cooke-ham" (pp. 39-45).

Travitsky, Betty, ed. *The Paradise of Women: Writings by Englishwomen of the Renais-sance.* Westport, Conn.: Greenwood Press, 1981; rpt., New York: Columbia Uni-versity Press Morningside Edition, 1989.

General anthology of excerpted writings of sixteenth- and seventeenth-century women writers. Entries for Lanyer in sections on "Religious Compositions" and on "Secular Writings" include short biography (pp. 28-29); excerpts from *Salve Deus Rex Judaeorum* (pp. 29-30, 97-103); brief contextualization and reading of text as a whole (p. 97).

Criticism

Barnstone, Aliki. "Women and the Garden: Andrew Marvell, Emilia Lanier, and Emily Dickinson." *Women & Literature* 2 (1982): 147-67.

The essays in this special issue "investigate the topic of male characters and male-ness . . . by women authors who have found 'man' interesting" (p. 2). Barnstone sug-gests that Lanyer "seeks to subvert the meaning of the myth of Eden in order to re-deem women in the name of Eve, and to bring harmony and equality to women and men. . . . [Lanyer] refutes all the main attitudes about womanhood found in both Marvell and his source, the Bible, which she courageously reinterprets" (p. 149). Sees Lanyer as "an unorthodox Christian" (p. 154). Compares Lanyer's treatment of Eden to Emily Dickinson's.

Beilin, Elaine. *Redeeming Eve: Women Writers of the English Renaissance.* Princeton: Princeton University Press, 1987.

Analyzes English women writers of the sixteenth and seventeenth centuries as a group instead of as isolated exempla to suggest that they form an early modern tradi-tion of women's writing. Sees them not as proto-feminists but as women representing women's roles and place in culture (pp. xvi-xvii). In chapter 7, "The Feminization of Praise: Aemilia Lanyer" (pp. 177-207), Beilin proposes that "Lanyer wrote specifically to praise women, and more precisely, to redeem for them their pivotal importance as Christians. To accomplish her task, Lanyer called upon her considerable knowledge of English poetry, her scriptural reading, and a familiarity with traditional debate mate-rial on the woman question" (p. 179). Contrasts *Salve Deus Rex Judaeorum* with Donne's *Anniversaries;* reads the texts—dedications, "Salve Deus Rex Judaeorum," "The Description of Cooke-ham"—as a triptych of mixed genres. Biographical material (pp. 181-82).

—————. "Current Bibliography of English Women Writers, 1500-1640." In *The Renaissance Englishwoman in Print: Counterbalancing the Canon*, Anne M. Haselkorn and Betty S. Travitsky, eds., pp. 347-60. Amherst: University of Massachusetts Press, 1990.
Beilin "lists works by women printed between 1500 and 1640." Includes Lanyer's work in section on verse (p. 355).

Bell, Maureen, George Parfitt, and Simon Shepherd. *A Biographical Dictionary of English Women Writers, 1580-1720*. Boston: Hall, 1990.
Dictionary of over 550 women writers; each entry limited to approximately two hundred words. For "Lanyer, Aemilia," lists poem titles; refers reader to Greer et al. for "To Cooke-ham" (p. 123).

Blain, Virginia, Patricia Clements, and Isobel Grundy. *The Feminist Companion to Literature in English: Women Writers from the Middle Ages to the Present*. New Haven and London: Yale University Press, 1990.
Over 2700 entries surveying women writing in English; defines literature to include letters, diaries, writing for children. Brief biography of Lanyer; describes poems and mentions their feminist aspects. Cites Rowse's edition of Lanyer's poetry, Beilin, Lewalski in *Silent But for the Word*.

Bradbrook, Muriel C. Review of *The Paradise of Women*, Betty Travitsky, ed. *Tulsa Studies of Women's Literature* 1 (1982): 89-93.
Summarizes contents of *The Paradise of Women;* suggests other methods of organization; questions Travitsky's editorial representations concerning Lanyer's work (p. 92).

Buck, Claire, ed. *The Bloomsbury Guide to Women's Literature*. New York: Prentice Hall, 1992.
Guide to women writers from "the huge range of cultural groups from across the world and throughout all ages" (p. ix). Entries for "Lanyer, Aemilia" (p. 719) and *Salve Deus, Rex Judaeorum* (p. 986). Compares "To Cooke-ham" to country-house poems; reports Rowse's contention that Lanyer was Shakespeare's "dark lady" and questions it; summarily analyzes three sections of work; lists brief bibliography.

Coiro, Ann Baynes. "Writing in Service: Sexual Politics and Class Position in the Poetry of Aemilia Lanyer and Ben Jonson." *Criticism* 35 (1993): 357-76.
Considers implications of class and race (accepts Prior's identification of Bassano family as Jewish) as well as gender for writers in the seventeenth century; compares Ben Jonson's *The Forrest* with Aemilia Lanyer's *Salve Deus Rex Judaeorum* to "learn more about concepts of authorship in the late Renaissance, more about the strains (both sexual and social) which, within three decades, would change English society, and more about the relationship of genre to social crisis" (p. 360). Questions critical approaches of early 1990s: "the politics of current literary criticism in Renaissance studies and feminist criticism in particular, . . . which have left largely unchallenged

the orthodoxies of traditional literary history so that women writers remain the lacy, decorative frill on the edge of a fabric that has not changed"(p. 358).

Cornell, Christine Anne. "Unparadised Women: Royal Mistresses in Early Modern English Literature (Rosamund Clifford, Jane Shore)." *Dissertation Abstracts International* 56.9 (1996): 3591A.

Cornell examines "the careers" of Anne Boleyn and Aemilia Lanyer to establish the historical context surrounding cultural constructions of mistresses (p. 3591), arguing that "the representations of mistresses become a forum for cultural debate. The interaction of sexuality, gender, and power in these stories provides . . . an opportunity to observe a range of recuperative and subversive responses to patriarchy and its discontents" (p. 3591). Focuses on Rosamund Clifford and "Jane," actually Elizabeth, Shore.

David, Alfred. *Teaching with "The Norton Anthology of English Literature": A Guide for Instructors.* New York: W.W. Norton & Company, 1993.

This manual of teaching strategies for college-level surveys of English literature proposes the inclusion of Lanyer's "To Cooke-ham" as an example of description of landscape in a thematic study of nature (p. 73) and the use of "Eves Apologie" in a unit on "Women as Readers and Authors" in the Renaissance (p. 125).

De Lafontaine, H.C., ed. *The King's Musick: A Transcript of Records Relating to Music and Musicians (1460-1700).* London: Novello, 1909, rpt., New York: Da Capo Press, 1973.

Selected documents concerning musicians attached to the English Court, collected from the records of the Lord Chamberlain preserved in the Records Office. Includes Aemilia Lanyer's 1635 petition against Clement Lanyer (p. 92); lists her husband, Alfonso Lanyer, as a recorder for whom mourning livery was purchased for the funeral of Queen Elizabeth in 1603 (p. 45); also records numerous references to the Bassano family members, among them Aemilia Lanyer's father, Baptista Bassano (pp. 6, 8, 9, 11, 12, 14-18, 478-79), and to other Lanyer family members.

Ezell, Margaret J.M. *Writing Women's Literary History.* Baltimore: The Johns Hopkins University Press, 1993.

Questions the marginalization of pre-1700 women's writing by literary historians of women: "too often the twentieth century's perceptions of works by Renaissance and seventeenth-century women rest on a set of anachronistic and restrictive presumptions . . . [and] assumptions about literary practice, production, and genre" (pp. 40-41). Recent anthologies of women's writing "perpetuate the [notion] that—with the exception of anomalous and isolated figures such as Aphra Behn . . . —the women of the sixteenth and seventeenth centuries did not write for an audience, if indeed they wrote at all" (p. 41). Says of the *Norton Anthology of Literature by Women* that it "neutralizes [the women it includes in its section on pre-1700 writers, including Lanyer,] by depicting them as amateurs, merely aristocrats amusing themselves with scribbling. . . . Although these early women's writings are thus preserved as part of the canon, such commentary automatically lessens their value and significance in the 'tradition'" (p.

50). Interrogates twentieth-century assumptions about social class, writing for an audience, professionalism, and suggests that women's studies tends to read the Renaissance with assumptions developed for nineteenth-century literature.

Fraser, Antonia. *The Weaker Vessel.* New York: Alfred A. Knopf, 1984, rpt., New York: Random House, 1985.

General analysis of seventeenth-century English women's history; "a study of women's lot" (p. xii). Quotes Lanyer's construction of Adam (p. 2); mentions her connection to Anne Clifford and records Lanyer's praises of Clifford (p. 95).

Garrett, Cynthia E. Review of *The Poems of Aemilia Lanyer: "Salve Deus Rex Judaeorum,"* Susanne Woods, ed. *Renaissance Quarterly* 49.3 (1996): 666-67.

Praises Woods's text and says that it "provides a much-needed authoritative edition of Lanyer's work for scholarly and classroom use in seventeenth-century English studies" (p. 666). Judges its critical introduction and editing exemplary (p. 667).

Goreau, Angeline, ed. *The Whole Duty of a Woman: Female Writers in Seventeenth Century England.* Garden City, New York: Dial Press, 1984.

Includes Lanyer in "an expanded list of women who published during the seventeenth century, whose texts either did not provide sufficient interests for the questions under examination, or were simply excluded because space was limited" (p. 333).

Guibbory, Achsah. "The Gospel According to Aemilia: Women and the Sacred in Aemilia Lanyer's *Salve Deus Rex Judaeorum.*" In *Sacred and Profane: The Interplay of Secular and Devotional Literature, 1500-1700,* Helen Wilcox, Richard Todd, Alasdair McDonald, eds. Amsterdam: VU Press, 1995, rev. and rpt. for this volume (chapter 10).

Guibbory argues that Lanyer presents her poem "as a true Gospel, inspired and authorized by God." Lanyer reads Christ's message regarding the place of women in Christian devotion with respect to the contradictory construals of women's connection with God in the Protestant culture of early-modern England.

Hageman, Elizabeth. "Recent Studies in Women Writers of the English Seventeenth Century (1604-1674): Part I: 1945-1986." In *Women in the Renaissance: Selections from "English Literary Renaissance,"* Kirby Farrell, Elizabeth H. Hageman, and Arthur F. Kinney, eds., Amherst: University of Massachusetts Press, 1990, pp. 269-98.

An extremely useful survey of background studies, editions, general studies, studies of individual genres, studies of individual writers, state of criticism, and anthologies including women's writing.

―――. "Recent Studies in Women Writers of the English Seventeenth Century (1604-1674): Part II: 1987-April 1990." In *Women in the Renaissance: Selections from "English Literary Renaissance,"* Kirby Farrell, Elizabeth H. Hageman, and Arthur F. Kinney, eds., Amherst: University of Massachusetts Press, 1990, pp. 299-309.

A continuation of the extensive survey Hageman completed for materials from 1945-1986.

Hull, Suzanne W. *Chaste, Silent and Obedient: English Books for Women, 1475-1640.* San Marino: Huntington Library, 1982.

Examines books printed 1475 to 1640 aimed at audiences of women. Hull includes chapters on "an emerging female literature," guide books, devotional books, recreational literature, *querelle des femmes.* Mentions Lanyer's dedications to female patrons (p. 25), discusses *Salve Deus Rex Judaeorum* as devotional literature (pp. 98-99). Excellent bibliography of primary sources, divided into two categories: "Basic List of Books for Women, 1475-1640" (pp. 144-217) with annotations and owners' lists, information on frontispieces and dedications; and "supplemental List" (pp. 218-233) designed "for those wishing a broader definition of women's literature" (p. 218).

Hutson, Lorna. "Why the Lady's Eyes Are Nothing Like the Sun." In *Women, Texts & Histories, 1575-1760,* Clare Brant and Diane Purkiss, eds., pp. 13-38. London: Routledge, 1992. Also published in *New Feminist Discourses: Critical Essays on Theories and Texts,* Isobel Armstrong, ed. London: Routledge, 1992, pp. 154-75.

Hutson argues that *Salve Deus Rex Judaeorum* is "a poem which celebrates woman as an effective reader and agent, rather than offering her as a dark secret to be disclosed" (p. 14). Also establishes Lanyer's credibility as poet; contextualizes her with male poets, especially Shakespeare and Jonson, and with Protestant, humanist discourse.

———. "Aemilia Lanier." *The Dictionary of National Biography: Missing Persons,* C.S. Nicholls, ed., pp. 388-89. Oxford: Oxford University Press, 1993.

Notes that Lanyer's "outstanding achievement is undoubtedly the composition of the first original poetry by a woman to be published in the seventeenth century (p. 388), and suggests that Lanyer "has become notorious as a result of attempts to identify her as the 'dark lady' of Shakespeare's *Sonnets,* on the conjectural grounds of her racial colouring, musical ability, and promiscuity" (pp. 388-389). Proposes that "the ambiguity of an elegy which laments the loss of constancy in relations between household and patron, and yet offers itself in the public marketplace as a suit for favour, aptly characterizes the circumstance of Emilia Lanier's life" (p. 389). Refers reader to Rowse, *Poems of Shakespeare's Dark Lady,* and Prior, "Jewish Musicians at the Tudor Court."

Jarvis, Simon. "Lanier, Emilia." In *British Women Writers: A Critical Reference Guide,* Janet Todd, ed., pp. 396-98. A Frederick Unger Book. New York: Continuum, 1989.

Biographical dictionary. Lanyer entry based on Lewalski in *Silent But for the Word,* and Rowse, *The Poems of Shakespeare's Dark Lady.* Brief biography; questions Rowse's theory that Lanyer was Shakespeare's "dark lady." Notes feminist aspect of dedicatory, title poems; suggests that Lanyer's "feminism is often accompanied by a more defensive insistence on the importance of chastity" (p. 398).

Jones, Ann Rosalind. *The Currency of Eros: Women's Love Lyric, 1520-1640.* Bloomington: Indiana University Press, 1991.

An analysis of eight women writers that "studies negotiations between two complex institutions: the mixed gender ideologies produced by political and social transformations in early modern Europe, and the network of classical, early Renaissance and contemporary texts composing the discursive territory of sixteenth-century love poetry" (p. 3). Chapter 4, "Feminine Pastoral as Heroic Martyrdom: Gaspara Stampa and Mary Wroth," includes the example of "To Cooke-ham" to support the assertion that "pastoral offered women poets . . . its double status as the genre of the humblest form of life and as an elite discourse validated by earlier poets" (p. 124).

Katz, David S. *The Jews in the History of England, 1485-1850.* Oxford: Clarendon Press, 1994.

Extensive, detailed historical analysis of Jewish communities in England mentions the Bassano brothers and other Jewish musicians (pp. 7-9) in "Introduction: The New Beginnings of Anglo-Jewry" (pp. 1-14). Chapter 1, "The Jewish Advocates of Henry VIII's Divorce," and chapter 2, "The Jewish Conspirators of Elizabethan England," offer useful information about the Jewish community and its treatment.

Krontiris, Tina. *Oppositional Voices: Women as Writers and Translators of Literature in the English Renaissance.* London and New York: Routledge, 1992.

Krontiris analyzes the writings of Isabella Whitney, Margaret Tyler, Mary Herbert, Elizabeth Cary, Aemilia Lanyer, and Mary Wroth to answer the question, "How is it that the same culture which produced a prohibitive ideology also produced the possibility of even a few women writing, publishing, and sometimes voicing criticism of their oppressors?" (p. 1). In a chapter entitled "Women of the Jacobean Court Defending Their Sex" (pp. 102-40), Krontiris pairs Aemilia Lanyer with Mary Wroth and suggests that, "For Lanyer, then, as for other women who wrote for publication, gaining acceptance as a female writer was a precondition for, as well as a means to, achieving various aims" (p. 105). In *Salve Deus Rex Judaeorum,* "opposition to cultural norms appears to be inevitably circumscribed by the use of the oppositional voice as a strategy in soliciting patronage" (p. 105).

Lamb, Mary Ellen. "Patronage and Class in Aemilia Lanyer's *Salve Deus Rex Judaeorum.*" In *Women, Writing, and the Reproduction of Culture,* Jane Donawerth, Mary Burke, Linda Dove, and Karen Nelson, eds., pp. 77-104. Syracuse University Press, 1998.

Examines the writing of Aemilia Lanyer to posit a woman's desire for professional compensation as well as patronage. Lamb considers issues of class in order to discuss the importance of an individual woman's experience, instead of generalizing all women's conditions from an individual example. Argues against attributing only proto-feminism or the need for patronage as the sole justifications for women's writing.

Lasocki, David. "Professional Recorder Playing in England, 1540-1740." *Early Music* 10 (1982): 23-29.

Overview of recorder playing at court, as part of the waits, at the theaters. Mentions Baptista Bassano, Aemilia Lanyer's father, and his brothers as originators of recorder consort; briefly describes family of Alfonso Lanyer, a later member of the consort and Aemilia Lanyer's husband: "Alfonso and Clement Lanier were two of the seven musical sons of Nicholas Lanier, a Huguenot refugee who joined the court flute consort in 1561" (p. 24). Refers to Aemilia Bassano Lanyer; also includes her in family tree (p. 25). Table 1, "The Royal Recorder Consort," includes Baptista Bassano and Alfonso Lanyer (p. 25). Supports Prior's assertion that Bassano family members were Jewish refugees (p. 24).

————. "The Anglo-Venetian Bassano Family as Instrument Makers and Repairers." *Galpin Society Journal* 38 (1985): 112-32.

Focuses on the Bassano family's involvement in instrument-making at the court of Henry VIII and afterwards; discusses Aemilia Bassano Lanyer's uncles; her father, Baptista, seems to have been less involved in that aspect of the family business. Family tree includes Aemilia (1569-1645) and her husband, Alfonso Lanyer (p. 113). Also offers illustrations of London Charterhouse (pp. 118-19), which Lasocki claims was used as workshop, home of Bassano brothers while employed by Henry VIII. Agrees with Roger Prior's speculation that the Bassanos were Jewish refugees (pp. 114-15).

————. "The Bassanos: Anglo-Venetian and Venetian." *Early Music* 14 (1986): 558-60.

Presents archival evidence connecting Aemilia Bassano Lanyer's father's family with Venetian instrument-makers and musicians.

————. *The Bassanos: Venetian Musicians and Instrument Makers in England, 1531-1665.* With Roger Prior. Aldershot: Scolar Press, 1995.

Most useful for its introduction of extensive, detailed family context for Lanyer and for the Bassano family as Court musicians. Establishes case for Bassanos as a Jewish family. In chapter 7, "Emilia Bassano and Alfonso Lanier," Lasocki and Prior develop the connection between Lanyer's poetry and that of "Anne Locke" (or Anne Lok); "Anne's brother, Stephen Vaughan, was a trusted friend of Emilia's parents. Moreover, Anne dedicated her translation of Calvin to Catherine Bertie, the mother of Emilia's guardian, Susan, Countess of Kent" (pp. 101-2). Relates biographical material from Simon Forman's diaries; also offers information regarding Alfonso Lanyer (pp. 106-10).

In chapter 8, "Was Emilia Bassano the Dark Lady of Shakespeare's Sonnets?" Prior uses evidence from Shakespeare's sonnets and Forman's diaries to support Rowse's assertions that Lanyer was the "dark lady": "not only do the pair in many ways resemble each other; there is no respect in which they an be shown to differ" (p. 129). Includes, as similarities, their "colouring, marital status, acquaintance with Shakespeare, and musicality . . . and their sexual behavior" (pp. 119, 120). Prior uses Lanyer's "book of poems," which he does not name, as evidence of Lanyer's "pride, her love of the aristocracy and her shameless pursuit of them" (pp. 122-23), qualities he suggests she shares with the "dark lady." Also compares "Emilia's poems" to the sonnets to show that "the mistress *collects* people, just as Emilia does" (p. 125), and sees "verbal and conceptual parallels [which] are too numerous and unusual to be explained by coincidence" (p. 126). Then uses "her bastardy (and her son's), her Jewishness and her Bassano coat of arms" (p. 129), as well as her Italian origins (pp. 136-37), to "throw new light on Shakespeare" (p. 129).

Lewalski, Barbara K. "Of God and Good Women: The Poems of Aemilia Lanyer." In *Silent But for the Word: Tudor Women as Patrons, Translators, and Writers of Religious Works,* Margaret P. Hannay, ed., pp. 203-24. Kent, Oh.: Kent State University Press, 1985.

Responds to Rowse and examines *Salve Deus Rex Judaeorum* to assess its achievement on its own terms instead of as the work of Shakespeare's "dark lady," a claim

Lewalski finds questionable. Notes contribution of "Epistle to the Vertuous Reader" to the *querelle des femmes* (p. 212); categorizes the dedicatory poem to Mary Sidney, Countess of Pembroke, as especially "well conceived, well made and charming" (p. 210); declares the title poem conceptually interesting but stylistically uneven (p. 213), and calls "The Description of Cooke-ham" "the gem of the volume" (p. 220).

―――. "The Lady of the Country-House Poem." In *The Fashioning and Functioning of the British Country House,* Gervase Jackson-Stops, Gordon J. Schochet, Lena Cowen Orlin, and Elisabeth Blair MacDougall, eds., pp. 261-75. Hanover and London: National Gallery of Art, 1989.

Lewalski compares representation of Margaret and Anne Clifford in "To Cooke-ham" with Ben Jonson's portrait of Barbara Gamage Sidney in "To Penshurst," with Andrew Marvell's construction of Sir Thomas Fairfax's daughter Mary in "Upon Appleton House," and with Richard Lovelace's characterization of Olivia Boteler Porter, wife of Endymion Porter, in "Amyntor's Grove." Defines genre of country-house poem and theorizes that praises of the lady of the house "occur only when the woman in question is of some special importance to her husband or family, or in her own right . . . [to] recast [their social roles] in mythic terms . . . [and relate] these ladies in various and complex ways to nature and culture" (p. 261). Includes portrait of Margaret Russell Clifford (p. 266).

―――. "Re-writing Patriarchy and Patronage: Margaret Clifford, Anne Clifford, and Aemilia Lanyer." *The Yearbook of English Studies* 21 (1991): 87-106.

Lewalski examines archival materials relating to Clifford family, including Anne Clifford's diaries, and *Salve Deus Rex Judaeorum* to analyze connections between the three women. Suggests "the texts . . . afford some insight into three women's construction of self and world as they sought to rewrite patriarchy and patronage, supported on the one hand by a sense of female community, and on the other by the firm conviction that God the Divine Patriarch was their ally against the many earthly patriarchs who oppressed them" (p. 89). Focuses on Lanyer (pp. 97-106); sees Cookham as lost female Eden (pp. 104-6).

―――. *Writing Women in Jacobean England.* Cambridge: Harvard University Press, 1993.

Lewalski studies nine women "whose active involvement with Jacobean culture can be read through some of the texts of their own making" (p. 1). Chapter 8, "Imagining Female Community: Aemilia Lanyer's Poems" (pp. 213-41) argues that: "[*Salve Deus Rex Judaeorum*] is of particular interest for its feminist conceptual frame: it is a defense and celebration of the enduring community of good women that reaches from Eve to contemporary Jacobean patronesses. Lanyer imagines that community as distinctively separate from male society and its evils, and proclaims herself its poet" (p. 213). Also includes biography (pp. 213-18); readings, which emphasize genre tradition and historical contexts, of "The Dedications," "The Title Poem," and "The Country-House Poem: 'Cooke-ham'." Appendix B, "Presentation Copies of Lanyer's *Salve Deus Rex Judaeorum,*" describes texts (pp. 321-22). Includes reproduction of title page from Huntington Library copy of the 1611 edition (pp. 212).

Marder, Louis. "The Dark Lady: Demise of a Theory." *Shakespeare Newsletter* 23 (1973): 24.

Reviews responses to Rowse's proposal of Lanyer as Shakespeare's "dark lady."

McBride, Kari Boyd. "Engendering Authority in Aemilia Lanyer's *Salve Deus Rex Judaeorum.*" Ph.D. diss., University of Arizona. *Dissertation Abstracts International* 55.5 (1994): 1267A.

McBride theorizes that "Aemilia Lanyer subverted traditional understandings of poetic subjectivity and altered received generic forms in order to construct herself as poet in a culture that reserved that vocation to men . . . by creating in her poems a tradition of female poetic subjectivity through the imaginative construction of a community of women" (p. 1267A). McBride also examines Lanyer's "alliance" with Christ, her "remaking of the initiatory pastoral poem," her alteration of the genre of the country-house poem, and her use of the Geneva Bible and the *Book of Common Prayer.*

McBride, Phyllis. Review of *The Poems of Aemilia Lanyer: "Salve Deus Rex Judaeorum,"* Susanne Woods, ed. *Seventeenth-Century News* 54.3-4 (1995): 50.

Praises Woods's text: "[the volume] stands as a fine introduction to and new edition of the poet's work."

McGrath, Lynette. "Metaphoric Subversions: Feasts and Mirrors in Amelia Lanier's *Salve Deus Rex Judaeorum.*" *LIT: Literature Interpretation Theory* 3.2 (1991): 101-13.

Explains ways in which Lanyer, as a woman limited by patriarchal constraints, exploits religious discourse to "code . . . a subversive message" (p. 101). McGrath focuses on the way that "the rhetorical device of metaphor provides a strategy which reinforces Lanyer's radical project to construct poetically within a female community a sense of self that subverts the public construction for women of an image not their own" (p. 102).

―――. "'Let Us Have Our Libertie Againe': Amelia Lanier's 17th-Century Feminist Voice." *Women's Studies: An Interdisciplinary Journal* 20.3-4 (1992): 331-48.

McGrath reads *Salve Deus Rex Judaeorum* in terms of feminist theories of Luce Irigaray and Josephine Donovan. Argues "that although Lanyer lacked the terms to describe her politics, she forced the grounds of protest available in her culture to their most radical possible feminist expression. Appropriating the most powerful Christian ideological icon as authorization, she textually established a supportive female community under whose auspices she urged women to embark on a process of self-definition beyond the power of male construction and outside the range of male desire" (p. 345).

Morton, Lynn Moorhead. "'Vertue Cladde in Constant Love's Attire': The Countess of Pembroke as a Model for Renaissance Women Writers." Ph.D. diss., University of South Carolina. *Dissertation Abstracts International* 54.7 (1994): 2590A-91A.

Examines ways in which Mary Sidney, Countess of Pembroke, influenced the choices of genre and the construction of female characters in the works of Aemilia Lanyer, Elizabeth Cary, and Mary Wroth. Morton suggests that *Salve Deus Rex Judaeorum* "combines devotion, political concerns, and a vision of female heroism in ways which suggest the inspiration of the Countess's role in the Sidneian Psalms, which Lanyer specifically mentions" (p. 2590). Morton also addresses issues of genre and literary conventions and "suggests that the use of specific conventions signals women's membership within a literary coterie rather than exclusion from the literary world . . . [and] identifies a female authorial 'voice' which creates a vision of female heroism based on the traditionally passive value of constancy in love" (p. 2590).

Mueller, Janel. "The Feminist Poetics of Aemilia Lanyer's *Salve Deus Rex Judaeorum.*"
In *Feminist Measures: Soundings in Poetry and Theory,* Lynn Keller and Cristianne
Miller, eds., pp. 208-36. Ann Arbor: University of Michigan Press, 1993, rev. and
rpt. for this volume (chapter 6).
Suggests that Lanyer's poetry overlaps with postmodern interests in two ways.
First, Lanyer formulates "political, critical, and poetic projects" based on her "cultural
embeddedness . . . even though her notion of culture is Christian world history and
her understanding of embeddedness finds two sexes locked in domination-subordination relationship that shows everywhere as a given of social organization" (p. 210).
Second, Lanyer articulates "transformative possibilities in gender relations that will
carry their own secure imperative for actualization . . . [for which] she looks to the
figure of Christ in history" (p. 211). Compares Lanyer to Christine de Pizan to identify the ground of their poetic authority. Contrasts Lanyer's poetics with those of Samuel
Daniel and of Giles Fletcher's *Christs Victorie and Triumph in Heaven, and Earth, over
and after Death* (1610), to argue for the feminine and feminist nature of Lanyer's work.

Ongaro, Giulio M. "New Documents on the Bassano Family." *Early Music* 20 (1992):
409-13.
Constructs possible Bassano family genealogy. Uses Venetian family wills to establish connections between Aemilia Bassano Lanyer's father, Baptista Bassano, his
brothers, and the Bassanos of Venice, including the instrument-maker Jacomo Bassano
and the musician and composer Giovani Bassano. Reviews evidence used to theorize
that the Bassano family was Jewish (p. 412, n. 5).

———. "Sixteenth-Century Venetian Wind Instrument Makers and Their Clients."
Early Music 13 (1985): 391-97.
Ongaro describes business partnerships between Venetian businessmen; speculates on possible connection of Jacamo Bassano of Venice and Bassano brothers of
England, including Baptista Bassano, Aemila Bassano Lanyer's father.

Parfitt, George. "Poetry by Women." In *English Poetry of the Seventeenth Century.* 2d
ed., pp. 222-49. London and New York: Longman, 1992.
Includes this chapter on women writers as part of a critical introduction to poetic
genres of the seventeenth century. Discusses "The Description of Cooke-ham" in section entitled "Women and 'Politics.'" Resists reading it as a country-house poem, since
"such poetry includes a strong sense of specific place" and "has a socio-political dimension," both of which Parfitt finds lacking in Lanyer's text (pp. 241-43). Refers reader to
Greer et al., *Kissing the Rod.*

Prior, Roger. "Was Emilia Lanier the Dark Lady?" *Shakespeare Newsletter* 25 (1975): 26.

Supports Rowse and draws connections between Shakespeare's *Merchant of Venice* and Lanier's biography. Points to Shakespeare's characters Bassanio and Solanio. Prior reads Solanio as an anagram for Alfonso Lanier.

———. "Jewish Musicians at the Tudor Court." *Musical Quarterly* 69 (1983): 253-65.

Prior identifies nineteen of Henry VIII's Court musicians as Jewish and argues that this discovery "changes the traditional picture both of the Jews under the Tudors and of musical life at the Tudor Court; it allows us to solve a long-standing problem of Anglo-Jewish history; and it adds considerably to our understanding of some works of Shakespeare" (p. 254). Includes the Bassanos in his discussion.

———. "More (Moor? Moro?) Light on the Dark Lady." *Financial Times* (10 October 1987): 17.

Prior reads a Bassano coat of arms, consisting of a silkworm as the family crest, three silkworm moths on the upper half of the shield, and a tree on the lower half described in an early seventeenth-century document as a mulberry. Uses this coat of arms to assert that Bassanos were Jewish, "since it was Jews who introduced silk-farming into Italy and dominated the industry" and also to support Rowse's theory of Lanier as the "dark lady." Coat of arms is figured.

———. "Second Jewish Community in Tudor London." *Jewish Historical Studies* 31 (1988-90): 137-52.

Defines two distinct Jewish communities in London in the sixteenth century, one with Portuguese roots and one with Italian origins. Asserts that while both benefited from court patronage, Portuguese Jews tended towards professions of medicine or trade, while Italian Jews made music and instruments. Argues that Italian Jews were more quickly assimilated into English society and illustrates this point with a reference to Lanier: "In the 1590s, Emilia Bassono dreamed of Jews and entitled the poems which she published in 1611 describing her religious conversion *Salve Deus Rex Judaeorum*" (p. 138).

Ramsey, Paul. *The Fickle Glass: A Study of Shakespeare's Sonnets*. New York: AMS Press, 1979.

In the chapter discussing "Biographical Questions," Ramsey relates Rowse's claim that Lanier is Shakespeare's "dark lady," and observes that while Rowse's "opponents have scored some points [against his case, they] certainly have not proved that she was not Shakespeare's dark lady" (p. 20). Argues that Lanier "remains a possible candidate" (p. 21).

———. "Darkness Lightened: A.L. Rowse's Dark Lady Once More." *The Upstart Crow* 5 (1984): 143-45.

Offers evidence against Rowse's suggestion that Lanier was Shakespeare's "dark lady." Rowse bases part of this claim on the fact that Lanier's family was of Venetian origin; Ramsey argues that this background does not necessarily mean that she was dark-haired and dark-eyed.

Reed, Nancy Ellen Elizabeth. "Reclaiming the Garden: The Poetry of a Christian Feminist." *Masters Abstracts International* 31.2 (1993): 577.

Explores the ways in which Lanyer "revised the mythology and symbols of the Christian Church (under the guise of epideictic poetry) in order to place women at the centre, and liberate the 'faire' sex from the tyranny of men." Contextualizes Lanyer's work with that of Sidney, Spenser, Shakespeare, and Donne and studies her construction of ideals of love, death, and art.

Richey, Esther Gilman. "'To Undoe the Booke': Cornelius Agrippa, Aemilia Lanyer and the Subversion of Pauline Authority." *English Literary Renaissance* 27.1 (1997): 105-208.

Notes relationship of *Salve Deus Rex Judaeorum* to *querelle des femmes*; traces to hermaneutics of Cornelius Agrippa's interpretation of Genesis in Nobilitie and Excellencie of Womankinde (1542). Richey suggests that "In form as well as content *Salve Deus Rex Judaeorum* embodies Agrippa's subversive re-reading of Paul, but it goes one step further: it records the voices of women who have been silenced in the pages of the New Testament and it uncovers the politics of that suppression" (p. 128).

Roberts, Jospehine A. "'My Inward House': Women's Autobiographical Poetry in the Early Seventeenth Century." In *"The Muses females are": Martha Moulsworth and Other Women Writers of the English Renaissance,* Robert C. Evans and Anne C. Little, ed., pp. 129-37. Locust Hill Literary Studies, no. 20. West Cornwall, Conn.: Locust Hill Press, 1995.

Interprets "The Authors Dreame," a dedicatory poem to Mary Sidney, Countess of Pembroke, and "The Description of Cooke-ham," within the context of dream-vision poetry (pp. 130-31); compares to work of other women writers such as Elizabeth Melville, Rachel Speght, and Mary Wroth, as well as to that of Martha Moulsworth.

Rowse, A.L. "Revealed at Last, Shakespeare's Dark Lady." *London Times* (29 January 1973): 12.

Announces discovery of Lanyer as Shakespeare's "dark lady": "She was lying in wait for me in the manuscripts [of Simon Forman] and forced herself upon my attention." Misidentifies her as "the wife of William Lanier." Asserts that the discovery implies: "The Sonnets *are* autobiographical; they contain the secrets of the private life of our greatest writer" (p. 12). Makes a case for new editions of Shakespeare, new readings of the sonnets, and new versions of Shakespeare's biography.

―――. *Shakespeare the Man.* New York: Harper & Row, 1973.

In chapter 6, "The Dark Lady" (pp. 74-99), Rowse restates his case for Lanyer's identity as the "dark lady."

―――. *Simon Forman: Sex and Society in Shakespeare's Age.* London: Weidenfeld & Nicolson, 1974.

Rowse's biography of Simon Forman based on Forman's diaries and other writings; "Part II" includes excerpts from these primary materials. Advances theory that Aemilia Lanyer is Shakespeare's "dark lady," based on Forman's notations (pp. 15-16, 99-117); reads *Salve Deus Rex Judaeorum* "with its passionate address against men's defaming of women" (p. 106) as a response to Shakespeare's sonnets (pp. 105-16).

————. *What Shakespeare Read—and Thought.* New York: Coward, McCann & Geoghegan, 1981.

Rowse conflates Lanyer with the "dark lady" throughout, so that index entries for Lanyer lead to discussions of the "dark lady." For example, the first index entry for Lanyer sends the reader to page 5: "Here we go beyond the region of phrases to penetrate into Shakespeare's thought; for Berowne speaks for Shakespeare in *Love's Labour Lost,* is in fact Shakespeare himself. Berowne's dark Rosaline is the Dark Lady of the sonnets," and is, therefore, Lanyer.

————. *Prefaces to Shakespeare's Plays.* London: Orbis, 1984.

As he does in *What Shakespeare Read—and Thought,* Rowse here collapses Lanyer and the "dark lady" into the same persona.

————, ed. *Shakespeare's Sonnets: The Problems Solved.* 2d ed. New York: Harper & Row, 1973.

Reads sonnets as autobiography; discusses identity of "dark lady," revealed by Forman's manuscripts (pp. xxiv-xli). Offers modernizations of sonnets along with Shakespeare's text; annotations to Sonnets 127 through 153 support Rowse's reading of Lanyer as the "dark lady" (pp. 264-317).

————. *Annotated Shakespeare.* 2 vols. New York: C.N. Potter, 1978.

In volume 2, "Histories, Sonnets and Other Poems," Rowse identifes Lanyer as Shakespeare's "dark lady" and reads her into a narrative interpretation of Shakespeare's sonnets: "Emilia Lanier was a bad lot—no doubt about that; Shakespeare had no doubt of it, but, a strongly sexed heterosexual, he could not help himself" (p. 749).

Schleiner, Louise. *Tudor and Stuart Women Writers.* Bloomington: Indiana University Press, 1994.

Explores writing of fifteen early modern women in terms of the question of "how Tudor and Stuart women came to write anything for public or semipublic circulation when they faced so many obstacles for doing so" (p. xvii). Chapter 1, "Women's Household Circles as a Gendered Reading Formation: Whitney, Tyler, and Lanyer" (pp. 1-29), discusses Lanyer's associations with Lady Anne Clifford and the Countess of Cumberland at Cookham Dean, and argues that "in the 'Salve Deus Rex Judaeorum' poem . . . we saw how a relationship of waiting woman to lady-of-service could empower a woman to write a poem revising Christian male typology about guilty Eve, through celebrating a beloved lady who had encouraged her writing" (p. 29). Also includes excerpts from *Salve Deus Rex Judaeorum* with spelling modernized (pp. 231-43).

Schnell, Lisa. "The Fetter'd Muse: Renaissance Women Writers and the Idea of a Literary Career (Sidney, Lanyer, Speght)." Princeton University. *Dissertation Abstracts International* 51.9 (1991): 3087A.

Schnell "considers the individual works of three Renaissance women devotional poets as they represent the struggle to fashion female literary careers" (p. 3087). She establishes a context of generic traditions for devotional manuals written by men for women, and contrasts the career of Mary Sidney, Countess of Pembroke, with those of Aemilia Lanyer and Rachel Speght. Schnell suggests that "Lanyer demonstrates a sophisticated sense of female fame and reputation that often finds expression in brilliant and subversive irony. Her preoccupation with her social placement—or displacement— leads to a vision of a new community that both occasions and authorizes her own literary activity" (p. 3087).

————. "So Great a Difference Is There in Degree": Aemilia Lanyer and the Aims of Feminist Criticism." *Modern Language Quarterly* 57.1 (1996): 23-35.
Schnell calls for moving beyond generalizing "women's experience" from individual women writers and suggests that critics "recognize the places in women's writing where the search for commonality breaks down because material differences—class or race, for instance—have come to be understood as insurmountable" (p. 25). She examines "The Description of Cooke-ham" and analyzes "what happens when discursive and material rehearsals of difference in Lanyer's work are allowed to compete with the poet's attempts to advance a united female community" (p. 25). She sees as especially important the implications of Lanyer's social position.

Schoenbaum, Samuel. *Shakespeare and Others.* Washington, D.C.: Folger Shakespeare Library, 1985.
Chapter 4, "Shakespeare, Dr. Forman, and Dr. Rowse," collects Schoenbaum's critiques of Rowse over the years. Questions whether Rowse's *Shakespeare the Man,* aimed at "an essentially uncritical readership," was "a suitable vehicle for a new and controversial thesis . . . [concerning] Emilia Lanier, neé Bassano" (p. 54). Refutes Rowse's thesis for a variety of reasons, including misidentification of Lanyer's husband as Will, instead of Alfonso (pp. 74-79); praises Rowse for recovering Lanyer's poetry (p. 77).

————. *William Shakespeare: A Compact Documentary Life.* 1977. Oxford: Oxford University Press, 1987.
Briefly mentions Rowse's case for Lanyer as "dark lady" and refutes it (p. 170).

————. *Shakespeare's Lives.* New edition. Oxford: Clarendon Press, 1991.
In this extensive survey of critical speculation about Shakespeare's life, Schoenbaum relates a summary of Rowse's case for Lanyer as Shakespeare's "dark lady," and questions it (pp. 558-59).

Shattock, Joanne. *The Oxford Guide to British Women Writers.* Oxford and New York: Oxford University Press, 1993.
Survey of over four hundred British women writers and criticism concerning them. Very brief biography of Lanyer and overview of her poems; notes feminist tone: "At the same time her feminism is informed by her belief in women's pivotal importance in Christianity. She stressed women's spirituality, chastity, and virtue, in other words, the traditional feminine attributes, but also their learning, knowledge, and wisdom" (p. 253). Refers reader to Rowse, *The Poems of Shakespeare's Dark Lady*; Lewalski in *Silent But for the Word,* Beilin, Krontiris.

Sterling, Eric. "Women Writers of the English Renaissance: A Chronology of Texts and Contexts." In *"The Muses females are": Martha Moulsworth and Other Women Writers of the English Renaissance,* Robert C. Evans and Anne C. Little, eds., pp.

281-310. Locust Hill Literary Studies, no. 20. West Cornwall, Conn.: Locust Hill Press, 1995.

Includes information about Lanyer's encounters with Simon Forman, publication of *Salve Deus Rex Judaeorum,* operation of a school, and death.

Travitsky, Betty, and Adele F. Seeff, eds. *Attending to Women in Early Modern England.* Newark: University of Delaware Press, 1994.

Reports proceedings of interdisciplinary symposium held at University of Maryland, November 1991, and sponsored by the University's Center for Renaissance and Baroque Studies. In "Workshop #9: Constructing a Public Self: Women's Religious Writing," Lynette McGrath uses psychoanalytic theory to "read Lanyer's mirror metaphor as encoding and enhancing women's self-defining relationship with this feminized Christ and with each other, her subversive message justifying the public's activity of writing. The mirror metaphor assists Lanyer's project of constructing privately within a female community a sense of self that subverts the public construction for women of a passive voice not their own" (pp. 198-99). Also includes suggestions for teaching Lanyer in various undergraduate survey courses as part of "Appendix: Responses to Pedagogy Survey" (pp. 323-24, 332, 334, 335). Catherine Schuler and Sharon Ammen used an excerpt from Lanyer's "Eves Apologie" as a part of a dramatic performance entitled "Attending to Renaissance Women" written for the occasion (pp. 344, 350-51).

Wall, Wendy. "The Shapes of Desire: Politics, Publication and Renaissance Texts (Mulcaster, Gascoigne, Sidney, Lyly)." University of Pennsylvania. *Dissertation Abstracts International* 50.9 (1990): 2913A.

Studies various cultural forms such as pageants, sonnets, miscellanies, and complaint poems and "investigate[s] the authorial power made possible by print and how that power was complicated by the privilege attached to coterie circulation." In the last chapter, analyzes the work of Mary Sidney, Lanyer, Isabella Whitney, and Mary Wroth to show how women writers "concocted printed genres capable of interrogating and responding to . . . masculine tropes of authorship."

————. *The Imprint of Gender: Authorship and Publication in the English Renaissance.* Ithaca and London: Cornell University Presses, 1993.

In this extensive study of the impact of the printing press on late sixteenth- and early seventeenth-century notions of authorship, Wall includes analysis of "The Body of Christ: Aemilia Lanyer's Passion" (pp. 319-30). As she does in "Our Bodies/Our Texts?", Wall explores the ways in which Lanyer authorizes her own public voice by appropriating the body of Christ. Wall places Lanyer's text within the traditions of defenses of women, of appropriations of the *Song of Songs,* and of Petrarchan conventions, and argues that "*Salve Deus Rex Judaeorum* thus shows us one strategy by which a woman writer combined the stances of religious devotee, mourner, and an apologist in creating an authorial role in print" (p. 329).

————. "Our Bodies/Our Texts? Renaissance Women and the Trials of Authorship." In *Anxious Power: Reading, Writing, and Ambivalence in Narrative by Women,* Carol

J. Singley and Susan Elizabeth Sweeney, eds., pp. 51-71. Albany: State University of New York Press, 1993.

Wall sets Mary Sidney's prefatorial poem to her translation of the *Psalms* and Aemilia Lanyer's *Salve Deus Rex Judaeorum* within the tradition of the blazon and suggests that: "What Sidney and Lanyer do in these religious works is startling: they devise novel ways of imagining the male body so as to renegotiate the relationship between writer, text, and reader. Their works stage the anxieties of female writing by playfully reconstructing the techniques of corporeal representation dear to authorial presentation" (p. 52). For Lanyer's text, Wall focuses on representations of the body of Christ and asserts, "The crucifixion, then, becomes the site of a contest between the sexes, an agonistic moment in history that makes woman's virtue visible" (p. 60).

Weisner, Merry E. "Women's Defense of Their Public Role." In *Women in the Middle Ages and the Renaissance: Literary and Historical Perspectives,* Mary Beth Rose, ed. Syracuse: Syracuse University Press, 1986.

Defines freedom for women as "the ability to participate in public life," and examines "the contradictions of women's public role, and their responses to it" (p. 3). Uses one of Lanyer's dedications to illustrate the assertion that "a woman's [special] gift [of writing] could also be the inspirations provided by the life of another, a motivation for writing frequently expressed in dedicatory prefaces" (p. 16).

Woods, Susanne. "Aemilia Lanyer and Ben Jonson: Patronage, Authority, and Gender." *The Ben Jonson Journal* 1 (1994): 15-30.

Uses biographical information about Lanyer's Bassano family and its involvement as Court musicians to discuss parallels between Ben Jonson's "well-documented aspirations" (p. 15) and Lanyer's. Compares the ways that the two poets used systems of patronage and suggests that while Jonson manipulated the system "to validate Jonson's own role as definer of his own culture [and] to serve conventional social advancement" (p. 19), Lanyer's position was complicated by issues of gender, both her own and her patrons'. Woods notes two main differences, which include Lanyer's "apparent inability to bridge the social gap between herself and her dedicatees, and her use of the inability to obscure the audacity of 'A Womans writing of divinest things'" as well as "her set of strategies for rendering female gender a source of authority" (p. 20).

―――. "Aemilia Lanyer." *Seventeenth-Century British Nondramatic Poets, First Series. Dictionary of Literary Biography,* vol. 121, M. Thomas Hester, ed., pp. 213-20. Detroit, London: Bruccoli Clark Layman, 1992.

This volume of "literary biographies of the first generation of seventeenth-century non-dramatic poets" (p. ix) treats Lanyer as a major figure and includes an extensive article on Lanyer and her work. Woods claims that *Salve Deus Rex Judaeorum* is "arguably the first genuinely feminist publication in England: all of its dedicatees are women, the poem on the Passion specifically argues the virtues of women as opposed to the vices of men, and Lanyer's own authorial voice is assured and unapologetic" (p. 213). Offers biographical information (pp. 213-14), description of the *Salve* and its historical contexts as well as its feminist implications. Provides overview and analysis of poems, especially in the context of the system of female patrons and in terms of genre conventions of dedicatory poetry, religious lamentations, and country-house poetic tradition. Includes illustrations: title page of 1611 edition (p. 213) and portraits of Margaret Russell, Countess of Cumberland and Anne Clifford, Countess of Dorset. Bibliography of criticism (p. 220).

————. *Lanyer: A Renaissance Poet in her Context*. Oxford University Press, 1999.

Woods uses archival records and Lasocki's work on the Bassano family to draw a number of connections between Lanyer and her contemporaries, including patrons such as Susan Bertie, radical Protestants such as Stephen Vaughan, and women writers such as Anne Lok. Woods examines links between the *Salve Deus Rex Judaeorum* and narrative poems including Samuel Daniel's "Letter from Octavius to Marcus Antonius," *Cleopatra,* and the *Complaint of Rosamund;* Edmund Spenser's *The Faerie Queene,* especially books one and three; William Shakespeare's *Venus and Adonis* and *Rape of Lucrece;* and Michael Drayton's *Legend of Matilda*. Woods refutes Prior's support of Rowse in "Was Emilia Bassano the Dark Lady of Shakespeare's Sonnets?" and elsewhere, in part because she "find[s] Prior's readings of both the sonnets and the plays naive about literary conventions of the period and unpersuasive in their claims for simple biographical correspondences."

Woods shows how Lanyer's text, like Shakespeare's, benefits from an understanding of genre, suggesting that "at least three specific areas of Lanyer's work . . . owe something to a reading of Spenser: her approach to patrons, her analysis of earthly versions of heavenly love and beauty, and her use of marginal voices to decenter and recenter narrative action."

Contributors

LEEDS BARROLL is professor of English at the University of Maryland, Baltimore County. He is editor of the annual volume *Shakespeare Studies* and the author of books and articles on Shakespeare and his times. His book on Anne of Denmark is in press and he is currently working on censorship and the drama.

BOYD BERRY, associate professor of English at Virginia Commonwealth University, in Richmond, Virginia, is the author of *Process of Speech: Puritan Religious Writing and Paradise Lost* (Johns Hopkins University Press, 1976) and has recently sent off a manuscript studying changes in the representation of the poor in Tudor England. He has published essays on the representation of childhood, the poetry of Henry Vaughan, and on Elizabeth Cary's *The Tragedy of Mariam;* an essay on Anne Askew's writing is in press.

DAVID BEVINGTON is Phyllis Fay Horton Professor in the Humanities at the University of Chicago, where he has taught since 1967. His studies include *From "Mankind" to Marlowe* (1962), *Tudor Drama and Politics* (1968), and *Action Is Eloquence: Shakespeare's Language of Gesture* (1985). He is also the editor of *The Bantam Shakespeare* in twenty-nine paperback volumes (1988), and *The Complete Works of Shakespeare* (Harper Collins, 1992; updated, Longman, 1996), as well as the Oxford *1 Henry IV* (1987) and the Cambridge *Antony and Cleopatra* (1990). His *Troilus and Cressida* is forthcoming in the Arden Shakespeare Series.

MARSHALL GROSSMAN is professor of English at the University of Maryland, College Park. He is the author of *"Authors to themselves": Milton and the Revelation of History* (Cambridge, 1987) and *The Story of All Things: Writing the Self in English Renaissance Narrative Poetry* (Duke, 1998), as well as numerous articles on early modern literary history and the history and theory of literary criticism.

ACHSAH GUIBBORY is professor of English at the University of Illinois and managing editor of *The Journal of English and Germanic Philology.* The author of *The Map of Time: Seventeenth-Century English Literature and Ideas of Pattern in History* (Illinois, 1986) as well as numerous articles on seventeenth-century literature, she has recently completed a book on *Literature, Religion, and Cultural Conflict in Seventeenth-Century England,* forthcoming from Cambridge University Press.

MICHAEL MORGAN HOLMES is currently a postdoctoral fellow in the Department of English at Georgetown University. He has published on lesbian and gay literature and culture in the early modern period and is currently engaged in a project on seduction and roguery in seventeenth-century England.

BARBARA KIEFER LEWALSKI is William R. Kenan Professor of English Literature at Harvard University. Her publications include several books on Milton, Donne, and other early modern writers, as well as *Writing Women in Jacobean England* (Harvard, 1993) and an edition of *The Polemics and Poems of Rachel Speght* (Oxford, 1996).

KARI BOYD MCBRIDE is a lecturer in women's studies at the University of Arizona, where she teaches Women and Western Culture and Feminist Theories. Her other work on Lanyer includes "Remembering Orpheus in the Poems of Aemilia Lanyer" and *Aemilia Lanyer,* an Internet resource for scholars and teachers (http://www.u.arizona.edu/~kari/lanyer.htm).

NAOMI J. MILLER is associate professor of English and women's studies at the University of Arizona. Her research interests center on early modern women writers, and constructions of gender in early modern England. Her publications include a book-length study of Lady Mary Wroth (c. 1587-1653), entitled *Changing the Subject* (Kentucky, 1996), as well as a collection of essays on Wroth, and several articles on other women writers, such as Elizabeth Cary, Aemilia Lanyer, and Anne Clifford. She is currently working on a book on representations of maternity in sixteenth- and seventeenth-century English literature and society.

JANEL MUELLER is William Rainey Harper Professor of Humanities at the University of Chicago and editor of *Modern Philology.* Her books include *Donne's Prebend Sermons* (Harvard, 1979) and *The Native Tongue and the Word: Developments in English Prose Style, 1380-1580* (Chicago, 1984). She has published numerous articles on the formative phases of the English Reformation, on Donne and Milton, and on earlier English women authors (Margery Kempe, Katherine Parr, Elizabeth I, Aemilia Lanyer). She is currently working on editions of Katherine Parr and Elizabeth I.

SUSANNE WOODS is professor of English at Franklin & Marshall College and chair of the executive committee of the Women Writers Project at Brown University, where she taught for many years.

Index